Lecture Notes in Computer Science   10577

Commenced Publication in 1973
Founding and Former Series Editors:
Gerhard Goos, Juris Hartmanis, and Jan van Leeuwen

More information about this series at http://www.springer.com/series/7409

Eva Blomqvist · Katja Hose
Heiko Paulheim · Agnieszka Ławrynowicz
Fabio Ciravegna · Olaf Hartig (Eds.)

The Semantic Web: ESWC 2017 Satellite Events

ESWC 2017 Satellite Events
Portorož, Slovenia, May 28 – June 1, 2017
Revised Selected Papers

 Springer

Editors
Eva Blomqvist
Linköping University
Linköping
Sweden

Agnieszka Ławrynowicz
Poznan University of Technology
Poznan
Poland

Katja Hose
Aalborg University
Aalborg
Denmark

Fabio Ciravegna
University of Sheffield
Sheffield
UK

Heiko Paulheim
University of Mannheim
Mannheim
Germany

Olaf Hartig
Linköping University
Linköping
Sweden

ISSN 0302-9743   ISSN 1611-3349   (electronic)
Lecture Notes in Computer Science
ISBN 978-3-319-70406-7   ISBN 978-3-319-70407-4   (eBook)
https://doi.org/10.1007/978-3-319-70407-4

Library of Congress Control Number: 2017957990

LNCS Sublibrary: SL3 – Information Systems and Applications, incl. Internet/Web, and HCI

Preface

The 14th edition of ESWC took place in Portorož, Slovenia, from May 28 to June 1, 2017. The program included three keynotes by Lora Aroyo (Vrije Universiteit Amsterdam, The Netherlands, and Columbia University, New York, USA), Kevin Crosbie (RavenPack), and John Sheridan (The National Archives). The main scientific program of the conference comprised 51 papers, which have been published by Springer as LNCS volumes 10249 and 10250: 40 research and 11 in-use and application papers, selected out of 183 reviewed submissions, corresponding to an acceptance rate of 25% for the research papers submitted and 52% for the in-use papers. This program was completed by a demonstration and poster session, in which researchers had the chance to present their latest results and advances in the form of live demos. In addition, the conference program included 12 workshops, six tutorials, a challenge track with five challenges (revised selected papers published by Springer as an upcoming CCIS volume), an EU project networking session, and a PhD symposium. The PhD symposium program included ten contributions, selected out of 14 submissions.

This volume includes the accepted contributions to the demonstration and poster track: eight poster and 24 demonstration papers, selected out of 51 submissions (20 posters and 31 demos), which corresponds to an overall acceptance rate of 63%. Each submission was reviewed by at least four, and on average five, Program Committee members. During the poster session the students from the PhD symposium were invited to display a poster about their work. This resulted in ten additional posters being presented during the session.

Additionally, this book includes a selection of the best papers from the workshops co-located with the conference, which are distinguished meeting points for discussing ongoing work and the latest ideas in the context of the Semantic Web. The ESWC 2017 Workshops Program Committee carefully selected 12 workshops focusing on specific research issues related to the Semantic Web, organized by internationally renowned experts in their respective fields:

- Querying the Web of Data (QuWeDa 2017), published by CEUR-WS.org as a part of volume 1870
- Managing the Evolution and Preservation of the Data Web (MEPDaW 2017), published by CEUR-WS.org as a part of volume 1824
- Workshop on Semantic Web Solutions for Large-Scale Biomedical Data Analytics (SeWeBMeDA)
- Scientometrics Workshop
- Second RDF Stream Processing Workshop (RSP 2017), published by CEUR-WS. org as a part of volume+1870
- Third International Workshop on Emotions, Modality, Sentiment Analysis and the Semantic Web (EMSASW 2017), published by CEUR-WS.org as a part of volume 1874

- First International Workshop on Applications of Semantic Web Technologies in Robotics (ANSWER 2017)
- Second International Workshop on Linked Data and Distributed Ledgers (LD-DL 2017)
- Enabling Decentralized Scholarly Communication
- Third International Workshop on Semantic Web for Scientific Heritage (SW4SH 2017)
- 4th Workshop on Linked Data Quality (LDQ 2017)
- Workshop on Semantic Deep Learning (SemDeep)

From the overall set of 54 papers that were accepted for these workshops, a selection of the best papers has been included in this volume. Each workshop's Organizing Committee evaluated the papers accepted in their workshop to propose those to be included in this volume. The authors of the selected papers improved their original submissions, taking into account the comments and feedback obtained during the workshop and the conference. As a result, 12 papers were selected for this volume.

Finally, this volume also includes the revised and improved version of one of the best papers of the First Workshop on Humanities in the Semantic Web at ESWC 2016 (WHiSE 2016, initial papers published by CEUR-WS.org as volume 1608). This paper should have been included in LNCS volume 9989 ("The Semantic Web. ESWC 2016 Satellite Events") but was omitted by mistake.

As general chair, poster and demo chairs, and workshop chairs, we would like to thank everybody who was involved in the organization of ESWC 2017. Special thanks go to the Poster and Demo Program Committee and to all the workshop organizers and their respective Program Committees who contributed to making the ESWC 2017 workshops a real success. We would also like to thank the Organizing Committee and especially the local organizers and the program chairs for supporting the day-to-day operation and execution of the workshops.

A special thanks also to our proceedings chair, Olaf Hartig, who did an excellent job in preparing this volume with the kind support of Springer.

Last but not least, thanks to all our sponsors listed herein, for their trust in ESWC.

August 2017

Eva Blomqvist
Katja Hose
Heiko Paulheim
Agnieszka Ławrynowicz
Fabio Ciravegna

Organization

Organizing Committee

General Chair

Eva Blomqvist   Linköping University, Sweden

Program Chairs

Diana Maynard   University of Sheffield, UK
Aldo Gangemi   Paris Nord University, France and ISTC-CNR, Italy

Workshops Chairs

Agnieszka Ławrynowicz   Poznan University of Technology, Poland
Fabio Ciravegna   University of Sheffield, UK

Poster and Demo Chairs

Katja Hose   Aalborg University, Denmark
Heiko Paulheim   University of Mannheim, Germany

Tutorials Chairs

Anna Lisa Gentile   University of Mannheim, Germany
Sebastian Rudolph   TU Dresden, Germany

PhD Symposium Chairs

Rinke Hoekstra   Vrije Universiteit Amsterdam, The Netherlands
Pascal Hitzler   Wright State University, USA

Challenge Chairs

Monika Solanki   University of Oxford, UK
Mauro Dragoni   Fondazione Bruno Kessler, Italy

Semantic Technologies Coordinators

Lionel Medini   University of Lyon, France
Luigi Asprino   University of Bologna, Italy

EU Project Networking Session Chairs

Lyndon Nixon   Modul Universität Vienna, Austria
Maria Maleshkova   Karlsruhe Institute of Technology (KIT), Germany

Process Improvement Chair

Derek Doran   Wright State University, USA

Publicity Chair

Ruben Verborgh   Ghent University, Belgium

Web Presence

Venislav Georgiev   STI International, Austria

Proceedings Chair

Olaf Hartig   Linköping University, Sweden

Treasurer

Alexander Wahler   STI, Austria

Local Organization Chair

Marko Grobelnik   Jožef Stefan Institute, Slovenia

Local Organization and Conference Administration

Katharina Vosberg   YouVivo GmbH, Germany
Marija Kokelj   PITEA, Slovenia
Monika Kropej   Jožef Stefan Institute, Slovenia
Spela Sitar   Jožef Stefan Institute, Slovenia

Program Committee

Program Chairs

Diana Maynard   University of Sheffield, UK
Aldo Gangemi   Paris Nord University, France and ISTC-CNR, Italy

Track Chairs

Vocabularies, Schemas, Ontologies

Helena Sofia Pinto   Universidade de Lisboa, Portugal
Silvio Peroni   University of Bologna, Italy

Reasoning

Uli Sattler   University of Manchester, UK
Umberto Straccia   ISTI-CNR, Italy

Linked Data

Jun Zhao   University of Oxford, UK
Axel Ngonga Ngomo   Universität Leipzig, Germany

Social Web and Web Science

Harith Alani   The Open University, UK
Wolfgang Nejdl   Leibniz Universität Hannover, Germany

Semantic Data Management, Big Data, Scalability

Maria Esther Vidal   University of Bonn, Germany and Universidad Simón
                         Bolívar, Venezuela
Jürgen Umbrich   Vienna University of Economics and Business, Austria

Natural Language Processing and Information Retrieval

Claire Gardent   CNRS, France
Udo Kruschwitz   University of Essex, UK

Machine Learning

Claudia d'Amato   University of Bari, Italy
Michael Cochez   Fraunhofer Institute for Applied Information
                         Technology FIT, Germany

Mobile Web, Sensors, and Semantic Streams

Emanuele Della Valle   Politecnico di Milano, Italy
Manfred Hauswirth   TU Berlin, Germany

Services, APIs, Processes, and Cloud Computing

Peter Haase   metaphacts GmbH, Germany
Barry Norton   Elsevier, UK

Multilinguality

Philipp Cimiano   Universität Bielefeld, Germany
Roberto Navigli   Sapienza University of Rome, Italy

Semantic Web and Transparency

Mathieu d'Aquin   The Open University, UK
Giorgia Lodi   CNR, Italy

In-Use and Industrial Track

Paul Groth   Elsevier Labs, The Netherlands
Paolo Bouquet   Trento University, Italy

Steering Committee

Chair

John Domingue   The Open University, UK and STI International, Austria

Members

Claudia d'Amato   Universià degli Studi di Bari, Italy
Mathieu d'Aquin   Knowledge Media Institute KMI, UK
Philipp Cimiano   Bielefeld University, Germany
Oscar Corcho   Universidad Politécnica de Madrid, Spain
Fabien Gandon   Inria, W3C, Ecole Polytechnique de l'Université de
                       Nice Sophia Antipolis, France
Valentina Presutti   CNR, Italy
Marta Sabou   Vienna University of Technology, Austria
Harald Sack   FIZ Karlsruhe and KIT Karlsruhe, Germany

Workshop Organization

Workshop Chairs

Agnieszka Ławrynowicz   Poznan University of Technology, Poland
Fabio Ciravegna   University of Sheffield, UK

QuWeDa Workshop Organizers

Muhammad Saleem   University of Leipzig, Germany
Ricardo Usbeck   University of Leipzig, Germany
Ruben Verborgh   Ghent University, Belgium
Axel Ngonga Ngomo   Institute for Applied Informatics, Germany

MEPDaW Workshop Organizers

Jeremy Debattista   Trinity College Dublin, Ireland
Javier D. Fernández Vienna University of Economics and Business, Austria
Jürgen Umbrich   Vienna University of Economics and Business, Austria

SeWeBMeDA Workshop Organizers

Ali Hasnain   National University of Ireland, Galway, Ireland
Amit Sheth   Wright State University, USA
Michel Dumontier   Maastricht University, The Netherlands
Dietrich   National University of Ireland, Galway, Ireland
  Rebholz-Schuhmann

Scientometrics Workshop Organizers

Sabrina Kirrane	Vienna University of Economics and Business, Austria
Aliaksandr Birukou	Springer, Germany
Paul Buitelaar	National University of Ireland, Galway, Ireland
Javier D. Fernández	Vienna University of Economics and Business, Austria
Anna Lisa Gentile	IBM Research Almaden, USA
Paul Groth	Elsevier Labs, The Netherlands
Pascal Hitzler	Wright State University, USA
Ioana Hulpus	Universität Mannheim, Germany
Krzysztof Janowicz	University of California, Santa Barbara, USA
Elmar Kiesling	TU Vienna, Austria
Andrea Nuzzolese	ISTC-CNR, Italy
Francesco Osborne	The Open University, UK
Axel Polleres	Vienna University of Economics and Business, Austria
Marta Sabou	TU Vienna, Austria
Harald Sack	FIZ Karlsruhe and KIT Karlsruhe, Germany

RSP Workshop Organizers

Jean-Paul Calbimonte	University of Applied Sciences Western Switzerland, Switzerland
Minh Dao-Tran	Vienna University of Technology, Austria
Daniele Dell'Aglio	University of Zurich, Switzerland
Danh Le Phuoc	Technical University of Berlin, Germany

EMSASW Workshop Organizers

Mauro Dragoni	Fondazione Bruno Kessler, Italy
Diego Reforgiato	University of Cagliari, Italy

ANSWER Workshop Organizers

Emanuele Bastianelli	The Open University, UK
Mathieu d'Aquin	The Open University, UK
Daniele Nardi	Sapienza University of Rome, Italy

LD-DL Workshop Organizers

Luis Daniel Ibáñez	University of Southampton, UK
Elena Simperl	University of Southampton, UK
Fabien Gandon	Inria, W3C, Ecole Polytechnique de l'Université de Nice Sophia Antipolis, France
John Domingue	The Open University, UK and STI International, Austria

Decentralized Scholarly Communication Workshop Organizers

Sarven Capadisli	University of Bonn, Germany
Amy Guy	University of Edinburgh, UK
David De Roure	University of Oxford, UK

SW4SH Workshop Organizers

Catherine Faron Zucker   Université Nice Sophia Antipolis, France
Isabelle Draelants   CNRS, IRHT, France
Alexandre Monnin   Inria, France
Arnaud Zucker   Université Nice Sophia Antipolis, France

LDQ Workshop Organizers

Amrapali Zaveri   Maastricht University, The Netherlands
Anisa Rula   University of Milano-Bicocca, Italy
Anastasia Dimou   Ghent University, Belgium
Wouter Beek   VU Amsterdam, The Netherlands

SemDeep Workshop Organizers

Georg Heigold   DFKI, Germany
Dagmar Gromann   IIIA – CSIC, Spain
Thierry Declerck   Saarland University and DFKI, Germany

Sponsoring Institutions

Gold Sponsors

http://www.iospress.nl/   http://www.sti2.org/

Silver Sponsors

https://www.elsevier.com/

Contents

Poster Papers

Ontology-Based Photogrammetric Survey in Underwater Archaeology

Pierre Drap[1](✉), Odile Papini[1], Jean-Chrisophe Sourisseau[2], and Timmy Gambin[3]

[1] Aix-Marseille Université, CNRS, ENSAM, Université De Toulon, LSIS UMR 7296,
Domaine Universitaire de Saint-Jérôme, Bâtiment Polytech, 13397 Marseille, France
{Pierre.Drap,Odile.Papini}@univ-amu.fr
[2] Aix-Marseille Université, CNRS, Ministère de la Culture et de la Communication,
CCJ UMR 7299, 13094 Aix En Provence, France
Jean-Christophe.Sourisseau@univ-amu.fr
[3] University of Malta, Msidi, Malta
Timmy.Gambin@um.edu.mt

Abstract. This work addresses the problem of underwater archaeological surveys from the point of view of knowledge. We propose an approach based on underwater photogrammetry guided by a representation of knowledge used, as structured by ontologies. Survey data feed into to ontologies and photogrammetry in order to produce graphical results. This paper focuses on the use of ontologies during the exploitation of 3D results. JAVA software dedicated to photogrammetry and archaeological survey has been mapped onto an OWL formalism. The use of procedural attachment in a dual representation (JAVA - OWL) of the involved concepts allows us to access computational facilities directly from OWL. As SWRL The use of rules illustrates very well such 'double formalism' as well as the use of computational capabilities of 'rules logical expression'. We present an application that is able to read the ontology populated with a photogrammetric survey data. Once the ontology is read, it is possible to produce a 3D representation of the individuals and observing graphically the results of logical spatial queries on the ontology. This work is done on a very important underwater archaeological site in Malta named Xlendi, probably the most ancient shipwreck of the central Mediterranean Sea.

Keywords: Underwater archaeology · Photogrammetry · Ontology · JAVA

1 Introduction

Recent developments in computer vision and photogrammetry, make the latter technique a near-ideal tool, or at the very least an essential one, for archaeological survey. In underwater context, it is undeniably a must as there is no efficient alternative.

The main idea of this project is based on the fact that the survey, whether it takes place in the scope of underwater archaeology, relies on a complex well-established corpus, even though it evolves over time. A formalisation of the archaeological knowledge involved, is used to guide the survey.

© Springer International Publishing AG 2017
E. Blomqvist et al. (Eds.): ESWC 2017 Satellite Events, LNCS 10577, pp. 3–6, 2017.
https://doi.org/10.1007/978-3-319-70407-4_1

The photogrammetry survey carried out is based on an original approach of underwater photogrammetry that was deployed with the help of a specific instrumental infrastructure provided by COMEX, a partner in the GROPLAN[1] project [1]. This photogrammetry process, as well as the body of surveyed objects, were formalized in an ontology expressed in OWL2. Our approach is based on procedural attachment; the ontology being seen as a dual of the JAVA class structure that manages the photogrammetric survey and the measurement of artefacts. This allows the establishment of a reasoning for the ontologies as well as intensive calculations using JAVA programming language with the same interface. Furthermore, the ontology used to describe the archaeological artefacts from a measurement point of view is aligned with CIDOC-CRM ontology used for museo-graphical objects [2, 3].

The focus of this experimental project is the *Xlendi* shipwreck, named after the place where it was found off the Gozo coast in Malta. The shipwreck was located by during an offshore survey in 2008. The shipwreck is located near a coastline known for its limestone cliffs that plunge into the sea and whose foundation rests on a continental shelf at an average depth of 100 m below sea level. The shipwreck itself is therefore exceptional; first due to its configuration as well as its state of preservation which is particularly well-suited for our experimental 3D modelling project. The examination of the first layer of amphorae also reveals a mixed cargo, consisting of items from Western Phoenicia and Tyrrhenian-style containers which are both well-matched with other archaeological excavations from the Archaic, that is between the end of the VIII and the first half of the VII centuries BC. The historical interest of this wreck, which has been highlighted by our work, is the first to be performed on this site and creates real added-value in terms of innovation. In turn, this contributes to the international reputation of the project.

2   The Use of Ontologies

The ontology has been developed to represent the photogrammetric process used for the survey, the process identification, measure and representation of visible archaeological objects. The final ontology is, on the one hand, an ontology built from a JAVA program modeling the entire photogrammetric process. On the other hand, we also present an ontology describing the archaeological artefacts from the point of view of the photogrammetric measure.

Our goal is to link the measured artefacts with all the observations used to measure and identify them. One of the main advantages of the photogrammetric process is to provide several 2D representations of the measured artefacts. We build this ontology from an existing JAVA code in order to represent the concepts used in photogrammetry and to be able to use a reasoner on ABox photogrammetric data. Initial mapping from an Object Oriented (OO) formalism to a Description Logic (DL) is relatively easy according to the fact that we have to map a poor semantic formalism toward a richer one [4]. In order to do this, we need to manage both the computational aspects (often heavy in photogrammetry) implemented in the artefacts and measurable by

---

[1] http://www.groplan.eu.

photogrammetry and the ontological representation of the same photogrammetric process and surveyed artifacts.

Our implementation is based on a double formalism, JAVA, used for computation, photogrammetric algorithms, 3D visualization of photogrammetric data and patrimonial objects, and OWL for the definition of ontologies describing the concepts involved in the measurement process and the link with the measured objects.

The ontology construction in OWL - dual to the JAVA taxonomy - cannot be produced automatically. Each concept of ontology has been constructed with concern for the representation of fine knowledge from a specific point of view: measurement. Indeed, the same point of view presides over the development of the JAVA taxonomy, but software engineering constraints are superimposed on a point of view strictly linked to knowledge of concepts.

We have abandoned an automatic mapping using JAVA annotation and JAVA beans for a manual extraction even if this is a common way in literature [4–8]. The main advantage of our approach is that it is possible to perform logical queries on both the ontology and the JAVA representation. We can thus read an ontology, visualize the artefacts in 3D present in the ontology as well as the result of SQWRL queries in the

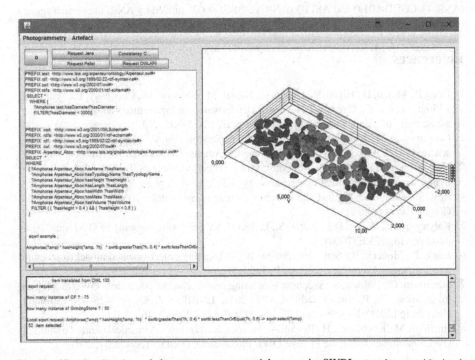

Fig. 1. 3D visualization of the answer to a spatial query in SWRL: Amphorae(?a) ^ swrlArp:isCloseTo(?a, "IdTargetAmphora", 6.2) ^ hasTypologyName (?a, "Pitecusse_365") -> sqwrl:select(?a). Means select all amphorae with the typology *Pitecusse_365* and at a maximum distance of 6.2 m from the amphorae labelled *IdTargetAmphora*

JAVA viewer. A representation of the artefacts measured on the *Xlendi* wreck as well as an answer to a SWRL query is shown in Fig. 1.

The approach we have chosen so far, using OWLAPI and the Pellet reasoner, allows for handling SQWRL queries using an extension of SWRL Built-In[2] packages. SWRL provides a very powerful extension mechanism that allows for implementing user-defined methods in the rules. We have built some spatial operators allowing us to express spatial queries in SWRL, as for example the operator *isCloseTo* with three arguments which allows for selecting all the amphorae present in a sphere centered on a specific amphora and belonging to a certain typology (Fig. 1).

3 Conclusions and Future Work

Based on a procedural attachment approach we built a mechanism which allows for evaluating and visualizing spatial queries from SWRL rules. We are currently extending this approach in a 3D Information System dedicated to archaeological survey based on photogrammetric survey and knowledge representation for spatial reasoning.

Acknowledgement. This work is partially done in the framework of the projects GROPLAN (ANR-13-CORD-0014) and ASPIQ (ANR-12-BS02-0003) funded by ANR, the French agency for scientific research.

References

1. Drap, P., Merad, D., Hijazi, B., Gaoua, L., Nawaf, M., Saccone, M., Chemisky, B., Seinturier, J., Sourisseau, J.-C., Gambin, T., Castro, F.: Underwater photogrammetry and object modeling: a case study of xlendi wreck in Malta. Sensors **15**(12), 29802 (2015)
2. Gergatsoulis, M., Bountouri, L., Gaitanou, P., Papatheodorou, C.: Mapping cultural metadata schemas to CIDOC conceptual reference model, Athens, pp. 321–326 (2010)
3. Niccolucci, F., D'Andrea, A.: An ontology for 3D cultural objects. In: The 7th International Symposium on Virtual Reality, Archaeology and Cultural Heritage VAST (2006)
4. Roy, S., Yan, M.F.: Method and system for creating owl ontology from java. I.T. Limited, Google Patents (2012)
5. Kalyanpur, A., Pastor, D.J., Battle, S., Padget, J.A.: Automatic mapping of OWL ontologies into Java. In: SEKE (2004)
6. Ježek, P., Mouček, R.: Semantic framework for mapping object-oriented model to semantic web languages. Front. Neuroinform. **9**, 3 (2015)
7. Stevenson, G., Dobson, S.: Sapphire: generating java runtime artefacts from OWL ontologies. In: Salinesi, C., Pastor, O. (eds.) CAiSE 2011. LNBIP, vol. 83, pp. 425–436. Springer, Heidelberg (2011). https://doi.org/10.1007/978-3-642-22056-2_46
8. Horridge, M., Knublauch, H., Rector, A., Stevens, R., Wroe, C.: A Practical Guide To Building OWL Ontologies Using the Protege-OWL Plugin and CO-ODE Tools. 1.0 (2004)

---

[2] https://github.com/protegeproject/swrlapi/wiki/SWRLBuiltInBridge#SWRL_BuiltIns

Assessing the Completeness of Entities in Knowledge Bases

Albin Ahmeti[1]([✉]), Simon Razniewski[2]([✉]), and Axel Polleres[1]

[1] Vienna University of Economics and Business, Vienna, Austria
albin.ahmeti@gmail.com
[2] Free University of Bozen-Bolzano, Bolzano, Italy
razniewski@inf.unibz.it

Abstract. While human-created knowledge bases (KBs) such as Wikidata provide usually high-quality data (precision), it is generally hard to understand their completeness. In this paper we propose to assess the relative completeness of entities in knowledge bases, based on comparing the extent of information with other similar entities. We outline building blocks of this approach, and present a prototypical implementation.

1 Introduction

Knowledge bases such as Wikidata, YAGO or DBpedia are becoming increasingly popular as structured sources of data, and are used in a variety of tasks such as structured search, question answering, or entity recognition, even though they are generally highly *incomplete* [8]. In particular, when incomplete KBs are combined with query languages that contain negation such as SPARQL, the result easily yields unsound answers [6]. Understanding how complete KBs are on different aspects is important for KB curators so they know where to focus their efforts, and for consumers to know to which extent they can rely on a KB.

It is difficult to talk about the completeness of KBs because completeness can be investigated on various levels and with varying semantics. While it is relatively easy to understand when a knowledge base is complete for children of Obama (when Malia and Sasha are there), it is not clear what completeness of Obama himself, or of US politicians as a whole, could mean. Previous work on knowledge base completeness has focused on the lowest level, i.e., finding out when a subject is complete for a predicate (like Obama for *child*) [2,4,7], whereas more abstract levels have not been investigated so far.

In this paper we propose investigating completeness on the level of entities, i.e., to give statements about how complete entities such as Barack Obama or Portoroz are. We propose to compute these statements by comparison with other, similar entities. More specifically, for a designated entity we check its coverage of frequent properties, computed among similar entities. We have implemented a prototype as *Recoin (Relative Completeness Indicator)* in Wikidata.

E. Blomqvist et al. (Eds.): ESWC 2017 Satellite Events, LNCS 10577, pp. 7–11, 2017.
https://doi.org/10.1007/978-3-319-70407-4_2

2   Background

While general-purpose knowledge bases already find application in a variety of tasks, due to their ill-defined scope (for instance, unlike Wikipedia, Wikidata has no relevance criteria other that new items should be linked to at least one existing item) and/or ambition to capture as much knowledge as possible, they are in general highly incomplete. In Wikidata, for instance, only 48% of politicians are member of a party, or only 0.02% of people do have a child.

Previous work on assessing KB completeness has focused on the level of subject-predicate pairs. [7] provides a plugin for Wikidata that allows to assert completeness for such pairs directly on the Wikidata website. [2] has used association rule mining for automatically determining complete pairs. [4] used Wikipedia texts to mine the cardinalities of such pairs, using these cardinalities in turn to assess completeness. A recent survey paper, [5], provides a comprehensive overview on the state-of-the-art KB refinement approaches aimed at improving the KB completeness.

For more holistic descriptions of quality, Wikipedia has so-called status indicators (like "Featured article", "Good article"). For Wikidata, such indicators do not yet exist, but their introduction is planned.[1]

3   Relative Completeness Indicators

For basic granularities, such as children of Obama, as discussed in [2,4,7], boolean completeness annotations generally suffice. In contrast, on the entity level, given that Wikidata contains over 2700 properties, of which 101 are used at least 1000 times for the class *human*, containing further ill-defined properties such as *medical condition*, *notable work* and *participant of*, it is clear that boolean statements such as "Data about Obama is complete", or "Data about Trump is incomplete", are not meaningful.

To allow statements for entities, we thus propose to define a relative completeness measure. More specifically, we propose to compare the extent of information about an entity with the extent of information that is available for other, similar entities. For instance, in assessing the completeness of Obama, we would compare the information available about him with that available for other politicians, while when assessing the completeness of Slovenia, we would compare with other countries.

There are three crucial components to this approach, (i) the definition of similar entities, (ii) the way how the extent of information is compared among similar entities, and (iii) the way how explanations are provided.

(i) For similarity, classes are a natural baseline, and class-like properties such as *occupation* allow a further refinement. Semantic similarity measures [9] could provide even better way to find similar entities.

---

[1] https://en.wikipedia.org/wiki/Wikipedia:Wikidata#Article_status_indicators.

(ii) Baselines for comparison could be counts of facts or properties, while better results can be expected if the relevance or importance of properties and facts is taken into account [1].

(iii) The way explanations are generated depends highly on the choices made for (i) and (ii), and will in turn impact usability for knowledge base authors and users. We may expect a tradeoff between accuracy and complexity, i.e., more complex choices may lead to more accurate assertions, which however are harder to explain, thus not necessarily increasing usability.

4 Wikidata Implementation

We have implemented a relative completeness indicator called *Recoin* in Wikidata.[2] It is provided as user script, i.e., logged in Wikimedia users can enable it in a user configuration file. It consists of two components. The core component, which adds a relative completeness indicator to the status indicator section of Wikidata articles, is shown in Fig. 1. The indicator is a color-coded progress bar, which can show 5 levels of completeness, ranging from "very detailed" to "very basic". An explanation module adds information about the relevant missing properties, based on which the completeness level is calculated. Further details about the architecture are on the tools website. It is currently available on the Wikidata pages of all *humans* that have a profession. Internally, the completeness level is computed as follows:

1. Each entity is compared with the set of all entities that have at least one profession in common.
2. For that set, the 50 most frequent properties are computed. The completeness level is then computed using fixed thresholds, i.e., if the entity has more than 40 out of these 50 properties, completeness is on the highest level, if it has between 30 and 40 of these properties, second highest level, and so on.
3. As explanation, the properties absent wrt. the comparison set are shown along with their frequency in the comparison set.

The tool was made available to the Wikidata community on 15th of November, 2016. An expansion to all *humans* and other classes of entities are planned.

5 Evaluation and Future Work

Some completeness levels computed by Recoin are for Obama 4 (detailed), for Trump 3 (fair), for Jimmy Wales 3 (fair), or for Dijkstra 2 (basic). While many levels appear reasonable (more popular entities are more complete, less popular ones less), others can only be understood using the explanations. The comparably low level for Jimmy Wales, for instance, is based on the fact that he misses properties such as *member of political party, position held* and *father*, which in the comparison set, exist for 10%, 8% and 6% of entities.

---

[2] https://www.wikidata.org/wiki/User:Ls1g/Recoin.

10   A. Ahmeti et al.

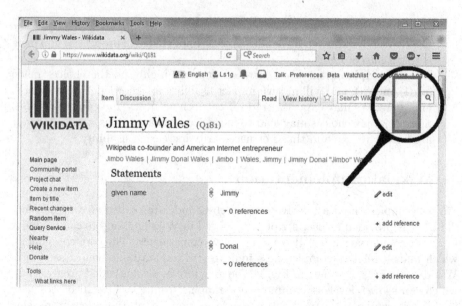

Fig. 1. Recoin core module on the Wikidata page of Jimmy Wales.

To further evaluate the levels computed by Recoin, in a crowdsourcing experiment, we compared a three-level scheme with levels that human annotators would give. Using 20 entities and 7 opinions per entity, we found that Recoin agreed in 60% of cases with the majority opinion, while in 25% it was off by one level, and in 15% off by two levels.

As future work, we aim to evaluate how methods based on semantic similarity can provide more meaningful sets of entities for comparison, and how relevance and importance of properties can be taken into account when comparing entities. More specifically, we aim to investigate [3], which uses statistical analysis of predicate-value pairs in order to find similar entities.

Acknowledgment. We thank Werner Nutt for comments, and Fariz Darari for technical help. This work has been partially supported by the project "TaDaQua", funded by the Free University of Bozen-Bolzano.

References

1. Dessi, A., Atzori, M.: A machine-learning approach to ranking RDF properties. Future Gener. Comput. Syst. **54**, 366–377 (2016)
2. Galárraga, L., Razniewski, S., Amarilli, A., Suchanek, F.M.: Predicting completeness in knowledge bases. In: WSDM (2017)
3. Hogan, A., Polleres, A., Umbrich, J., Zimmermann, A.: Some entities are more equal than others: statistical methods to consolidate linked data. In: NeFoRS (2010)
4. Mirza, P., Razniewski, S., Nutt, W.: Expanding Wikidata's parenthood information by 178%, or how to mine relation cardinalities. In: ISWC Posters & Demos (2016)

5. Paulheim, H.: Knowledge graph refinement: a survey of approaches and evaluation methods. Semant. Web **8**(3), 489–508 (2017)
6. Polleres, A., Feier, C., Harth, A.: Rules with contextually scoped negation. In: Sure, Y., Domingue, J. (eds.) ESWC 2006. LNCS, vol. 4011, pp. 332–347. Springer, Heidelberg (2006). doi:10.1007/11762256_26
7. Prasojo, R.E., Darari, F., Razniewski, S., Nutt, W.: Managing and consuming completeness information for wikidata using COOL-WD. In: COLD (2016)
8. Razniewski, S., Suchanek, F.M., Nutt, W.: But what do we actually know. In: AKBC (2016)
9. Rodríguez, M.A., Egenhofer, M.J.: Determining semantic similarity among entity classes from different ontologies. TKDE **15**(2), 442–456 (2003)

Unsupervised Open Relation Extraction

Hady Elsahar[1]([✉]), Elena Demidova[2], Simon Gottschalk[2], Christophe Gravier[1],
and Frederique Laforest[1]

[1] Univ Lyon, UJM-Saint-Etienne, CNRS, Laboratoire Hubert Curien, Lyon, France
{hady.elsahar,christophe.gravier,frederique.laforest}@univ-st-etienne.fr
[2] L3S Research Center, Leibniz Universität Hannover, Hannover, Germany
{demidova,gottschalk}@L3S.de

Abstract. We explore methods to extract relations between named entities from free text in an unsupervised setting. In addition to standard feature extraction, we develop a novel method to re-weight word embeddings. We alleviate the problem of features sparsity using an individual feature reduction. Our approach exhibits a significant improvement by 5.8% over the state-of-the-art relation clustering scoring a F1-score of 0.416 on the NYT-FB dataset.

Keywords: Relation extraction · Word embedding · NLP

1 Introduction

Relation extraction (RE) is the task of identification and classification of relations between named entities (such as persons, locations or organizations) in free text. RE is of utmost practical interest for various fields including event detection, knowledge base construction and question answering. Figure 1 illustrates a typical RE task. For the first two sentences, RE should identify the semantic relation type *birth place* between the named entity pairs regardless of the surface pattern used to express the relation such as *hometown is* or *was born in*. RE should also distinguish it from the album production relation between the same named entities in the third sentence.

Distant supervision techniques for RE [1,4] have proven to be very efficient in solving that problem. However, distant supervision is limited to a fixed set of relations in a given knowledge base, which hinders its adaptation to new domains. Unsupervised approaches [3,7] can potentially overcome these limitations by applying purely unsupervised methods enabling extraction of open relations (relations unknown in the knowledge base in advance). In this paper, we propose an unsupervised approach to extract and cluster open relations between named entities from free text by re-weighting word embeddings and using the types of named entities as additional features.

© Springer International Publishing AG 2017
E. Blomqvist et al. (Eds.): ESWC 2017 Satellite Events, LNCS 10577, pp. 12–16, 2017.
https://doi.org/10.1007/978-3-319-70407-4_3

1. ***David Bowie***'s <u>hometown is</u> ***London***, United Kingdom.
2. ***Axel Rose***, also known as "William Bruce", <u>was born in</u> ***Lafayette***, Indiana.
3. ***David Bowie*** <u>produced his first album in</u> ***London***, United Kingdom.

Fig. 1. Sentences containing textual <u>relations</u> between ***named entities***.

2   Proposed Method

Our system builds sentence representations based on the types of the involved named entities, and the terms forming the relations. For the latter, we use pretrained word embeddings after re-weighting them according to the dependency path between the named entities. These representations are clustered so that different representations of the semantically equivalent relations are mapped to the same cluster. Figure 2 presents an overview of our system for unsupervised open relation extraction, consisting of four stages: preprocessing, feature extraction, sparse feature reduction and relation clustering described in the following.

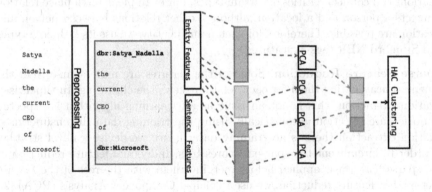

Fig. 2. System overview

Preprocessing. For each sentence in the dataset, we extract named entities using DBpedia Spotlight and consider all sentences containing at least two entities. For this set of sentences, the Stanford CoreNLP dependency parser is utilized to extract the lexicalized dependency path between each pair of named entities.

Feature Extraction. For each sentence, our method outputs a vector representation of the textual relation between each named entity pair. Features include word embeddings, dependency paths between named entities, and named entity types. Word embeddings provide an estimation of the semantic similarity between terms using vector proximity. Sentence representations are typically built by averaging word vectors. However, not all words in a sentence equally

contribute to the expression of the relation between two named entities. Therefore we develop a novel method to re-weight the pre-trained word embeddings.
Terms that appear within the lexicalized dependency path between the two
named entities are given a higher weight. Intuitively, shorter dependency paths
are more likely to represent true relationships between the named entities. The
vector representation $s(W, D)$ of each sentence is calculated through the following function:

$$s(W, D) = \sum_{w_i \in W} f(w_i, W, D) \cdot v(w_i), \quad f(w_i, W, D) = \begin{cases} \frac{C_{in} \cdot |W|}{|D|}, & \text{if } w_i \epsilon D \\ C_{out}, & \text{otherwise} \end{cases},$$

where $W = \{w_1, ..., w_n\}$ is the set of terms in the sentence, $D \subset W$ is the set
of terms in the lexicalized dependency path between the named entities in the
sentence, and $v(w_i)$ is the pre-trained word embedding vector for w_i. $C_{in} \geq 1$ and
C_{out} are constant values experimentally set to 1.85 and 0.02. We use Glove[1] word
embeddings of size 100. As a baseline, we compare these representations with
standard sentence representations features such as: TF-IDF, the sum of word
embeddings, and the sum of IDF re-weighted word embeddings [5]. Intuitively,
relations can connect entities of certain types. For example, a birth place relation
connects a person and a location, although other relations between person and
location are possible. Therefore, for each named entity, we use its DBpedia types
and Stanford NER tags as features.

Sparse Feature Reduction. Some of the features are more sparse than the
others; concatenating them for each relation skews the clustering. In supervised
relation extraction, this is not an issue as any learning algorithm is expected
to do feature selection automatically using the training data. In unsupervised
relation extraction there is no training data, hence we devise a novel strategy
in order to circumvent the sparse features bias. Individual feature reduction of
the sparse features is applied before merging them with the rest of the feature
vectors. For feature reduction, we use Principal Component Analysis (PCA) [2].

Relation Clustering. We use Hierarchical Agglomerative Clustering (HAC) to
cluster the feature representations of each relation, with Ward's [6] linkage criteria[2], which yields slightly better results than the k-means clustering algorithm.

3 Evaluation

To evaluate our system, we use the NYT-FB dataset [3]. This dataset contains
approximately 1.8M sentences divided into 80%–20% test-validation splits and
aligned automatically to the statements (triples) from Freebase. The alignment
between sentences and the properties of the Freebase triples in this dataset is
considered as the gold standard for the relation clustering algorithm.

---

[1] http://nlp.stanford.edu/projects/glove/.
[2] Accessing the clustering output by HAC at rank k giving k clusters.

We use the validation split to tune the parameters for re-weighting word vectors and the PCA algorithm, and the test set for evaluating relation discovery methods. We compare our method using the best identified feature combination with the state-of-the-art models for unsupervised Relation Discovery, namely the variational autoencoders model [3] and two other systems, Rel-LDA [7], and Hierarchical Agglomerative Clustering (HAC) baseline with standard features [8]. To make our results comparable we set the number of relations to induce (number of clusters k) to 100, following the SOA systems.

Table 1 shows the performance of the clustering algorithm by relying only on sentence representations as features. Results demonstrate that our method of word embeddings re-weighted by the dependency path shows a significant improvement over other traditional sentence representations. Table 2 shows the performance when the dependency re-weighted word embeddings are merged with the rest of the proposed features and applying individual feature reduction. Our method outperforms the state-of-the-art relation discovery algorithm scoring a pairwise F1 score of 41.6%.

Table 1. Comparison between different features for clustering.

Feature	F_1
TF-IDF	12.2
Word-Emb.	7.4
IDF-Emb.	10.3
Dependency Re-Weighted Emb.	**19.5**

Table 2. Pairwise F_1 (%) scores of different models on the test set of the NYT-FB dataset.

Var. Autoencoder	Rel-LDA	HAC	Our
35.8	29.6	28.3	**41.6**

4   Conclusion

In this paper, we proposed an approach for unsupervised relation extraction from free text. Our approach is based on a novel method of re-weighting word vectors according to the dependency parse tree of the sentence. As additional features, we use the types of named entities involved in the relations. A final HAC clustering is applied to the sentence representations so that similar representation of a relation are mapped to the same cluster. Our evaluation results demonstrate that our method outperforms the state-of-the-art relation clustering method by 5.8% pairwise F1 score. The code for feature building and dimensionality reduction is publicly available[3].

---

[3] https://github.com/hadyelsahar/relation-discovery-2-entities.git

Acknowledgements. This work was partially funded by H2020-MSCA-ITN-2014 WDAqua (64279), ALEXANDRIA (ERC 339233) and Data4UrbanMobility (BMBF).

References

1. Augenstein, I., Maynard, D., Ciravegna, F.: Distantly supervised web relation extraction for knowledge base population. Semant. Web **7**(4), 335–349 (2016)
2. Jolliffe, I.T.: Principal component analysis. In: Lovric, M. (ed.) International Encyclopedia of Statistical Science, pp. 1094–1096. Springer, Heidelberg (2011). doi:10.1007/978-3-642-04898-2_455
3. Marcheggiani, D., Titov, I.: Discrete-state variational autoencoders for joint discovery and factorization of relations. Trans. ACL **4**, 231–244 (2016)
4. Mintz, M., Bills, S., Snow, R., Jurafsky, D.: Distant supervision for relation extraction without labeled data. In: Proceedings of ACL 2009, pp. 1003–1011 (2009)
5. Rei, M., Cummins, R.: Sentence similarity measures for fine-grained estimation of topical relevance in learner essays. In: Proceedings of the BEA Workshop (2016)
6. Ward Jr., J.H.: Hierarchical grouping to optimize an objective function. J. Am. Statist. Assoc. **58**(301), 236–244 (1963)
7. Yao, L., Haghighi, A., Riedel, S., McCallum, A.: Structured relation discovery using generative models. In: Proceedings of EMNLP 2011 (2011)
8. Yao, L., Riedel, S., McCallum, A.: Unsupervised relation discovery with sense disambiguation. In: Proceedings of ACL 2012 (2012)

REPRODUCE-ME: Ontology-Based Data Access for Reproducibility of Microscopy Experiments

Sheeba Samuel[(⊠)] and Birgitta König-Ries

Heinz-Nixdorf Chair for Distributed Information Systems,
Friedrich-Schiller University, Jena, Germany
{sheeba.samuel,birgitta.koenig-ries}@uni-jena.de

Abstract. It has always been the aim of every scientist to make their work reproducible so that the scientific community can verify and trust the experiment results. With more complex *in vivo* and *in vitro* studies, achieving reproducibility has become more challenging over the last decades. In this work, we focus on integrative data management for reproducibility aspects related to execution environment conservation taking into account the use case of microscopy experiments. We use Semantic Web technologies to describe the experiment and its execution environment. We have developed an ontology, REPRODUCE-ME (Reproduce Microscopy Experiments) by extending the existing vocabulary PROV-O. Scientists can use this ontology to make semantic queries related to reproducibility of experiments on the microscopic data. To ensure efficient execution of these queries, we rely on ontology-based data access to source data stored in a relational DBMS.

Keywords: Reproducibility · Experiments · Ontology · OBDA · Microscopy

1 Introduction

The latest advancements in the field of science have brought new challenges to achieving reproducibility. Interviews with the scientists in the CRC ReceptorLight[1] helped us to understand the different scientific practices followed in their experiments and their requirements concerning reproducibility, data management and data reuse [6]. The results of an experiment performed by a scientist can show different anomalies and inconsistencies. This can be due to different reasons like a specific device configuration, a certain property of a material, procedural or human error. Scientists would like to be able to track errors and expose only those datasets which resulted in the error by querying from the large volume of data. Examples of such evaluation queries are "Which experiment used the material which was referenced in journal X but was not verified?" or "Which

---

[1] http://www.receptorlight.uni-jena.de/.

© Springer International Publishing AG 2017
E. Blomqvist et al. (Eds.): ESWC 2017 Satellite Events, LNCS 10577, pp. 17–20, 2017.
https://doi.org/10.1007/978-3-319-70407-4_4

experiment materials do not have the citation of the paper where the material was described?". The scientists would like to get answers for these questions for later analysis and reproducibility of their experiments. Currently, this is only partially possible by manually browsing through (hopefully thoroughly written) lab books.

The aim of our work is to enable end-to-end reproducibility of scientific experiments taking into account the use case of microscopy. As an initial step towards reproducibility, we set up an information system, that stores not only relevant experiment data, but also captures provenance of experiments. This includes all resources, activities, agents and their roles in the experiment. We introduce the REPRODUCE-ME ontology, which is extended from the W3C PROV-O to make this information available in a structured and queryable way. Scientists who use microscopic relational database management platforms like OMERO [1] can benefit from this approach which allows them to pose competency questions related to their experiment and its execution environment.

2   State of the Art

Many semantic vocabularies have been developed to capture provenance for different applications of science. PROV-O [4] provides high flexibility to align between different ontologies [2] making it general-purpose and domain-independent. There are a few works which capture some aspects of scientific experiments like design and methodology but not others like execution environment [7]. To the best of our knowledge, there are only few microscopy domain ontologies [3] which model data related to biological structures and microscopy images. Research is continuing to enable reproducibility of experiments with the help of Semantic Web technologies. The goal of our work is to capture the provenance of the experiment, execution environment and agents responsible for the experiment and to be able to share the data with other scientists based on the roles and permissions assigned to them. We achieve this by augmenting our OMERO based data management platform with a semantic layer which allows scientists to represent and query the data with the help of an ontology and ontology-based data access.

3   REPRODUCE-ME Ontology: Ontology for Reproducibility of Microscopy Experiments

We extended PROV-O to build the REPRODUCE-ME Ontology to describe microscopy experiments, procedures, instruments used, people involved and results [5]. The prefix "repr:" is used to indicate the terms. PROV-O makes a clear distinction between agents, entities and activities involved in producing a piece of data or thing. The main concepts in the REPRODUCE-ME ontology are extended from the starting point terms of PROV-O which include prov:Entity, prov:Agent and prov:Activity. The main entity `repr:Experiment` which extends from `prov:Entity`, connects various concepts and relations in the ontology. The execution environment is described using `repr:ExperimentMaterial`, `repr:Device` and `repr:Setting`. The class `prov:Person` is extended to introduce entities like `repr:Supervisor`, `repr:Experimenter` etc. These are some of the agents who are responsible for performing, supervising, investigating, designing the experiment or manufacturing or distributing the materials needed for an experiment. In addition, the ontology introduces various roles for these agents by extending the `prov:Role` to include classes like `repr:Verification`. Various object properties like `prov:actedOnBehalfOf`, `repr:wasVerifiedBy`, `prov:wasAssociatedWith` are used to describe the interaction between agents, entities and activities.

In Fig. 1, entities are represented in ovals, activities in rectangles and agents in pentagons. The example shows a part of a scientific experiment which involves the activities, agents and its execution environment. The entities, agents, and activities can be references to linked data on the web like DOI, ORCID.

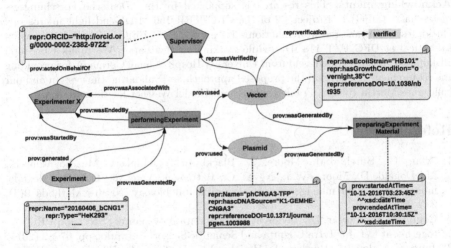

Fig. 1. REPRODUCE-ME ontology

There is a need for a stable data management system which can handle a large volume of data as well as all the formats of microscopic images. So we develop our system by extending features of OMERO, an image data management platform, which uses PostgreSQL. In order to avoid replicating the same data to RDF, we use OBDA techniques to access data from the data layer through a conceptual layer. The terms in the ontology are semantically linked with the data which is stored in the relational database. The OBDA system helps in the question answering without the need of replicating the relational data to the conceptual layer. The OBDA system will make a transformation of the queries in the conceptual layer to the query language for the data layer.

In our work, the conceptual layer, expressed by the REPRODUCE-ME ontology was mapped to the data layer which is in the form of relational database,

PostgreSQL. The mappings are written using Ontop[2]. The model was validated by testing with the list of competency questions provided by the scientists. The REPRODUCE-ME Ontology and the list of evaluation questions expressed in SPARQL are publicly available[3].

4   Conclusion and Future Work

This paper presents the REPRODUCE-ME ontology which is developed taking the real case scenario of modeling a microscopy experiment. This work provides a conceptual layer to map the data stored in relational database so that scientists can make semantic queries related to experiments. This proof-of-concept was tested with limited data. Future work includes scalability and performance test and developing a visual user interface for the scientists who have less background in the computer science domain to make queries in human readable format.

Acknowledgements. This research is supported by the "Deutsche Forschungsgemeinschaft" (DFG) in Project Z2 of the CRC/TRR 166 "High-end light microscopy elucidates membrane receptor function - ReceptorLight". Birgitta König-Ries was on sabbatical at DFG FZT 118 iDiv while working on this paper. We thank Christoph Biskup and Kathrin Groeneveld from University Hospital Jena, Germany, for providing the requirements to develop the proposed approach and validating the system and our colleagues Martin Bücker, Frank Taubert und Daniel Walther for their feedback.

References

1. Allan, C., Burel, J.M., Moore, J., Blackburn, C., Linkert, M., Loynton, S., MacDonald, D., Moore, W.J., Neves, C., Patterson, A., et al.: OMERO: flexible, model-driven data management for experimental biology. Nature Methods 9(3), 245–253 (2012)
2. Compton, M., Corsar, D., Taylor, K.: Sensor data provenance: SSNO and PROV-O together at last. In: Terra Cognita and Semantic Sensor, Networks, pp. 67–82 (2014)
3. Jupp, S., Malone, J., Burdett, T., Heriche, J.K., Williams, E., Ellenberg, J., Parkinson, H., Rustici, G.: The cellular microscopy phenotype ontology. J. Biomed. Semant. 7(1), 28 (2016). http://dx.doi.org/10.1186/s13326-016-0074-0
4. Lebo, T., Sahoo, S., McGuinness, D., Belhajjame, K., Cheney, J., Corsar, D., Garijo, D., Soiland-Reyes, S., Zednik, S., Zhao, J.: PROV-O: the PROV ontology. W3C Recommendation 30 (2013)
5. Samuel, S.: Integrative data management for reproducibility of microscopy experiments. In: Blomqvist, E., Maynard, D., Gangemi, A., Hoekstra, R., Hitzler, P., Hartig, O. (eds.) ESWC 2017. LNCS, vol. 10250, pp. 246–255. Springer, Cham (2017). doi:10.1007/978-3-319-58451-5_19
6. Samuel, S., Taubert, F., Walther, D., König-Ries, B., Bücker, H.M.: Towards reproducibility of microscopy experiments. D-Lib Magaz. 23(1/2) (2017)
7. Soldatova, L.N., King, R.D.: An ontology of scientific experiments. J. R. Soc. Interface 3(11), 795–803 (2006)

---

[2] http://ontop.inf.unibz.it/.
[3] http://fusion.cs.uni-jena.de/fusion/repr/.

Leveraging Cognitive Computing for Multi-class Classification of E-learning Videos

Danilo Dessì[✉], Gianni Fenu, Mirko Marras, and Diego Reforgiato Recupero

Department of Mathematics and Computer Science, University of Cagliari,
Via Ospedale 72, 09124 Cagliari, Italy
{danilo_dessi,fenu,mirko.marras,diego.reforgiato}@unica.it

Abstract. Multi-class classification aims at assigning each sample to one category chosen among a set of different options. In this paper, we present our work for the development of a novel system for multi-class classification of e-learning videos based on the covered educational subjects. The audio transcripts and the text depicted into visual frames are extracted and analyzed by Cognitive Computing tools, going over the traditional term-based similarity approaches. Preliminary experiments demonstrate effectiveness and capabilities of the system, suggesting that semantic analysis improves the performance of multi-class classification.

Keywords: Cognitive computing · Multi-class classification · E-learning video classification · Semantic classification

1 Introduction

Digital videos have become one of the most important e-learning formats. The growing popularity of online course providers, such as Coursera[1] and edX[2], has enabled learners to experience smart video-based lectures which are rapidly increasing in number. They mainly provide knowledge through the teacher's voice and the content is usually depicted by presentation slides or digital whiteboards. This has led to specific approaches for the analysis of their educational content.

The maturity of Automatic Speech Recognition (ASR) and Optical Character Recognition (OCR) services has made possible the extraction of text from audio and visual frames. As a result, several studies have tried to address content-based video lecture analysis as text analysis for various purposes (e.g. clustering, classification, retrieval). For instance, [1] applied topic modeling to cluster videos from their audio transcripts and [2] extracted key-phrases and topic-based segments that effectively summarize the content of a video lecture. In [3], ASR and OCR results were subsequently analyzed to detect keywords based on Term Frequency Inverse Document Frequency (TF-IDF) scores. Similar approaches were

---

[1] https://www.coursera.org/.
[2] http://edx.org/.

E. Blomqvist et al. (Eds.): ESWC 2017 Satellite Events, LNCS 10577, pp. 21–25, 2017.
https://doi.org/10.1007/978-3-319-70407-4_5

integrated in [4,5] for video lecture retrieval. However, they tend to adopt traditional term-based similarity approaches. In contrast, knowledge extraction from natural language text can detect insights out of the video data. State-of-the-art cognitive systems, such as IBM Watson[3] and Microsoft Cognitive Services[4], have the ability to infer semantic information rather than simple word frequencies and they can enable systems to better learn about resources.

In this paper, we introduce a supervised multi-class classification system for e-learning videos which uses semantic content together with textual data extracted from audio transcripts and text depicted in visual frames. The goal is to assign each sample to one category chosen from a predefined list according to the covered educational subjects. The text derived from videos is processed to extract semantic content pertaining to concepts. It is the first attempt of mixing text features and semantics for performing multi-class classification of video lectures following the methodology and the tools stated below. For this purpose, we developed a prototype and performed a first evaluation, showing that enriching textual data with semantic content improves classification performances.

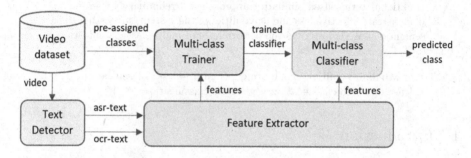

Fig. 1. A reference schema for the proposed system.

2 System Overview

The proposed system is depicted in Fig. 1. It is built on top of three main foundations: (i) the use of textual data derived from videos, (ii) its content-based semantic analysis through cognitive computing services, and (iii) the high modularity for easy customization in terms of feature types and classification algorithms. The modules work in a pipelined work-flow. At this stage, we have implemented a Python prototype following the design described as follows.

Text Detector. The module takes a *video* as input and returns two texts namely *asr-texts* and *ocr-texts* extracted from its audio and its visual frames respectively. It gets the video transcript from ASR computation and the text depicted in the images from OCR. Both raw texts are spell-checked and eventually corrected.

---

[3] https://www.ibm.com/watson/.
[4] https://www.microsoft.com/cognitive-services.

The module employs IBM Speech-to-Text API[5] and Google Text Recognition API[6] for text detection, WordNet[7] for spell-checking.

Feature Extractor. The module receives two texts namely *asr-texts* and *ocr-texts* as input and returns a set of *features*. Each feature is a pair whose first element is the string identifier of that feature and the second element is its relevance score. The relevance value spans in the range [0, 1] where a value closer to 0 represents a low relevance and a value closer to 1 represents a high relevance of the corresponding feature into the text. The module extracts concepts through IBM Alchemy Language APIs[8] in addition to TF-IDF scores. As default, it returns a set of features resulting from their concatenation where the TF-IDF scores are first row-by-row normalized in the range [0, 1] through a min-max technique. However, the returned type of features can be selected as a parameter.

Multi-class Trainer. The module takes a set of *features* together with the *pre-assigned class* for each video in a training set. The features are employed to represent each video as a vector in a N-dimensional space, where N is the number of different features detected from training videos. Using these vectors, the module trains a classifier and returns it. The module can be set to use a subset of videos for validation. The algorithm underling the classifier can be selected from a list of alternatives we have implemented. At this stage, some variants of support vector machines have been integrated.

Multi-class Classifier. The module takes the *features* associated to a no-labeled video together with a *trained classifier* and returns the predicted class from the set of possible classes derived during training. The module works on the same N-dimensional space used for training the classifier; therefore, new unseen features extracted from the no-labeled video are ignored.

The system is designed to be modular and extensible. Each module is independent from the other ones and the addition and the update of feature types, feature fusion methods, or classification algorithms involve almost no changes to the base architecture. Moreover, each module is properly parametrized, with in mind that the system could be used via a graphical user interface in the future.

3   Preliminary Evaluation

We preliminarily evaluated precision, recall and f-measure of the system using support vector machine as classification algorithm and concepts and TF-IDF as feature types (10-fold cross-validation). The system was tested on a Coursera video dataset which is composed by more than 10,000 pre-annotated videos. For each video, the associated class consists of the category assigned to the course in which the video is provided. Due to unequal category distribution, the

---

[5] https://www.ibm.com/watson/developercloud/speech-to-text.html.

[6] https://developers.google.com/vision/text-overview.

[7] https://wordnet.princeton.edu/.

[8] https://www.ibm.com/watson/developercloud/alchemy-language.html.

metrics are locally calculated for each category, then their average is obtained by weighting each category metric with the number of instances of the category in the dataset. In Table 1, the preliminary evaluation we conducted shows that the combination of TF-IDF and concepts obtains the highest F-measure.

Table 1. System performance using weighted average computation of metrics.

Features	Precision	Recall	F-Measure
TF-IDF	0.6852	0.6817	0.6741
Concepts	0.6320	0.6205	0.6138
TF-IDF + Concepts	0.6984	0.6951	0.6873

4 Conclusion and Future Work

In this paper, we described our work on developing a system for assigning content-based categories to educational videos from a pre-defined taxonomy based on audio transcripts and text in visual frames. Preliminary results suggest semantic analysis can improve the performance over using textual data only.

In next steps, we would investigate new approaches for assigning relevant scores depending on additional features (e.g. text fonts size), the use of other semantic analysis tools (e.g. frame semantic) and classification algorithms (e.g. neural networks), and larger datasets where to test our system. Moreover, we plan to employ Big Data architectures to support large-scale fast computations. Our system can be applied to other domains where the extraction of content-based categories from videos is essential.

Acknowledgments. Danilo Dessì and Mirko Marras gratefully acknowledge Sardinia Regional Government for the financial support of their PhD scholarship (P.O.R. Sardegna F.S.E. Operational Programme of the Autonomous Region of Sardinia, European Social Fund 2014–2020 - Axis III Education and Training, Thematic Goal 10, Priority of Investment 10ii, Specific Goal 10.5).

References

1. Basu, S., Yu, Y., Zimmermann, R.: Fuzzy clustering of lecture videos based on topic modeling. In: 2016 14th International Workshop on Content-Based Multimedia Indexing (CBMI), pp. 1–6. IEEE (2016)
2. Balasubramanian, V., Doraisamy, S.G., Kanakarajan, N.K.: A multimodal approach for extracting content descriptive metadata from lecture videos. J. Intell. Inf. Syst. **46**(1), 121–145 (2016)
3. Yang, H., Meinel, C.: Content based lecture video retrieval using speech and video text information. IEEE Trans. Learn. Technol. **7**(2), 142–154 (2014)

4. Kothawade, A.Y., Patil, D.R.: Retrieving instructional video content from speech and text information. In: Satapathy, S.C., Bhatt, Y.C., Joshi, A., Mishra, D.K. (eds.) Proceedings of the International Congress on Information and Communication Technology. AISC, vol. 439, pp. 311–322. Springer, Singapore (2016). doi:10.1007/978-981-10-0755-2_33
5. Radha, N.: Video retrieval using speech and text in video. In: International Conference on Inventive Computation Technologies, vol. 2, pp. 1–6. IEEE (2016)

The datAcron Ontology for Semantic Trajectories

Georgios M. Santipantakis$^{(\boxtimes)}$, George A. Vouros, Apostolos Glenis,
Christos Doulkeridis, and Akrivi Vlachou

University of Piraeus, Piraeus, Greece
{gsant,georgev,cdoulk}@unipi.gr,
apostglen46@gmail.com, avlachou@aueb.gr

Abstract. Motivated by real-life emerging needs in critical domains, this paper proposes a coherent and generic ontology for the representation of semantic trajectories, in association with related events and contextual information. *The main contribution of the proposed ontology is the representation of semantic trajectories at different levels of spatio-temporal analysis.*

1 Introduction

Many critical domains w.r.t. economy and safety, such as the Maritime and the Aviation domains, where Situation Awareness (MSA) and Air Traffic Management (ATM), respectively, are of importance, require analysis of moving objects' behaviour over time: Challenges concern effective detection and forecasting of moving entities' trajectories, as well as recognition and prediction of important events by exploiting information about entities' behaviour and contextual data. Due to these needs, semantic trajectories are turned into "first-class citizens", forming a paradigm shift towards operations that are built and revolve around the notion of trajectory. Our work focuses on trajectories and aims to build solutions towards managing data that are connected via, and contribute to enriched views of trajectories: Doing so, we revisit the notion of semantic trajectory and build on it. Specifically, it is expected that we will be able to *represent, store and manipulate the wealth of information available in disparate and heterogeneous data sources, integrated in a representation where trajectories are the main entities, towards computing meaningful moving patterns so as to recognize and predict the behaviour and states of moving objects.* Therefore, motivated by real-life emerging needs in MSA and ATM domains, this paper proposes a coherent and generic ontology for the representation of semantic trajectories, in association with related events and contextual information. *The main contribution of the proposed ontology is the representation of semantic trajectories at different levels of spatio-temporal analysis: Trajectories may be seen as temporal sequences of moving objects' positions derived from raw data, of mere geometries, of temporal sequences of raw data aggregations signifying meaningful events (generalizing on the stops and moves model [8]), providing a synoptic view of raw trajectories [7],*

© Springer International Publishing AG 2017
E. Blomqvist et al. (Eds.): ESWC 2017 Satellite Events, LNCS 10577, pp. 26–30, 2017.
https://doi.org/10.1007/978-3-319-70407-4_6

and as temporal sequences of non-overlapping meaningful trajectories segments (each revealing specific behaviour, event, goal, activity etc.). Representations at any such level of analysis should be linked to each other, as well as to contextual information and co-occurring events: These are important features for performing informed analysis tasks at different levels of detail/analysis, consulting raw data and/or semantic information associated with it.

Existing approaches for the representation of semantic trajectories either (a) use plain textual annotations instead of semantic links to other entities [1–3], hindering the provision of a fully-fledged representation where trajectories are semantically linked with other data or with semantic resources associated with moving objects' behaviour; (b) constrain the types of events that can be used for structuring a trajectory [1,2]; or (c) make assumptions on the constituents of trajectories [3,4,6] (e.g. semantic trajectories in [3] are sequences of sub-trajectories, while in [4] are sequences of episodes). To a greater extent than previous proposals, the proposed ontology *supports the representation of trajectories at multiple, interlinked levels of analysis*: For instance, although [4] provides a rich set of constructs for the representation of semantic trajectories, these are sequences of episodes, each associated with raw trajectory data, and optionally, with a spatio-temporal model of movement. However, there is no fine association between abstract models of movements and raw data. On the other hand, [3] provides a two-levels analysis where semantic trajectories are lists of semantic sub-trajectories, and each sub-trajectory in its own turn is a list of semantic points. Regarding events and episodes, these are connected to specific resources at specific levels of analysis: In [3] events -mostly related to the environment rather than to the trajectory itself- are connected to points only (something that may lead to ambiguities in some cases), while in [4] episodes concern things happening in the trajectory itself, and may be associated to specific models of movement: It is not clear how multiple models of a single trajectory -each at a different level of analysis- connected to a single episode, are associated. Finally, contextual information in [4] is related to movement models, episodes or semantic trajectories, which is quite generic, while in [3] environment attributes are associated to points only, and are assigned specific values.

2 The datAcron Ontology

The datAcron ontology (http://ai-group.ds.unipi.gr/datacron_ontology/) was developed by group consensus over a period of 12 months following the HCOME methodology [5]. It has been designed to be used as a core ontology for the MSA and ATM domains, following a data-driven approach towards supporting analysis tasks. Its development has been driven by ontologies related to our objectives (e.g. DUL, SimpleFeature, NASA Sweet and SSN) as well as schemas and specifications regarding data sources from the different domains.

The main concepts and properties in the datAcron ontology regarding trajectories, are depicted in Fig. 1. Starting from the definitions about *raw, structured* and *semantic trajectories* provided in [7], a *raw trajectory* is a temporal sequence of raw data specifying the moving object's spatio-temporal positions. Raw data can be aggregated, analyzed and semantically annotated, providing multiple abstractions of a trajectory. A maximal sequence of raw data that comply with a given pattern, define an *episode*. In this work we focus on *events* as a generalisation of episodes, taking also into consideration -in conjunction to movement data- *contextual information* (i.e. any information -mostly about the environment of an object- that affects its movement). *Events* represent specific, aggregated or abstract happenings instantiating an event pattern (whose description is not part of the ontology) and are distinguished to *low-level events* regarding information about a single trajectory, isolated from its context, and *high-level events* regarding information from multiple objects' trajectories and/or contextual information. Each event is associated with one or more moving objects, and it has spatial, temporal and domain-specific properties.

A *semantic trajectory* consists of a sequence of temporally non-overlapping *trajectory parts* that can be either *semantic nodes, raw positions* reported from sensing devises, or *trajectory segments*. Each trajectory part may be associated to a specific *geometry*, representing a point or region of occurrence, and a *temporal entity* specifying an instant or time interval of occurrence. A *semantic node* provides a meaningful abstraction or aggregation of raw positions. E.g. a set of raw positions may signify a "turn" event: This set can be represented as a single semantic node, associated to a low-level event of type "turn". Each semantic node or trajectory segment, may be associated with any trajectory part at a finer level of analysis; e.g. with a set of raw positions representing a "turn" or the last and first point of a "gap of communication". A *trajectory segment* is a trajectory itself, part of a whole trajectory. Segmentation of trajectories can be done with different objectives depending on the application and target analysis. A *structured trajectory* is a meaningful sequence of non-overlapping semantic trajectory parts. Any trajectory part may be associated with an event that co-occurs with it spatially and/or temporally: E.g. A bad weather region may co-occur with a trajectory crossing-it (thus, related spatially) during a time period (related temporally). It must be pointed out that each trajectory part can be associated with different trajectories of the same moving object: E.g. with the planned and with the actual trajectory of that object.

According to the above specifications, and as Fig. 1 shows, a trajectory -for instance- can be segmented to non-overlapping semantic trajectory segments, each corresponding to one or more semantic nodes. Each semantic node may be associated with a specific raw position or a temporally ordered sequence of raw positions of a moving object. Trajectory parts can be associated with contextual information, and they can be associated with events that happen independently from the trajectory but co-occur with the trajectory affecting the moving object's behaviour. In such a representation, one may consider a trajectory either as a list of non-overlapping trajectory segments, or as lists of semantic nodes, or even lists of raw trajectory data, or as a simple geometric object occurring in a specific time interval, also considering different mixtures of these levels of analysis, depending on analysis needs. Furthermore, it must be

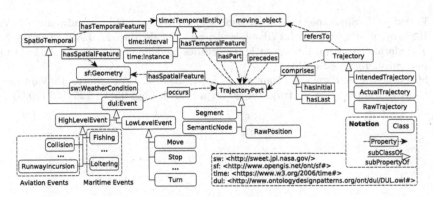

Fig. 1. The main concepts and relations of the proposed ontology.

noticed that the notion of event comprises happenings due to the trajectory itself (e.g. a "gap of communication") also in conjunction to contextual information (e.g. vessel in a protected or in a bad-weather area). Such events, associated to constructs at any level of abstraction can be further inspected and justified by information at lower-levels of analysis, or be further abstracted and generalised to more abstract levels.

Acknowledgement. This work is supported by the datAcron project, which has received funding from the European Union's Horizon 2020 research and innovation programme under grant agreement No. 687591.

References

1. Alvares, L.O., Bogorny, V., Kuijpers, B., de Macêdo, J.A.F., Moelans, B., Vaisman, A.A.: A model for enriching trajectories with semantic geographical information. In: GIS, p. 22 (2007)
2. Baglioni, M., de Macêdo, J.A.F., Renso, C., Trasarti, R., Wachowicz, M.: Towards semantic interpretation of movement behavior. In: Sester, M., Bernard, L., Paelke, V. (eds.) Advances in GIScience. Lecture Notes in Geoinformation and Cartography, pp. 271–288. Springer, Heidelberg (2009). doi:10.1007/978-3-642-00318-9_14
3. Bogorny, V., Renso, C., de Aquino, A.R., de Lucca Siqueira, F., Alvares, L.O.: Constant - a conceptual data model for semantic trajectories of moving objects. Trans. GIS **18**(1), 66–88 (2014)
4. Fileto, R., May, C., Renso, C., Pelekis, N., Klein, D., Theodoridis, Y.: The baquara[2] knowledge-based framework for semantic enrichment and analysis of movement data. Data Knowl. Eng. **98**, 104–122 (2015)
5. Kotis, K., Vouros, G.A.: Human-centered ontology engineering: the HCOME methodology. Knowl. Inf. Syst. **10**(1), 109–131 (2006)
6. Nogueira, T.P., Martin, H.: Querying semantic trajectory episodes. In: Proceedings of MobiGIS, pp. 23–30 (2015)

7. Parent, C., Spaccapietra, S., Renso, C., Andrienko, G.L., Andrienko, N.V., Bogorny, V., Damiani, M.L., Gkoulalas-Divanis, A., de Macêdo, J.A.F., Pelekis, N., Theodoridis, Y., Yan, Z.: Semantic trajectories modeling and analysis. ACM Comput. Surv. **45**(4), 42 (2013)
8. Spaccapietra, S., Parent, C., Damiani, M.L., de Macêdo, J.A.F., Porto, F., Vangenot, C.: A conceptual view on trajectories. Data Knowl. Eng. **65**(1), 126–146 (2008)

Dynamic Semantic Music Notation
Using Linked Data to Enhance Music Performance

David M. Weigl[(✉)] and Kevin R. Page

Oxford e-Research Centre, University of Oxford, Oxford, UK
{david.weigl,kevin.page}@oerc.ox.ac.uk

Abstract. The Music Encoding Initiative (MEI) XML schema expresses musical structure addressing score elements at musically meaningful levels of granularity (e.g., individual systems, measures, or notes). While this provides a comprehensive representation of music content, only concepts and relationships provided by the MEI schema can be encoded. Here, we present our Music Encoding and Linked Data (MELD) framework which applies RDF Web Annotations to targetted portions of the MEI structure. Concepts and relationships from the Semantic Web can be included alongside MEI in an expanded musical knowledge graph. We have implemented a music performance scenario which collects, distributes, and displays semantic annotations, enhancing a digital musical score used by performers in a live music jam session.

1 Introduction: Describing Music (with Linked Data)

Linked Data applications for multimedia link descriptive metadata to videos, images, or audio–including music [11]. Examples include catalogue descriptions of musical works (e.g. songs, albums) or performances, or biographical descriptions of the agents involved in the creation of music (composers, performers) [4,10]. Alternatively, they may describe (portions of) musical *content*, e.g., the first verse of a song. Media fragments[1] [12] can specify image regions (e.g., of musical score), temporal sections, named elements, or collection of tracks (in the case of multitrack recordings) of an audio or MIDI resource. Such fragments can be referenced within Linked Data structures incorporating arbitrary semantic descriptors. Typically, fragments are addressed according to timeline anchors expressed in milliseconds, beat instances, or MIDI clock ticks (e.g. [2,6,9]; see also SMIL [1]). Some of these have been directly transcribed into RDF [5]. However, such time positions are not *musically* meaningful.

The Music Encoding Initiative (MEI; [3]), an XML schema focussing on musical content, addresses this issue. MEI defines an XML hierarchy encompassing a comprehensive representation of musical structure at many levels of granularity, from an entire composition, via an individual measure, to an articulating staccato mark on a particular note. Content is cleanly separated from presentation [7], allowing the identification and addressing of fragments of a musical *work* (e.g., a collection of notes constituting a phrase within a particular measure

---

[1] http://www.w3.org/TR/media-frags/.

© Springer International Publishing AG 2017
E. Blomqvist et al. (Eds.): ESWC 2017 Satellite Events, LNCS 10577, pp. 31–34, 2017.
https://doi.org/10.1007/978-3-319-70407-4_7

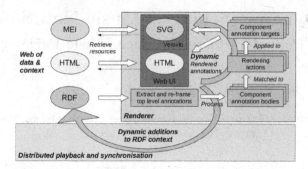

Fig. 1. Dynamic rendering of musical notation and semantic markup corresponding to user interactions

played by a specified instrument), rather than, e.g., a section of an audio recording of that work. MEI is embraced by music scholars, librarians, and technologists concerned with encoding fine-grained, machine-readable representations of musical meaning. While the classes, attributes, and data types required to encode a broad range of musical documents and structures are comprehensively expressed, MEI does not include or reference concepts, relationships, or existing descriptive forms of multimedia Linked Data external to its schema.

2   Music Encoding and Linked Data (MELD) Framework

Our Linked Data framework extends MEI-encoded musical structures with semantic Web Annotations[2] targetting named elements (fragments) within an MEI resource. Annotation bodies encode rendering and interactivity instructions according to `oa:semanticTag` graph nodes; for example, instances of the `meldterm:Jump` class comprise RDF data structures representing the requirements to render a hyperlink from one specified section of the score to another. Each annotation is itself a body of a *top-level* annotation targeting the URI of the MEI resource to be rendered. A RESTful web API supports dynamic collection, distribution, and presentation of annotations among a group of clients. A web renderer interprets these annotations, employing the open-source Verovio [8] MEI engraver to produce SVG renditions of musical score. Verovio retains the hierarchy and identifiers of MEI XML elements in its output, allowing for visual markup and dynamic interaction with score elements, identified in our Linked Data, through a web browser.

The procedure is illustrated in Fig. 1. The client processes a framed[3] JSON-LD representation of the RDF graph instantiating the data model. It then performs an HTTP GET call to acquire the MEI resource targeted by a top-level

---

[2] http://www.w3.org/TR/annotation-model/.
[3] http://json-ld.org/spec/latest/json-ld-framing/.

annotation, and renders the corresponding musical score to SVG using Verovio. Capture of user interactions and visual display of annotations is handled using HTML divs drawn as bounding boxes over portions of the SVG corresponding to MEI elements of interest; this is simplified by Verovio's retention of MEI identifiers in the produced SVG output. Such interactions generate further Web Annotations which are pushed to the server (HTTP POST), where they are incorporated into the RDF graph. The client then repeats this sequence in an iterative polling procedure, enabling multiple performers to interact dynamically with a shared representation of the score and knowledge graph, broadcasting new annotations to each performer's client in near-real-time.

3   Scenario: Supporting a Live Music Jam Session

Our implemented prototype scenario supports an ensemble of musicians performing from music notation enhanced by MELD semantic annotations. The annotated score is dynamically presented on a touchscreen to each performer. The renderer applies XML transformations on multi-voiced MEI files to show only the portions of score relevant to a respective performer. During a jam session, a performer can signal (via Web Annotations generated by the MELD web client) for the group to transition to a new piece by selecting from a drop-down menu populated by the results of external SPARQL queries—e.g., other songs associated with the artist URI referenced by a pointer element within the current MEI header's responsibility statement. The performer can also call out direction to shape the structural elements of the current song's performance, such as to jump to a particular chorus or verse.

Figure 2 illustrates this latter "jump" functionality: a performer "calls out" a jump action by tapping on a score element and selecting a musically meaningful destinations (e.g. Intro, Verse 1) specified as Linked Data (see Fig. 2; jump source highlighted in red, destination in green). Web Annotation RDF triples instantiating the corresponding `meldterm:Jump` action, along with provenance information, are generated and pushed to the server; where they are integrated into the shared knowledge graph, and distributed to the entire ensemble. Each performer taps on the jump source when they are ready, instructing their client

Fig. 2. Rendering of a Web Annotation expressing `meldterm:Jump`. (Color figure online)

to display the page of score containing the destination. Each client polls on a resource representing the set of annotations remaining to be actioned by the corresponding performer, and patches this list upon completing an action to ensure that a drop in connectivity does not "break" a performance.

Ongoing work is focussed on extending the system with additional semantic actions, as well as addressing user interaction constraints within a live performance context.

Acknowledgements. Undertaken as part of the Fusing Audio and Semantic Technologies for Intelligent Music Production and Consumption project. Funder: UK EPSRC (EP/L019981/1).

References

1. Bulterman, D.C., Rutledge, L.W.: SMIL 3.0: Flexible Multimedia for Web, Mobile Devices and Daisy Talking Books. Springer, Heidelberg (2009)
2. Gasser, M., Arzt, A., Gadermaier, T., Grachten, M., Widmer, G.: Classical music on the web-user interfaces and data representations. In: Proceedings of the 16th International Society for Music Information Retrieval Conference (2015)
3. Hankinson, A., Roland, P., Fujinaga, I.: The music encoding initiative as a document-encoding framework. In: Proceedings of the 12th International Society for Music Information Retrieval Conference, pp. 293–298 (2011)
4. Kobilarov, G., et al.: Media meets semantic web – how the BBC uses DBpedia and Linked Data to make connections. In: Aroyo, L., et al. (eds.) ESWC 2009. LNCS, vol. 5554, pp. 723–737. Springer, Heidelberg (2009). doi:10.1007/978-3-642-02121-3_53
5. Meroño-Peñuela, A., Hoekstra, R.: The song remains the same: lossless conversion and streaming of MIDI to RDF and back. In: Sack, H., Rizzo, G., Steinmetz, N., Mladenić, D., Auer, S., Lange, C. (eds.) ESWC 2016. LNCS, vol. 9989, pp. 194–199. Springer, Cham (2016). doi:10.1007/978-3-319-47602-5_38
6. Nurmikko-Fuller, T., Weigl, D.M., Page, K.R.: On organising multimedia performance corpora for musicological study using Linked Data. In: Proceedings of the 2nd International Workshop on Digital Libraries for Musicology (DLfM 2015), pp. 25–28, New York. ACM (2015)
7. Pugin, L., Kepper, J., Roland, P., Hartwig, M., Hankinson, A.: Separating presentation and content in MEI. In: Proceedings of the 13th International Society for Music Information Retrieval Conference, pp. 505–510 (2012)
8. Pugin, L., Zitellini, R., Roland, P.: Verovio: a library for engraving MEI music notation into SVG. In: Proceedings of the 15th International Society for Music Information Retrieval Conference, pp. 107–112 (2014)
9. Rahman, F., Siddiqi, J.: Semantic annotation of digital music. J. Comput. Syst. Sci. **78**(4), 1219–1231 (2012)
10. Raimond, Y., Abdallah, S.A., Sandler, M.B., Giasson, F.: The music ontology. In: Proceedings of the 8th International Conference on Music Information Retrieval, pp. 417–422 (2007)
11. Schandl, B., Haslhofer, B., Bürger, T., Langegger, A., Halb, W.: Linked Data and multimedia: the state of affairs. Multimed. Tools Appl. **59**(2), 523–556 (2012)
12. Troncy, R., Hardman, L., Van Ossenbruggen, J., Hausenblas, M.: Identifying spatial and temporal media fragments on the web. In: W3C Video on the Web Workshop, pp. 4–9 (2007)

Towards Learning Commonalities in SPARQL

Sara El Hassad, François Goasdoué[✉], and Hélène Jaudoin

IRISA, Univ. Rennes 1, Lannion, France
{sara.el-hassad,fg,helene.jaudoin}@irisa.fr

Abstract. Finding the commonalities between descriptions of data or knowledge is a foundational reasoning problem of Machine Learning, which amounts to computing a *least general generalization (*lgg*)* of such descriptions. We revisit this old problem in the popular conjunctive fragment of SPARQL, a.k.a. Basic Graph Pattern Queries (BGPQs). In particular, we define this problem in all its generality by considering general BGPQs, while the literature considers unary tree-shaped BGPQs only. Further, when *ontological knowledge* is available as RDF Schema constraints, we take advantage of it to devise much more pregnant lggs.

Keywords: BGP queries · RDF · RDFS · Least general generalization

1 Introduction

Finding commonalities between descriptions of data and knowledge is a fundamental Machine Learning problem. It was formalized in early 70's as computing a *least general generalization* (lgg) of First Order Logic formulae [4].

We revisit this old reasoning problem in the setting of SPARQL, the RDF query language by W3C, which may have varied theoretical and practical applications. For instance, an lgg of queries is a best upper approximation thereof by a single query in *knowledge approximation*, is the largest set of commonalities that may be recommended for view materialization or shared processing in *query optimization*, or may help recommending users to each other, especially in a social context, if what they ask for is enough related in *recommendation*, etc.

Our contribution is to carefully study and define a pregnant notion of lgg for the well-established conjunctive fragment of SPARQL, a.k.a. Basic Graph Pattern Queries (BGPQs). Our results significantly depart from the literature by considering *general* BGPQs, instead of *unary tree-shaped* BGPQs [1,3], and crucially by taking advantage of *ontological knowledge* formalized as RDF Schema constraints, when available. Proofs for this paper's claims are delegated to [2].

2 Preliminaries

The RDF data model allows specifying *RDF graphs*, which are sets of *well-formed triples* from $(\mathcal{U} \cup \mathcal{B}) \times \mathcal{U} \times (\mathcal{U} \cup \mathcal{B} \cup \mathcal{L})$ with $\mathcal{U}$, $\mathcal{B}$, $\mathcal{L}$ pairwise disjoint sets of URIs, of blank nodes (unknown values) and of literals (constants)

© Springer International Publishing AG 2017
E. Blomqvist et al. (Eds.): ESWC 2017 Satellite Events, LNCS 10577, pp. 35–39, 2017.
https://doi.org/10.1007/978-3-319-70407-4_8

respectively [5]. A triple (s, p, o) states that its *subject* s has *property* p whose value is the *object* o. Importantly, the RDF standard provides built-in property URIs to state facts for classes (unary relations) and properties (binary relations), called *RDF statements*, and ontological constraints relating classes and properties, called *RDF Schema (RDFS) statements*, as shown in Table 1. Hereafter, we use the shorthands τ, $\preceq_{sc}$, $\preceq_{sp}$, $\hookleftarrow_d$ and $\hookrightarrow_r$ for the built-in property URIs rdf:type, rdfs:subClassOf, rdfs:subPropertyOf, rdfs:domain and rdfs:range respectively. The semantics of an RDF graph $\mathcal{G}$ is its *saturation* (a.k.a. *closure*), denoted $\mathcal{G}^\infty$, defined as the set of $\mathcal{G}$ triples together with all the *implicit* triples that can be derived from them and entailment rules from the RDF standard. Table 2 shows some rules that use RDFS constraints to derive implicit facts and constraints.

Table 1. RDF & RDFS statements.

RDF statement	Triple
Class assertion	$(s, \text{rdf:type}, o)$
Property assertion	(s, p, o) with $p \neq$ rdf:type
RDFS statement	Triple
Subclass	$(s, \text{rdfs:subClassOf}, o)$
Subproperty	$(s, \text{rdfs:subPropertyOf}, o)$
Domain typing	$(s, \text{rdfs:domain}, o)$
Range typing	$(s, \text{rdfs:range}, o)$

Table 2. Sample RDF entailment rules.

Rule [6]	Entailment rule
rdfs2	$(p, \hookleftarrow_d, o), (s_1, p, o_1) \rightarrow (s_1, \tau, o)$
rdfs3	$(p, \hookrightarrow_r, o), (s_1, p, o_1) \rightarrow (o_1, \tau, o)$
rdfs5	$(p_1, \preceq_{sp}, p_2), (p_2, \preceq_{sp}, p_3) \rightarrow (p_1, \preceq_{sp}, p_3)$
rdfs7	$(p_1, \preceq_{sp}, p_2), (s, p_1, o) \rightarrow (s, p_2, o)$
rdfs9	$(s, \preceq_{sc}, o), (s_1, \tau, s) \rightarrow (s_1, \tau, o)$
rdfs11	$(s, \preceq_{sc}, o), (o, \preceq_{sc}, o_1) \rightarrow (s, \preceq_{sc}, o_1)$
ext1	$(p, \hookleftarrow_d, o), (o, \preceq_{sc}, o_1) \rightarrow (p, \hookleftarrow_d, o_1)$
ext2	$(p, \hookrightarrow_r, o), (o, \preceq_{sc}, o_1) \rightarrow (p, \hookrightarrow_r, o_1)$
ext3	$(p, \preceq_{sp}, p_1), (p_1, \hookleftarrow_d, o) \rightarrow (p, \hookleftarrow_d, o)$
ext4	$(p, \preceq_{sp}, p_1), (p_1, \hookrightarrow_r, o) \rightarrow (p, \hookrightarrow_r, o)$

The *Basic Graph Pattern Queries (BGPQs)* form the conjunctive (or select-project-join) fragment of SPARQL. A BGPQ is of the form $q(\bar{x})_1, \ldots, t_\alpha$, where $\{t_1, \ldots, t_\alpha\}$ is a subset of $(\mathcal{U} \cup \mathcal{B} \cup \mathcal{V}) \times (\mathcal{U} \cup \mathcal{V}) \times (\mathcal{U} \cup \mathcal{B} \cup \mathcal{L} \cup \mathcal{V})$ with $\mathcal{V}$ a set of variables pairwise disjoint with $\mathcal{U}, \mathcal{B}, \mathcal{L}$, and $\bar{x}$ is a subset of the variables occurring in $t_1, \ldots, t_\alpha$ called *answer variables*; for boolean queries, $\bar{x}$ is empty. The head of q is $head(q) = q(\bar{x})$ and the body of q is $body(q) = \{t_1, \ldots, t_\alpha\}$.

Two standard reasoning tasks characterize how RDF graphs contribute to queries. *Query entailment* indicates if an RDF graph holds some answer(s) to a query. Given a BGPQ q, an RDF graph $\mathcal{G}$ and a set $\mathcal{R}$ of RDF entailment rules, $\mathcal{G}$ *entails* q, noted $\mathcal{G} \models_\mathcal{R} q$, iff $\mathcal{G} \models_\mathcal{R} body(q)$ holds, i.e., there exists a homomorphism ϕ from q's variables and blank nodes to $\mathcal{G}^\infty$'s values (URIs, literals and blank nodes) such that $[body(q)]_\phi \subseteq \mathcal{G}^\infty$. Importantly, $\mathcal{G} \models_\mathcal{R} q$ holds iff $\mathcal{G}^\infty \models_\emptyset q$ holds. We note $\mathcal{G} \models_\mathcal{R}^\phi q$ the entailment $\mathcal{G} \models_\mathcal{R} q$ due to the homomorphism ϕ. *Query answering* identifies *all* the answers to a query that an RDF graph holds. Given a BGPQ q with head $q(\bar{x})$, the *answer set of* q *against* $\mathcal{G}$ is $q(\mathcal{G}) = \{(\bar{x})_\phi \mid \mathcal{G} \models_\mathcal{R}^\phi body(q)\}$ where we denote by $(\bar{x})_\phi$ the tuple of $\mathcal{G}^\infty$ values obtained by replacing every answer variable $x_i \in \bar{x}$ by its image $\phi(x_i)$.

Finally, queries can be compared through the generalization/specialization relationship of *entailment between queries*, which is the obvious adaptation of query entailment to the presence of variables in queries. Given two BGPQs q, q' with *same* arity, whose heads are $q(\bar{x})$ and $q'(\bar{x}')$, and a set $\mathcal{R}$ of RDF entailment rules at hand, q *entails* q', noted $q \models_\mathcal{R} q'$, iff $body(q) \models_\mathcal{R}^\phi body(q')$ with $(\bar{x}')_\phi = \bar{x}$.

3   Least General Generalization of BGPQs

A *least general generalization* (lgg) of two[1] descriptions d_1, d_2 is a most specific description d generalizing d_1, d_2 for some generalization/specialization relation [4]. In our SPARQL setting, we use BGPQs as descriptions and entailment between BGPQs as generalization/specialization relation:

Definition 1 (lgg of BGPQs). *Let q_1, q_2 be two BGPQs with the same arity and $\mathcal{R}$ a set of RDF entailment rules.*
- *A generalization of q_1, q_2 is a BGPQ q_g such that $q_1 \models_\mathcal{R} q_g$ and $q_2 \models_\mathcal{R} q_g$.*
- *A least general generalization of q_1, q_2 is a generalization q_{lgg} of q_1, q_2 such that for any other generalization q_g of q_1, q_2: $q_{\text{lgg}} \models_\mathcal{R} q_g$.*

Unfortunately, this natural definition is of limited practical interest as exemplified next. Consider the BGPQs q_1 and q_2 in Fig. 1, which respectively ask for the conference papers having some contact author, and for the journal papers having some author. Clearly, with the RDF entailment rules shown in Table 2, an lgg of q_1 and q_2 is the *very* general BGPQ $q_{\text{lgg}}(x) \leftarrow (x, \tau, y)$ asking for *the resources having some type*. However, by considering the ontological constraints displayed in Fig. 1 that hold in the scientific publication domain, i.e., the context in which the queries are asked, a more pregnant lgg would be $q_{\text{lgg}}(x) \leftarrow (x, \tau, \text{Publication}), (x, \text{hasAuthor}, y), (y, \tau, \text{Researcher})$ asking for *the publications having some researcher as author*, since (i) having a contact author

---

[1] This easily generalizes to lggs of n descriptions [2].

is having an author, (*ii*) only publications have authors, (*iii*) only researchers are authors, and (*iv*) conference (resp. journal) papers are publications.

To devise such elaborate lggs that rely on ontological knowledge, we revisit the notion of entailment between BGPQs in order to account for extra RDFS constraints. We first complement a BGPQ w.r.t. ontological knowledge:

Definition 2 (BGPQ saturation w.r.t. RDFS constraints). *Let $\mathcal{R}$ be a set of RDF entailment rules, $\mathcal{O}$ a set of RDFS statements, and q a BGPQ the body of which, without loss of generality, does not contain blank nodes[2]. The saturation of q w.r.t. $\mathcal{O}$, denoted $q_{\mathcal{O}}^{\infty}$, is a BGPQ with the same answer variables as q and whose body, denoted $body(q_{\mathcal{O}}^{\infty})$, is the maximal subset of $(\mathcal{O} \cup body(q))^{\infty}$ such that for any of its subset $\mathcal{S}$: if $\mathcal{O} \models_{\mathcal{R}} \mathcal{S}$ holds then $body(q) \models_{\mathcal{R}} \mathcal{S}$ holds.*

Intuitively, the saturation of a BGPQ comprises all the triples in the saturation of its body augmented with the constraints, except those triples that only follow from the ontological constraints, i.e., which are not related to what the query is asking for. This corresponds to the *non-hatched* subset of $(\mathcal{O} \cup body(q))^{\infty}$ shown in Fig. 2. This Figure also displays the saturations $q_{1\mathcal{O}}^{\infty}, q_{2\mathcal{O}}^{\infty}$ of the two BGPQs q_1, q_2 w.r.t. the constraints $\mathcal{O}$ shown in Fig. 1. Importantly, we proved that a BGPQ and its saturation w.r.t. ontological constraints are *equivalent for the central RDF reasoning tasks of query entailment and query answering* [2]:

Theorem 1. *Let $\mathcal{R}$ be a set of RDF entailment rules, $\mathcal{O}$ a set of RDFS statements, and q a BGPQ whose saturation w.r.t. $\mathcal{O}$ is $q_{\mathcal{O}}^{\infty}$. For any RDF graph $\mathcal{G}$ whose set of RDFS statements is $\mathcal{O}$, (i) $\mathcal{G} \models_{\mathcal{R}} q$ holds iff $\mathcal{G} \models_{\mathcal{R}} q_{\mathcal{O}}^{\infty}$ holds, and (ii) $q(\mathcal{G}) = q_{\mathcal{O}}^{\infty}(\mathcal{G})$ holds.*

Building on BGPQ saturation, we generalize entailment between BGPQs to:

Definition 3 (Entailment between BGPQs w.r.t. RDFS constraints). *Given a set $\mathcal{R}$ of RDF entailment rules, a set $\mathcal{O}$ of RDFS statements, and two BGPQs q and q' with the same arity, q entails q' w.r.t. $\mathcal{O}$, denoted $q \models_{\mathcal{R},\mathcal{O}} q'$, iff $q_{\mathcal{O}}^{\infty} \models_{\emptyset} q'$ holds.*

When $\mathcal{O}$ is empty, the above definition coincides with standard entailment between BGPQs. Further, we proved fundamental properties for a BGPQ entailed by another w.r.t. ontological constraints: the former *generalizes* the latter for the central RDF reasoning tasks of query entailment and query answering [2]:

Theorem 2. *Let $\mathcal{R}$ be a set of RDF entailment rules, $\mathcal{O}$ a set of RDFS statements, and two BGPQs q and q' such that $q \models_{\mathcal{R},\mathcal{O}} q'$. For any RDF graph $\mathcal{G}$ whose set of RDFS statements is $\mathcal{O}$, (i) if $\mathcal{G} \models_{\mathcal{R}} q$ holds then $\mathcal{G} \models_{\mathcal{R}} q'$ holds, and (ii) $q(\mathcal{G}) \subseteq q'(\mathcal{G})$ holds.*

With the above notion of entailment between BGPQs endowed with ontological knowledge, we revise the definition of lgg (Definition 1) in order to use $\models_{\mathcal{R},\mathcal{O}}$ instead of $\models_{\mathcal{R}}$. We therefore propose to investigate as next challenge:

---

[2] In SPARQL queries, blank nodes are equivalent to non-answer variables [7].

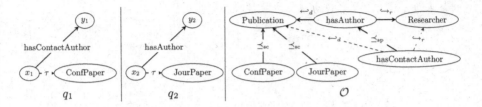

Fig. 1. Sample BGPQs q_1 and q_2; sample set of ontological constraints $\mathcal{O}$.

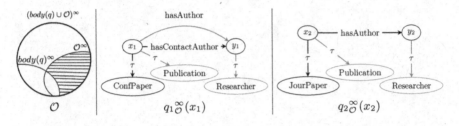

Fig. 2. Characterization of the body of a saturated BGPQ q w.r.t. a set $\mathcal{O}$ of RDFS constraints; saturations of q_1 and q_2 w.r.t. $\mathcal{O}$, triples in grey are added by saturation.

Problem 1. Given *two* BGPQs q_1, q_2 with same arity, a set $\mathcal{O}$ of RDFS statements, and a set $\mathcal{R}$ of RDF entailment rules, compute an **lgg** of q_1, q_2 w.r.t. $\mathcal{O}$.

References

1. Bühmann, L., Lehmann, J., Westphal, P.: DL-learner - a framework for inductive learning on the semantic web. J. Web Semant. **39**, 15–24 (2016)
2. El Hassad, S., Goasdoué, F., Jaudoin, H.: Learning commonalities in RDF and SPARQL (research report) (2016). https://hal.inria.fr/hal-01386237
3. Lehmann, J., Bühmann, L.: AutoSPARQL: let users query your knowledge base. In: Antoniou, G., Grobelnik, M., Simperl, E., Parsia, B., Plexousakis, D., Leenheer, P., Pan, J. (eds.) ESWC 2011. LNCS, vol. 6643, pp. 63–79. Springer, Heidelberg (2011). https://doi.org/10.1007/978-3-642-21034-1_5
4. Plotkin, G.D.: A note on inductive generalization. Mach. Intell. **5**, 153–163 (1970)
5. Resource description framework 1.1. https://www.w3.org/TR/rdf11-concepts
6. RDF 1.1 semantics. https://www.w3.org/TR/rdf11-mt/
7. SPARQL. http://www.w3.org/TR/rdf-sparql-query

Demo Papers

AMR2FRED, A Tool for Translating Abstract Meaning Representation to Motif-Based Linguistic Knowledge Graphs

Antonello Meloni[1], Diego Reforgiato Recupero[1(✉)], and Aldo Gangemi[2]

[1] Department of Mathematics and Computer Science, University of Cagliari,
Via Ospedale 72, 09124 Cagliari, Italy
diego.reforgiato@unica.it
[2] Université Paris 13, 99 avenue JB Clément, 93430 Villetaneuse, France
aldo.gangemi@lipn.univ-paris13.fr

Abstract. In this paper we present AMR2FRED, a software application to translate Abstract Meaning Representation (AMR) to RDF using the knowledge patterns applied by the FRED machine reading method. AMR and FRED representations are both graph-based, and event-centric (neo-Davidsonian), but they differ in several logical, conceptual, and design assumptions. The former has become a de facto standard for the Natural Language Processing community, whereas FRED adds semantics to the extracted information using several ontologies and best practices from the Semantic Web. With the increasing availability of manually AMR-annotated datasets, this tool provides straightforward means to adapt annotated datasets for AMR according to the design patterns used by FRED, and to evaluate machine reading tools with gold-standard data. AMR2FRED takes as input an AMR representation of a text, and prints a FRED-like RDF output. The system is open source and can be freely downloaded from https://github.com/infovillasimius/amr2Fred.

Keywords: Abstract Meaning Representation · RDF · Machine reading

1 Introduction

Abstract Meaning Representation (AMR) graphs have been introduced [7] to represent sentence-level semantics. AMR has gained popularity in computational linguistics [1–6] for several reasons: (i) its tree structure easily shows the connections between the semantic elements of a sentence, (ii) it can be expressed as directed acyclic graphs, which simplifies the evaluation for machine-generated output, (iii) it is much easier to manually produce AMRs than traditional formal meaning representations, and as a consequence there are now several gold-standard corpora available. AMR graphs are directed and acyclic, where leaves represent concepts whereas internal nodes represent variables, which denote instances of those concepts. Edges represent roles that relate pairs of instances or concepts. Each AMR has a unique root node. A slash denotes instantiation:

© Springer International Publishing AG 2017
E. Blomqvist et al. (Eds.): ESWC 2017 Satellite Events, LNCS 10577, pp. 43–47, 2017.
https://doi.org/10.1007/978-3-319-70407-4_9

the fact that x is an instance of the concept *child* is represented as $x/child$. A colon denotes a role, which is predicated to event instances within brackets. For example, the sentence *It may rain* can be expressed as: *(p / possible-01 :ARG1 (r / rain-01))* (the reader notices that there might be multiple AMR representations for a given sentence). AMR implements a neo-Davidsonian semantics [8] using standard feature structure representation.

FRED is a reference Semantic Web (SW) machine reader [9] that automatically generates RDF/OWL ontologies and Linked Data (LD) from natural language text. The resulting RDF/OWL graph is enriched with links to existing SW knowledge, by means of ontology alignment, word sense disambiguation, and entity linking techniques, as well as with an RDF encoding of syntactic annotations based on Earmark [10] and the NLP Interchange Format (NIF) [11] vocabularies. The core of FRED takes as input a neo-Davidsonian variety of Discourse Representation Structures (DRS) for event and role representation, but substantially extends it with compositional semantics of terms, event relations, a novel adjective semantics [14], and many other features described in [9]. FRED and its REST APIs are available online[1]. FRED performs several basic semantic tasks {e.g. named entity resolution and recognition, terminology resolution and extraction, sense tagging, taxonomy induction, relation extraction, event detection and semantic role labeling, frame detection}. Its OWL/RDF graphs are constructed by means of *motifs* [12] that correspond to the hybrid linguistic-logical semantics that can be pragmatically extracted from sentences, and represented in a fragment of OWL. FRED has been used for ontology population and learning, and as a middleware for opinion mining, automated summarization, etc.

On the one hand, creating an annotated corpus for FRED is not an easy task because of all the varieties of knowledge extracted by FRED, which are often outside the scope of AMR and mainstream NLP. Other knowledge extraction tools for the SW are typically more restricted in scope, but they also concentrate on data and ontology-related features rather than linguistic semantics (cf. [13]). On the other hand, human annotators have created datasets of more than 10000 AMR/English sentence pairs. Thus, AMR2FRED, by translating AMR into RDF/OWL, can quickly provide large gold-standard datasets for evaluating the linguistic reliability of SW machine readers and knowledge extractors, by reusing the datasets natively developed by the Natural Language community.

2   AMR2FRED at Work

AMR2FRED takes as input a valid AMR of a text, and outputs RDF triples in a specific serialisation (RDF/OWL, Turtle, NTriples), after a number of steps of translation, mapping, processing, and application of SW and LD best practices.

First, AMR2FRED creates an internal data structure of the input AMR graph representation (labeled nodes and edges).

---

[1] http://wit.istc.cnr.it/stlab-tools/fred.

Then, each rule[2] of AMR is analyzed: the following heuristics show the mapping and translation steps performed in order to have a proper FRED-oriented representation of the input AMR.

- **Nodes containing an inverse pattern :X-of.** If the root has an inverse pattern as relationship, then the root and the node referred by the inverse pattern are swapped and the role is rewritten in direct form. For example, *(b / boy :quant 4 :ARG0-of (m / make-01 :ARG1 (p / pie)))* becomes *(m / make-01 :ARG0 (b / boy :quant 4) :ARG1 (p / pie))*. Otherwise (it is not root), the node with the inverse relation becomes the new root, and the node having the inverse pattern is added to it through a direct relation. E.g. *(s / see-01 :ARG0 (b / boy) :ARG1 (g / girl :ARG0-of (w / want-01 :ARG1 b)))* becomes *(s / see-01 :ARG0 (b / boy) :ARG1 (g / girl)), (w / want-01 :ARG0 g :ARG1 b)*. The reader notices that other usages of the preposition *of* are properly handled with different heuristics: for example, *:prep-on-behalf-of* becomes *fred:on-behalf-of*, *:subevent-of* becomes *fred:in*, *:subset-of* becomes *fred:of*, *:part-of* becomes *fred:nameOfThePartOf*. Some AMR nodes are not yet translated to FRED (because new FRED motifs might be necessary). They are removed from internal structures, and listed in a window in the top right part of the output. They include: *:mode* with imperative or interrogative form, *:timezone, :conj-as-if, (a / amr-unknown).*
- **Rules involving root node and some of the internal nodes** are recursively processed. To translate them we need to add/remove nodes to make the resulting graph compliant with FRED's motifs and design patterns. In this category we have the rule *date-entity* and its children *:calendar :century :day :dayperiod :decade :era :month :quarter :season :time :timezone :weekday :year :year2*. We have also the following cases: *relative-position, :scale, :ord, :concession, :condition,* expressions when we have either the verb *have-org-role-91* or *have rel-role-91, and* and *or* followed by *:opx, :mod + :degree + :compared-to, :degree* without *:compared-to, :degree + :domain + :compared-to,* nominal predicates, *X-quantity + :unit,* sums and products.
- **Rules involving internal nodes but not root** are also recursively processed. We include: *:domain+adjective* or *:domain+name, personal pronouns and demonstrative adjectives, :name, :wiki + schemaorg on wiki node, :wiki + schemaorg on root node, :poss, :quant* and *:frequency* with numeric value, *:quant* with numeric value, *:mod, :age, :degree, :time* with not null value, *:manner* with verbal form, *:manner* with no verbal form.
- **Roles** from AMR to FRED are directly translated as there is a 1 to 1 correspondence between the two syntaxes. 27 rules belong to this category and are contained within the class *Glossary.java* of the source code. In particular, each AMR role (ARG0, ARG1, etc.) is translated in FRED's roles using VerbNet (ARG0, ARG1, etc. are mapped to Agent, Patient, Theme, etc.).[3]
- **AMR instance nodes** are converted to FRED's individual nodes. As an example, in AMR, *(b / boy)* indicates a variable followed by an instance name.

---

[2] https://github.com/amrisi/amr-guidelines/blob/master/amr.md.
[3] The resource we have used, predmatrix.txt, is included in the github of AMR2FRED.

All the references to *b* are translated in FRED with the name of the instance *boy* followed by an underscore and a progressive number (if *b* is referenced then in FRED we will have *boy_1*; if the AMR includes a reference to *b2* then we will translate in FRED *boy_2*, etc.)

Once an AMR rule has been translated according to FRED's RDF/OWL patterns, we employ JENA[4] to properly print the output in a RDF serialisation. Nodes not processed by any of our heuristics are displayed separately, and a further button in the GUI allows getting rid of them in the output.

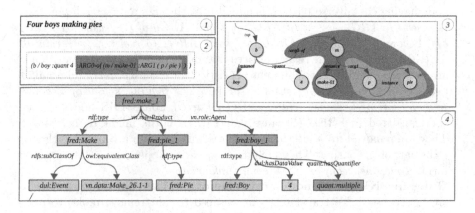

Fig. 1. How AMR2FRED translates the sentence *Four boys making pies*.

Figure 1 shows an example of translation from AMR to FRED for the input sentence *Four boys making pies*. The top left side shows an AMR representation for that sentence is given as input. On the top right side, the corresponding graph representation is displayed. The bottom shows the final FRED representation, after the application of the rules and heuristics of AMR2FRED.

AMR2FRED has been tested and evaluated on more than 100 AMR texts (extended evaluation ongoing). This corpus is available in Github within the package containing the source code (the corpus is called tested_input).

3   Conclusions

In this paper we have shown AMR2FRED, an open source application to translate AMR to FRED. FRED is a machine reader that produces RDF/OWL enriched with semantic predicates extracted from Verbnet, Framenet, using a mapping model and a set of heuristics following Ontology Design Patterns best-practice of OWL ontologies and RDF data design. The huge amount of annotated datasets available for AMR triggered the development of AMR2FRED, for a linguistically sound evaluation of knowledge extraction tools for the SW.

---

[4] https://jena.apache.org/.

References

1. Artzi, Y., Lee, K., Zettlemoyer, L.: Broad-coverage CCG semantic parsing with AMR. In: Proceedings of the 2015 Conference on Empirical Methods in Natural Language Processing, Lisbon, pp. 1699–1710 (2015)
2. Chen, W.-T.: Learning to map dependency parses to abstract meaning representations. In: Proceedings of the ACL-IJCNLP 2015 Student Research Workshop, Beijing, pp. 41–46 (2015)
3. Pust, M., Hermjakob, U., Knight, K., Marcu, D., May, J.: Parsing English into abstract meaning representation using syntax-based machine translation. In: Proceedings of the EMNLP 2015, Lisbon, pp. 1143–1154 (2015)
4. Peng, X., Song, L., Gildea, D.: A synchronous hyperedge replacement grammar based approach for AMR parsing. In: Proceedings of the Nineteenth Conference on Computational Natural Language Learning, Beijing, pp. 32–41 (2015)
5. Sawai, Y., Shindo, H., Matsumoto, Y.: Semantic structure analysis of noun phrases using abstract meaning representation. In: Proceedings of the 53rd Annual Meeting of the ACL (Short Papers), Beijing, vol. 2, pp 851–856 (2015)
6. Werling, K., Angeli, G., Manning, C.D.: Robust subgraph generation improves abstract meaning representation parsing. In: Proceedings of the 53rd Annual Meeting of the ACL (Long Papers), Beijing, vol. 1, pp. 982–991 (2015)
7. Banarescu, L., Bonial, C., Cai, S., Georgescu, M., Griffitt, K., Hermjakob, U., Knight, K., Koehn, P., Palmer, M., Schneider, N.: Abstract meaning representation for sembanking. In: Proceedings ACL Linguistic Annotation Workshop (LAW) (2013)
8. Kamp, H.: A theory of truth and semantic representation. In: Groenendijk, J.A.G., Janssen, T.M.V., Stokhof, M.B.J. (eds.) Formal Methods in the Study of Language, Part I, pp. 277–322. Mathematisch Centrum (1981)
9. Gangemi, A., Presutti, V., Reforgiato Recupero, D., Nuzzolese, A.G., Draicchio, F., Mongioví, M.: Semantic web machine reading with FRED. Semant. Web J. (2016). https://doi.org/10.3233/SW-160240
10. Peroni, S., Gangemi, A., Vitali, F.: Dealing with markup semantics. In: Proceedings of the 7th International Conference on Semantic Systems, Graz, Austria, pp. 111–118. ACM (2011)
11. Hellmann, S., Lehmann, J., Auer, S., Brümmer, M.: Integrating NLP using linked data. In: Alani, H., Kagal, L., Fokoue, A., Groth, P., Biemann, C., Parreira, J.X., Aroyo, L., Noy, N., Welty, C., Janowicz, K. (eds.) ISWC 2013. LNCS, vol. 8219, pp. 98–113. Springer, Heidelberg (2013). https://doi.org/10.1007/978-3-642-41338-4_7
12. Gangemi, A., Mongiovi, M., Nuzzolese, A.G., Presutti, V., Reforgiato, D.: Identifying motifs for evaluating open knowledge extraction on the web. Knowl.-Based Syst. **108**, 33–41 (2016)
13. Gangemi, A.: A comparison of knowledge extraction tools for the semantic web. In: Cimiano, P., Corcho, O., Presutti, V., Hollink, L., Rudolph, S. (eds.) ESWC 2013. LNCS, vol. 7882, pp. 351–366. Springer, Heidelberg (2013). https://doi.org/10.1007/978-3-642-38288-8_24
14. Gangemi, A., Nuzzolese, A.G., Presutti, V., Reforgiato, D.: Adjective semantics in open knowledge extraction. In: Formal Ontology in Information Systems Conference (FOIS 2106). IOS Press (2016)

Trill: A Reusable Front-End for QA Systems

Dennis Diefenbach[1]([⊠]), Shanzay Amjad[2], Andreas Both[3], Kamal Singh[1],
and Pierre Maret[1]

[1] Laboratoire Hubert Curien, Saint Etienne, France
{dennis.diefenbach,kamal.singh,pierre.maret}@univ-st-etienne.fr
[2] University of Ottawa, Ottawa, Canada
samja088@uottawa.ca
[3] DATEV eG, Nuremberg, Germany
contact@andreasboth.de

Abstract. The Semantic Web contains an enormous amount of information in the form of knowledge bases. To make this information available to
end-users many question answering (QA) systems over knowledge bases
were created in the last years. Their goal is to enable users to access large
amounts of structured data in the Semantic Web by bridging the gap
between natural language and formal query languages like SPARQL.

But automatically generating a SPARQL query from a user's question is not sufficient to bridge the gap between Semantic Web data and
the end-users. The result of a SPARQL query consists of a list of URIs
and/or literals, which is not a user-friendly presentation of the answer.
Such a presentation includes the representation of the URI in the right
language and additional information like images, maps, entity summaries
and more.

We present Trill, the first reusable user-interface (UI) for QA systems
over knowledge bases supporting text and audio input, able to present
answers from DBpedia and Wikidata in 4 languages (English, French,
German, and Italian). It is designed to be used together with Qanary,
an infrastructure for composing QA pipelines. This front-end enables
the QA community to show their results to end-users and enables the
research community to explore new research directions like studying and
designing user-interactions with QA systems.

Keywords: Question answering systems · Front-end · User interaction ·
Answer presentation

1 Introduction

Users' experience is an important factor for the success of a given application.
Thus, the front-end of QA systems, which highly impacts the users' experience,
is an important part of a QA system. On one side the research community
has made a lot of efforts to increase the F-score over different benchmarks,
i.e., the accuracy of the translation of a natural language question in a formal
representation like a SPARQL query. On the other side not much attention has

© Springer International Publishing AG 2017
E. Blomqvist et al. (Eds.): ESWC 2017 Satellite Events, LNCS 10577, pp. 48–53, 2017.
https://doi.org/10.1007/978-3-319-70407-4_10

been paid to how the answer is presented and how users can interact with a QA system.

On a technical level one could say that a lot of attention has been paid to services in the back-end but little attention has been paid to the front-end. We hope to change this trend by presenting the first reusable front-end for QA systems over knowledge bases, i.e. a front-end that can be reused easily by any new QA system. It can currently be used for QA systems over DBpedia and Wikidata and supports 4 different languages.

2   Related Work

In the last years a large number of QA systems were created by the research community. This is for example shown by the number of QA systems (more then 20 in the last 5 years) that were evaluated against the QALD benchmark[1]. Unfortunately only very few of them have a UI and even fewer are available as web services. Some exceptions that we are aware of are *SINA* [8], QAKiS [2] and *Platypus*[2]. Also industrial UI were created for well known systems like *Apple Siri, Microsoft Cortana, Google Search, Ok Google,* and *WolframAlpha*[3].

All the UIs mentioned above are tightly integrated with the corresponding QA systems. This is not the case for Trill. Trill can be used as a front-end for new QA systems. To achieve the modularity by making the front-end independent from the back-end of the QA system, we build Trill on top of a framework that provides a reusable architecture for QA systems. We are aware of four such architectures namely: QALL-ME [6], openQA [7], the Open KnowledgeBase and Question-Answering (OKBQA) challenge[4] and Qanary [1,4,9]. We choose to build Trill on top of the last mentioned framework, Qanary, since it allows the highest flexibility to integrate new QA components.

3   Description of Trill

In this section, we first describe the interaction of the front-end with the Qanary back-end. Then we describe which functionalities/presentational elements are implemented in the front-end. A screenshot showing most of the presentational elements is shown in Fig. 1. A live demo can be found at www.wdaqua.eu/qa.

Trill builds on the APIs offered by Qanary. Qanary is a framework for composing QA pipelines. A QA system can be seen as a pipeline, i.e., as a sequence of services that are called one after the other and finally are able (or not) to

---

[1] http://qald.sebastianwalter.org.

[2] http://sina.aksw.org, http://live.ailao.eu, http://qakis.org/qakis2/, https://askplatyp.us/?.

[3] http://www.apple.com/ios/siri, http://www.wolframalpha.com, http://windows.microsoft.com/en-us/windows-10/getstarted-what-is-cortana,   www.google.com https://support.google.com/websearch/answer/2940021?hl=en.

[4] http://www.okbqa.org/.

50   D. Diefenbach et al.

compute the answer for a given question. Qanary has APIs that allow to combine components integrated in Qanary starting from a text or an audio question. The human accessible versions are exposed for example under:

www.wdaqua.eu/qanary/startquestionansweringwithtextquestion,
www.wdaqua.eu/qanary/startquestionansweringwithaudioquestion

A call to these APIs require as parameters both the question and a list of Qanary components. A call will activate the mentioned components which will be executed as a pipeline in the defined order. Trill accesses the Qanary back-end using these APIs. In particular the demo running under www.wdaqua.eu/qa calls a Qanary component called WDAqua-core0 [5] created in the frame of the WDAqua project[5].

Now we give a list of all the functionalities and presentational elements that are available in Trill. The numbers in the item list correspond to the numbers in Fig. 1.

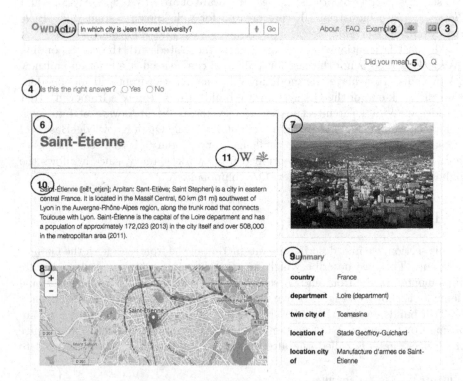

Fig. 1. Screenshot of Trill for the question "In which city is Jean Monnet University?". The numbers refer to the item list in Sect. 3

---

[5] http://www.wdaqua.eu.

1. **Text and audio input:** The front-end contains a search-bar component. This allows the user to input a text question using a text bar or a vocal question using a microphone[6].

2. **Language selection:** The user has the possibility to change between 4 languages (English, French, German, and Italian) by selecting the flag of the corresponding country. The whole webpage will re-render using labels of the selected language and also the answers to a question will be adapted to the corresponding language.

3. **Knowledge-base selection:** The user has the option to choose an available knowledge base to query. Actually this is limited to DBpedia and Wikidata. Note that the answer presentation is coupled to the knowledge base since different properties are used to express the same information, i.e., the image can be retrieved in DBpedia using the property `dbo:thumbnail` while in Wikidata it is the property `wdt:P18`.

4. **Feedback functionality:** We implemented an easy-to-use feedback functionality where a user can choose if the answer is correct or not. This information is logged in the back-end and can be used to create a training set.
Answer presentation We implemented several components to display information about the answer that can be useful for a user. Here is a list.

5. **Generated query:** For expert users, we give the possibility to see the generated SPARQL query for the question.

6. **Label:** In the case the answer is a URI, we display its label in the corresponding language, i.e., `wd:Q90` will be displayed as "Paris" in English and "Parigi" in Italian. If the answer is a literal, we display it directly.

7. **Image:** One component retrieves the image (if it exists) of the answer and displays it.

8. **Map:** If available the geo-coordinates are used to display the position of the answer on a map. The map is showed using Leaflet[7] Javascript Library which retrieves maps from OpenStreetMap[8].

9. **Top-k Properties:** A summary of the entity is visualized using an external service called LinkSUM [10] provided by Andreas Thalhammer.

10. **Text description from Wikipedia abstract**: Every entity in DBpedia is linked to the corresponding Wikipedia page and for many Wikidata entities this is also the case. Following these links we use the Wikipedia API to retrieve the introduction of the article.

11. **External Links:** If available, we present some external links to the user. This include links to DBpedia, Wikidata and Wikipedia.

12. **Ranking of list answers:** In the case of a list of answers, we rank them in the case of DBpedia. For example, if a user asks about "italian lakes" the result will be a long list of answers. Without ranking, the first answer will probably be a small unknown lake in Italy. For this reason we reorder

---

[6] This feature is supported only for Chrome and Firefox due to dependencies on the MediaStream Recording API.

[7] http://leafletjs.com.

[8] http://openstreetmap.org/.

the results using the page rank scores presented in [11] that are available online[9]. Hence, if a user asks for "italian lakes", he will get at a first position in the result list the entity "Lake Como" followed by "Lake Maggiore".

The code can be found under https://github.com/WDAqua/Trill. Table 1 compares the features of other open source front-ends with Trill.

Table 1. Table comparing the features of Trill with other open source UIs.

	Audio input	Language sel.	KB sel.	Feedback func	Generated query	Entity label	Image	Map	Top-k properties	Text description	External links	Language support	KB support
SINA						x	x	x		x	x	en	dbpedia
QAKiS			x			x	x				x	en	dbpedia
Platypus	x					x	x	x		x	x	en	wikidata
Trill	x	x	x	x	x	x	x	x	x	x	x	en, de, fr, it	dbpedia, wikidata

4   Conclusion

We have presented Trill, a reusable user-interface for QA systems over knowledge bases that can be used on top of Qanary. While many efforts were made to develop better QA technology in the back-end, little work was done in the front-end.
We hope that Trill can change this trend. Trill can be used for any future QA pipeline integrated into Qanary as an off-the-shelf front-end. Moreover, it can be used to deeply study the interactions of the end-users with QA systems. This includes: 1. collect end-user queries to create easily large and realistic benchmarks, 2. studies to analyze which questions users ask, 3. study how much context information should be presented to a user together with the answer, 4. create interfaces, like the disambiguation interfaces in [3], to allow users to interact with QA systems. These examples shows how advances on the front-end can also be beneficial for classical QA research in the back-end.

Acknowledgments. Parts of this work received funding from the European Union's Horizon 2020 research and innovation programme under the Marie Skodowska-Curie grant agreement No. 642795, project: Answering Questions using Web Data (WDAqua).

---

[9] http://people.aifb.kit.edu/ath/#DBpedia_PageRank.

References

1. Both, A., Diefenbach, D., Singh, K., Shekarpour, S., Cherix, D., Lange, C.: Qanary – a methodology for vocabulary-driven open question answering systems. In: Sack, H., Blomqvist, E., d'Aquin, M., Ghidini, C., Ponzetto, S.P., Lange, C. (eds.) ESWC 2016. LNCS, vol. 9678, pp. 625–641. Springer, Cham (2016). doi:10.1007/978-3-319-34129-3_38
2. Cabrio, E., Cojan, J., Aprosio, A.P., Magnini, B., Lavelli, A., Gandon, F.: QAKiS: an open domain QA system based on relational patterns. In: Proceedings of the 2012th International Conference on Posters & Demonstrations Track, vol. 914 (2012)
3. Diefenbach, D., Hormozi, N., Amjad, S., Both, A.: Introducing feedback in Qanary: how users can interact with QA systems. In: ESWC P&D (2017)
4. Diefenbach, D., Singh, K., Both, A., Cherix, D., Lange, C., Auer, S.: The Qanary ecosystem: getting new insights by composing question answering pipelines. In: Cabot, J., Virgilio, R., Torlone, R. (eds.) ICWE 2017. LNCS, vol. 10360, pp. 171–189. Springer, Cham (2017). doi:10.1007/978-3-319-60131-1_10
5. Diefenbach, D., Singh, K., Maret, P.: WDAqua-core0: a question answering component for the research community. In: ESWC, 7th Open Challenge on Question Answering over Linked Data (QALD-7) (2017)
6. Ferrández, Ó., Spurk, C., Kouylekov, M., Dornescu, I., Ferrández, S., Negri, M., Izquierdo, R., Tomás, D., Orasan, C., Neumann, G., Magnini, B., González, J.: The QALL-ME framework: a specifiable-domain multilingual Question Answering architecture. J. Web Sem. 9(2), 137–145 (2011)
7. Marx, E., Usbeck, R., Ngonga Ngomo, A., Höffner, K., Lehmann, J., Auer, S.: Towards an open question answering architecture. In: SEMANTiCS (2014)
8. Shekarpour, S., Marx, E., Ngomo, A.C.N., Auer, S.: Sina: semantic interpretation of user queries for question answering on interlinked data. Web Semant. Sci. Serv. Agents World Wide Web 30, 39–51 (2015)
9. Singh, K., Both, A., Diefenbach, D., Shekarpour, S.: Towards a message-driven vocabulary for promoting the interoperability of question answering systems. In: ICSC 2016 (2016)
10. Thalhammer, A., Lasierra, N., Rettinger, A.: LinkSUM: using link analysis to summarize entity data. In: Bozzon, A., Cudre-Maroux, P., Pautasso, C. (eds.) ICWE 2016. LNCS, vol. 9671, pp. 244–261. Springer, Cham (2016). doi:10.1007/978-3-319-38791-8_14
11. Thalhammer, A., Rettinger, A.: PageRank on wikipedia: towards general importance scores for entities. In: Sack, H., Rizzo, G., Steinmetz, N., Mladenić, D., Auer, S., Lange, C. (eds.) ESWC 2016. LNCS, vol. 9989, pp. 227–240. Springer, Cham (2016). doi:10.1007/978-3-319-47602-5_41

KBox: Distributing Ready-to-Query RDF Knowledge Graphs

Edgard Marx[1,2]([✉]), Tommaso Soru[2], Ciro Baron[2], and Sandro Athaide Coelho[3]

[1] Leipzig University of Applied Sciences (HTWK), Leipzig, Germany
edgard.marx@htwk-leipzig.de
[2] AKSW, University of Leipzig, Leipzig, Germany
[3] Universidade Federal de Juiz de Fora, Juiz de Fora, Brazil
http://kbox.tech

Abstract. The Semantic Web community has successfully contributed to a remarkable number of RDF datasets published on the Web. However, to use and build applications on top of Linked Data is still a cumbersome and time-demanding task. We present KBox, an open-source platform that facilitates the distribution and consumption of RDF data. We show the different APIs implemented by KBox, as well as the processing steps from a SPARQL query to its corresponding result. Additionally, we demonstrate how KBox can be used to share RDF knowledge graphs and to instantiate SPARQL endpoints.

1 Introduction

The advances in the Web of Data lead to an avalanche of open knowledge graphs made available in RDF format, such as DBpedia [3], Freebase [1] and Wikidata [7]. Together, these knowledge graphs encompass millions of facts from a multitude of domains. However, consuming RDF data is still a very cumbersome and time-demanding task.

SPARQL endpoints must handle very complex operations [5] which makes high demand services expensive to host and difficult to maintain [6]. Manifold research efforts have proposed solutions to tackle the reliability of SPARQL endpoints [2,6,8]. However, these methods often imposed limitations [4], as consuming RDF from dump files is a very cumbersome, time-consuming and resource-demanding task.

In this demo, we present KBox [4], an open-source platform that allows users to share and consume ready-to-query RDF knowledge graphs (KGs). We show the functionalities implemented by our software, as well as the different stages from a query to its result. We demonstrate how KBox can be used to facilitate the implementation, integration, and evaluation of Semantic Web systems. KBox source code is available online.[1]

---

[1] https://github.com/AKSW/KBox.

© Springer International Publishing AG 2017
E. Blomqvist et al. (Eds.): ESWC 2017 Satellite Events, LNCS 10577, pp. 54–58, 2017.
https://doi.org/10.1007/978-3-319-70407-4_11

2 Demonstration

The goal of the demonstration will be to show how to share and query RDF knowledge graphs using the KBox platform.

2.1 The Knowledge Box (KBox)

The KBox architecture comprises five components, shown in Fig. 1:

1. *Knowledge Graph Name System* (KNS): The KNS is designed to allow users and applications to share and dereference ready-to-query RDF knowledge graphs. With the KNS, a KG can have different names, be distributed by various authorities, as well as stored at several Web Addresses in a decentralized manner. For instance, a version of the DBpedia KG can be distributed not only by DBpedia but also by other authorities. The KNS is composed of different components: The KNS Server, the Knowledge Graph Name (KN), and the target KG.
2. *Knowledge Graph Name (KN)*: The Knowledge Graph Name is the name of the graph represented by an IRI. A KG can have different names. For instance, a KG can be named as http://example.org or simply *example*.
3. *KNS Server*: The KNS Server is an HTTP server that stores records containing the Knowledge Graph Name and its Web Address (URL) in format (KN, URL) that enables the KBox Client to dereference KGs.
4. *Client*: The client is where KBox is running; it interfaces between the User/Application, the Operational System, the Network as well as the KNS.
5. *User/Application (Edge)*: The edge is the KBox Client user, i.e. one or more applications running on a server or a standard user machine.

With KBox, users or applications perform queries targeting Knowledge Graph Names. The KNs are the target ready-to-query RDF KGs that the user or application desire to use.

The KBox client is built upon the KBox Core, Kibe and Fusca libraries. The Core library contains the core functions to dereference and uniquely identify resources in the Network (Web/Intranet) as well as in the File System. The Kibe library extends the Core and adds the capability to manipulate RDF Knowledge Graphs. Such library contains both the SPARQL and the Resource Description Framework (RDF) layers. The RDF and SPARQL layers allow KBox to deal with RDF data through operations such as reading, serialization and processing. The Fusca library enables User/Applications to instantiate SPARQL endpoints using any available KG in KBox. The User/Application performs operations over the previous layers such as dynamically dereference, aggregate, uniquely identify and execute SPARQL query operations over published KGs.

2.2 Querying

In the KBox architecture, all intelligence is shifted to the client. The process starts when the User/Application provides the KBox Client with a SPARQL

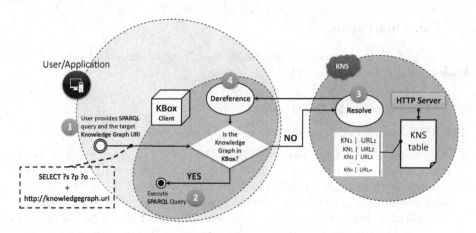

Fig. 1. KBox

query along with a KG Name (see ①). The KBox client first checks the availability of the KN. If the KG is locally available, the Client executes the SPARQL query (see ②). Otherwise, if the KG is not available locally, the Client uses the KNS table to resolve the KN (see ③). That is, it locates the ready-to-query KG in one of the available entries in the KNS table. If the KG is located, the KBox Client dereferences it (see ④) and finally executes the SPARQL query (see ②).

KBox can also be used to query multiple knowledge graphs (Listing 1.2). This functionality enables users to execute federated SPARQL queries, better define the target data as well as perform more efficient queries.

In this demo, we are going to show how to query single and multiple knowledge graphs. Furthermore, we are going to demonstrate how to use and build applications using KBox API natively (Listing 1.3) or from the command line interface (Listing 1.1).

```
1 $ java -jar kbox-v0.0.1-alpha3.jar -sparql "Select (count(
     distinct ?s) as ?n) where {?s ?p ?o}" -kb "https://www.
     w3.org/2000/01/rdf-schema" -install
```

Listing 1.1. Querying RDF knowledge graphs in command line interface using KBox runnable JAR file.

```
1 $ java -jar kbox-v0.0.1-alpha3.jar -sparql "Select (count(
     distinct ?s) as ?n) where {?s ?p ?o}" -kb "https://www.
     w3.org/2000/01/rdf-schema,http://xmlns.com/foaf/0.1" -
     install
```

Listing 1.2. Federated Querying RDF knowledge graphs in command line interface using KBox runnable JAR file.

```
1 KBox.query("Select (count(distinct ?s) as ?n) where {?s ?p
    ?o}", true, "https://www.w3.org/2000/01/rdf-schema");
```

Listing 1.3. Querying RDF knowledge graphs using KBox Java library.

2.3 Instantiating

KBox also facilitates the instatiation of SPARQL endpoints thanks to the `Fusca` library. KBox is distributed as executable JAR file (Listing 1.1), library (Listing 1.3), and `Docker` container (Listing 1.4). In this demo, we are going to show how to instantiate a SPARQL endpoint using each of these interfaces.

```
1 docker pull aksw/kbox
2 docker run aksw/kbox -server -kb "https://www.w3.org
    /2000/01/rdf-schema" -install
3 Loading Model...
4 Publishing service on http://localhost:8080/kbox/query
5 Service running ;-) ...
```

Listing 1.4. Instantiating a SPARQL endpoint using KBox Docker container.

3 Conclusion

During the demo, we will present KBox, an open-source platform that allows users to share and consume ready-to-query RDF knowledge graphs. We will explain the steps between an SPARQL query and its result, the available APIs, as well as how to instantiate a SPARQL endpoint using different interfaces. Finally, we will show practical examples of applications using KBox and queries using the latest version of large datasets such as DBpedia 2015-10.[2]

Acknowledgments. This work was partly supported by a grant from the German Research Foundation (DFG) for the project *Professorial Career Patterns of the Early Modern History: Development of a scientific method for research on online available and distributed research databases of academic history* under the grant agreement No GL 225/9-1, by CNPq under the program *Ciências Sem Fronteiras* process 200527/2012-6.

References

1. Bollacker, K., Evans, C., Paritosh, P., Sturge, T., Taylor, J.: Freebase: a collaboratively created graph database for structuring human knowledge. In: SIGMOD, pp. 1247–1250. ACM (2008)
2. Fernández, J.D., Martínez-Prieto, M.A., Gutiérrez, C., Polleres, A., Arias, M.: Binary RDF representation for publication and exchange (HDT). Web Semant. Sci. Serv. Agents World Wide Web **19**, 22–41 (2013)

---

[2] Available at the Knowledge Graph Name http://dbpedia.org/2015-10/en.

3. Lehmann, J., Isele, R., Jakob, M., Jentzsch, A., Kontokostas, D., Mendes, P.N., Hellmann, S., Morsey, M., van Kleef, P., Auer, S., Bizer, C.: DBpedia - a large-scale, multilingual knowledge base extracted from wikipedia. Semant. Web J. **6**(2), 167–195 (2015)

4. Marx, E., Baron, C., Soru, T., Auer, S.: KBox: transparently shifting query execution on knowledge graphs to the edge. In: ICSC (2017)

5. Pérez, J., Arenas, M., Gutierrez, C.: Semantics and complexity of SPARQL. ACM Trans. Database Syst. **34**(3), 16:1–16:45 (2009)

6. Verborgh, R.: Querying datasets on the web with high availability. In: Mika, P., et al. (eds.) ISWC 2014. LNCS, vol. 8796, pp. 180–196. Springer, Cham (2014). doi:10.1007/978-3-319-11964-9_12

7. Vrandečić, D., Krötzsch, M.: Wikidata: a free collaborative knowledgebase. Commun. ACM **57**(10), 78–85 (2014)

8. Yuan, P., Liu, P., Wu, B., Jin, H., Zhang, W., Liu, L.: TripleBit: a fast and compact system for large scale RDF data. Proc. VLDB Endow. **6**(7), 517–528 (2013)

Verbalising OWL Ontologies in IsiZulu with Python

C. Maria Keet[1]([✉]), Musa Xakaza[1], and Langa Khumalo[2]

[1] Department of Computer Science, University of Cape Town,
Cape Town, South Africa
mkeet@cs.uct.ac.za, XKZMUS001@myuct.ac.za
[2] Linguistics Program, University of KwaZulu-Natal, Durban, South Africa
khumalol@ukzn.ac.za

Abstract. Ontologies as a component of Semantic Web technologies are used in Sub-Saharan Africa mainly as part of ontology-driven information systems that may include an interface in a local language. IsiZulu is one such local language, which is spoken by about 23 million people in South Africa, and for which verbalisation patterns to verbalise an ontology exist. We have implemented the algorithms corresponding to these patterns in Python so as to link it most easily to the various technologies that use ontologies and for other NLP tasks. This was linked to Owlready, a new Python-based OWL API, so as to verbalise an ontology in isiZulu. The verbaliser can run in 'ontology inside' mode, outputting the sentences in the terminal for further processing in an ontology-driven information system, and in GUI mode that displays colour-coded natural language sentences for users such as domain experts and linguists. The demo will showcase its features.

1 Introduction

The use of Semantic Web technologies in Sub-Saharan Africa focuses predominantly on ontology-driven information systems. Examples include the integration of flower-visiting biodiversity data from natural history museums [3], agriculture and health data in Senegal [9], e-government monitoring for development projects [5], learning platforms [4], and localisation of OpenMRS[1] that uses the medical ontology SNOMED CT [11]. While some existing ontologies obviously can be reused, others are being developed to represent the knowledge more relevant for the region, and several existing ontologies would benefit from localisation. For instance, with a localised SNOMED CT and OpenMRS, one should be able to use it to generate patient discharge notes in an indigenous language.

To accommodate the varied use of ontologies especially for ontology-mediated natural language interfaces, an OWL verbaliser was developed for isiZulu, which is one of the 11 official languages in South Africa and the most popular language by first language speakers. This was based on the isiZulu verbalisation patterns

---

[1] https://www.transifex.com/openmrs/OpenMRS/.

© Springer International Publishing AG 2017
E. Blomqvist et al. (Eds.): ESWC 2017 Satellite Events, LNCS 10577, pp. 59–64, 2017.
https://doi.org/10.1007/978-3-319-70407-4_12

and algorithms presented in [6,7] and the Python OWL API Owlready [8]. It is a proof-of-concept verbaliser that shows it can be done, despite having a grammar that does neither fit in existing language annotation models nor in pre-existing verbalisers, and in such a way that the core linguistic knowledge as well as the data and technologies can be reused independently.

We will describe the system design and implementation, provide brief notes on evaluation and what an attendee may expect from the demo.

2 System Design and Implementation

Design considerations. Unlike ontology verbalisation for English that uses mostly a template-based approach to insert the vocabulary elements, for isiZulu, there are verbalisation *patterns* that take into account context, such as verb conjugation and the strings for the quantifiers (examples further below). Also, the verbaliser had to meet multiple use case scenarios. This made it unfeasible to implement it with one or more existing technologies. Importantly, the use cases focus on text generation in intelligent user interfaces and patient discharge notes from electronic health records, rather than the sole purpose of facilitating user interaction with the ontology (knowledge acquisition, validation, documentation). This means that the language and linguistics components have to be reusable across applications, rather than tailor-made to OWL. Noting that isiZulu (and related languages) are under-resourced, any 'most generic' design and technology possible was preferred, so that the few resources available can be reused, cf. highly specialised formats that still would need to be adapted to accommodate the grammar [2]. For instance, it is helpful to make a separate list of nouns with their respective noun class (there are 17 for isiZulu), rather than extending, e.g., *lemon* [10]: the noun class of the noun determines the surface realisation for universal and existential quantification, conjugation, and negation, yet that list of nouns with their respective noun class can be reused in morphological analysers and in computer-assisted language learning.

Architecture and implementation. The components of the verbaliser and their interaction are shown in Fig. 1. The *verbaliser algorithms* file consists of the algorithms for named class subsumption ($C \sqsubseteq D$) and disjointness ($C \sqsubseteq \neg D$), simple existential quantification in the 'all-some' pattern ($C \sqsubseteq \exists R.D$) and negation thereof ($C \sqsubseteq \neg \exists R.D$) and simple conjunction ($C \sqcap D$), based on the algorithms and patterns in [6] and extended with the patterns for part-whole relations [7]. Some of these patterns require the name of the OWL class—assumed to be in the singular, as by good design practices—to be pluralised, hence requiring the isiZulu *pluraliser* of [1]. The implementation of the algorithms in Python is such that the corresponding functions can be linked to a variety of source files as well as individual statements in the interpreter for quick generation of a single sentence. For instance, for some axiom of the pattern $C \sqsubseteq \exists R.D$, e.g., uSolwazi $\sqsubseteq$ ∃fundisa.Isifundo, then the input would be

```
>>> exists_zu('uSolwazi','fundisa','isifundo')
```
that will instantly generate *Bonke* oSolwazi bafundisa isifundo *esisodwa* 'all professors teach at least one course'.

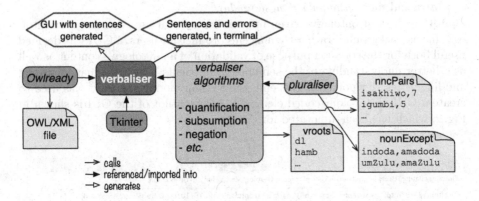

Fig. 1. Principal components of the OWL verbaliser.

To make it truly Semantic Web enabled, we have linked the verbalisation module to the novel OWL API for Python, Owlready [8], which works with OWL/XML serialisations. Using Owlready, the verbaliser fetches automatically the knowledge from the ontology and passes it on to the verbalisation module so as to compute the sentences and output the generated sentences in batch to the terminal for possible further processing. Consider, e.g., named class subsumption, whose serialisation in OWL/XML is <SubClassOf><Class IRI="..."/> <Class IRI="..."/> </SubClassOf>, which is mapped to the isa_zu(sub,super) function in the .py file. For instance, the serialisation of impala ⊑ isilwane,

```
<SubClassOf>
    <Class IRI="http://www.example.org/ex.owl#impala"/>
    <Class IRI="http://www.example.org/ex.owl#isilwane"/>
</SubClassOf>
```

is fetched and passed on and processed as isa_zu('impala','isilwane') to generate *impala* yisilwane 'impala is an animal'. This holds likewise for the other supported types of axioms, with one category of exceptions: part-whole relations. There is no single string for the 'has part' object property in isiZulu. Therefore, a stub is used that is mapped to a specific part-whole relation and corresponding function; e.g., 'has portion' is realised with an object property named eeee in the OWL/XML file, which is mapped to the Python function wp_solid_p(whole,part) that, when used in an axiom, will generate the correct isiZulu surface realisation of 'has portion'. For instance, in shorthand notation, isinkwa ⊑ ∃eeee.ucezu_isinkwa generates, with the 'has portion' underlined,

Sonke isinkwa ~~sino~~cezu lwesinkwa *olulodwa* yet igazi ⊑ ∃eeee.isampula_igazi generates *Lonke* igazi ~~line~~sampula legazi *elilodwa*, where the difference is due to the conjugation determined by the noun class (*si-* for the noun *isinkwa* in noun class 7 and *li-* for *igazi* in noun class 5) and phonological conditioning (*na- + ucezu = nocezu* and *na + isampula = nesampula*).

Although most ontology-driven information system use cases have an ontology 'in the background' rather than as end product for users, a GUI was deemed useful both for the common purpose of validation of an ontology's content as well as a better understanding of the sentence components from a language learning and linguistics viewpoint. To this end, the Python module Tkinter[2] was used to create a GUI with colour-coded elements. A screenshot of the GUI is shown in Fig. 2, which has been annotated for clarity.

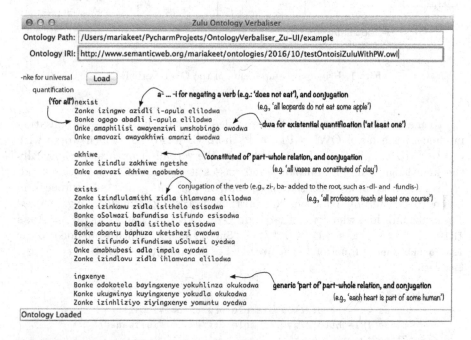

Fig. 2. Section of the GUI interface of the Semantic Web-enabled isiZulu verbaliser. Colour coding: existential and universal quantification is shown in blue, the classes (nouns) in red, and the object properties and simple subsumption (verbs) in green. (Color figure online)

Evaluation. Evaluation of the tool consisted of internal verification of correctness of encoding and external validation in the sense of testing it with more examples as described in [6], i.e., with more axioms. We represented in OWL all test cases of [6,7], and the axioms used in their respective user evaluations, which were

---

[2] https://wiki.python.org/moin/TkInter.

based on existing ontologies and selected to ensure coverage of permutations for noun classes, verbs, and part-whole relations. This totalled to 82 logical axioms. The tool, source code, sample ontology, and screencast video showing the working code are available from http://www.meteck.org/files/geni/.

Benefits of the chosen design and implementation The principal benefits are: (1) the ease with which the *verbaliser algorithms* file can be swapped for an analogous file in another language (e.g., isiXhosa, which is similar to isiZulu), (2) the reusability of the algorithms beyond OWL files when needed, and (3) the two modes of operation for users (GUI) and further processing in ontology-driven information systems (terminal output).

3 The Demo

The main aim of the demo is to present the functioning proof-of-concept OWL verbaliser. Given that isiZulu is not a familiar language to most people, an English-isiZulu dictionary will be available so that attendees can select terms and declare axioms that then will be verbalised on the fly. It is also an opportunity to discuss details of the implementation of the verbalisation patterns that present challenges to other existing OWL verbalisers and ontology editor tools.

Acknowledgments. This work is based on the research supported in part by the National Research Foundation of South Africa (Grant Number 93397).

References

1. Byamugisha, J., Keet, C.M., Khumalo, L.: Pluralising nouns in isiZulu and similar languages. In: Gelbkuh, A. (ed.) Proceedings of CICLing 2016. Springer (2016, in print)
2. Chavula, C., Keet, C.M.: Is lemon sufficient for building multilingual ontologies for Bantu languages? In: Proceedings of OWLED 2014, CEUR-WS, Riva del Garda, Italy, 17–18 October 2014, vol. 1265, pp. 61–72 (2014)
3. Coetzer, W., Moodley, D., Gerber, A.: A case-study of ontology-driven semantic mediation of flower-visiting data from heterogeneous data-stores in three South African natural history collections. In: Semantics for Biodiversity (S4BioDiv 2013), 27 May 2013, Montpellier, France (2013)
4. Dalvit, L., Gunzo, F.T., Maema, M.K.V., Slay, H.: Exploring the use of ontologies in creating learning platforms: HIV and AIDS Education at a South African University. In: Proceedings of ICCSSE 2008, vol. 5, pp. 407–410, December 2008
5. Dombeu, J.V.F.: A conceptual ontology for e-Government monitoring of development projects in Sub Saharan Africa. IST-Africa **2010**, 1–8 (2010)
6. Keet, C.M., Khumalo, L.: Toward a knowledge-to-text controlled natural language of isiZulu. Language Resources and Evaluation (2016, in print)
7. Keet, C.M., Khumalo, L.: On the verbalization patterns of part-whole relations in isiZulu. In: Proceedings of INLG 2016, 5–8 September 2016, Edinburgh, UK, pp. 174–183. ACL (2016)
8. Lamy, J.: Ontology-oriented programming for biomedical informatics. Stud. Health Technol. Inform. **221**, 64–68 (2016)

64   C.M. Keet et al.

9. Lo, M., Camara, G., Niang, C.A.T., Ndiaye, S.M., Sall, O.: Towards an ontology-based framework for data integration: application to agriculture and health domains in Senegal. In: Gamatié, A. (ed.) Computing in Research and Development in Africa, pp. 41–57. Springer, Cham (2015). doi:10.1007/978-3-319-08239-4_3
10. McCrae, J., et al.: Interchanging lexical resources on the semantic web. Lang. Resour. Eval. **46**(4), 701–719 (2012)
11. SNOMED CT: http://www.ihtsdo.org/snomed-ct/. Accessed 27 Jan 2012

ComSem: Digitization and Semantic Annotation of Comic Books

Joachim Van Herwegen$^{(\boxtimes)}$, Ruben Verborgh, and Erik Mannens

IDLab, imec, Ghent University,
Sint-Pietersnieuwstraat 41, B-9000 Ghent, Belgium
`joachim.vanherwegen@ugent.be`

Abstract. The popularity of digital comic books keeps rising, causing an increase in interest from traditional publishers. Digitizing existing comic books can require much work though, since older comic books were made when digital versions were not taken into account. Additions such as digital panel segmentation and semantic annotation, which increase the discoverability and functionality, were only introduced at a later point in time. To this end, we made ComSem: a tool to support publishers in this task by automating certain steps in the process and making others more accessible. In this paper we present our demo and how it can be used to easily detect comic book panels and annotate them with semantic metadata.

Keywords: Digital publishing · EPUB3 · Comic book

1 Introduction

Digital comic books are becoming more and more popular. Comic book sales keep increasing every year, both physically and digitally[1]. Because of this, more and more publishers are interested in entering this digital market, both with their new releases and their older backlog. Unfortunately, most of their backlog was designed in a time when there was no demand for digital comics. This means that at most they might have an archive of images corresponding to the complete pages of the comics. These images are not enough to create a pleasant reading experience: it is for example often infeasible to display an entire comic page on a mobile device, meaning additional steps have to be taken to create a pleasant reading experience.

Publishers are also often not that aware of how they can annotate their comic books with semantic data or what advantages this offers. Adding meta-information to comics can greatly increase their discoverability and usability [5].

In this paper we showcase our Comic Semantifier, ComSem, which assists publishers in their digital production pipeline, starting from a set of images and

---

[1] http://www.cnbc.com/2016/06/05/comic-books-buck-trend-as-print-and-digital-sales-flourish.html.

© Springer International Publishing AG 2017
E. Blomqvist et al. (Eds.): ESWC 2017 Satellite Events, LNCS 10577, pp. 65–70, 2017.
https://doi.org/10.1007/978-3-319-70407-4_13

ending with a semantically annotated EPUB3 file. The demo itself can be found at http://comsem.demo.idlab.technology/[2]. ComSem was made in cooperation with actual comic book publishers and is based on their workflow and needs.

2   Related Work

2.1   Digital Comic Book Tools

There are many tools available for creating digital comic books[3], but most of these focus on creating the comic itself in their tool, instead of adapting an existing comic book to a digital format, making them less suited for publishers looking to digitize their existing backlog. Others still require much manual labour to specify where all the panels are located on a page. There is also very little focus on the semantic aspect of the comic books, providing publishers with no option to embed this in their work, which limits their potential as described in Sect. 2.3.

2.2   EPUB3 and RDFa

EPUB3 [2] is a standard for the digital publication of e-books. It consists of an archive of HTML files, describing both the content and metadata, combined with relevant assets. Although the format was originally designed for e-books, work has been put into extending the format for digital comic books[4].

RDFa[5] is a format designed to embed RDF data into HTML pages. Since EPUB3 is a collection of HTML, RDFa can also be used to enrich EPUB3 files, which is how ComSem annotates comic books.

2.3   Metadata

Research has shown that the addition of metadata to digital publications can have several positive impacts, such as increasing discovery, supporting dynamic content and providing semantic search [1,3,5].

Discoverability plays a big role in digital publications. With a surplus of offerings available, it becomes harder to stand out in the crowd. In his study on optimizing digital publications, Wischenbart [5] explains the importance of metadata to improve the chances of people discovering your work.

An example tool showcasing the advantages of metadata is the digital authoring environment created by De Meester et al. [1], supporting content creators by providing easy to use tools for enhancing their text with semantic metadata.

---

[2] An example comic can be found at http://comsem.demo.idlab.technology/dnd.html?comic=1 (Saving changes and NER are disabled on this specific comic for demo reasons).
[3] http://networkcultures.org/longform/2016/11/21/digital-comics-harder-better-faster-stronger/.
[4] https://idpf.github.io/epub-vocabs/structure/#h_comics.
[5] https://rdfa.info/.

Similarly, Heyvaert et al. have created a tool making use of comic book metadata to improve the user experience [3] by allowing them to apply specific filters on comic book collections.

3   Comic Book Digitization

ComSem starts from a set of digital images, and ends with a valid EPUB3 containing all the relevant metadata. The user begins by uploading a set of images, which can be done by dragging them to the relevant area, after which ComSem automatically detects the specific panels on each of them. Afterwards these can be annotated with additional semantic metadata. Then, once the user has finished, the result can be exported as EPUB3.

3.1   Automated Panel Detection

Our implementation is currently based on a flood-fill implementation, making use of the OpenCV[6] library, with additional support for detecting overlapping panels, similar to the method described by Ho et al. [4]

Figure 1 shows an example of the panel detection done by ComSem after uploading a page. As can be seen, the detection is not completely correct. This

Fig. 1. Automated panel detection. The borders, number of panels, and order of the panels can easily be changed by right-clicking the panels.

---

[6] http://opencv.org/.

can be caused by panel lines not being 100% straight, or by having components extending outside of the panel, as is the case for the bottom-right panel in this figure. The handles on the sides of the panels allow the user to manually fine-tune the panel positioning in the cases where this is deemed necessary.

The order of the panels is also determined automatically, based on their relative positioning. This order can easily be changed by right-clicking on the panels in the order they should appear.

Should the number of detected panels be incorrect, new panels can quickly be added by double-clicking, while superfluous panels can be deleted by double-clicking them while holding the ALT key.

3.2   Semantic Annotation

During the creation of an EPUB3, we provide the user with ample opportunity to enrich the content with RDFa, using the tools described below. In ComSem, we have mostly focused on metadata such as the characters appearing in the story, using metadata to indicate their appearance on specific panels, and transcribing the textual contents of a panel, allowing for translations to be present. But we also support custom RDF tags, making it possible to describe other components.

Annotation Tools: There are two types of metadata that can be added in ComSem: panel-specific and global. Panel-specific metadata pertains to the events depicted in a specific panel, while global metadata describes information corresponding to the entire comic book, such as the author.

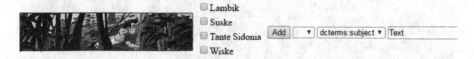

Fig. 2. Panel metadata. The panels are automatically generated based on the selection made before.

In the panel-specific tab (Fig. 2), the check-boxes can be used to indicate the presence of a specific character in the given panel. This metadata gets stored using the `schema:about`[7] tag, while the text-boxes provide the user with the option of adding additional non-character tags, using, among others, `schema:text` and `schema:url`. Users can also update the list of characters and metadata to choose from, which is not pictured here.

Besides the panel editor, there is also the global metadata editor (Fig. 3). There the user can add global metadata, such as ISBN, title, and author. A short description of the comic book can also be written in the given text field. This description can then be used for enriching the comic with additional metadata.

---

[7] https://schema.org/.

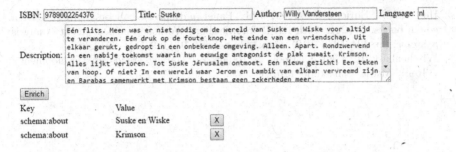

Fig. 3. Global metadata. New tags can easily be added or removed.

When the `Enrich` button is pressed, the description text is sent to a Named Entity Recognition (NER) engine, after which all recognized entities are added using the `schema:about` tag. The NER engine is currently configured for the Dutch language, but will be adapted to depend on the value of the language tag provided by the user. There is also the option for users to add extra tags, should more specific predicates be required. All this metadata is then added to the EPUB3 file once it is generated.

4 Conclusion

ComSem supports publishers in digitizing and annotating their existing backlog of comic books. It also provides them with the opportunity to add metadata in those comic books, enriching their content and providing the possibility of integrating with new applications to improve the user experience. It was made in such a way that it can easily be used by someone with no Semantic Web background, while still having full RDF support.

Due to the automated panel detection, the digitization process can be sped up, since only minor adjustments are required to perfectly mark the panel locations, after which the comic book can immediately be converted to a valid EPUB3 file.

References

1. De Meester, B., De Nies, T., Ghaem Sigarchian, H., Vander Sande, M., Van Campen, J., Van Impe, B., De Neve, W., Mannens, E., Van de Walle, R.: A digital-first authoring environment for enriched e-Books using EPUB 3. Information services and use, pp. 259–268 (2014). http://dx.doi.org/10.3233/ISU-140748
2. Gylling, M., McCoy, W., Garrish, M.: Epub publications 3.0. Recommended specification IDPF (2011). http://www.idpf.org/epub/30/spec/epub30-publications.html
3. Heyvaert, P., De Nies, T., Van Herwegen, J., Vander Sande, M., Verborgh, R., De Neve, W., Mannens, E., Van de Walle, R.: Using EPUB 3 and the open web platform for enhanced presentation and machine-understandable metadata for digital comics. ELPUB 2015, pp. 37–46 (2015)

4. Ho, A.K.N., Burie, J.C., Ogier, J.M.: Panel and speech balloon extraction from comic books. In: 2012 10th IAPR International Workshop on Document Analysis Systems, pp. 424–428 (2012). http://dx.doi.org/10.1109/DAS.2012.66
5. Wischenbart, R.: Global EBook: A Report on Market Trends an Developments. O'Reilly Media, Sebastopol (2014)

Live Storage and Querying of Versioned Datasets on the Web

Ruben Taelman[(✉)], Miel Vander Sande, Ruben Verborgh, and Erik Mannens

IDLab, imec, Department of Electronics and Information Systems,
Ghent University, Ghent, Belgium
{ruben.taelman,miel.vandersande,
ruben.verborgh,erik.mannens}@ugent.be

Abstract. Linked Datasets often evolve over time for a variety of reasons. While typical scenarios rely on the latest version only, useful knowledge may still be contained within or between older versions, such as the historical information of biomedical patient data. In order to make this historical information cost-efficiently available on the Web, a low-cost interface is required for providing access to versioned datasets. For our demonstration, we set up a live Triple Pattern Fragments interface for a versioned dataset with queryable access. We explain different version query types of this interface, and how it communicates with a storage solution that can handle these queries efficiently.

Keywords: Linked data · Versioning · Triple pattern fragments · OSTRICH · SPARQL

1 Introduction

Linked Datasets often change over time [7], because the underlying information changes, or mistakes are corrected. Currently, most data publishers provide queryable access to only the latest version of their datasets. Other data publishers, such as DBpedia [1], provide data dumps of previous versions of their datasets. Historical information and its evolution might still contain a lot of useful knowledge, such as historical information of biomedical patient data, or for the analysis of concept drift. Because of this, we need queryable access to this data at different versions.

Querying on the Web is possible using the Triple Pattern Fragments (TPF) framework [8], which was introduced as an alternative to SPARQL endpoints [2] for publishing Linked Data at a low cost, while still enabling queryable access. The TPF approach limits server interfaces to triple pattern queries and moves the effort of full SPARQL query evaluation to the client. TPF interfaces are based on the REST principles and provide declarative hypermedia controls with the Hydra Core Vocabulary [5] using which clients can discover the triple pattern query controls. Furthermore, each response contains metadata to help client-side query evaluation, such as an estimated query result counts.

E. Blomqvist et al. (Eds.): ESWC 2017 Satellite Events, LNCS 10577, pp. 71–75, 2017.
https://doi.org/10.1007/978-3-319-70407-4_14

Querying versioned datasets is possible using different query atoms [4]. In this demo, we focus on the following realistic query atoms:

- *Version Materialization* (VM) queries *at* a single version.
- *Delta Materialization* (DM) queries differences *between* versions.
- *Version Queries* (VQ) annotate results *for* different versions.

Each query engine needs some form of storage solution behind it. Strategies for storing different dataset versions can be categorized in the following storage policies [3]:

1. *Independent copies* (IC) for storing fully materialized snapshots for each version.
2. *Change-based* (CB) will only store differences between consecutive versions.
3. *Timestamp-based* (TB) annotates each triple with the versions for which it exists.

In this paper, we demonstrate an extension of the TPF interface that has support for the three versioned query atoms, which is discussed in Sect. 2. We illustrate the feasibility of this interface by publishing a large versioned dataset publicly, using a new storage solution that is optimized for triple pattern queries for each of these query atoms, as shown in Sect. 3. Finally, in Sect. 4, we demonstrate example usage of the interface.

2   Interface

In this section, we discuss *Versioned Triple Pattern Fragments* (VTPF), a versioning feature for the TPF interface that supports VM, DM and VQ queries.

Support for these query atoms is possible by adding three new query forms to the interface. Each of these forms supports the basic triple patterns. The VM form adds a *version* parameter for selecting the version in which the triple pattern query should be evaluated. For the DM form, a *start* and *end* parameter is added for selecting the version range in between which changes should be queried given a triple pattern. Triples are then annotated as *addition* or *deletion*. Finally, for VQ queries, no additional parameter is added but triples matching a given triple pattern are annotated with versions.

These forms are made available both in HTML and RDF representations. An example of the HTML form for VM queries can be seen in Fig. 1. Listing 1.1 shows a hypermedia control for VM queries in RDF. We use the *version* vocabulary[1] for these hypermedia controls, metadata and result representation.

---

[1] http://w3id.org/version/ontology.

```
<http://versioned.linkeddatafragments.org/bear#metadata> {
 <http://versioned.linkeddatafragments.org/bear#dataset> hydra:search [
   hydra:template "http://versioned.linkeddatafragments.org/bear?versionType=
   VersionMaterialized{&s,p,o,v}";
   hydra:variableRepresentation hydra:ExplicitRepresentation;
   hydra:mapping [ hydra:variable "s"; hydra:property rdf:subject       ],
                 [ hydra:variable "p"; hydra:property rdf:predicate     ],
                 [ hydra:variable "o"; hydra:property rdf:object        ],
                 [ hydra:variable "v"; hydra:property ver:relatedVersion ]
 ].
}
```

Listing 1.1. The VM query RDF form using the Hydra Core Vocabulary.

Search Versioned BEAR dataset by triple pattern   **For version**

subject: _____ 🔳   within between all

predicate: _____   version: 6 ↕

object: "WebDeveloper1"_____

[Search]

Matches in Versioned BEAR dataset for *{ ?s ?p "WebDeveloper1". }*

Showing items 1 to 4 of 4 with 100 items per page.

```
TwitterAccount    accountName    "WebDeveloper1".
Bhttpx3Ax2Fx2Fbrucewhealtonx2Eusx2Ffoafx2Erdfxxbnode6    accountName    "WebDeveloper1".
Bhttpx3Ax2Fx2Fpersonalprofilesx2Efwwebdevx2Ecomx2FBruceWhealtonJrx2Ffoafx2Erdfxxbnode6    ac...
me    nick    "WebDeveloper1".
```

Fig. 1. VM query HTML form and results.

3 Storage

In this section, we give a high-level overview of OSTRICH, which is a new storage solution that is used as a back-end for our VTPF instance.

Previous work [4,6] has shown that the complexity for different versioning query atoms depends on the storage policy. VTPF supports the VM, DM and VQ query atoms, where each of them can be disabled in case the cost for publishing would be too high, when for example a storage policy is in place that is inefficient for certain query atoms. For our demonstration, we enable the three query atoms, because OSTRICH is a hybrid IC–CB–TB approach, which enables efficient VM, DM and VQ querying. OSTRICH supports these query atoms for simple triple pattern queries, which is the only type of query that is required for a back-end TPF datasource. Furthermore, the TPF approach requires each fragment to contain metadata about the estimated number of matching triples for each triple pattern. For this, OSTRICH supports (approximate) count queries for all query atoms for triple patterns.

For our demonstration, we used the first ten versions of the RDF archive provided by the BEAR benchmark [4]. Each version in this dataset is a weekly snapshot from the Dynamic Linked Data Observatory[2]. When combined, these

---

[2] http://swse.deri.org/dyldo/.

ten versions are approximately 45 GB large in N-Triples format, and 3 GB when gzipped. OSTRICH requires less than 6 GB for storing these versions, which is significantly less than the N-Triples format, i.e., it only requires 13% of the storage space. Even though OSTRICH requires twice as much storage space for this dataset when compared to gzip, it still provides queryable access, which is not possible with gzip. On average, OSTRICH evaluates triple pattern queries for any of the versions in approximately 1ms, which is sufficiently fast for a Web interface back-end system.

4   Demonstration Overview

We published the first ten versions of the BEAR dataset using a VTPF interface with an OSTRICH back-end at http://versioned.linkeddatafragments.org/bear. This enables queryable access to this dataset *at*, *between* and *for* different versions using triple patterns. Visiting the interface using a webbrowser allows humans to consume the data as shown in Fig. 1. Machines can also consume the data by setting an RDF serialization format in the accept header[3].

We list several example queries about "WebDeveloper1" that can be performed using the interface:

- Information in version 6:
  http://versioned.linkeddatafragments.org/bear?object=%22WebDeveloper
  1\%22\&versionType=VersionMaterialized\&version=6
- Changes between version 6 and 9:
  http://versioned.linkeddatafragments.org/bear?object=%22WebDeveloper
  1\%22\&versionType=DeltaMaterialized\&versionStart=6\&versionEnd=9
- Version query for all information:
  http://versioned.linkeddatafragments.org/bear?
  object=%22WebDeveloper1%22\&versionType=Version

With this demonstration, we show the feasibility of the VTPF interface for exposing versioned Linked Datasets on the Web, with queryable triple pattern access. In future work, we will extend the TPF client [8] with support for this interface, so that it is able to consume data using the version query atoms for more complex queries, using an appropriate query language.

References

1. Auer, S., Bizer, C., Kobilarov, G., Lehmann, J., Cyganiak, R., Ives, Z.: DBpedia: a nucleus for a web of open data. In: Aberer, K., Choi, K.-S., Noy, N., Allemang, D., Lee, K.-I., Nixon, L., Golbeck, J., Mika, P., Maynard, D., Mizoguchi, R., Schreiber, G., Cudré-Mauroux, P. (eds.) ASWC/ISWC -2007. LNCS, vol. 4825, pp. 722–735. Springer, Heidelberg (2007). doi:10.1007/978-3-540-76298-0_52

---

[3] Request data in TriG using curl: `curl -H "Accept: application/trig"` "http://versioned.linkeddatafragments.org/bear".

2. Feigenbaum, L., Todd Williams, G., Grant Clark, K., Torres, E.: SPARQL 1.1 protocol. Recommendation W3C, Mar 2013. http://www.w3.org/TR/2013/REC-sparql11-protocol-20130321/
3. Fernández, J.D., Polleres, A., Umbrich, J.: Towards efficient archiving of dynamic linked open data. In: Proceedings of DIACHRON (2015)
4. Fernández, J.D., Umbrich, J., Polleres, A., Knuth, M.: Evaluating query and storage strategies for RDF archives. In: Proceedings of the 12th International Conference on Semantic Systems (2016)
5. Lanthaler, M., Gütl, C.: Hydra: a vocabulary for hypermedia-driven Web APIS. In: Proceedings of the 6th Workshop on Linked Data on the Web, May 2013
6. Taelman, R., Verborgh, R., Mannens, E.: Exposing RDF archives using Triple Pattern Fragments. In: Proceedings of the 20th International Conference on Knowledge Engineering and Knowledge Management: Posters and Demos, Nov 2016
7. Umbrich, J., Decker, S., Hausenblas, M., Polleres, A., Hogan, A.: Towards dataset dynamics: change frequency of linked open data sources. In: 3rd International Workshop on Linked Data on the Web LDOW (2010)
8. Verborgh, R., Vander Sande, M., Hartig, O., Van Herwegen, J., De Vocht, L., De Meester, B., Haesendonck, G., Colpaert, P.: Triple pattern fragments: a low-cost knowledge graph interface for the web. J. Web Semant. 37(38), 184–206 (2016)

μRDF Store: Towards Extending the Semantic Web to Embedded Devices

Victor Charpenay[1,2(✉)], Sebastian Käbisch[1], and Harald Kosch[2]

[1] Siemens AG — Corporate Technology, Munich, Germany
{victor.charpenay,sebastian.kaebisch}@siemens.com
[2] Fakultät für Informatik und Mathematik, Universität Passau, Passau, Germany
harald.kosch@uni-passau.de

Abstract. This paper presents the μRDF store, a triple store designed for micro-controllers with limited memory, typically 8 to 64 kB. The μRDF store exposes a query interface inspired by SPARQL that supports basic graph pattern queries. Data is sent over CoAP and serialized in EXI, a binary format for XML.

The performances of its processing engine are demonstrated in a Web chat application where the μRDF store can be submitted queries. The application is available at: https://vcharpenay.github.io/urdf-amaa/.

Keywords: Web of things · Internet of things · SPARQL · RDF · EXI · CoAP

1 Introduction

In the past few years, Semantic Web technologies have been successfuly applied to the domain of the Internet of Things (IoT). Various systems such as SPIT-FIRE [6], mixing RDF and machine-generated data, were developed with promising results.

In this paper, we explore the possibility of exchanging RDF data in constrained environments, in order to extend the scope of the Semantic Web for the IoT. In particular, we are interested in the problem of storing and querying RDF data on micro-controllers with IP connectivity (8 to 64 kB RAM).

2 Related Work

Until recently, no realistic use case could be found where computational devices had limited resources but still IP connectivity. As a consequence, the problem of storing RDF in constraind environments, as opposed to storing billions of statements in very large databases, has remained mostly unexplored. The situation has changed with the coming of the IoT where RDF has found new usages.

The first work that addressed constrained devices —and to the best of our knowledge, the only one— is the Wiselib TupleStore (as part of SPITFIRE) [4].

© Springer International Publishing AG 2017
E. Blomqvist et al. (Eds.): ESWC 2017 Satellite Events, LNCS 10577, pp. 76–80, 2017.
https://doi.org/10.1007/978-3-319-70407-4_15

It compares the performance of various C++ data structures to compress URIs, inherent to any RDF document.

The Wiselib TupleStore features insertion and removal operations. There exists other proposals to compress RDF data but none of them have these characteristics. The most notable ones are the Header Dictionary Triples (HDT) binary representation for RDF [2] and k^2-triples, a variant of HDT [1]. The main objective of HDT was to compress large RDF datasets. e.g. to fit in the main memory of a standard PC. But its compression scheme could reasonably be used on small datasets as well.

In the original proposal for HDT, triples are stored using bitmaps on which compression is applied. k^2-triples indexes triples in subject-object indexes (vertical partitioning) and applies k^2-tree compression on the two-dimensional arrays.

HDT and k^2-triples show high compression ratios. However, in a typical IoT configuration, RDF data might be dynamically updated, which requires insertion and removal operations. Moreover, neither the Wiselib Tuplestore nor HDT/k^2-triples go beyond triple pattern matching to query RDF. Our proposal, the μRDF store, combines both a small memory footprint with insertion/removal operations and Basic Graph Pattern (BGP) processing. It is presented next.

3   Overview of the μRDF Store

A few assumptions were made in the design of the μRDF store. First, it is expected that datasets contain a limited number of triples, to fit in the RAM of a micro-controller. Second, we expect datasets to contain mostly assertional data, as opposed to terminological data.

3.1   Data Structure

The data structure underlying the μRDF store is optimized for navigational queries (i.e. with bound predicates) against datasets having few distinct properties (max. n properties). Each resource is given an index number where the first n indices are reserved for predicates (in practice, $n = 32$ or 64, i.e. a multiple of the size of a machine word). Triples are stored with variable-length byte (vbyte) encoding in a way that navigation from every resource to its neighbors in the RDF graph is possible both forward and backward. Triples with literals are only stored once.

Formally, for I, B and L mutually disjoint sets of IRIs, blank nodes and literals respectively, a μRDF resource $\rho \in P$ is the pair (R, L) where $R \subset I \times (I \cup B) \times \{0,1\}$ is the set of direct and reverse relations to other resources and $L \subset I \times L$ is the set of literal relations associated to ρ. An instance of the μRDF store is a map $\mu : (I \cup B) \rightarrow P$.

3.2   Query Interface

The μRDF store supports BGP queries (given that at least one subject or object is bound). Queries are processed in a greedy fashion: as soon as a binding is found for a triple pattern, the next triple pattern is processed. This guarantees an upper bound of $O(|V|)$ for intermediate storage, where V is the set of variables in the query. This process, that might lead to duplicated calls, avoids managing arbitrarily large intermediary results (e.g. for patterns with the `rdf:type` predicate), which is critical in constrained environments.

To exchange data over the network, data is serialized in the Efficient XML Interchange (EXI) format. Our original proposal for the μRDF store suggests that EXI, that can take advantage of schema information from RDF/XML, offers satisfactory compression ratios [5].

Moreover, a straightforward mapping of the HTTP SPARQL 1.1 protocol can be defined for the Constrained Application Protocol (CoAP), where both query and update are supported. The CoAP specification limits the payload size to 1024 bytes. If the serialized result set is above this value, the algorithm described above allows data to be sent "block-wise": each full mapping found by the algorithm is sent in a separate block[1].

4   Evaluation

We implemented the μRDF store for the ESP8266, a microcontroller with an integrated Wi-Fi chip (64 kB RAM, 80 MHz). To test its performances, we used the dataset generator and the query mix provided by the Lehigh University Benchmark (LUBM) [3]. The generator had to be adapted to small datasets[2]. All fourteen queries of the benchmark can be processed by our implementation.

We compared the memory footprint of our implementation to the Wiselib tuplestore, HDT and k^2-triples (Fig. 1a). The comparison suggests that, overall, HDT performs best, followed by the μRDF store, in the range we consider of interest (up to 10,000 triples). It is reported in the literature that k^2-triples performs better but the graphic shows that this does not apply to small RDF datasets. It also shows that URI compression as performed by the Wiselib tuplestore performs poorly for datasets with less than 1,000 triples.

The original idea behind the μRDF store is to explore SPARQL as a decentralized discovery mechanism among IoT devices. This requires at least BGPs to be supported by individual nodes. As mentioned before, no work in the state-of-the-art has proposed an implementation of BGP processing at the scale of a micro-controller.

On the MSP8266, all queries from the LUBM benchmark —especially Q9 that requires many intermadiary joins—are processed in less than 20 ms, including EXI coding. In comparison, sending static RDF/EXI data over CoAP takes at least 500 ms and this number grows with the number of triples being sent (Fig. 1b), which means that query processing has no significant impact on the overall exchange between two devices. On the contrary, local BGP processing,

---

[1] The demonstration presented in this paper also exploits this partitioning of the result set with MQTT, another IoT protocol: each mapping is published in a separate MQTT message.
[2] See https://github.com/vcharpenay/urdf-store-exp for more details.

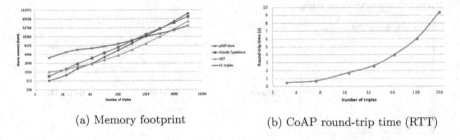

(a) Memory footprint   (b) CoAP round-trip time (RTT)

Fig. 1. Evaluation of the µRDF store with LUBM synthetic data

in constrat to other RDF query mechanisms such as Triple Pattern Fragments (TPFs) [7], can significantly improve the rapidity of an exchange by reducing the total amount of exchanged data.

Our work on the µRDF store has led us to the following conclusion: with today's hardware, an "Embedded Semantic Web" is possible. As opposed to HDT, the µRDF store supports updates and BGP processing; without degrading data transmission; with a limited overhead in memory.

5 Demonstration: Ask Me (almost) Anything

The purpose of this demonstration is to illustrate the conclusions of our evaluation in an interactive fashion. We developed a simple chat application that allows one to submit queries in a simplified manner to an instance of the µRDF store from their Web browser. Its design is inspired by a concept popularized by Reddit called Ask Me Anything (AMA). Here, a microcontroller invites you to an AMA session to let you discover its name, its capabilites and the "Things" it is semantically connected to.

Figure 2a shows the Web interface on which queries can be formulated. The technical details of the demonstration are given in Fig. 2b. A client query is first pre-processed by the so-called "advisor", a non-constrained machine that first translates the query into SPARQL, then serializes it in EXI; the EXI is processed by the micro-controller which responds with another EXI message; the server response is post-processed by the advisor to print it in a human-readable form. All the messages are sent via the Message Queue Telemetry Transport (MQTT) protocol following a simple publish-subscribe interaction pattern. The delay between requests and responses does not exceed a few seconds.

6 Conclusion

IoT devices that embed a full IP-based communication stack usually come with unused computational power. As current applications mostly concentrate on sending sensor data to the Cloud as fast as possible, the capacities of edge devices remain untapped. With the µRDF store, we aim at relocating intelligence to the

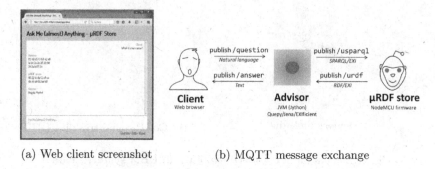

(a) Web client screenshot   (b) MQTT message exchange

Fig. 2. Overview of the ask me (almost) anything (AMaA) application

edge, starting with semantic processing. Our demonstration underlines the relevance of an Embedded Semantic Web for the IoT.

Another aspect that this demonstration tends to show is that human–to–machine communication is tedious. IoT systems might be much more performant if machines themselves formulated the queries. This is our next line of research. Support for the OPTIONAL operator is also being considered in our implementation.

References

1. Álvarez-García, S., Brisaboa, N.R., Fernández, J.D., Martínez-Prieto, M.A.: Compressed k2-triples for full-in-memory RDF engines. CoRR, abs/1105.4004 (2011)
2. Fernández, J.D., Martínez-Prieto, M.A., Arias, M., Gutierrez, C., Álvarez-García, S., Brisaboa, N.R.: Lightweighting the web of data through compact RDF/HDT. In: Lozano, J.A., Gómez, J.A., Moreno, J.A. (eds.) Advances in Artificial Intelligence. volume 7023, pp. 483–493. Springer, Berlin (2011)
3. Guo, Y., Pan, Z., Heflin, J.: LUBM: a benchmark for OWL knowledge base systems. Web Semant. Sci. Serv. Agents World Wide Web **3**(23), 158–182 (2005)
4. Hasemann, H., Kröller, A., Pagel, M.: The wiselib tuplestore: a modular RDF database for the internet of things. CoRR, abs/1402.7228 (2014)
5. Käbisch, S., Peintner, D., Anicic, D.: Standardized and efficient RDF encoding for constrained embedded networks. In: Gandon, F., Sabou, M., Sack, H., dAmato, C., Cudré-Mauroux, P., Zimmermann, A. (eds.) ESWC 2015. LNCS, vol. 9088, pp. 437–452. Springer, Cham (2015). doi:10.1007/978-3-319-18818-8_27
6. Pfisterer, D., Romer, K., Bimschas, D., Kleine, O., Mietz, R., Truong, C., Hasemann, H., Kröller, A., Pagel, M., Hauswirth, M., Karnstedt, M., Leggieri, M., Passant, A., Richardson, R.: SPITFIRE: toward a semantic web of things. **49**(11), pp. 40–48 (2011)
7. Verborgh, R., Hartig, O., Meester, B., Haesendonck, G., Vocht, L., Vander Sande, M., Cyganiak, R., Colpaert, P., Mannens, E., Walle, R.: Querying datasets on the web with high availability. In: Mika, P., et al. (eds.) ISWC 2014. LNCS, vol. 8796, pp. 180–196. Springer, Cham (2014). doi:10.1007/978-3-319-11964-9_12

Introducing Feedback in Qanary: How Users Can Interact with QA Systems

Dennis Diefenbach[1], Niousha Hormozi[2], Shanzay Amjad[3], and Andreas Both[4(✉)]

[1] Lab. Hubert Curien, Saint Etienne, France
dennis.diefenbach@univ-st-etienne.fr
[2] University of Athens, Athens, Greece
nhormozi@di.uoa.gr
[3] University of Ottawa, Ottawa, Canada
samja088@uottawa.ca
[4] DATEV eG, Nuremberg, Germany
contact@andreasboth.de

Abstract. Providing a general and efficient Question Answering system over Knowledge Bases (KB) has been studied for years. Most of the works concentrated on the automatic translation of a natural language question into a formal query. However, few works address the problem on how users can interact with Question Answering systems during this translation process. We present a general mechanism that allows users to interact with Question Answering systems. It is built on top of Qanary, a framework for integrating Question Answering components. We show how the mechanism can be applied in a generalized way. In particular, we show how it can be used when the user asks ambiguous questions.

Keywords: User interaction · Question answering systems · User interface

1 Introduction

In recent years, there has been a fast growth in available data sets. One very important use case is finding relevant results for a user's requests, and by using different data sets. The field of Question Answering (QA) tackles this information retrieval use case by providing a (natural language) interface aiming at easy-to-use fact retrieval from large data sets in knowledge bases (KB). While following this path it could be observed that additional challenges are rising while the data sets are growing. For example, while having only recent geospatial information a term like "Germany" can be identified directly without ambiguity. However, after adding historic data several instances called "Germany" will be available, representing different entities (over time).

In the past years several question answering systems were published working on-top of linked data, cf., Question Answering over Linked Data (QALD) [8].

E. Blomqvist et al. (Eds.): ESWC 2017 Satellite Events, LNCS 10577, pp. 81–86, 2017.
https://doi.org/10.1007/978-3-319-70407-4_16

Many QA systems follow a single interaction approach, where the user asks a question and retrieves an answer. However, many questions cannot be understood because the context is only clear in the users' mind, or because the ambiguity of the considered data set is not known by the user. Hence, not any kind of question can be interpreted correctly following an ad hoc single-interaction approach. User interaction in QA systems (i.e., how users can influence a QA process) is not well explored. Only a few QA systems exists involving the user in the retrieval process, e.g., Querix [7], Freya [2], and Canalis [10].

In this paper we extend the Qanary methodology [1] a framework for integrating Question Answering components. Our main contribution is a generalized user feedback mechanism in Qanary.

2   Related Work

In the context of QA, a large number of systems have been developed in the last years. For example, more than twenty QA systems were evaluated against the QALD benchmark (cf., http://qald.sebastianwalter.org). However, only few of them address user interaction. Freya [2] uses syntactic parsing in combination with the KB-based look-up in order to interpret the question, and involves the user if necessary. The user's choices are used for training the system in order to improve its performance. Querix [7] is a domain-independent natural language interface (NLI) that uses clarification dialogs to query KBs. Querix is not "intelligent" by interpreting and understanding the input queries; it only employs a reduced set of NLP tools and consults the user when hitting its limitations. Canali [10] shows completions for a user's query in a drop-down menu appearing under the input window. The user has the option of clicking on any such completion, whereby its text is added to the input window.

Since QA systems often reuse existing techniques, the idea to develop QA systems in a modular way arise. Besides Qanary, three frameworks tried to achieve this goal: QALL-ME [6], openQA [9] and the Open Knowledge Base and Question-Answering (OKBQA) challenge (cf., http://www.okbqa.org/). To the best of our knowledge these frameworks do not address the problem of integrating user interaction.

3   A Generalized Feedback Mechanism On-Top of Qanary

3.1   The Qanary Methodology

QA systems are generally made up by several components that are executed in a pipeline. Qanary offers a framework to easily integrate and reuse such components. Here, we briefly describe the Qanary methodology. Qanary components interact with each other by exchanging annotations (following the W3C WADM[1]) expressed in the qa vocabulary [11] and stored in a central triplestore T.

---

[1] Web Annotation Data Model: https://www.w3.org/TR/annotation-model/.

For example, an annotation expressing that the sub-string between character 19 and 32 of the question "Who is the wife of Barack Obama?" refers to
dbr:Barack_Obama is expressed as:

```
PREFIX qa: <https://w3id.org/wdaqua/qanary#>
PREFIX oa: <http://www.w3.org/ns/oa#>
<anno1>  a   qa:AnnotationOfInstance;
  oa:hasTarget [ a                   oa:SpecificResource;
                oa:hasSource     <URIQuestion>;
                oa:hasSelector [ a oa:TextPositionSelector;
                          oa:start "9"^^xsd:nonNegativeInteger;
                          oa:end   "21"^^xsd:nonNegativeInteger ]];
  oa:hasBody     dbr:Barack_Obama .
  oa:annotatedBy <http://wdaqua.eu/component1> .
  oa:annotatedAt "2017-02-22T21:40:51+01:00" .
```

Note that each annotation also contains information about the components that created them (oa:annotatedBy) and the time when this happened
(oa:annotatedAt). We consider a QA system with several components $C_1,...,C_n$.
Running these components over a new question q would lead to the following workflow: (1) Qanary is called through an API saying that it should process question
q using the components $C_1, ...,C_n$ (this API can be found under: http://www.
wdaqua.eu/qanary/startquestionansweringwithtextquestion). (2) Qanary generates in a triplestore T a new named graph G where q is stored (using the qa vocabulary). (3) The components are subsequently called, i.e., the address of the triplestore T and the named graph G is passed to C_i. Component C_i retrieves annotations from G and uses them to generate new knowledge about the question. This
is written back to G in the form of new annotations. (4) When all the components
have been called, the address of T and G are returned. This way full access to all
knowledge generated during the process is possible.

The vocabulary that is used for the annotations is described in [11]. The
Qanary methodology and their services are described in [1,4].

3.2 Collecting User Feedback Within a Qanary Process

A user cannot change the internal algorithm of a component, but only affect
the behavior of a component by the annotations it uses as input. Assume that
the user wants to interact with the process after component C_i. The generalized
workflow would be as follows: (1) Components $C_1,...,C_i$ are called (cf., Sect. 3.1).
(2) All the generated knowledge is stored in G. The user or the application
accesses G and retrieves the annotation needed and creates new ones. (3) The QA
system is restarted from component C_{i+1}, i.e., a QA process executing $C_{i+1},...,$
C_n is started using T and G.

To avoid conflicting annotations of the same type, we enforce that both the
components and the user create annotation with a timestamp, and the components read only the annotations with the last timestamp. Note that during the
QA process existing annotations are not deleted, s.t., G contains a full history
of all the information generated at the different point in time by any component
and by the user.

4   Use Cases

We created some user interface components that follow the approach described in Sect. 3.2. In the back-end we used WDAqua-core0 [5]. It consists of two components: C_1 a query generator that translate a question (in keywords or natural language) into SPARQL queries and C_2 a query executor. The interfaces are integrated in Trill [3], a reusable front-end for QA systems that can be used for QA pipelines integrated in Qanary. The code can be found under https://github. com/WDAqua/Trill. We first describe in detail one of the interface components we implemented. It can be used by users to resolve the ambiguity of a question. We then briefly describe the other interfaces.

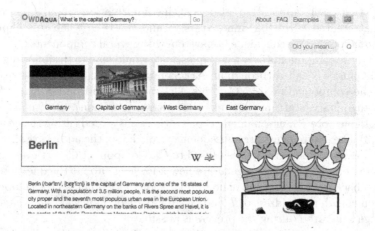

Fig. 1. Snapshot of the disambiguation interface for the question: "What is the capital of Germany?". By clicking on "Did you mean" several entities, the question might refereed to, are shown. These include the actual "Federal Republic of Germany" but also the "Capital of Germany" (as an entity), "West Germany", "East Germany", "Allied-Occupied Germany" and others. By clicking on the entity, the question is interpreted differently and a new answer is presented, e.g., if the user clicks on "West Germany", the answer "Bonn" is computed.

Example: Removing Entity Ambiguity from a Qanary process One of the main problems in QA systems is to disambiguate between different meanings associated to a user's question. Given "What is the capital of Germany?", the substring "Germany" can refer to the actual "Federated Republic of Germany" but also to "East Germany" (former GDR) or "West Germany", which will lead to different answers. To allow the user to choose between different options we use the workflow presented in Sect. 3.2. In the example implementation, C_1 produces 30 SPARQL query candidates which are ranked based on relevance and stored in T using the annotations qa:AnnotationOfSparqlQueries. E.g., for the given question the first 3 candidates are:

```
1. SELECT ?x WHERE { dbr:Germany dbo:capital ?x . }
2. SELECT ?x { VALUES ?x { dbr:Capital_of_Germany } }
3. SELECT ?x WHERE { dbr:West_Germany dbp:capital ?x . }
```

For the disambiguation interface we extract 30 queries from the end-point, extract the resources from them (in the example dbr:Germany, dbr:Capital_of_Germany, dbr:West_Germany) and show them to the user. By clicking on one of the resources, the corresponding query is ranked first and the re-ranked queries are written to the triple-store using again the annotations qa:AnnotationOfSparqlQueries. C_2 is called which executes the first-ranked query. Finally the answer is shown. The example is implemented as a user interface component in Trill and shown in Fig. 1.

Additional Examples Similarly to the above interface we have also created a user interface component that allows a user to directly choose between SPARQL queries. This interface component can for example be used, by expert users, to construct a training data set to learn how to rank SPARQL queries. We created also two interfaces components for language and knowledge base selection. They are easy-to-use drop down menus. The user selects the knowledge base or the language. Each time a new question is sent to the back-end the corresponding annotations selecting the language or the knowledge base are generated. A demo with the different interface components can be found under www.wdaqua.eu/qa.

5   Conclusion and Future Work

In this paper we have showed a generalized feedback for QA processes. It is an approach on-top of the Qanary framework. Qanary provides an established paradigm for collecting knowledge about a given user question in a triplestore. Our extension provides a mechanism for the user to interact with any type of information that is stored in the triplestore. Hence, computing the correct answer through the feedback of the user is thereby enabled on various steps during the QA process. This leads to the novel option not only to create a QA system from the Qanary ecosystem, but also to establish an interactive QA process on-top of it. All these arrangements are dedicated to support the QA research community in improving QA processes.

In the future, we will extend the user interface components and collect training sets for the community to be used for improving the involved back-end components, the overall QA process, and particularly the quality of QA.

Acknowledgments. This project has received funding from the European Union's Horizon 2020 research and innovation program under the Marie Sklodowska-Curie grant agreement No 642795.

References

1. Both, A., Diefenbach, D., Singh, K., Shekarpour, S., Cherix, D., Lange, C.: Qanary
   – a methodology for vocabulary-driven open question answering systems. In: Sack,
   H., Blomqvist, E., dAquin, M., Ghidini, C., Ponzetto, S.P., Lange, C. (eds.)
   ESWC 2016. LNCS, vol. 9678, pp. 625–641. Springer, Cham (2016). doi:10.1007/
   978-3-319-34129-3_38
2. Damljanovic, D., Agatonovic, M., Cunningham, H.: Freya: an interactive way
   of querying linked data using natural language. In: García-Castro, R., Fensel,
   D., Antoniou, G. (eds.) ESWC 2011. LNCS, vol. 7117, pp. 125–138. Springer,
   Heidelberg (2012). doi:10.1007/978-3-642-25953-1_11
3. Diefenbach, D., Amjad, S., Both, A., Singh, K., Maret, P.: Trill: a reusable Front-
   End for QA systems. In: ESWC P&D (2017)
4. Diefenbach, D., Singh, K., Both, A., Cherix, D., Lange, C., Auer, S.: The qanary
   ecosystem: getting new insights by composing question answering pipelines. In:
   ICWE (2017)
5. Diefenbach, D., Singh, K., Maret, P.: WDAqua-core0: a question answering component for the research community. In: ESWC, 7th Open Challenge on Question
   Answering over Linked Data (QALD-7) (2017)
6. Ferrández, Ó., Spurk, C.H., Kouylekov, M., Dornescu, I., Ferrández, S., Negri, M.,
   Izquierdo, R., Tomás, T., Orasan, C., Neumann, G., Magnini, B., González, J.L.V.:
   The QALL-ME framework: a specifiable-domain multilingual question answering
   architecture
7. Kaufmann, E., Bernstein, A., Zumstein, R.: Querix: a natural language interface
   to query ontologies based on clarification dialogs. In: ISWC (2006)
8. Lopez, V., Unger, C., Cimiano, P., Motta, E.: Evaluating question answering over
   linked data. Web Semant. Sci. Serv. Agents World Wide Web (2013)
9. Marx, E., Usbeck, R., Ngonga Ngomo, A., Höffner, K., Lehmann, J., Auer, S.:
   Towards an open question answering architecture. In: SEMANTICS (2014)
10. Mazzeo, G.M., Zaniolo, C.: Question answering on RDF KBs using controlled
    natural language and semantic auto completion. Semant. Web J. (2016)
11. Singh, K., Both, A., Diefenbach, D., Shekarpour, S.: Towards a message-driven
    vocabulary for promoting the interoperability of question answering systems. In:
    ICSC (2016)

Juma: An Editor that Uses a Block Metaphor to Facilitate the Creation and Editing of R2RML Mappings

Ademar Crotti Junior[(✉)], Christophe Debruyne,
and Declan O'Sullivan

ADAPT Centre, Trinity College Dublin, Dublin 2, Ireland
{crottija,debruync,declan.osullivan}@scss.tcd.ie

Abstract. R2RML is the W3C standard mapping language used to define customized mappings from relational databases into RDF. One issue that hampers its adoption is the effort needed in the creation of such mappings, as they are stored as RDF documents. To address this problem, several tools that represent mappings as graphs have been proposed in the literature. In this paper, we describe a visual representation based on a block metaphor for creating and editing such mappings that is fully compliant with the R2RML specification. Preliminary findings from users using the tool indicate that the visual representation was helpful in the creation of R2RML mappings with good usability results. In future work, we intend to conduct more experiments focusing on different types of users and to abstract the visual representation from the R2RML mapping language so that it supports the serialization of other uplift mapping languages.

Keywords: R2RML · Visual representation · Data mapping

1 Introduction

A significant part of the Linked Data web is achieved by converting non-RDF resources into RDF. This conversion process is typically called *uplift*. For relational databases, one can rely on the W3C Recommendation R2RML[1] for creating mappings from relational databases into RDF datasets. Though useful, some problems with its adoption can be observed. Firstly, R2RML mappings are stored as RDF. We argue that writing any RDF graph by hand can be troublesome and prone to errors. Secondly, the R2RML mapping language has a steep learning curve, where the creation of mappings is time consuming, and syntactically heavy in various cases [9]. Initiatives have emerged to address these problems and make the technology more accessible such as visual *graph* representations for engaging with mappings [6, 7] and others that will be discussed in Sect. 2.

In this paper, we describe a visual representation for mappings called Juma. Our representation is based on the block (or jigsaw) metaphor that has become popular with

---

[1] https://www.w3.org/TR/r2rml/.

© Springer International Publishing AG 2017
E. Blomqvist et al. (Eds.): ESWC 2017 Satellite Events, LNCS 10577, pp. 87–92, 2017.
https://doi.org/10.1007/978-3-319-70407-4_17

visual programming languages – where it is called the block paradigm – such as Scratch[2]. This metaphor allows one to focus on the logic instead of the language's syntax and it has been successfully used in introducing programming to non-experts. We have applied this representation for the R2RML mapping language, being fully compliant with its specification. The main contributions of this research to date are: (1) a visual representation for mappings based on a block metaphor; (2) a tool that uses this representation for creating and managing R2RML mappings and (3) an initial user evaluation of the approach.

The remainder of this paper is structured as follows: Sect. 2 reviews the related work. Section 3 presents our visual representation. Section 4 presents an initial user evaluation and Sect. 5 concludes the paper.

2 Related Work

In this section, we discuss the different mapping tools developed and the mapping representations used for R2RML mappings.

Karma [6] is a web-based application where the data is loaded before it can be mapped into RDF. The ontologies used during the mapping process are represented in a tree structure and the data as a table. A graph visualization of the mapping is available while the user creates them. The creation of mappings using Karma can be troublesome because of the data centric approach, where every input is shown in a different table. This makes the interlinking between tables unnecessarily complex. OntopPro[3] [11] is a Protégé plugin that uses a proprietary mapping language internally to create mappings. Lembo et al. [7] also uses a graph representation for R2RML mappings. The tool is fully compliant with R2RML's specification and offers support for syntactic and semantic checking of mappings. Even though the tool offers a graph visualization of mappings, its creation and/or editing is done through text, which may make the mapping process prone to errors. RMLeditor [5] has support for R2RML and RML [4] mapping languages. The RMLeditor also uses a graph representation for the mapping. The input data and RDF output are shown as tables. MapOn [10] is yet another graph representation tool for R2RML mappings. It also provides a graph visualization for ontologies and databases. SQuaRE [1] is a tool that provides a visual environment for the creation of R2RML mappings. This tool also uses a graph visual representation for mappings, similar to RMLeditor and MapOn. Ontologies and RDF vocabularies that will be used in the mapping process are shown as a tree.

These tools offer different abstractions for the creation of R2RML mappings. In [2], the authors proposed the use of the block metaphor for SPARQL. To the best of our knowledge, no other tool has yet used the block metaphor for representing R2RML mappings. In Sect. 3, we discuss how we use the metaphor in our design.

---

[2] https://scratch.mit.edu/, last accessed March 2017.

[3] http://ontop.inf.unibz.it .

3   Juma: A Visual Representation for Mappings

In this section, we introduce a method called **J**igsaw p**u**zzles for representing **map**pings, Juma, applied to the R2RML mapping language. As outlined in Sect. 1, there are a number of issues with how R2RML mappings are created. For example, creating mappings with a text editor – even with support for RDF – is a time consuming process, being syntactically heavy even for simple mappings in various cases. Moreover, it has a steep learning curve if one is not acquainted with the R2RML vocabulary and RDF, amongst others. To facilitate the creation and maintenance of mappings, and to leverage the uptake of R2RML to a wider set of stakeholders, we have developed a tool[4] that applies the Juma method to the R2RML mapping language. For the development of the visual representation, we derived some requirements:

1. users should be able to create a mapping without being preoccupied with R2RML's vocabulary or with a particular RDF serialization format's syntax;
2. the visual representation should guide users in creating and editing valid R2RML mappings, according to the standard specification;
3. common patterns, which are completed by a user for a given context, should be available.

Our implementation (screenshot shown in Fig. 1) uses Google's Blockly API[5]. In our tool, each block has been designed to represent an R2RML statement that automatically generates a correspondent R2RML construct, as specified in requirement 1. For requirement 2, when a user drags a block near other blocks, if that is valid according to the R2RML specification, then the visual representation highlights this. For requirement 3, we have defined a menu option called **templates**. This option shows one complete triple map and one complete predicate object map. The other menu options provide one with all other possibilities within the R2RML mapping language.

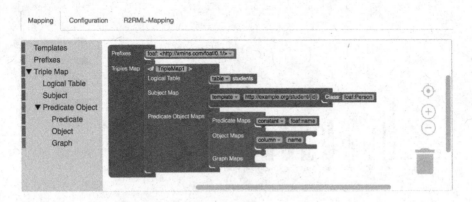

Fig. 1. Visual representation of an R2RML mapping

---

[4] https://www.scss.tcd.ie/ ~ crottija/juma/.

[5] https://developers.google.com/blockly/ .

We have defined the menu using a tree structure, which gives users a hint of how the blocks connect to each other.

4   User Study

We have initially evaluated two aspects of the tool: the accuracy of the mappings created and the usability of the tool using a standard usability test.

This initial user study was built on top of the Northwind[6] database for MySQL and it involved 15 participants split into 3 groups of 5. The first group had no knowledge of Semantic Web technologies. The second group was familiar with Semantic Web technologies, such as RDF and OWL, but not R2RML. The last group was familiar with the R2RML mapping language. Participants were asked to create one R2RML mapping. The task involved the use of different R2RML constructs, such as *parent triples maps* and others, in order to explore the visual representation. A sample RDF output was shown to participants. In addition, they could run the mapping and compare the output from the tool to the sample provided. To enable this in the experiment, we integrated an R2RML processor [3] into the tool.

The accuracy of the mappings created was calculated by counting the number of correct triples in the respective RDF output. Additionally, any help needed during the execution of the task was recorded. The high accuracy of the mappings (95.5%) indicates that the visual representation was helpful to participants. In relation to the help needed, the most common need found was how to interlink triples maps with the use of the *parent triples map* construct. Participants were able to create the R2RML construct using the visual representation but they had difficulties defining the parent and child values for the join condition, which required knowledge on SQL joins.

We also evaluated the usability of the tool using the Post-Study System Usability Questionnaire (PSSUQ). PSSUQ evaluates a system in 4 aspects using a questionnaire with a Likert scale from 1 (strongly agree) to 7 (strongly disagree) (see [8]). The PSSUQ

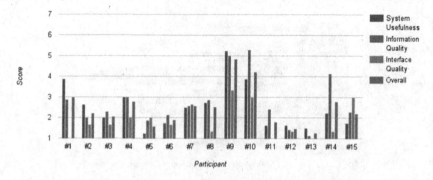

Fig. 2. PSSUQ questionnaire responses by participant

---

[6] https://github.com/dalers/mywind .

scores by participant can be seen in Fig. 2. Participants 1, 11 and 13 had a score of 1 for interface quality.

The scores indicate that the visual representation in the tool has good usability results for most participants, where these are less than half the scale (3.5).

5   Conclusions and Future Work

In this paper, we have presented a visual representation applied to the R2RML mappings language that is fully compliant with its specification. Our representation is based on the block metaphor, where each R2RML construct is represented as a block. An initial user study indicated that the visual representation was beneficial in the creation of R2RML mappings and shows promising usability results.

Future work includes more extensive experimentation including using the representation in managing uplift mappings. We also intend to implement the loading of existing mappings into the tool, incorporation of function representation in mappings and to abstract our implementation from R2RML to support other uplift mapping languages. One limitation of our approach is the reuse of resources, which are supported by R2RML mappings written using Turtle syntax.

Acknowledgements. This paper was supported by CNPQ, National Counsel of Technological and Scientific Development – Brazil and by the Science Foundation Ireland (Grant 13/RC/2106) as part of the ADAPT Centre for Digital Content Technology (http://www.adaptcentre.ie/) at Trinity College Dublin.

References

1. Blinkiewicz, M., Bak, J.: Square: a visual support for OBDA approach. In: Proceedings of the Second International Workshop on Visualization and Interaction for Ontologies and Linked Data (VOILA@ISWC 2016) (2016)
2. Bottoni, P., Ceriani, M.: SPARQL playground: a block programming tool to experiment with SPARQL. In: Proceedings of the International Workshop on Visualizations and User Interfaces for Ontologies and Linked Data (VOILA@ISWC 2015) (2015)
3. Debruyne, C., O'Sullivan, D.: R2RML-F: towards sharing and executing domain logic in R2RML mappings. In: Proceedings of the Workshop on Linked Data on the Web, LDOW 2016, co-located with the 25th International World Wide Web Conference (WWW 2016) (2016)
4. Dimou, A., Vander Sande, M., Colpaert, P., Verborgh, R., Mannens, E., Van de Walle, R.: RML: a generic language for integrated RDF mappings of heterogeneous data. In: Workshop on Linked Data on the Web (LDOW 2014) (2014)
5. Heyvaert, P., Dimou, A., Herregodts, A.-L., Verborgh, R., Schuurman, D., Mannens, E., Van de Walle, R.: RMLEditor: a graph-based mapping editor for linked data mappings. In: Sack, H., Blomqvist, E., d'Aquin, M., Ghidini, C., Ponzetto, S.P., Lange, C. (eds.) ESWC 2016. LNCS, vol. 9678, pp. 709–723. Springer, Cham (2016). doi:10.1007/978-3-319-34129-3_43

6. Knoblock, C.A., et al.: Semi-automatically mapping structured sources into the semantic web. In: Simperl, E., Cimiano, P., Polleres, A., Corcho, O., Presutti, V. (eds.) ESWC 2012. LNCS, vol. 7295, pp. 375–390. Springer, Heidelberg (2012). doi:10.1007/978-3-642-30284-8_32

7. Lembo, D., Rosati, R., Ruzzi, M., Savo, D.F., Tocci, E.: Visualization and management of mappings in ontology-based data access (progress report). In: Informal Proceedings of the 27th International Workshop on Description Logics (2014)

8. Lewis, J.R.: Psychometric evaluation of the post-study system usability questionnaire: the PSSUQ. In: Proceedings of the Human Factors and Ergonomics Society Annual Meeting, vol. 36, No. 16, pp. 1259–1260. SAGE Publications (1992)

9. Pinkel, C., Binnig, C., Haase, P., Martin, C., Sengupta, K., Trame, J.: How to best find a partner? an evaluation of editing approaches to construct R2RML mappings. In: Presutti, V., d'Amato, C., Gandon, F., d'Aquin, M., Staab, S., Tordai, A. (eds.) ESWC 2014. LNCS, vol. 8465, pp. 675–690. Springer, Cham (2014). doi:10.1007/978-3-319-07443-6_45

10. Siciliaa, Á., Nemirovskib, G., Nolleb, A.: Map-on: a web-based editor for visual ontology mapping. Semant. Web J. 1–12 (Preprint)

11. Rodriguez-Muro, M., Hardi, J., Calvanese, D.: Quest: efficient SPARQL-to-SQL for RDF and OWL. In: 11th International Semantic Web Conference on Posters and Demonstrations (ISWC 2012) (2012)

Automated UML-Based Ontology Generation in OSLO²

Dieter De Paepe[1](✉), Geert Thijs[2](✉), Raf Buyle[1](✉), Ruben Verborgh[1](✉), and Erik Mannens[1](✉)

[1] IDLab, Department of Electronics and Information Systems,
Ghent University – imec, Sint-Pietersnieuwstraat 41, 9000 Ghent, Belgium
{dieter.depaepe,raf.buyle,ruben.verborgh,erik.mannens}@ugent.be
[2] Flanders Information, Koningin Maria Hendrikaplein 70, 9000 Ghent, Belgium
geert.thijs@kb.vlaanderen.be

Abstract. In 2015, Flanders Information started the OSLO² project, aimed at easing the exchange of data and increasing the interoperability of Belgian government services. RDF ontologies were developed to break apart the government data silos and stimulate data reuse. However, ontology design still encounters a number of difficulties. Since domain experts are generally unfamiliar with RDF, a design process is needed that allows these experts to efficiently contribute to intermediate ontology prototypes. We designed the OSLO² ontologies using UML, a modeling language well known within the government, as a single source specification. From this source, the ontology and other relevant documents are generated. This paper describes the conversion tooling and the pragmatic approaches that were taken into account in its design. While this tooling is somewhat focused on the design principles used in the OSLO² project, it can serve as the basis for a generic conversion tool. All source code and documentation are available online.

Keywords: Linked Data · UML · Ontology design · RDF generation · OSLO²

1 Introduction

In 2015, the Flemish government started a project to stimulate data reuse between Belgian governments and improving semantic interoperability between government services. They initiated the OSLO² project as a continuation of OSLO [2], the aim of OSLO² was to define multiple ontologies to model 4 core government domains. The project was led by the Flanders Information agency and involved local, regional, federal, European and private stakeholders in the process through working groups.

Governments are slowly finding their way to the Semantic Web. Working with Semantic Web still requires a lot of technical knowledge not familiar to domain experts. Yet, the input of these domain experts is essential to model an ontology in line with business requirements. As such it is very important to

E. Blomqvist et al. (Eds.): ESWC 2017 Satellite Events, LNCS 10577, pp. 93–97, 2017.
https://doi.org/10.1007/978-3-319-70407-4_18

either train domain experts or to use more familiar techniques for modeling. This led us to the decision to use UML, a well known formal modeling language. The UML model was familiar enough to domain experts to understand it and provide feedback, while also serving as a source from which both the ontology and corresponding documentation could be generated.

In this demo, we will demonstrate the tool developed for and used in the OSLO[2] project. This tool is capable of transforming a UML diagram, intended for communication with stakeholders and domain experts rather than being modeled specifically for RDF generation, into an ontology. The tool is currently a command line tool with a focus on the design choices made by Information Flanders. Nevertheless, it displays great potential and could be extended into a fully generic tool in future work. All source code is available at https://github.com/Informatievlaanderen/OSLO-EA-to-RDF.

2 Related Work

Specialized ontology design tools such as Protégé [5] or TopBraid Composer are well known in the Semantic Web world. Because of their ontology-centered design method, these tools are powerful in the hands of experienced users but more obscure for users not familiar with ontologies.

UML[1] is a modeling language standardized by the Object Management Group (OMG). It originally focused on object oriented software engineering, but grew to cover more uses later on such as interaction or object diagrams. UML can be serialized to a machine readable format using the XML Metadata Interchange (XMI) format, also a standard created by the OMG.

UML has been already been investigated as a tool for assisting ontology development and has several advantages, mainly related to its adoption [4]. Cranefield et al. describe the use of XSLT transformations to transform UML represented in XMI into RDF-XML and supporting Java classes [3]. Stuckenschmidt et al. describe how UML could be used as a way of visualizing RDF as well as serving as a basis for generating RDF, again using an XSLT transformation [6]. They also describe the mismatch between both worlds, most notably the fact that properties are first class citizens in RDF but not in UML. Lastly, ISO 19150-2 describes how UML from geographical standards can be converted into OWL ontologies [1].

We see two shortcomings in the approaches described. Firstly, none of them demonstrate how to integrate existing ontologies in the design. Secondly, they rely on modeling the UML diagram very close to the RDF model, which will make the intended structure unfamiliar to domain experts.

---

[1] http://www.omg.org/spec/UML/.

3   RDF Transformation

3.1   Source Data Model

Because of its wide usability and simple representation, Flanders Information uses UML to model their data models. For this, they use Enterprise Architect (EA)[2], a commercial tool with extended UML features. EA uses an internal database to store the models and has the capability to export XMI.

Despite XMI being a common exchange format for UML, subtle differences cause information loss when importing this data into other tools, such as the freely available Visual Paradigm software[3]. Further difficulties arise when using XMI, as the XSLT transformations are very sensitive to the exact format of the source [6]. Lastly, the UML used in previously mentioned papers was mostly designed with an RDF model in mind, rather than following a data-modeling centric methodology. These reasons caused us to focus on the EA data model rather than the XMI format.

EA provides a Java API, giving access to the EA object model[4]. We found this API to be lacking in both usability and capabilities. Performance-wise, a noticeable load time is needed for the library and queries appear to become slower over time, possibly caused by the ActiveX COM implementation. Furthermore, the EA object model is not fully available through the API and no developer-friendly links are available between core classes. Instead, we created our own API for accessing the EA object model by directly querying the internal database.

3.2   Transforming UML to RDF

ISO 19150-2, Cranefield [3] and Stuckenschmidt [6] all describe similar ways of transforming UML into an ontology by mapping UML classes to RDF classes and UML attributes and associations to RDF properties. However, none provide any guidance for integrating existing terms into the ontology, a vital concept in the Linked Data world. Also, all seem to assume that the UML diagram will be created with the RDF model in mind: any UML attribute or association identifies a unique property, domain and range are determined by the related UML class, etc. While these assumptions are valid when strictly considering the modeling, they obstruct a workflow centered around expressive models, as demonstrated in Fig. 1.

In order to support this more pragmatic way of working, we extended the conversion rules from existing literature with extra customization options. Specifically, we allow the addition or customization of information through the use of tags that are added to the UML elements. These tags are stored as meta data in the EA data model. For example, it is possible to add multiple labels to each

---

[2] http://www.sparxsystems.com/products/ea/.

[3] https://www.visual-paradigm.com.

[4] http://www.sparxsystems.fr/resources/user-guides/automation/enterprise-architect-object-model.pdf.

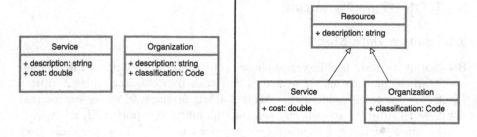

Fig. 1. Two UML versions of the same model. On the left as modeled in typical (non-RDF) contexts. On the right as modeled according to the RDF model.

element, to use a name for the RDF term that differs from the UML name or to specify the parent property of an association or attribute.

Through a configuration file, users can specify which tags map to which RDF terms, allowing them to customize the tool to their design needs instead of the other way around. The tool provides warnings for missing information or possible errors such as missing labels or multiple elements being mapped to the same URI. Nevertheless, any warnings can be ignored at the discretion of the user, giving them full control over the transformation.

A second addition to the tooling comprises the support for existing terms. In fact, because we were modeling 4 different domains that were reusing terms among themselves, we identified 3 types of terms being modeled:

In-scope terms. Terms defined by ourselves and contained within the package (ontology) being converted;
Out-of-scope terms. Terms defined by ourselves but contained outside the package being converted;
External terms. Terms used in the model but defined in external ontologies.

Each of these types has a different presence in the generated ontology: in-scope terms require all information to be included, out-of-scope terms do not require any information to be included and external terms may need to include some information such as additional translations. Again, this behavior can be customized using the configuration file.

Lastly, we allow the user to specify an RDF file containing *user terms*, which are simply added to the resulting ontology. This can be used to add additional information about the ontology itself (such as authors, revision date, changelist...) since this information varies a lot between ontologies and may contain a deeper linking structure. A complete workflow of the tool is shown in Fig. 2.

4   Demonstration

We will demonstrate our tool by converting different UML diagrams of varying complexity to RDF ontologies. We will focus on the integration with existing

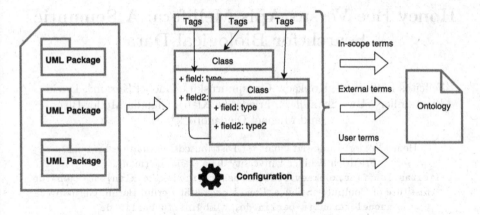

Fig. 2. Workflow of the tool. Starting from a project containing multiple, possibly interlinking packages, a single package is converted. RDF is generated based on the UML information, user specified tags present and the configuration. Depending on the type of the term, different statements are added to the ontology. Out-of-scope terms are not exported.

ontologies and UML intended for communication with stakeholders. An example transformation is available online at https://github.com/Informatievlaanderen/OSLO-EA-to-RDF/blob/v1.0/Example.md.

References

1. Geographic information - ontology - part 2: Rules for developing ontologies in the web ontology language (owl). https://www.iso.org/standard/57466.html
2. Buyle, R., De Vocht, L., Van Compernolle, M., De Paepe, D., Verborgh, R., Vanlishout, Z., De Vidts, B., Mechant, P., Mannens, E.: Oslo: open standards for linked organizations. In: Proceedings of the International Conference on Electronic Governance and Open Society: Challenges in Eurasia, EGOSE 2016, pp. 126–134. ACM, New York (2016). http://doi.acm.org/10.1145/3014087.3014096
3. Cranefield, S.: Uml and the semantic web. In: Proceedings of the First International Conference on Semantic Web Working, pp. 113–130. CEUR-WS. org (2001)
4. Kogut, P., Cranefield, S., Hart, L., Dutra, M., Baclawski, K., Kokar, M., Smith, J.: Uml for ontology development. Knowl. Eng. Rev. **17**(01), 61–64 (2002)
5. Noy, N.F., Sintek, M., Decker, S., Crubézy, M., Fergerson, R.W., Musen, M.A.: Creating semantic web contents with protege-2000. IEEE Intell. Syst. **16**(2), 60–71 (2001)
6. Stuckenschmidt, H., Falkovych, K., Sabou, M.: Uml for the semantic web: transformation-based approaches. Knowl. Transformation Semant. Web **95**, 92 (2003)

Honey Bee Versus Apis Mellifera: A Semantic Search for Biological Data

Felicitas Löffler[1]([✉]), Kobkaew Opasjumruskit[1], Naouel Karam[2], David Fichtmüller[3], Uwe Schindler[4], Friederike Klan[1], Claudia Müller-Birn[2], and Michael Diepenbroek[4]

[1] Heinz-Nixdorf Endowed Chair for Distributed Information Systems, Friedrich Schiller University Jena, Jena, Germany
{felicitas.loeffler,kobkaew.opasjumruskit,friederike.klan}@uni-jena.de
[2] Institute of Computer Science, Freie Universität Berlin, Berlin, Germany
naouel.karam@fu-berlin.de, clmb@inf.fu-berlin.de
[3] Botanic Garden and Botanical Museum (BGBM), Freie Universität Berlin, Berlin, Germany
d.fichtmueller@bgbm.org
[4] MARUM, University of Bremen, Bremen, Germany
{uschindler,mdiepenbroek}@pangaea.de

Abstract. While literature portals in the biomedical domain already enhance their search applications with ontological concepts, data portals offering biological primary data still use a classical keyword search. Similar to publications, biological primary data are described along meta information such as author, title, location and time which is stored in a separate file in XML format. Here, we introduce a semantic search for biological data based on metadata files. The search is running over 4.6 million datasets from GFBio - The German Federation for Biological Data (GFBio, https://www.gfbio.org), a national infrastructure for long-term preservation of biological data. The semantic search method used is query expansion. Instead of looking for originally entered keywords the search terms are expanded with related concepts from different biological vocabularies. Hosting our own Terminology Service with vocabularies that are tailored to the datasets, we demonstrate how ontological concepts are integrated into the search and how it improves the search result.

Keywords: Semantic search · Query expansion · Biological data · Life sciences · Biodiversity

1 Introduction

Scholars in life sciences are faced with an increasing amount of biological data. One example is the biodiversity domain dealing with the variety and variability of species, habitats and their relationships on earth. In this research area, different types and formats of data such as observational data, images or genome

© Springer International Publishing AG 2017
E. Blomqvist et al. (Eds.): ESWC 2017 Satellite Events, LNCS 10577, pp. 98–103, 2017.
https://doi.org/10.1007/978-3-319-70407-4_19

sequences need to be collected and analyzed. Enabling researchers to find relevant data for their information need requires effective filtering and search techniques that allow data retrieval across scientific domains. Even though a large number of ontologies exist in life sciences, only data portals offering biomedical literature such as MEDLINE articles enhance their search systems with semantic concepts and ontological filtering [4,5]. Data portals offering a search over biological datasets still rely on classical keyword-based techniques. Based on metadata files containing information about author, title, location and parameters of collected data, search applications in data portals such as GBIF[1], Data One[2] or Dryad[3] present datasets containing only user entered search terms. This does not allow cross-domain retrieval where keywords are used for searching and dataset descriptions refer to various terminologies. This hampers data retrieval, in particular, in the biodiversity domain which is inherently interdisciplinary.

Expanding search queries with semantically related concepts is a common technique for enhancing search engines. This idea is used in GFBio's [3] data search that currently contains around 4.6 million datasets from data centers specialized on nucleotide and environmental data, e.g., PANGAEA[4] and data centers focused on natural science collections, e.g., BGBM[5]. When entering a search term, the system calls web services from GFBio's open access Terminology Service [7]. Providing only vocabularies and ontologies that are tailored to biological datasets, the Terminology Service returns related terms that are added to the originally entered keywords. According to our previous findings [8] we only expand queries with synonyms, scientific and common names. For example, when looking for datasets about *Apis mellifera*, which is the scientific name of honey bee, the system also retrieves datasets with the common name *Honey bee* and synonyms such as *Bee*. This paper presents the underlying architecture of our semantic search feature, describes its components and use cases we will showcase to demonstrate how end users benefit from the system. A life demonstration can be found at https://www.gfbio.org/semantic-search.

2   Architecture

Figure 1 depicts the main components of GFBio's semantic search and the information flow between. Before calling the search engine, the system invokes web services from Terminology Service to get synonyms of the entered search terms. All terms, the originally entered and expanded ones, are finally sent to GFBio's standard search application (Sect. 2.4). In the following section, we describe all components individually.

---

[1] GBIF, http://www.gbif.org/.
[2] Data One, https://dataone.org/.
[3] Dryad, https://datadryad.org/.
[4] PANGAEA, https://www.pangaea.de/.
[5] BGBM, https://www.bgbm.org/.

2.1   Query Expansion with Synonyms

For a given search term t, we denote $\mathbf{S}_t = \{s_1, s_2, \ldots, s_n\}$ as a set of synonyms for t. From a linguistic point of view, synonyms are two different words with the same meaning including different spellings and different languages. In contrast to most biological literature, we also subsume common and scientific names under this term. All s in $\mathbf{S}_t$ are appended to t with a logical OR (Fig. 1). By default, several search terms are connected with a logical AND. If there is no result for AND, an OR search is processed.

Our experiments in a previous study [8] point out that scholars are experts in their research domain, however, they are not familiar with all taxonomic terms. Given a user's search query, datasets with broader (superclass label) or narrower terms (subclass label) in the result list were not considered as relevant. For instance, when looking for data about butterflies, datasets containing scientific names of butterfly species such as *Vanessa atalanta* (Red admiral) got low relevance ratings. Interviews afterwards revealed that those datasets were not irrelevant per se, however, the scholars marked them as 'not relevant' since they were not aware of the taxonomic relationship between the entered keywords and the expanded terms. In contrast, datasets with synonyms got high relevance ratings. Therefore, in a first version, we only expand the search terms with synonyms.

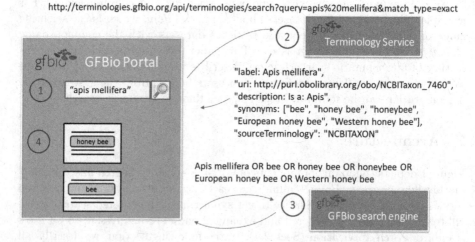

Fig. 1. (1) For all search terms, concepts from Terminology Service are looked up. (2) In a successful match, synonyms such as scientific and common names are extracted. (3) The expanded terms are sent to the search engine and (4) lead to a higher number of results.

2.2   User Interface

The user interface (Fig. 2) consists of a search field and two buttons for search, one for the ordinary keyword search and one for the semantic search. When entering a search term, auto-complete functionality suggests existing terms and phrases in the data repository. Quotes can be used to keep search terms together in the search result. All matched terms are highlighted in the result list.

2.3   Terminology Service

The GFBio Terminology Service (GFBio TS) [7] is the core semantic component of GFBio's infrastructure. It enables access to terminological knowledge necessary for annotation, semantic search, and integration of the increasingly heterogeneous project related datasets. Unlike existing terminology repositories like *Bioportal* or *Ontology Lookup Service* [2,9], the primary focus of GFBio TS is to provide tailored terminologies and services for the GFBio community. The GFBio community drives the selection and integration of terminologies, which can be either well-established ontologies like ENVO [1] or ontologies provided by the GFBio community like the KINGDOM ontology, describing a GFBio agreed list of species kingdoms. Terminologies are either internally hosted in a Semantic Web repository (Virtuoso) or externally accessed via their web services. Access to the GFBio TS is provided via a RESTful API, available terminologies can be accessed in a uniform way regardless of their degree of complexity and whether they are internally stored or externally accessed. An adapter component enables to harmonize the different internal and external schemas into a common Semantic Web compliant format. The service endpoints are grouped into four categories: metadata services, search services, information services and hierarchy-oriented services. The API documentation is available at: http://terminologies.gfbio.org/developer_section/api.html.

Fig. 2. User interface of GFBio's semantic search. The user's entered keywords are expanded in the background with related terms from GFBio's Terminology Service.

2.4   Search Engine

GFBio's metadata files are stored in *pansimple* format[6] which was primarily developed for PANGAEA. It is mainly based on Dublin Core metadata standard but contains additional fields such as parameters from primary data. An excerpt from an example file is presented in the listing below. GFBio uses *elasticsearch*[7] as search engine and TF-IDF weights as ranking function. Using elasticsearch's query-time boosting, originally entered keywords are higher ranked than expanded terms.

Listing 1.1. Excerpt from a biodiversity metadata file in pansimple format [6].

```
<dataset>
<dc:title>Wild bee monitoring in six agriculturally dominated landscapes of
    Saxony-Anhalt (Germany) in 2014</dc:title>
<dc:creator>Frenzel , Mark</dc:creator>
<dc:creator>[...]</dc:creator>
<dc:source>Helmholtz Centre for Environmental Research - UFZ</dc:source>
<dc:publisher>PANGAEA</dc:publisher>
<dataCenter>PANGAEA: [...]</dataCenter>
<dc:date>2016-09-29</dc:date>
<dc:type>Dataset</dc:type>
<dc:format>text/tab-separated-values , 47557 data points</dc:format>
<dc:identifier>doi:10.1594/PANGAEA.865100</dc:identifier>
<parentIdentifier>doi:10.1594/PANGAEA.864908</parentIdentifier>
<dc:relation>Papanikolaou , Alexandra D; Kuehn , Ingolf ; Frenzel , Mark;
    Schweiger , Oliver (2016): Semi-natural habitats mitigate the effects of
    temperature rise on wild bees. Journal of Applied Ecology , doi:10
    .1111/1365-2664.12763</dc:relation>
[...]
</dataset>
```

3   Demonstration

In this demo[8], visitors will be able to use the semantic search and to compare search results of the standard and the semantic search. We will provide users with example queries, but they are also welcome to explore on their own. If interested, users can also directly access the Terminology Service.

Acknowledgements. This work was funded by the Deutsche Forschungsgemeinschaft (DFG) within the scope of the GFBio project.

References

1. Buttigieg, P.L., Morrison, N., Smith, B., Mungall, C., Lewis, S., The ENVO Consortium: The environment ontology: contextualising biological and biomedical entities. J. Biomed. Semant. **4**, 43 (2013)

---

[6] Pansimple, https://ws.pangaea.de/schemas/pansimple/pansimple.xsd.
[7] Elasticsearch, https://www.elastic.co.
[8] https://www.gfbio.org/semantic-search.

2. Côté, R.G., Jones, P., Apweiler, R., Hermjakob, H.: The ontology lookup service, a lightweight cross-platform tool for controlled vocabulary queries. BMC Bioinform. **7**, 97 (2006)
3. Diepenbroek, M., Glöckner, F., Grobe, P., Güntsch, A., Huber, R., König-Ries, B., Kostadinov, I., Nieschulze, J., Seeger, B., Tolksdorf, R., Triebel, D.: Towards an integrated biodiversity and ecological research data management and archiving platform: GFBio. In: Informatik (2014)
4. Dietze, H., Schroeder, M.: Goweb: a semantic search engine for the life science web. BMC Bioinform. **10**(S-10), 7 (2009)
5. Faessler, E., Hahn, U.: Semedico: a comprehensive semantic search engine for the life sciences. In: ACL 2017 - Proceedings of the 55th Annual Meeting of the Association for Computational Linguistics: System Demonstrations, Vancouver, Canada, July 30–August 4 2017
6. Frenzel, M., Dussl, F., Höhne, R., Nickels, V., Creutzburg, F.: Wild bee monitoring in six agriculturally dominated landscapes of Saxony-Anhalt (Germany) (2014). doi:10.1594/PANGAEA.865100. In: Frenzel, M., Preiser, C., Dussl, F., Höhne, R., Nickels, V., Creutzburg, F.: (2016): TERENO (Terrestrial Environmental Observatories) wild bee monitoring in six agriculturally dominated landscapes of Saxony-Anhalt (Germany). Helmholtz Centre for Environmental Research - UFZ. doi:10.1594/PANGAEA.864908
7. Karam, N., Müller-Birn, C., Gleisberg, M., Fichtmüller, D., Tolksdorf, R., Güntsch, A.: A terminology service supporting semantic annotation, integration, discovery and analysis of interdisciplinary research data. Datenbank-Spektrum **16**(3), 195–205 (2016)
8. Löffler, F., Klan, F.: Does term expansion matter for the retrieval of biodiversity data? In: Martin, M., Cuquet, M., Folmer, E. (eds.) Joint Proceedings of the Posters and Demos Track of the 12th International Conference on Semantic Systems (SEMANTiCS 2016). CEUR Workshop Proceedings (2016)
9. Noy, N., Shah, N., Whetzel, P., Dai, B., Dorf, M., Griffith, N., Jonquet, C., Rubin, D., Storey, M., Chute, C., Musen, M.: Bioportal: ontologies and integrated data resources at the click of a mouse. Nucleic Acids Res. **37**(Web-Server-Issue), 170–173 (2009)

EvoRDF: A Framework for Exploring Ontology Evolution

Haridimos Kondylakis[1(✉)], Melidoni Despoina[2], Georgios Glykokokalos[2],
Eleftherios Kalykakis[2], Manos Karapiperakis[2], Michail-Angelos Lasithiotakis[2],
John Makridis[2], Panagiotis Moraitis[2], Aspasia Panteri[2], Maria Plevraki[2],
Antonios Providakis[2], Maria Skalidaki[2], Athanasiadis Stefanos[2],
Manolis Tampouratzis[2], Eleftherios Trivizakis[2], Fanis Zervakis[2],
Ekaterini Zervouraki[2], and Nikos Papadakis[2]

[1] Institute of Computer Science, FORTH, Heraklion, Crete, Greece
kondylak@ics.forth.gr
[2] Department of Informatics Engineering, Technological Educational Institute of Crete,
Heraklion, Greece

Abstract. The evolution of ontologies is a reality in current research community. The problem of understanding and exploring this evolution is a fundamental problem as maintainers of depending artifacts need to take a decision about possible changes and ontology engineers need to understand the reasons for this evolution. Recent research focuses on identifying and statically visualizing deltas between ontology versions using various low- or high-level language of changes. In this paper, we argue that this is not enough and we provide a complete solution enabling the active, dynamic exploration of the evolution of RDF/S ontologies using provenance queries. To this direction, we construct an ontology of changes for modeling the language of changes and we store all changes as instances of this ontology in a triple store. On top of this triple store two visualization modules, one individual app and one protégé plugin allow the exploration of the evolution using provenance queries. To the best of our knowledge our approach is unique in allowing the dynamic exploration of the evolution using provenance queries.

1 Introduction

Dynamicity is an indispensable part of the web. Ontologies are constantly evolving [8] for several reasons such as the inclusion of new experimental evidence or observations, or the correction of erroneous conceptualization. Understanding this evolution using the differences (deltas) between ontology versions has been proved to play a crucial role in various curation tasks, like the synchronization of autonomous developed dataset versions, the integration of interconnected linked datasets etc. To this direction, various approaches have been used for formally describing those deltas, ranging from low-level deltas (describing simple additions and deletions), to high-level ones (describing complex updates, such as for instance, different change patterns in the subsumption hierarchy) [5].

However, only listing those changes is insufficient for the purpose of understanding what actually happened. First attempts in the area, provide static statistical information

E. Blomqvist et al. (Eds.): ESWC 2017 Satellite Events, LNCS 10577, pp. 104–108, 2017.
https://doi.org/10.1007/978-3-319-70407-4_20

of the type of changes [4, 5]. In addition, in our past work [1] we provided algorithms for exploring ontology evolution using provenance queries without offering however a visualization/exploration interface.

In this demonstration, we present for the first time a framework enabling the dynamic exploration of RDF/S ontology evolution using provenance queries. The framework gets as input the change log and transforms it using a change ontology in order to be saved in a Virtuoso triple store. Then two visualization modules, one application and one Protégé plugin, enable the exploration of the evolution using provenance queries. Those queries can answer *when* a resource was introduced (which ontology version), and *how* (by which change operation) whereas the list of change operations that led to the creation of that specific resource can also be computed and presented.

The remaining of this paper is structured as follows: In Sect. 2 we present the architecture of the EvoRDF framework and we describe the corresponding components. Then in Sect. 3 we highlight the demonstration items that will be presented in the conference. Finally Sect. 4 concludes this paper and presents directions for future work.

2   Architecture

The workflow for exploring ontology evolution and the high-level architecture of the EvoRDF is shown in Fig. 1. The whole process starts by getting the change log constructed between two ontology versions output from a change detection algorithm similar to [3, 5]. The change log contains multiple change operations.

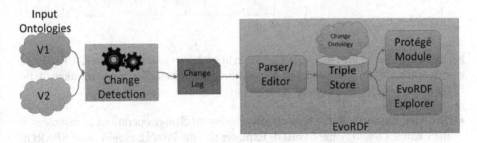

Fig. 1. Workflow for exploring ontology evolution

Definition (change operation): *A change operation u over an RDF ontology O, is any tuple* (δ_a, δ_d) *where* $\delta_a \cap O = \phi$ *and* $\delta_d \subseteq O$*. A change operation u from* O_1 *to* O_2 *is a change operation over* O_1 *such that* $\delta_a \subseteq O_2 \backslash O_1$ *and* $\delta_d \subseteq O_1 \backslash O_2$.

Obviously, δ_a and δ_d are sets of triples $\delta_a(u) \cap \delta_d(u) = \phi$ and $\delta_a(u) \cup \delta_d(u) \neq \phi$ if $O_1 \neq O_2$. The interested reader is forwarded to [3] for more information on the aforementioned language of changes. Two change operations for example are *Generalize_Domain(has_cont_point, Actor, Person)* and *Merge_Properties({street, city},address)*. The first one denotes that the domain of the *has_cont_point* property has been generalized from the *Actor* class to the *Person* class and the second one that the *street* and the *city* properties has been merged to formulate the *address* property.

The file containing these change operations is then provided as input to the EvoRDF framework, which is composed of the following components:

- **The Change Ontology:** In order to model all changes identified by the change detection mechanism a change ontology has been constructed (Fig. 2c). The ontology consists of 24 classes and 39 properties and depicts all different types of change operations available and their corresponding arguments. Additional meta-data are saved such as the authors, the ontology versions etc.

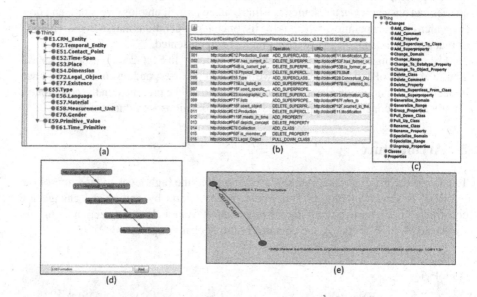

(a)   (b)   (c)

(d)   (e)

Fig. 2. Screenshots of the various parts presented in the demonstration: (a) CIDOC-CRM v3.2.1 in conjunction with (b) changes as they are identified by the change detection algorithm; (d) the Protégé plugin and (e) the individual application.

- **EvoRDF Explorer & Protégé plugin:** Having all change operations as instances of the Change Ontology the EvoRDF Explorer and the Protégé plugin issue SPARQL queries to the Virtuoso triple store in order to collect information about the change operations. These modules implement various algorithms, an initial version of which was presented in [1] for enabling ontology exploration using provenance queries. Three types of queries are available using these modules:
  - When queries: An end-user can search for the specific version that a resource was introduced. In order to return the corresponding answer the proper SPARQL query is formulated requesting the version of the change operation that introduced this resource.
  - How queries: In addition, an end-user can search for the change operation that introduced a specific resource (how). Again the proper SPARQL query is formulated and the answer is returned to the user.
  - Extended-how queries: Finally, the change path (i.e. the consecutive list of change operations) that led to the creation of a specific resource can be computed and

presented to the user allowing further exploration and understanding of the evolution of the ontology. Extended-how queries are possible not only for specific resources but for specific change operations as well.

Those queries can be formulated and answered either using the individual application EvoRDF Explorer shown in Fig. 2e or using the Protégé plugin shown in Fig. 2d.

3   Demonstration

To demonstrate the functionalities of the aforementioned platform, we will use three versions of the CIDOC-CRM[1] ontology (v.3.2.1, v3.3.2 and v.4.2) and the corresponding evolution log. CIDOC-CRM is an ISO standard modeling information about cultural heritage, which consists of nearly 80 classes and 250 properties. The demonstration will proceed in five phases shown in Fig. 2 whereas a video is available demonstrating some basic functionality[2].

(i)   *Visualizing ontology & Evolution log*: The demonstration will start by visualizing one version (v3.2.1) of the CIDOC-CRM ontology using Protégé. Then we will present the corresponding change log between CIDOC-CRM versions v3.2.1 and v4.2 using the developed parser explaining the identified changes. The detected change log contains 726 total changes among those versions making it impossible to explore evolution looking only this evolution log.

(ii) *Ontology for modeling evolution:* Next we will present the ontology for modeling evolution and we will show how the developed parser enables the transformation and storage, of all information available in the evolution log, in a triple store (Virtuoso).

(iii) *Exploring ontology evolution using EvoRDF plugin*: Then, we will demonstrate how the EvoRDF Protégé plugin works by loading CIDOC-CRM 3.2.1 and providing a Virtuoso connection endpoint. The visualization options will be explained and the idea behind the corresponding evolution exploration algorithms will be provided. In this phase some interesting observations will be commented. For example, we will show that in the evolution of the CIDOC-CRM ontology from version v3.2.1 to version v3.3.2, one ontology engineer renamed the class "*E11 Modification*" to "*E11 Modification Event*". A few years later another ontology engineer was employed to evolve the ontology. So in v4.2 we can see that the class "*E11 Modification Event*" was again renamed to "*E11 Modification*". If the second ontology engineer had an indication of the previous renaming he would avoid cycles and he would be able to identify possibly the reasons behind each renaming - we are also able to show comments from the ontology evolution. So, using provenance queries to explore ontology evolution can be a valuable tool reducing greatly the time spent on understanding evolution.

(iv) *"Hands-on" phase*: In this phase conference participants will be invited to directly interact with the plugin and explore ontology evolution

---

[1]   http://www.cidoc-crm.org/.
[2]   http://www.ics.forth.gr/~kondylak/ESWC2017/.

4   Conclusion

In this demonstration, we present a whole framework enabling the exploration of ontology evolution. Our framework gets as input the change log of the corresponding change detection algorithms and generates the corresponding instances of the ontology change. Those instances are saved to a triple store, on top of which two visualization modules allow the formulation of how, when and extended-how provenance queries for exploring ontology evolution. As future work several challenging issues need to be further investigated, for example extending our approach to OWL ontologies and presenting summaries [2, 6] of the overall evolution [7].

References

1. Kondylakis, H., Plexousakis, D.: Exploring RDF/S evolution using provenance queries. In: EDBT/ICDT Workshops (2014)
2. Pappas, A., Troullinou, G., Roussakis, G., Kondylakis, H., Plexousakis, D.: Exploring importance measures for summarizing RDF/S KBs. In: Blomqvist, E., Maynard, D., Gangemi, A., Hoekstra, R., Hitzler, P., Hartig, O. (eds.) ESWC 2017. LNCS, vol. 10249, pp. 387–403. Springer, Cham (2017). doi:10.1007/978-3-319-58068-5_24
3. Papavasileiou, V., Flouris, G., Fundulaki, I., Kotzinos, D., Christophides, V.: High-level change detection in RDF(S) KBs. ACM Trans. Database Syst. **38**(1), 1:1–1:42 (2013)
4. Roussakis, Y., Chrysakis, I., Stefanidis, K., Flouris, G.: D2 V: a tool for defining, detecting and visualizing changes on the data web. In: ISWC (Posters & Demos) (2015)
5. Roussakis, Y., Chrysakis, I., Stefanidis, K., Flouris, G., Stavrakas, Y.: A Flexible framework for understanding the dynamics of evolving RDF datasets. In: ISWC (2015)
6. Troullinoy, G., Kondylakis, H., Daskalaki, E., Plexousakis, D.: Ontology understanding without tears: the summarization approach. In: SWL (2017)
7. Troullinou, G., Roussakis, G., Kondylakis, H., Stefanidis, K., Flouris, G.: Understanding ontology evolution beyond deltas. In: EDBT/ICDT Workshops (2016)
8. Zablith, F., Antoniou, G., D'Aquin, M., Flouris, G., Kondylakis, H., Motta, E., Plexousakis, D., Sabou, M.: Ontology evolution: a process-centric survey. Knowl. Eng. Rev. **30**, 45–75 (2015)

Rendering OWL in Description Logic Syntax

Cogan Shimizu[1], Pascal Hitzler[1(✉)], and Matthew Horridge[2]

[1] Data Semantics (DaSe) Laboratory, Wright State University,
Dayton, OH, USA
pascal.hitzler@wright.edu

[2] Bio-Medical Informatics Research Group, Stanford University,
Stanford, CA, USA

Abstract. As ontology engineering is inherently a multidisciplinary process, it is necessary to utilize multiple vehicles to present an ontology to a user. In order to examine the formal logical content, description logic renderings of the axioms appear to be a very helpful approach for some. This paper introduces a number of changes made to the OWLAPI's LATEX rendering framework in order to improve the readability, concision, and correctness of translated OWL files, as well as increase the number of renderable OWL files.

1 Motivation

For ontology developers and consumers intimately familiar with the logical and formal semantic underpinnings of OWL, the presentation of OWL files in the form of description logic syntax appears to be a very useful one for a quick assessment of expressivity and formal content.

The OWLAPI [1], which is a powerful tool for the programmatic construction, manipulation, and rendering of ontologies, has for considerable time had limited support for the rendering of OWL ontologies in description logic syntax via LATEX. Unfortunately, this LATEX rendering framework, which outputs description logic in a LATEX source file, was never developed beyond an early experimental stage. As a consequence, translations suffered from a number of syntax errors and poor readbility of the output. In practice, translations were further impacted by the presence of illegal characters in the LATEX source, thus preventing nearly all renderings from typesetting. In Sect. 3 we see that in a test set of 117 OWL files, not a single one did typeset without error. This paper addresses changes made to the OWLAPI LATEX rendering framework in order to improve translations' succinctness, readability, and syntax, as well as ensuring that a larger number of translations will indeed typeset.

In Sect. 2 we describe in more detail the changes we made to the OWLAPI. Note that no changes were made to the rendering behaviour of SWRL or annotations. In Sect. 3 we describe the tools we developed, our test set, and rendering results.

© Springer International Publishing AG 2017
E. Blomqvist et al. (Eds.): ESWC 2017 Satellite Events, LNCS 10577, pp. 109–113, 2017.
https://doi.org/10.1007/978-3-319-70407-4_21

2   Improvements

For context, we provide a very brief overview of how the OWLAPI renders an ontology in LaTeX. First, the renderer examines a loaded ontology. Then, for each entity, (i.e. Class, Object Property, Data Property, Individual, and Datatype) in the ontology it prints associated axioms and facts. An axiom is associated to an entity if it appears somewhere in the axiom. For example, the axiom

$$DisjointClasses(A, B, C)$$

is associated with classes A, B, and C. While this does result in redundantly rendered axioms, we stress that the renderer is meant to summarize the *entities* in an ontology, rather than exhaustively enumerate all axioms in the ontology. Below, we describe the main changes made to enhance the framework's ability to do so.

Datatypes: With respect to the syntax of datatypes, there were a number of subtle changes necessary to align the LaTeX renderer with the OWL standard [3]. These changes are doubly important in that they prevent the writing of illegal characters (e.g. '#') and increase the readability of the rendering. For datatypes that are defined in the current namespace, their namespaces are omitted. Externally defined datatypes' namespaces are included using short-form notation. For example, datatypes specified as XML Schema Datatypes or in RDFS are prepended with the popular, shortened namespaces of xsd and rdfs, respectively.

Nominals: Literals, when used as nominals, are now properly rendered using set notation. In accordance with the above, the example below includes a shortform namespace for its datatype.

$$\exists hasSigrid3IceFormCode.\{\text{``05''}\hat{}\ \hat{}\ xsd:string\}$$

DatatypeRestriction Axiom: Previously, DatatypeRestriction axioms were not rendered in an intuitive manner. We have made changes in order to make it more similar to the functional syntax specified in [3]. However, we diverge slightly from the specification in the interest of readability. The constrained datatype is followed by a colon to differentiate it from its facets. Further, the constraining facets are rendered using their respective relational operators instead of keywords. In general, DatatypeRestriction axioms are now rendered using the following form, where the '+' indicates one or more of the preceding tokens.

$$DatatypeRestriction(datatype:\ (constrainingFacet\ restrictionValue)+)$$

HasKey Axiom: The HasKey axiom has no analog in description logic [2]. We also contend that the functional syntax in [3] is unwieldy and that distinguishing between Object Properties and Data Properties is unnecessary for axiomatic rendering. As such, we have adopted the following syntax for a HasKey axiom, where the '+' means one or more of the preceding token.

$$\text{ClassExpression } hasKey \text{ (Property+)}$$

Miscellaneous Fixes

- The Subproperty axiom now properly renders the subproperty.
- Extraneous spacing after logical symbols (e.g. $\neg$) has been fixed.
- Axioms expressing cardinality now correctly render cardinality.
- Role restriction axioms now have correct "." syntax.

Spacing & Math Mode: We have also made several general changes to increase both the quality of the LaTeX source and readability of the rendering itself. In particular, the amsmath package is now included in the preamble so that we may align related axioms over their principal relation (i.e. $\equiv$, $\neq$, $\sqsubseteq$) or after a function name. As such, axioms are now rendered in math mode.

Line Breaking Heuristics: In some cases, axioms would result in an excessively long rendering (i.e. result in hbox overflow, placing text in or even beyond the page margin). For the most part, LaTeX handles itself in knowing when to break a line. However, this behavior does not occur in the math environments. As such, it was necessary to look into methods for preventing unacceptable overflow.

The first option examined was the LaTeX package, breqn. This package is an experimental package that employs its own heuristics for breaking excessively long equations. Unfortunately, breqn's heuristics take into account only a select number of operators as potential breaking points. Due to the uncommon operators that description logic employs, breqn was unable to find appropriate breaking points.

The next option was the split environment from the LaTeX package amsmath. However, split does not dynamically split an equation; it is an entirely manual process. At this point, we developed our own heuristics to determine when the split environment would be necessary.

In the rendering tool, we have introduced a middle layer to the rendering system. The OWLAPI LaTeX framework renders normally, but to a special temporary file. From this temporary file, we examine the LaTeX source code. For our test set, this approach did not result in significant additional runtime. The heuristics is defined as follows.

First, we control for the LaTeX commands that are employed by the rendering framework and then count an empirically determined number of characters; we found 125 characters to be a reasonable equation length before a newline would be required. The following is an example rendering following this heuristics.

$$\text{DataGranule}(x_1) \rightarrow \geq 1x_2 \text{ hasDataSet}(x_1, x_2) \land \text{DataSet}(x_2)$$
$$\land \leq 1x_3 \text{ hasDataSet}(x_1, x_3) \land \text{DataSet}(x_3)$$

There are some limitations to this approach, as each entity's subsection is a single align environment. The split environment is, in turn, embedded in it. As such, if the antecedent of an axiom is very long, the line breaks may occur in or beyond the margin.

Reduction of Duplicate Axioms: Several OWL concepts provide a way for succinctly expressing pairwise relations (e.g. equivalence and disjointness). However, the translations of these concepts into description logic can potentially generate a huge number of axioms. For example, in order to express that n classes are mutually disjoint requires $2 \cdot \binom{n}{2}$ axioms. Furthermore, under the current framework all these axioms are related and will thus be printed in each class's section, for a total of $2n \cdot \binom{n}{2}$ axioms. This can quickly obscure the actual relationship between all the classes. As such, we adopt the functional syntax as defined in the specification as follows

$$disjoint(c_1, c_2, c_3, \cdots, c_n)$$

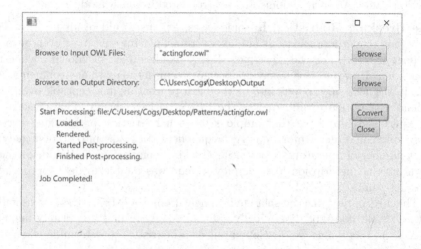

Fig. 1. Snapshot of the GUI tool.

3   Results

All tools, source code, the test set, and rendering results are available for download from the Data Semantics Lab website.[1]

Tools: In order to make these changes to the LaTeX renderer accessible, we have developed GUI and CLI interfaces. Figure 1 shows a capture of the developed GUI tool. The tool can take any number of files located in a single directory and output LaTeX source files into a user specified directory. A small log window is provided for monitoring job progress.

---

[1] http://daselab.org/content/owl2dl-rendering.

In addition, the changes described in this paper (and those used in the developed tools) have been submitted to the OWLAPI maintainers for review. At the time of this writing, the changes are visible on the GitHub repository and will appear in the version 5.0.6 release.

Test Set & Rendering Results: In order to test our changes, we pulled ontology design patterns from the www.ontologydesignpatterns.org website. In total, we collected 117 OWL files. These represent the subset of all Ontology Design Patterns from this site that are well-formed, syntactically correct, and have active download links. We chose to use Ontology Design Patterns as our test set, as they are ideal use cases for the rendering framework. That is, examining the logical structure of a module is an important step in ontology engineering.

First, we note that prior to our changes to the LaTeX renderer, none of the 117 OWL files would typeset without error due to illegal characters present in the expanded namespaces of the datatypes. Additionally, 2 of the 117 files generated lines in excess of the margins of the page when rendering was forced.

After translating all 117 files using the GUI tool, all LaTeX source files typeset without error and without needing manual modification. Further, the heuristic line breaking accurately and reasonably breaks the excessively long axioms found previously.

Future Work: The ontology engineering process necessarily includes domain experts. These domain experts are not expected to be experts in logic or OWL. We view this tool (and the changes to the OWLAPI) as a necessary step in providing multiple ways for domain experts to interface with OWL. Future work will consider adapting the LaTeX rendering framework and the lessons herein learned to other logical syntaxes. Furthermore, as these changes have been submitted to the OWLAPI, this is a perfect springboard to make the LaTeX rendering available via a plug-in to Protégé.

Demonstration: For the demonstration, we will provide a brief tutorial on acquiring the tool and its usage. Then, we will demonstrate its functionality via live renderings of some ontologies. Furthermore, we will invite users to provide their own ontology to view performance on ontologies outside of our testset.

Acknowledgement. The first two authors acknowledge support by the National Science Foundation award 1440202 EarthCube Building Blocks: Collaborative Proposal: GeoLink – Leveraging Semantics and Linked Data for Data Sharing and Discovery in the Geosciences.

References

1. Horridge, M., Bechhofer, S.: The OWL API: a java API for OWL ontologies. Semantic Web **2**(1), 11–21 (2011)
2. Krötzsch, M., Simančík, F., Horrocks, I.: A description logic primer. In: Lehmann, J., Völker, J.(eds.) Perspectives on Ontology Learning, chapter 1. IOS Press (2014)
3. Motik, B., Patel-Schneider, P., Parsia, B. (eds.): OWL 2 Web Ontology Language: Structural Specification and Functional-Style Syntax (Second Edition). W3C Recommendation, 11 Dec 2012

MappingPedia: A Collaborative Environment for R2RML Mappings

Freddy Priyatna[1], Edna Ruckhaus[1], Nandana Mihindukulasooriya[1],
Oscar Corcho[1], and Nelson Saturno[2(✉)]

[1] Ontology Engineering Group, Universidad Politécnica de Madrid, Madrid, Spain
{fpriyatna,eruckhaus,nmihindu,ocorcho}@fi.upm.es
[2] Dep. de Computación y T. I., Universidad Simón Bolívar, Caracas, Venezuela
nelsonsaturno@gmail.com

Abstract. Most of Semantic Web data is being generated from legacy datasets with the help of mappings, some of which may have been specified declaratively in languages such as R2RML or its extensions: RML and xR2RML. Most of these mappings are kept locally in each organization, and to the best to our knowledge, a shared repository that would facilitate the discovery, registration, execution, request and analysis of mappings doesn't exist. Additionally, many R2RML users do not have sufficient knowledge of the mapping language, and would probably benefit from collaborating with others. We present a demo of MappingPedia, a collaborative environment for storing and sharing R2RML mappings. It is comprised of five main functionalities: (1) Discover, (2) Share, (3) Execute, (4) Request, and (5) Analyze.

1 Introduction

Most Semantic Web data is being generated from existing legacy datasets with the help of R2RML mappings (https://www.w3.org/TR/r2rml/) or extensions, such as RML [2] and xR2RML [4].

Currently, a significant number of users have developed R2RML mappings but they have been kept locally in each organization, and to the best to our knowledge, a shared repository that would facilitate the registration, discovery, exploration and execution of mappings doesn't exist. Additionally, many R2RML users do not have sufficient knowledge of the mapping language, and would probably benefit from collaborative work with users who have experience in the development and specification of mappings in similar contexts. MappingPedia[1] provides such an environment where users may browse mappings that have used concepts in their domain of interest or request their development by other users.

This research is supported by the MobileAge (H2020/693319) project & the BES-2014-068449 FPI grant. We'd like to thank Boris and Ahmad for fruitful discussions.

[1] MappingPedia is available at http://demo.mappingpedia.linkeddata.es/ and is currently in MobileAge (http://www.mobile-age.eu/) and Retele (http://retele.linked data.es/).

E. Blomqvist et al. (Eds.): ESWC 2017 Satellite Events, LNCS 10577, pp. 114–119, 2017.
https://doi.org/10.1007/978-3-319-70407-4_22

The work in [6] points out the difficulties encountered during the development of R2RML mappings, and presents two approaches for mapping construction: Ontology-driven and Database-driven; [3] extends them with the Model-driven and Result-driven approaches. MappingPedia is a tool to support collaborative mapping development and is independent of a specific editing approach.

MappingPedia integrates several tools developed for the exploitation of RDF data. The core of the integrated tools is morph-RDB [7], an RDB2RDF engine that follows the R2RML specification. It supports two operational modes: (1) RDF data generation from a relational database or CSV file, and (2) SPARQL to SQL Query translation according to R2RML mapping descriptions. MIRROR [1] is a system that generates two sets of R2RML mappings: First, it creates a set of mappings similar to the W3C Direct Mappings (https://www.w3.org/TR/rdb-direct-mapping/), and second, a set of R2RML mappings that result from the implicit knowledge encoded in relational database schemas. Loupe [5] is a tool that is aimed at the exploration of data sources that have been annotated, and their ontologies. Loupe conducts an inspection of the classes, properties and triples to gather explicit vocabulary, classes and property usage, and to discover implicit data patterns through a fine grained set of metrics.

We demonstrate the capabilities of MappingPedia for a set of use cases that take into account three key elements: the dataset, the ontologies used for the mappings and the mapping files themselves.

2 Architecture

Figure 1 presents the MappingPedia architecture. MappingPedia consists of two components: the Engine and the Interface. The MappingPedia Engine is responsible for storing mappings as RDF graphs in a Virtuoso server, executing mappings by connecting to morph-RDB, and taking care of the evolution of mappings through their storage in a GitHub repository. The MappingPedia Interface provides a web interface for end-users and REST interfaces for external applications. Additionally, it stores user data in a MySQL database and calls the Loupe API

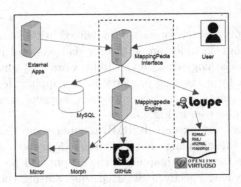

Fig. 1. Architecture of MappingPedia

to gather statistics. Loupe has been extended in order to analyze not only classes and properties, but also the value distribution of properties. This is the case of the R2RML properties `rr:class` and `rr:predicate`, where their values are the classes and properties used in mappings.

3   Use Cases

Table 1 presents eight use cases for MappingPedia and the actions that can be performed. A description of the functionalities follow:

Table 1. Scenarios in MappingPedia

Functionality	Use case	What the user has			MappingPedia allows to
		Dataset info	Mappings	Ontologies to map to	
Browse	UC1	No	No	No	Browse/Search mappings by metadata and ontology classes/properties
	UC2	No	No	Yes	
	UC3	No	Yes	Yes	*Mappings without dataset info not considered currently*
	UC4	No	Yes	Yes	
Request	UC5	Yes	No	No	Request the development of mappings
	UC6	Yes	No	Yes	
Share/Execute	UC7	Yes	Yes	No	Register Mappings and Generate RDF or SPARQL→SQL query translation
	UC8	Yes	Yes	Yes	

- **Browse.** Users may search for metadata defined in the MappingPedia ontology[2]. The ontology includes properties for datasets and mapping files and reuses the Data Catalog (dcat) and Dublin Core (dc) ontologies. The user may also search by a class or property in a mapping; for example a user may search the mappings that contain `foaf:Person`. A screenshot of this functionality can be seen in Fig. 2.
- **Execute.** A user may execute R2RML mappings on MappingPedia using morph-RDB. If the mappings have not been developed, MIRROR can be used to generate the initial mappings; the output will be an RDF dataset. Additionally she may specify a SPARQL query using the concepts in the

---

[2] http://ontoology.linkeddata.es/publish/MappingpediaVocabulary/index-en.html).

ontologies mapped, and the query will be rewritten into SQL according to
the R2RML mapping descriptions.
- **Share**. A user may register mappings and dataset information.
- **Request**. A user may request the development of mappings. This resembles
  a ticket system where a request may be Open, In progress, Resolved (Fixed,
  Incomplete, Not Fixed) and Closed.
- **Analyze**. Statistics are gathered on all the classes and properties of ontologies
  that have been used in the mappings (e.g. MappingPedia, R2RML, Data
  Catalog, etc.); also, statistics may be requested over a period of time.

Fig. 2. Screenshot browse UI

3.1   Request and Analyze Functionalities

In the demo we will show the functionalities of MappingPedia with an emphasis
on two cases: mapping request and mapping analysis.

Mapping request. There are two actors in a mapping request: the data owner
and the mapping creator. The data owner wants to publish his dataset as Linked
Data. He creates a request for mappings and provides information on his dataset.
A mapping creator may assign himself a request for mappings, the dataset owner
will be notified. Once the mappings have been uploaded the owner will again
be notified. He may execute the mappings and according the outcome of the
execution he may decide to close the request or reopen it.

Mapping analysis. The objective of mapping analysis is to provide a generic
overview and analytics about the mappings to a user who is browsing. Mapping-
Pedia uses Loupe profiling services to generate information such as the number
of mappings available, top classes being mapped, top properties being mapped,
and the number of columns mapped for each mapping. Currently MappingPedia

is populated with the 685 English DBpedia mappings that are available in the RML format[3]. The analysis of those mappings is presented in the "Statistics" option. A screenshot of this functionality is illustrated in Fig. 3.

Fig. 3. Screenshot analyze UI

4   Conclusions and Future Work

We have presented MappingPedia, a collaborative environment that integrates various R2RML-based tools for the purpose of discovery, sharing, requesting and executing R2RML mappings. MappingPedia is in its first version and we envision several features that we will implement.

In the future we will integrate an R2RML mapping editor so that a mapping creator is able to work directly on MappingPedia once he has been assigned a mapping request. We will also integrate MappingPedia with data characterization tools in order to propose mappings based on the content of a dataset. Finally, we also plan to integrate MappingPedia with RML and xR2RML engines.

References

1. de Medeiros, L.F., Priyatna, F., Corcho, Ó.: MIRROR: automatic R2RML mapping generation from relational databases. In: Engineering the Web in the Big Data Era. ICWE 2015 (2015)
2. Dimou, A., Vander Sande, M., Colpaert, P., Verborgh, R., Mannens, E., Van de Walle, R.: RML: a generic language for integrated RDF mappings of heterogeneous data. In: Linked Data on the Web LDOW 2014 Co-located with WWW 2014

---

[3] http://mappings.dbpedia.org/server/mappings/en/pages/rdf/all.

3. Heyvaert, P., Dimou, A., Verborgh, R., Mannens, E., de Walle, R.V.: Towards approaches for generating RDF mapping definitions. In: Posters & Demonstrations Track Co-located with International Semantic Web Conference ISWC 2015
4. Michel, F., Djimenou, L., Faron-Zucker, C., Montagnat, J.: Translation of relational and non-relational databases into RDF with xR2RML. In: International Conference on Web Information Systems and Technologies WEBIST 2015
5. Mihindukulasooriya, N., Poveda-Villalón, M., García-Castro, R., Gómez-Pérez, A.: Loupe - an online tool for inspecting datasets in the linked data cloud. In: Posters & Demonstrations Track Co-located with the International Semantic Web Conference ISWC 2015
6. Pinkel, C., Binnig, C., Haase, P., Martin, C., Sengupta, K., Trame, J.: How to best find a partner? an evaluation of editing approaches to construct R2RML mappings. In: Extended Semantic Web Conference ESWC 2014
7. Priyatna, F., Corcho, Ó., Sequeda, J.: Formalisation and experiences of R2RML-based SPARQL to SQL query translation using morph. In: WWW 2014

TDDonto2: A Test-Driven Development Plugin for Arbitrary TBox and ABox Axioms

Kieren Davies[1], C. Maria Keet[1(✉)], and Agnieszka Ławrynowicz[2]

[1] Department of Computer Science, University of Cape Town,
Cape Town, South Africa
{kdavies,mkeet}@cs.uct.ac.za
[2] Institute of Computing Science, Poznan University of Technology,
Poznań, Poland
agnieszka.lawrynowicz@cs.put.poznan.pl

Abstract. Ontology authoring is a complex task where modellers rely heavily on the automated reasoner for verification of changes, using effectively a time-consuming test-last approach. Test-first with Test-Driven Development aims to speed up such processes, but tools to date covered only a subset of possible OWL 2 DL axioms and provide limited feedback. We have addressed these issues with a model for TDD testing to give more feedback to the modeller and seven new, generic, TDD algorithms that also cover OWL 2 DL class expressions on the left-hand side of inclusions and ABox assertions by availing of several reasoner methods. The model and algorithms have been implemented as a Protégé plugin, TDDonto2.

1 Introduction

With most automated reasoners for OWL having become stable and reliable over the years, ontology engineers are exploring their creative uses to assist the ontology authoring process of ontology development. For instance, the possible world explorer examining negations [4], the entailment differences of an ontology edit [3,8], and proposing the feasible object properties [7]. This is in a considerable part motivated by the time-consuming trial-and-error approach in the authoring process where many modellers invoke the reasoner even after each single edit [11], noting also that aforementioned methods still require classification for each assessment step. Such practices are unsustainable when the ontology becomes large or complex and classifying the ontology prohibitively long. Analysing such modeller behaviour, this actually amounts to a *test-last* mode, alike unit testing in software development. In that regard, ontology engineering methodologies lag behind software engineering methodologies in terms of both maturity and adoption [5]. In particular, there is only one tentative methodology that explicitly incorporates automated testing as a *test-first* approach (that reduces the number of times a reasoner has to be invoked) [6], which is a staple of software engineering as test-driven development (TDD) [1]. There are a few tools for TDD unit testing ontologies in this manner [6,10,12], i.e., (in short) checking whether

E. Blomqvist et al. (Eds.): ESWC 2017 Satellite Events, LNCS 10577, pp. 120–125, 2017.
https://doi.org/10.1007/978-3-319-70407-4_23

an axiom is entailed before adding it. They all share two notable shortcomings, however: certain axioms are not supported as TDD unit tests even though they are permitted in OWL 2, such as $\forall R.C \sqsubseteq D$, and test results are mostly just "pass" or "fail" with no further information about the nature of failure. Moreover, no rigorous theoretical analysis of the techniques used for such test-first ontology testing has been carried out. However, for modellers to be able to fully rely on reasoner-driven TDD in the ontology authoring process—as they do with test-last ontology authoring—such rigour is an imperative.

In this demo-paper, we present TDDOnto2, which fills this gap in rigour and coverage. It relies on a succinct logic-based model of TDD unit testing as a prerequisite and generalised versions of the algorithms of [6] to cover also *any* OWL 2 class expression in the axiom under test for not only the TBox, as in [6], but also ABox assertions. The model details and proofs of correctness of the algorithms are described in [2]. These algorithms do not require reclassification of an ontology in any test after a first single classification before executing one or more TDD unit test, and are such that the algorithms are compliant with any OWL 2 compliant reasoner. This is feasible through 'bypassing' the ontology editor functionality and availing directly of a set of methods available from the OWL reasoners in a carefully orchestrated way.

We have implemented both the model for testing and the novel algorithms by extending TDDonto [6] as a proof-of-concept to ascertain their correct functioning practically. It uses the OWL API [9] and a subset of its functions, including ISSATISFIABLE(C), GETSUBCLASSES(C), GETINSTANCES(C), and GETTYPES(a), for the 'convenience method' ISENTAILED is not mandatory for reasoners to implement, and most do not. This open source Protégé 5 plugin, TDDonto2, is accessible at https://github.com/kierendavies/tddonto2, which also has a screencast of the working code. A screenshot is included in Fig. 1.

The remainder of this demo paper describes several scenarios where TDD aspects are useful (Sect. 2), and then introduces TDDonto2 and illustrates several of its algorithms through brief examples (Sect. 3). We close with conclusions and what an attendee may expect from the demo (Sect. 4).

2 Scenarios for Testing During Ontology Development

Ontologies, like computer programs, can become complex so that it is difficult for a human author to predict the consequences of changes. Automated tests are therefore useful to detect unintended consequences. For instance, suppose an author creates the following classes and subsumptions: Giraffe $\sqsubseteq$ Herbivore $\sqsubseteq$ Mammal $\sqsubseteq$ Animal, but then realises that not all herbivores are mammals, so shortens the hierarchy to Herbivore $\sqsubseteq$ Animal, thereby losing the Giraffe $\sqsubseteq$ Mammal derivation. An application that uses this ontology to retrieve mammals would then erroneously exclude giraffes. This issue can be caught by a simple automated test to check whether Giraffe $\sqsubseteq$ Mammal is still entailed. It may seem like this problem can be solved just adding those axioms directly to the ontology. However, adding such axioms introduces a lot of redundancy, making modification of the ontology more difficult. Adding only a test instead ensures correctness without bloating the ontology.

Tests may also be used to explore and understand an ontology. For example, an author might be assessing an ontology of animals for reuse and wants to verify that `Giraffe ⊑ Mammal`. The author can simply create a corresponding temporary test and observe the result, saving the time it would take to browse the inferred class hierarchy. A similar approach can be employed when developing a new ontology: create a temporary test to determine whether the axiom (i) is already entailed, (ii) would result in a contradiction or unsatisfiable class if it were to be added to the ontology, or (iii) can be added safely. The standard approach of adding an axiom and then observing the consequences involves reclassification, which is typically very slow, and which a TDD unit test can avoid.

Overall, there are thus two broad use cases: (1) Declare many tests alongside an ontology and evaluate them in order to demonstrate quality or detect regressions; (2) Evaluate temporary tests in order to explore an ontology or predict the consequences of adding a new axiom. Such scenarios are made possible with test-driven development with the TDDonto2 tool.

3   Illustration of TDDonto2's Algorithms

The simple workflow for an actual test in TDDonto2 is to type an axiom in the test text box; e.g., eats some Animal SubClassOf: (Carnivore or Omnivore), and either "Evaluate" it immediately (as with giraffe SubClassOf: mammal in Fig. 1) or "Add" it to the test suite (middle of the screen), then either select a subset of the tests (Shift-/Ctrl-click), or all tests, and test them by pressing the "Evaluate selected" or "Evaluate all" button, respectively. The "Result" can be one of the following: the knowledge is already in the ontology (*entailed*), adding the axiom will make the ontology *inconsistent*, adding the axiom will make at least one class unsatisfiable (*incoherent*), the axiom is *absent* and will not lead to a contradiction if added, and *failed precondition* for if the ontology is already inconsistent or incoherent. Based on the results, one either can "Remove" the axiom under test or "Add selected to ontology".

In the remainder of this section we demonstrate examples of axioms being tested so as to illustrate how the algorithms are used and how they work (see also Fig. 1). Take a simple ontology O that consists of the following axioms:

Giraffe ⊑ Mammal	Carnivore ⊑ Animal
Mammal ⊑ Animal	Carnivore ⊓ Herbivore ⊑ ⊥
Animal ⊓ Plant ⊑ ⊥	Susan : Giraffe
Herbivore ≡ Animal ⊓ ∀eats.Plant	Max : owl:Thing

Example 1 is straightforward and falls into the use case of testing something a modeller expects to be entailed to ensure the quality of the ontology.

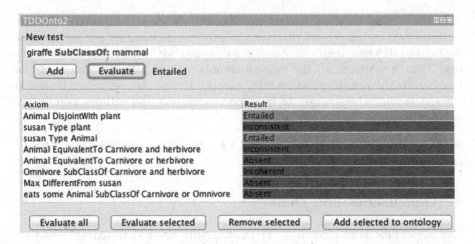

Fig. 1. Screenshot of TDDonto2 after having run several TDD unit tests on a sample ontology. Top: entering a test; middle: tests and their results; bottom: managing tests.

Example 1. Test that `Giraffe` is a subclass of `Animal`, hence, finding the result of test$_O$(`Giraffe` ⊑ `Animal`). It first checks if there are any instances of the class expression `Giraffe` ⊓ ¬`Animal`. There are none in this ontology, so it proceeds to check if the same class expression has any named subclasses or equivalent classes. Again there are none, so it checks if the class expression is satisfiable. It is not, so the algorithm returns entailed. ◇

Examples 2, 3, and 4 described below demonstrate testing of more interesting axioms that are not possible to test with any of the extant TDD tools, for (i) the left-hand side of the inclusion is not a named class (Example 2), (ii) have a test with individuals (Examples 3 and 4), and (iii) the axioms are not entailed for different reasons.

Example 2. Test that ∃`eats`.`Animal` ⊑ `Carnivore`. First, the algorithm checks if ∃`eats`.`Animal` ⊓ ¬`Carnivore` has instances (if so, then the ontology with this axiom would be inconsistent), which it does not, and then if it has named subclasses, which it does not (so, the ontology with this axiom would not cause the ontology to become incoherent). Then it checks if it is satisfiable, which it is because the ontology does not entail that it is empty, so the algorithm returns absent. Thus, the axiom is not entailed and it would not cause inconsistency or incoherence if added to the ontology. ◇

Example 3. Test whether `Susan` : `Plant`. TDDonto2 first checks if `Susan` is a known instance of `Plant`, which it is not. Then it checks if `Susan` is an instance of ¬`Plant`, which it is because `Giraffe` is disjoint with `Plant` because `Giraffe` ⊑ `Animal` and `Animal` ⊓ `Plant` ⊑ ⊥, so the algorithm returns inconsistent. ◇

Example 4. Test whether `Susan` and `Max` are different individuals. It first retrieves all the individuals that are the same as `Susan`; this set is empty, so adding the different individuals axiom will not result in an inconsistent ontology. Then it retrieves all the individuals different from `Susan`; `Max` is not in that set, so the algorithm will return 'absent', hence, the axiom can be added without causing the ontology to be come inconsistent and without introducing redundancy. ◇

More examples illustrating the tool and a screencast are available from https://github.com/kierendavies/tddonto2.

4   Conclusions and Demo

The algorithms implemented in TDDonto2 fully cover class axioms and partially cover assertions and object property axioms. They significantly broaden the coverage compared to the existing tools [6, 10, 12] and return more detailed test results. TDDonto2 easily could be extended or integrated with generating justifications of inconsistency or incoherence without the need to reclassify the ontology, and return more user-friendly explanations alike in [3].

In the demo, we will illustrate all possible permutations of the testing model's possible return values, as well as its coverage of types of axioms, and that it indeed does reduce the number of calls to the reasoner, hence, reduces ontology authoring time. Attendees can bring their own ontology and try it out, and we also will have several ontologies an attendee can test with.

Acknowledgments. This work has been partially supported by the National Science Centre, Poland, within grant 2014/13/D/ST6/02076. A. Ławrynowicz acknowledges support from grant 09/91/DSPB/0627.

References

1. Beck, K.: Test-Driven Development: By Example. Addison-Wesley, Boston (2004)
2. Davies, K.: Towards test-driven development of ontologies: an analysis of testing algorithms. Project report, University of Cape Town (2016). http://projects.cs.uct.ac.za/honsproj/cgi-bin/view/2016/allie_davies.zip/build/
3. Denaux, R., Thakker, D., Dimitrova, V., Cohn, A.G.: Interactive semantic feedback for intuitive ontology authoring. In: Proceedings of FOIS 2012, pp. 160–173. IOS Press (2012)
4. Ferré, S., Rudolph, S.: Advocatus diaboli – exploratory enrichment of ontologies with negative constraints. In: ten Teije, A., et al. (eds.) EKAW 2012. LNCS (LNAI), vol. 7603, pp. 42–56. Springer, Heidelberg (2012). https://doi.org/10.1007/978-3-642-33876-2_7
5. Iqbal, R., Murad, M.A.A., Mustapha, A., Sharef, N.M.: An analysis of ontology engineering methodologies: a literature review. Res. J. Appl. Sci. Eng. Technol. **6**(16), 2993–3000 (2013)

6. Keet, C.M., Lawrynowicz, A.: Test-driven development of ontologies. In: Sack, H., Blomqvist, E., d'Aquin, M., Ghidini, C., Ponzetto, S.P., Lange, C. (eds.) ESWC 2016. LNCS, vol. 9678, pp. 642–657. Springer, Cham (2016). https://doi.org/10.1007/978-3-319-34129-3_39
7. Keet, C.M., Khan, M.T., Ghidini, C.: Ontology authoring with FORZA. In: Proceedings of CIKM 2013, pp. 569–578. ACM (2013)
8. Matentzoglu, N., Vigo, M., Jay, C., Stevens, R.: Making entailment set changes explicit improves the understanding of consequences of ontology authoring actions. In: Blomqvist, E., Ciancarini, P., Poggi, F., Vitali, F. (eds.) EKAW 2016. LNCS (LNAI), vol. 10024, pp. 432–446. Springer, Cham (2016). https://doi.org/10.1007/978-3-319-49004-5_28
9. OWL API. http://owlcs.github.io/owlapi/. Accessed 1 Nov 2016
10. Scone Project. https://bitbucket.org/malefort/scone. Accessed 9 May 2016
11. Vigo, M., Bail, S., Jay, C., Stevens, R.D.: Overcoming the pitfalls of ontology authoring: strategies and implications for tool design. Int. J. Hum. Comput. Stud. 72(12), 835–845 (2014)
12. Warrender, J.D., Lord, P.: How, what and why to test an ontology. In: Bio-ontologies 2015 (2015)

Ladda: SPARQL Queries in the Fog of Browsers

Arnaud Grall[1(✉)], Pauline Folz[1,2], Gabriela Montoya[3], Hala Skaf-Molli[1],
Pascal Molli[1], Miel Vander Sande[4], and Ruben Verborgh[4]

[1] LS2N – Nantes University, Nantes, France
{arnaud.grall,pauline.folz,hala.skaf,pascal.molli}@univ-nantes.fr
[2] Nantes Métropole – Research, Innovation and Graduate Education Department,
Nantes, France
[3] Department of Computer Science, Aalborg University, Aalborg, Denmark
gmontoya@cs.aau.dk
[4] Ghent University – imec – IDLab, Ghent, Belgium
{miel.vandersande,ruben.verborgh}@ugent.be

Abstract. Clients of Triple Pattern Fragments (TPF) interfaces demonstrate how a SPARQL query engine can run within a browser and re-balance the load from the server to the clients. Imagine connecting these browsers using a browser-to-browser connection, sharing bandwidth and CPU. This builds a fog of browsers where end-user devices collaborate to process SPARQL queries over TPF servers. In this demo, we present Ladda: a framework for query execution in a fog of browsers. Thanks to client-side inter-query parallelism, Ladda reduces the makespan of the workload and improves the overall throughput of the system.

1 Introduction

Clients of Triple Pattern Fragments (TPF) interfaces demonstrate how a SPARQL query engine can run within a browser and re-balance the load from the server to the clients [4].

However, executing a workload composed of many queries with a single browser has intrinsic limitations regarding CPU and bandwidth. These limitations are severe as TPF potentially generates many calls and high network traffic.

Imagine connecting TPF clients using a browser-to-browser connection, sharing bandwidth and CPU. This realizes a *fog of browsers* [3] in which decentralized end-user devices cooperate to process SPARQL queries.

In this demo, we present Ladda; a framework for query execution in a fog of browsers. Ladda bypasses previous limitations and improves system throughput through the concurrent execution on multiple processors. Such *inter-query parallelism* was traditionally realized on the server-side. Ladda enables inter-query parallelism on the client-side, significantly reduces the time to obtain all results (*makespan*) and improves the overall *throughput*.

© Springer International Publishing AG 2017
E. Blomqvist et al. (Eds.): ESWC 2017 Satellite Events, LNCS 10577, pp. 126–131, 2017.
https://doi.org/10.1007/978-3-319-70407-4_24

2   Ladda: Query Delegation in the Fog

Continuing previous work [1], we introduce the Ladda framework for query execution in a fog of browsers. A federation of data consumers is connected through a Random Peer Sampling (RPS) overlay network [5]. Such a network approximates a random graph where each data consumer is connected to a fixed number of neighbors. It is resilient to churn, to failures and communication with neighbors is a zero-hop.

In the context of browsers, basic communications rely on WebRTC[1] to establish a data-channel between browsers and SPRAY [2] to enable RPS on WebRTC. Each browser maintains a set of neighbors K called a *view* that is a random subset of the whole network. To keep its view random, a data consumer renews it periodically by shuffling its view with the view of a random neighbor.

A browser executes an infinite stream of queries that arrive at any time. A data consumer can *execute* its query or *delegate* it to a neighbor. Given a fog of browsers and a workload of queries distributed in time across browsers, we aim to minimize the result time for data consumers, where, Δ, is the time elapsed between query results time $(Q.rt)$ and query arrival time $(Q.at)$. Ladda implements a load-balancing algorithm to balance the load among neighbors by executing queries on *free* neighbors.

Consider a federation of ten data consumers C_1 to C_{10}, where each data consumer has three neighbors, *i.e.*, $size(K) = 3$. Consider the data consumer C_1 has a workload of five queries, $C_1.W = [Q_1, ..., Q_5]$ and the following neighbors: C_4, C_6 and C_9.

Figure 1 illustrates how Ladda executes the workload of C_1.

- At time t_0, C_1 allocates its queries as follows: $(Q_1 \rightarrow C_1)$, $(Q_2 \rightarrow C_4)$, $(Q_3 \rightarrow C_6)$, and $(Q_4 \rightarrow C_9)$. Consequently, C_4, C_6 and C_9 belong to the list of *busy* neighbors of C_1: $C_1.B = [C_4, C_6, C_9]$.
- At time t_1, C_1 has finished the execution of Q_1, C_1 becomes *free* and it has only one waiting query, $C_1.W = [Q_5]$, therefore, C_1 executes Q_5: $(Q_5 \rightarrow C_1)$.
- At time t_2, Q_3 finished. As all queries are allocated, there is nothing to do.

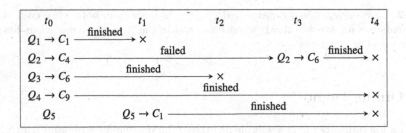

Fig. 1. Execution of C_1's workload of five queries with three neighbors among ten clients.

---

[1] https://webrtc.org/.

- At time t_3, Q_2 delegation fails. C_6 is no longer *busy* for C_1, so we allocate Q_2 to C_6.
- At time t_4, Q_2, Q_4 and Q_5 are finishing.

3   Evaluation

We evaluated Ladda on a local TPF server providing the DBpedia 3.8 dataset with the HDT back-end and four workers, a Web cache and different numbers of clients. NGINX is configured as a Web cache with a size of 1 GB. The TPF server, the Web cache, and all the TPF clients run on the same machine: a HPC server with 40 processors, 130 GB of memory, and Debian 7.8. From the DBpedia 3.8 query log, we extracted a full hour of queries from 50 clients (1,509 queries in total) on one day. We considered two setups as follows.

All loaded: 50 clients have their own query workload. This is considered as the worst case for Ladda, because at the beginning all clients are *busy*, so the first delegations to neighbors always fail.

One loaded: One client has the full workload. Since the client is the only one *busy* in the federation, all delegations succeed.

Figure 2 shows how Ladda improves the makespan for the two configurations.

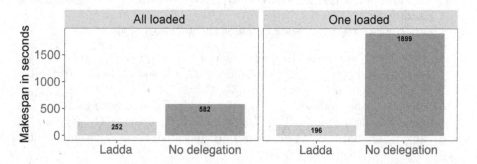

Fig. 2. Ladda delegation significantly decreases the makespan, both when each of the 50 clients has its own workload (worst case) and in the case where one client has the entire workload (best case).

4   Online Demo

The Ladda online demo is available at https://ladda-demo.herokuapp.com/, and the source code is available at https://github.com/folkvir/ladda-demo.

  When visiting https://ladda-demo.herokuapp.com/, the browser downloads and starts Ladda locally. Ladda connects the browser with other browsers in order to build a set of neighbors. Ladda needs to know at least one connected participant. A signaling service running on https://ladda-demo.herokuapp.com/ facilitates this process by keeping a random subset of connected browsers.

The number of neighbors "#Neighbors" appears in the timeline panel (see Fig. 3). Thanks to SPRAY [2], this number is bounded to $log(N)$ where N is the number of connected browsers.

Once connected, a browser can delegate queries to neighbors. The query workload appears in the "Queries" panel. Queries are executed against the TPF server defined in the "Queries panel". The delegation number dn determines the number of simultaneous delegation tentative. For instance, for a workload of 5 queries $q1$–$q5$, 3 neighbors and $dn = 2$, Ladda executes locally $q1$, delegates $q2$ and $q3$ to random neighbors and terminates its allocation process. A new allocation process takes place on the next event: receiving results, delegation failed or timeout on a delegation.

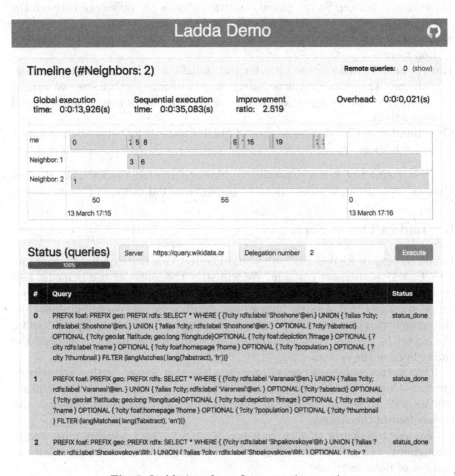

Fig. 3. Ladda interface after executing queries.

The button "Execute" allows to launch the execution of the local workload. The "Timeline" panel and the "Query" panel display in real-time the progression of the execution.

- The timeline allows to know in real-time when a participant executes a query. Each line represents a participant including "me". On a participant c, a query q starts at time $q.st$ and terminates at time $q.et$. The timeline displays for each participant $q.st$ and $q.et$.
- The "Query" panel displays the status of queries: waiting, done or delegated.

When the workload execution is terminated, Ladda computes the following statistics:

Global execution time is the makespan's workload. We suppose all queries in the workload arrive at the same time fixed when the user click on the "execute" button. So the global execution time is the difference between the result time of the last executed query and the arrival time.

Sequential execution time. For all Q_i in the workload, the sequential execution time is $\sum_{Q_i} Q_i.et - Q_i.st$.

Improvement ratio is the ratio for the global execution time to the sequential one. This comparison is barely an approximation because we cannot ensure that queries execution time would be the same if queries are executed sequentially.

Overhead is the total transfer time of queries and results between the browser and neighbors.

Once connected, it is also possible to receive delegated queries. The "Remote Queries" link in the timeline allows to display received queries.

5   Ladda Demo Scenario

In the context of ESWC 2017, we would like to run a live experiment that any ESWC 2017 participant can join. We will start the replay of the DBpedia logs available in USEWOD 2016 with TPF[2]. DBpedia logs contain hundreds of thousands of queries that a single browser can hardly execute. We will evaluate the throughput of a monitored TPF server according to the number of participants. We expect to see that collaboration between participants allows to increase the throughput of the system.

During the conference, we will tweet a link that anyone with a compatible browser (Chrome and Firefox) can click on and join the experiment. Participants will be able to see which queries they execute and observe in real-time the throughput of the system.

We aim to confirm that the number of participants positively impacts the throughput, *i.e.*, great improvements on the throughput are observed when the number of users increases.

---

[2] If compatible with the USEWOD usage agreement, otherwise, we will use synthetic queries.

6   Conclusion and Future Work

In this paper, we presented Ladda, an approach to execute SPARQL queries in the fog of browsers. Ladda enables inter-query parallelism on the client side. Ladda significantly reduces the overall makespan and improves the throughput of the federation.

In this demo, we did not take into accounts latencies in the network, neighbors are chosen randomly. A first perspective is to take into account network latencies to choose neighbors.

Second, it is interesting to study how collaborative caching as provided by Cyclades [1] and inter-query parallelism provided by Ladda contribute to performances improvements.

Finally, in Ladda, we focused on inter-query parallelism. Another research direction is to consider intra-query parallelism. Decomposition of SPARQL queries and delegation of subqueries open interesting perspectives.

Acknowledgement. We thank Thibaud Courtoison, Maël Quémard and Sylvain Vuylsteke, students of the Computer Science Department at the University of Nantes for implementing the interface of Ladda.

References

1. Folz, P., Skaf-Molli, H., Molli, P.: CyCLaDEs: a decentralized cache for Linked Data fragments. In: ESWC: Extended Semantic Web Conference (2016)
2. Nédelec, B., Molli, P., Mostefaoui, A.: Crate: writing stories together with our browsers. In: Proceedings of the 25th International Conference Companion on World Wide Web, pp. 231–234. International World Wide Web Conferences Steering Committee (2016)
3. Vaquero, L.M., Rodero-Merino, L.: Finding your way in the fog: towards a comprehensive definition of fog computing. ACM SIGCOMM Comput. Commun. Rev. **44**(5), 27–32 (2014)
4. Verborgh, R., Vander Sande, M., Hartig, O., Van Herwegen, J., De Vocht, L., De Meester, B., Haesendonck, G., Colpaert, P.: Triple pattern fragments: a low-cost knowledge graph interface for the web. J. Web Semant. **37–38**, 184–206 (2016)
5. Voulgaris, S., Gavidia, D., Van Steen, M.: CYCLON: inexpensive membership management for unstructured P2P overlays. J. Netw. Syst. Manag. **13**(2), 197–217 (2005)

Talking Open Data

Sebastian Neumaier, Vadim Savenkov, and Svitlana Vakulenko[✉]

Institute for Information Business, Vienna University of Economics and Business,
Vienna, Austria
{sebastian.neumaier,vadim.savenkov,svitlana.vakulenko}@wu.ac.at

Abstract. Enticing users into exploring Open Data remains an important challenge for the whole Open Data paradigm. Standard stock interfaces often used by Open Data portals are anything but inspiring even for tech-savvy users, let alone those without an articulated interest in data science. To address a broader range of citizens, we designed an open data search interface supporting natural language interactions via popular platforms like Facebook and Skype. Our data-aware chatbot answers search requests and suggests relevant open datasets, bringing fun factor and a potential of viral dissemination into Open Data exploration. The current system prototype is available for Facebook (https://m.me/OpenDataAssistant) and Skype (https://join.skype.com/bot/6db830ca-b365-44c4-9f4d-d423f728e741) users.

1 Introduction

The European Commission defines Open Data portals as "web-based interfaces designed to make it easier to find re-usable information"[1]. It is exactly the task of finding re-usable information, however, where current data portals fall short: they focus on supporting users to find files and not the information. It remains a tedious task for users to drill out and understand the information behind the data. According to the EU Data Portal study, 73% of the open data users characterize finding data as *Difficult* or *Very Difficult*[2].

Currently, the data is brought to end users not directly but through apps, each focusing on a specific service and based on a handful of open datasets. The app ecosystem, promoted by Open Data portals, is thriving. The downside of this approach, however, is that the data remains hidden from the users, who have to rely on IT professionals to get insights into it.

An orthogonal approach is to lower the entry barrier for working with open data for a broader audience. Being a moving target, as powerful data analysis methods become increasingly complicated, this approach still has a number of unique benefits. One can argue that it is embedded in the spirit of the Open Data movement itself, to enable and empower citizens to analyze the data, to be able to draw and share their own conclusions from it. Working with raw data is and will probably remain challenging for non-experts, and thus the easier it

---

[1] https://ec.europa.eu/digital-single-market/en/open-data-portals.
[2] https://www.europeandataportal.eu/en/highlights/barriers-working-open-data.

© Springer International Publishing AG 2017
E. Blomqvist et al. (Eds.): ESWC 2017 Satellite Events, LNCS 10577, pp. 132–136, 2017.
https://doi.org/10.1007/978-3-319-70407-4_25

is to find the right dataset and to understand its structure, the more energy a user has to actually work with it. Despite (or rather due to) the growing number of Open Data portals and ever increasing volumes of data served through them, their accessibility for non-technicians is still hampered by the lack of comprehensive and intuitive deep search, and means of integrating data across domains, languages and portals.

This demo showcases a novel natural-language interface, allowing users to search for open datasets by talking to the chatbot on a social network. We also address the challenge of cross-lingual dataset search that goes beyond the monolingual prototype[3] we developed earlier for two Austrian open data portals. To improve user experience, it embeds a state-of-the-art approach to semantic linking for natural language texts into a dialogue-based user interface.

Our hypothesis is that using a popular and convenient communication channel opens new possibilities for interactive search sessions. The inherent interactivity of a chat session makes it easy to enhance user experience with context-based and personalized elements. We envision our prototype to be the first step towards an intelligent dialogue system supporting contextual multilingual semantic search [1], focused on retrieval of datasets as well as the individual data items from them. In the future work we plan to extend the chatbot to search within the content of the datasets rather than merely in the metadata.

2   Chatbot Architecture

We implemented a prototype as a proof-of-concept by pooling and annotating 18 k datasets from seven Open Data portals with dataset descriptions in seven different languages (see Table 1). The front-end is designed using Microsoft Bot Framework[4], which connects the implementation to both Facebook Messenger and Skype platforms.

Table 1. List of selected data portals and respective languages

Portal	Country	Language	Datasets
dati.trentino.it	Italy	IT	5285
data.gov.ie	Ireland	EN	4796
datamx.io	Mexico	SP	2767
data.gv.at	Austria	DE	2323
dados.gov.br	Brazil	PT	2061
beta.avoindata.fi	Finland	FI	820
www.nosdonnees.fr	France	FR	290

---

[3] https://m.me/OpenDataATAssistant/.

[4] https://dev.botframework.com.

Collection and annotation of datasets. The search results of our chat-bot application are based on enrichment of dataset descriptions with BabelNet synsets [3]. Initially, we use the Open Data Portal Watch (ODPW) framework [4] to collect the dataset descriptions of the selected portals. ODPW harvests the metadata descriptions and maps them to the Schema.org standard vocabulary (cf. Fig. 1). We extract title, natural language description and keywords from these metadata and identify their language using langdetect[5] Python package. Then, we provide them as a single concatenated string (title, description, and keywords) for each dataset alongside the detected language to the Babelfy API[6] to detect and disambiguate entities and concepts within this string. The Babelfy API provides a list of corresponding "babelSynsetIDs" for an input string, language-independent entity identifiers in the BabelNet framework.

To deliver a good performance for the search functionality, we built an Elasticsearch index from the Schema.org dataset descriptions and the corresponding BabelNet entities. This allows us to retrieve all dataset descriptions that are annotated by a specific BabelNet entities and aggregate over the top co-occurring entities.

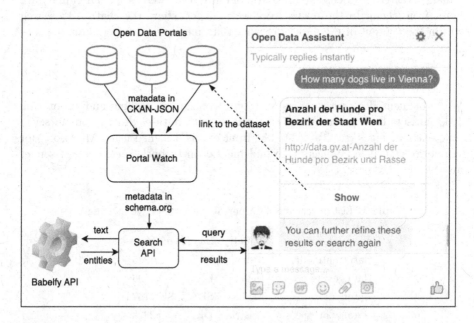

Fig. 1. Open Data Assistant chatbot. The system integrates metadata from different open data portals into a unified Schema.org format and enriches it with the concepts extracted from text via the Babelfly API. The chatbot interface provides access to the semantic (cross-lingual) open data Search API over the dataset metadata.

---

[5] https://pypi.python.org/pypi/langdetect.
[6] https://babelfy.org/guide.

Search API interactions. There are two modes of interaction and obtaining search results in the chatbot interface. First, the user can issue a free text search query. Our search API hands this input over to the Babelfy API which provides a list of disambiguated concepts and entities. We query our Elasticsearch index for *any* of these entities and return all matching datasets. The datasets get ranked by the number of matching entities. For instance, if a query includes the entites *dog* and *vienna*, then a dataset annotated with both of these gets ranked higher than a dataset annotated with either *dog* or *vienna*.

In the second interaction step the user can refine the search results by selecting one of the top co-occurring concepts and entities. We then use the selected entities to filter the result set, i.e., the selected entities *must* occur in the dataset description. This way we implicitly implement both AND/OR query operators.

3 Usability Study

Seven participants took part in a usability study designed to evaluate our system prototype. We asked the participants to complete a predefined search task and reflect on their experience of using the system. The search task was to find the official statistics data from different countries concerning climate change so that the participants could also experiment using various keywords related to the topic of climate change, e.g. air temperatures, snow level, etc.

Most of the participants found the system useful but in some cases limited in scope and functionality. Suggestions from the users include: (1) complementing open data with additional resources, such as Wikipedia; (2) user-specific answers, such as adjusting the language of interaction and geolocation-relevant queries; (3) context-specific answers, i.e. ability to follow up and refine the previous query. Often the participants were not able to assess the quality of the produced results when they were in an unfamiliar to the user language. More details on the evaluation task and results are available on-line[7].

4 Related Work

The originality of our system is in applying chatbot interface to the dataset search, which, as we believe based on our early evaluation, has large potential for popularizing and promoting open data, e.g. through easy access and gamification component.

Chatbots, e.g. Google Allo[8], recently gained an increased attention in the developers' communities worldwide. They integrate cutting-edge technologies, such as auto-reply, image and speech recognition, enhancing them with multimedia elements, which results in an attractive interface accessible also for users without IT background. Chatbot UI arguably provides a more natural and personalized way of human-computer interaction, as opposed to the traditional

---

[7] https://github.com/vendi12/oda_evaluation.
[8] https://allo.google.com.

"book-like" web page. To the best of our knowledge ours is the first chatbot focusing on dataset search.

The LingHub data portal[9] [2] is another example of cross-lingual data search implementation. It integrates language resources from Metashare, CLARIN, etc. using RDF, DCAT and SPARQL on the metadata level. Similar to our system, LingHub employs the Babelfy disambiguation algorithm.

5   Conclusion

We present a prototype of a conversational agent for Open Data search. The early user evaluation showed that such a cross-lingual dialog-based system has the potential to enable an easier access to Open Data resources.

The set of indexed portals can be easily extended since we rely on the ODPW framework that provides mapping of metadata from over 260 data portals into a homogenized schema, and Elasticsearch, which implements scalable search functionality. We also plan to extend the chatbot to search within the content of the datasets rather than merely in the metadata. Furthermore, the user query understanding needs to be enhanced to improve the results ranking. One way to facilitate it in the interactive chat context would be through asking user the questions to disambiguate the query, e.g. "Did you mean apple as a fruit or as a company Apple Inc.?"

Demonstration plan. Conference participants will be able to interact with the chatbot via Facebook and Skype. They will be free to experiment and come up with their own queries to the system. We will also provide the participants with the query samples that showcase both the strengths and the pitfalls of the current approach.

Acknowledgements. This work was supported by the Austrian Research Promotion Agency (FFG) under the projects ADEQUATe (grant no. 849982) and CommuniData (grant no. 855407).

References

1. Baeza-Yates, R.: Ten years of wisdom. In: Proceedings of the Tenth ACM International Conference on Web Search and Data Mining (WSDM 2017), Cambridge, 6–10 February 2017, pp. 1–2 (2017)
2. McCrae, J.P., Cimiano, P.: Linghub: a linked data based portal supporting the discovery of language resources. In: Joint Proceedings of the Posters and Demos Track and 1st Workshop on Data Science: Methods, Technology and Applications (DSci15) of 11th International Conference on Semantic Systems - SEMANTiCS 2015, Vienna, 15–17 September 2015, pp. 88–91 (2015)
3. Moro, A., Raganato, A., Navigli, R.: Entity linking meets word sense disambiguation: a unified approach. Trans. Assoc. Comput. Linguist. (TACL) **2**, 231–244 (2014)
4. Neumaier, S., Umbrich, J., Polleres, A.: Lifting data portals to the web of data. In: WWW 2017 Workshop on Linked Data on the Web (LDOW 2017), Perth, 3–7 April 2017

---

[9] http://linghub.lider-project.eu.

YAM++ *Online*: A Web Platform for Ontology and Thesaurus Matching and Mapping Validation

Zohra Bellahsene$^{(\boxtimes)}$, Vincent Emonet, Duyhoa Ngo, and Konstantin Todorov

University of Montpellier, LIRMM, Montpellier, France
{bella,todorov}@lirmm.fr

Abstract. We present the multi-task web platform YAM++ *online* for ontology and thesaurus matching, featuring a mapping validation and enrichment interface. The online matcher is based on the YAM++ system. The validator allows to visualize an alignment, edit the relation type and add new mappings discovered through a keyword-based search by a domain expert.

1 Introduction

Ontology matching, or alignment, is the process of (semi-) automatically discovering correspondences between entities belonging to different ontologies. Several approaches have been proposed and many matching systems have been designed in the past years [4]. However, few of them provide a user-friendly and easy to access interface that allows domain experts, having only basic technical knowledge of the semantic web field and the matching process per se, to execute and manipulate the alignments [1,2]. To take two examples, VOAR[1] allows to manually produce mappings or manipulate existing ones, whereas LogMap[2] allows to send a mapping request via a web platform, while the result (the alignment) is sent by email back to the user. In contrast, YAM++ *online*[3], provides an intuitive web environment for both the online execution *and* validation of ontology matching tasks, allowing for (not requiring) the active user participation.

2 Overview of the Platform

Matcher. We present concisely the main features of the YAM++ system [3], evaluated on several OAEI benchmarks in the past years, underlying the matcher module of YAM++ *online*. YAM++ ((not) Yet Another Matcher) is a multi-strategy and self-configuring system for discovering equivalence relations between ontology elements (classes, object properties and datatype properties). Figure 1 presents its architecture, described briefly below.

---

[1] http://voar.inf.pucrs.br.

[2] http://krrwebtools.cs.ox.ac.uk/logmap/.

[3] http://yamplusplus.lirmm.fr.

© Springer International Publishing AG 2017
E. Blomqvist et al. (Eds.): ESWC 2017 Satellite Events, LNCS 10577, pp. 137–142, 2017.
https://doi.org/10.1007/978-3-319-70407-4_26

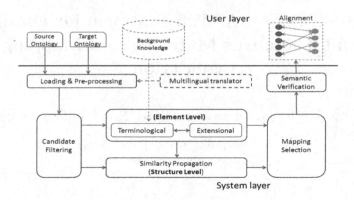

Fig. 1. Main components of YAM++.

Input ontologies are loaded and parsed by the *Ontology Loader* component; the ontology entities, according to their types, are indexed by the *Annotation Indexing*, the *Structure Indexing* and *Context Indexing* components; the *Candidates Pre-Filtering* component filters out all pairs of entities with highly similar descriptions; the candidate mappings are then passed into the *Similarity Computation* component, which includes: (i) a *Terminological Matcher* that produces a set of mappings by comparing the annotations of entities; (ii) an *Instance-based Matcher* that supplements new mappings through shared instances between ontologies and (iii) a *Contextual Matcher*, which is used to compute the similarity value of a pair of entities by comparing their context profiles. In YAM++, the matching results of the *Terminological Matcher*, the *Contextual Matcher* and the *Instance-based Matcher* are combined to produce a single merged set of mappings. The *Similarity Propagation* component then enhances the element level matching result by exploiting the structure of the ontologies. The *Candidate Post-Filtering* component is used to combine and select the potential candidate mappings from the element and the structural level results. Finally, the *Semantic Verification* component checks the consistency of the discovered mappings.

HTTP API. YAM++ *online* provides a way to perform the ontology matching programmatically by submitting the two ontology files through a HTTP request. Local files can be submitted using a HTTP POST request, while ontologies available on the web, through an URL, can be submitted using a HTTP GET request. Using the API requires an API key that is provided after creating an account. The HTTP response is provided using the alignment results in the XML EDOAL alignment format. The HTTP API allows users to easily integrate the matcher in their programs or workflow without having to install the YAM++ library. However, in case of an intensive use of the matcher, it is recommended to directly use the YAM++ library available on Maven.

Validator. An alignment produced by YAM++, or any other automatic system, can potentially contain erroneous mappings, or be incomplete. Therefore, the user participation at the mapping validation phase occurs to be important in real life situations, where the matching system will be seen as a generator of a (hopefully) significant in size and quality pool of candidates and the domain expert will have the final say. By domain here we mean the area of life that the aligned ontologies describe (e.g., biomedicine or music). The Validator module of YAM++ *online* allows for both the manual expert validation *and* enrichment of the automatically generated mappings.

3 Demonstration Scenario

We will go through the different components of the web interface of YAM++ *online*.

Fig. 2. The matcher GUI with the option "Show matcher parameters" on.

After login, **the Matcher** opens with a page where one can upload two ontologies to map by using a file path or a url, in one of the indicated input formats covering valid OWL and SKOS files, as shown in Fig. 2. A set of pairs of real-world ontologies are available for testing, including two medium-size pairs of SKOS vocabularies dedicated to musical instruments (IAML with 419 terms and DIABOLO – with 2117) and genres (REDOMI with 313 terms and RAMEAU – with 654)[4], respectively, issued from the DOREMUS project[5]. Further on the list, one finds pairs of (fragments of) larger ontologies from the OAEI campaign[6]: the

---

[4] https://github.com/DOREMUS-ANR/knowledge-base.
[5] http://www.doremus.org.
[6] www.oaei.org.

well-known *Anatomy* track ontologies (*Adult Mouse Anatomy* with 2744 concepts and a fragment of NCI with 3304 concepts) and three *Large bio* tasks ontologies (FMA with 10157 classes, SNOMED with 13412 and a larger fragment of NCI with 6488 concepts).

Before launching the execution, the user is able to determine whether the matching will be based on comparing only skos:prefLabel values or also synonyms from the skos:altLabel properties (Fig. 2, bottom left). The option of managing conflicts allows to improve recall (Fig. 2, bottom right). Once YAM++ has executed, the result is displayed on the Validator page (Fig. 3).

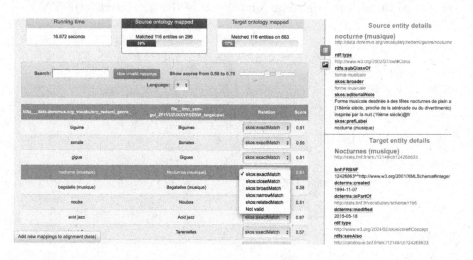

Fig. 3. The validator GUI. A text-based representation of the selected match pair on the right.

Note that the **the Validator interface** can be seen as a standalone tool, because it takes as an input a valid EDOAL alignment that is not necessarily produced by YAM++, together with its two ontologies (via an URL or a file path). A list of mappings (pairs of labels of aligned concepts) appears on the main page, together with information about the portions of the ontologies covered by the alignment (Fig. 3, above). A context description of each of the two concepts in each line is displayed (Fig. 3, right), containing all alternative labels, as well as the labels (or URIs) of parents and children. One can choose between a textual description (reaching a perimeter of distance 1 around the concept of interest) and a graphical visualization (reaching a distance 2). The confidence score, if available in the initial alignment, is provided for each pair of concepts (at the right end of each line) and the display of mappings can be filtered with respect to this score by the help of a horizontal cursor. For each concept pair, the expert is given the possibility to select a relation type from a list of SKOS relations (skos:exactMatch being the default choice), or simply discard the matching.

In case the expert feels that the provided list of mappings is incomplete or wants to look for a correct match to replace a mapping that they have invalidated, they can proceed to the alignment enrichment environment, by clicking on the "Add new mappings" button (Fig. 3, bottom left). A new page opens containing the full concept label lists of the two ontologies (Fig. 4). A key-word search on both lists, including preferred and alternative labels, allows to browse and select manually a pair of concepts and define their relation. Once done, the newly defined mappings are added to the initial alignment. Figure 4 also shows the alternative graphical visualization of the source and target concepts contexts.

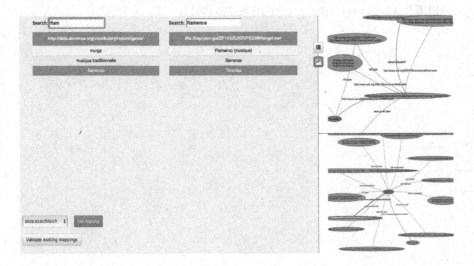

Fig. 4. Adding manually new mappings. A graph-based alternative representation of the selected classes contexts is seen on the right.

Finally, all modifications are added to the alignment file, which can be either saved in the default EDOAL internal format, or exported in the form of simple triples.

4   Future Work

In the future, we plan to extend the functionalities of YAM++ *online* by allowing for ontology recommendation, use and selection of background knowledge for a given matching task, alignment validation by crowdsourcing, as well as adding an interface for linkset validation in an instance matching scenario.

Acknowledgements. This work has been partially supported by the French National Research Agency (ANR) within the DOREMUS Project, under grant number ANR-14-CE24-0020.

References

1. Aumueller, D., Do, H.H., Massmann, S., Rahm, E.: Schema and ontology matching with COMA++. In: SIGMOD, pp. 906–908 (2005)
2. Dragisic, Z., Ivanova, V., Lambrix, P., Faria, D., Jiménez-Ruiz, E., Pesquita, C.: User validation in ontology alignment. In: Groth, P., et al. (eds.) ISWC 2016. LNCS, vol. 9981, pp. 200–217. Springer, Cham (2016). https://doi.org/10.1007/978-3-319-46523-4_13
3. Ngo, D.H., Bellahsene, Z.: Overview of YAM++ - (not) yet another matcher for ontology alignment task. J. Web Sem. **41**, 30–49 (2016)
4. Shvaiko, P., Euzenat, J.: Ontology matching: state of the art and future challenges. IEEE Trans. Knowl. Data Eng. **99**, 158–176 (2013)

SPARQL2Git: Transparent SPARQL and Linked Data API Curation via Git

Albert Meroño-Peñuela[1]([✉]) and Rinke Hoekstra[1,2]

[1] Department of Computer Science, Vrije Universiteit Amsterdam,
Amsterdam, The Netherlands
{albert.merono,rinke.hoekstra}@vu.nl
[2] Faculty of Law, University of Amsterdam, Amsterdam, The Netherlands

Abstract. In this demo, we show how an effective and application
agnostic way of curating SPARQL queries can be achieved by leveraging Git-based architectures. Often, SPARQL queries are hard-coded into
Linked Data consuming applications. This tight coupling poses issues in
code maintainability, since these queries are prone to change to adapt
to new situations; and *query reuse*, since queries that might be useful in
other applications remain inaccessible. In order to enable decoupling, version control, availability and accessibility of SPARQL queries, we propose
SPARQL2Git, an interface for editing, curating and storing SPARQL
queries that uses cloud based Git repositories (such as GitHub) as a back-
end. We describe the query management capabilities of SPARQL2Git,
its convenience for SPARQL users that lack Git knowledge, and its combination with grlc to easily generate Linked Data APIs.

Keywords: SPARQL · Git · Query curation · Query history

1 Introduction

The SPARQL Protocol and RDF Query Language [10] is a well known method of
accessing Linked Data that allows users to query a wide variety of Linked Data
sources [9]. Its implementation over HTTP, and the availability of libraries for
using it in various programming frameworks, has also enabled its use by *Linked
Data consuming applications*.

Usually, developers who want to retrieve Linked Data hard-code SPARQL
queries into their code. This gives raise to two important issues. First, SPARQL
queries become a critical component in the execution of such applications, making these applications *harder to maintain*. For instance, changes introduced in
datasets of the queried endpoints may oblige these queries to change accord-
ingly; often in more than one place, if the same query is used among various
applications. Secondly, queries buried into application source code are *harder to
discover and reuse*, even if the application is open source. Users are forced to
scan code and copy-paste these queries, with little attribution to the provenance
of the reused queries.

© Springer International Publishing AG 2017
E. Blomqvist et al. (Eds.): ESWC 2017 Satellite Events, LNCS 10577, pp. 143–148, 2017.
https://doi.org/10.1007/978-3-319-70407-4_27

Some query catalogs have been developed to overcome these issues. For instance, LinkedWiki[1] has a query sharing service where SPARQL queries can be found and reused, including code snippets for various programming languages. Another example is LSQ, the Linked SPARQL Queries dataset [8], which describes queries extracted from the logs of public SPARQL endpoints as Linked Data. In the CEDAR [4] and CLARIAH [3] projects, we have adopted a Git-centric approach, in which we curate queries independently of consuming applications. This query centralization has decoupled SPARQL queries from the various applications, like map visualizations[2], query interfaces[3], and even on-the-fly generated Linked Data APIs[4] with grlc [6], that depend on them to function. Moreover, by using Git and the API of Git repository managers such as GitHub, we enable *versioning*, *unique identification*, and *de-referenceability* of queries at a fine-grained, commit level, among other features of modern distributed version control systems.

In this paper, we describe SPARQL2Git, a system that builds on these foundations, and leverages the Web-based SPARQL editor libraries YASQE and YASR [7] and features of the Linked Data API generator grlc [5], to enable the curation of SPARQL queries, and their associated Linked Data APIs, in an effective, application-decoupled, and Git-agnostic way (Sect. 2). In Sect. 3 we show the contents of our demonstration, focusing on the user interaction workflow and the technology involved, and we discuss future work.

2   SPARQL2Git

SPARQL2Git is an open source[5] server and graphical user interface (GUI) for editing, documenting, and committing SPARQL queries to GitHub repositories, facilitating their versioning, dereferencing, decoupling from applications, and integration in Linked Data APIs. SPARQL2Git's GUI saves users from git interaction commands, and neatly documents SPARQL queries with relevant metadata (such as their target endpoint). SPARQL2Git allows to easily test the functionality of SPARQL queries from applications through their Linked Data APIs, using grlc [6]. SPARQL2Git's architecture consists of two parts: a Web front-end GUI; and a Python-flask backend, which deals with (1) receiving calls from and updating the GUI, and (2) manages authentication, repository access, and commits with GitHub's API. The public instance of SPARQL2Git is available at http://sparql2git.com.

The *welcome screen* asks the user to log in using GitHub's OAuth, thus a GitHub account is required in order to use SPARQL2Git. SPARQL2Git needs the user to grant permission to access the user's public repositories, username and

---

[1] See http://linkedwiki.com/searchExample.php.

[2] See http://www.nlgis.nl/.

[3] See http://lod.cedar-project.nl/data.html.

[4] See http://grlc.io/api/CEDAR-project/Queries/ and http://grlc.io/api/CLARIAH/ wp4-queries/.

[5] See https://github.com/albertmeronyo/SPARQL2Git.

email. Next, the *repository selection screen* shows the complete list of repositories of the authenticated user. The user can either choose an existing repository, or create a new one. This repository will be used to store SPARQL queries.

Next is the *query editing screen*, shown in Figs. 1 and 2. In this screen, users first select the query they are interested in editing, from the left pane (Fig. 1). Users can also create a new query, or delete an existing one. After this, users create or edit a query in two steps: query *metadata*, and query *body*. Query metadata are necessary to create compliant API specifications on top of SPARQL queries, and consist of (see Fig. 1): a query name; a brief summary; the SPARQL endpoint where the query should be sent; a MIME type (if the endpoint is an RDF dump or an HTML page with embedded RDFa); one or more tags, which are used to neatly organize queries in equivalent APIs; enumerations, which are used to create dropdown lists for parameter values in equivalent APIs; HTTP method (GET, POST, etc.); and a pagination number n, provided the user wants the query results to be returned in pages of n elements.

The query body is the SPARQL query itself, and can be edited below the metadata as shown in Fig. 2. We use the YASQE and YASR UI libraries [7] for prefix autocompletion, syntax highlighting, and other user friendly features. Users can press the *play* button to test their queries against the endpoint specified in Fig. 1, and see the results in the table below the SPARQL editor (Fig. 2). Once they are satisfied with the result, users can click on the commit button, which is placed on top of the query editor with a cloud sign (Fig. 2). After this, a dialog appears requesting a comment on the commit; this will be used as a commit message with the GitHub API interaction. After confirming, SPARQL2Git sends a request to the GitHub API to commit a new version of the file, with the

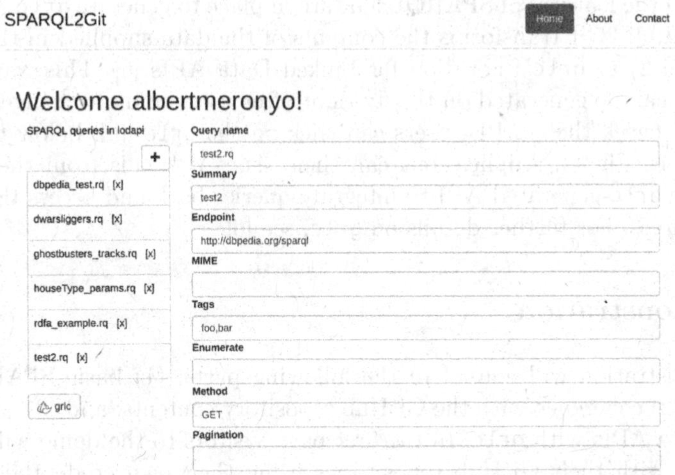

Fig. 1. SPARQL2Git metadata form. Users can select SPARQL queries in the left pane, and edit API metadata (name, summary, endpoint, etc.) on the right.

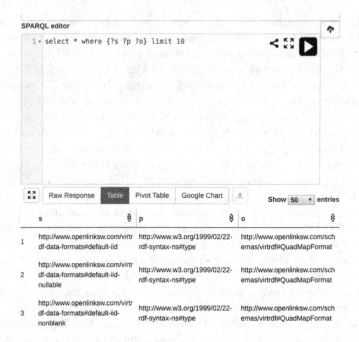

Fig. 2. SPARQL2Git query editor. The commit button at the top allows users to commit and push the query version to their GitHub repo.

supplied comment, metadata and body, over the file's last commit SHA hash. Users can click on the link to GitHub to check the result.

Many of the features of SPARQL2Git are in place to generate `grlc` compliant APIs. SPARQL2Git transforms the contents of the data supplied in this screen (Figs. 1 and 2) to `grlc`'s notation for Linked Data APIs [6]. This way, Linked Data APIs can be generated on the fly right after users commit changes to their queries. To check these APIs, users can click on the `grlc` link below the query list pane (see Fig. 1). Applications can then issue API calls from their source code to the `grlc`-generated API to integrate queries back and access the Linked Data resources. For further details on `grlc`, see [6].

3   Demonstration

The demonstration will consist of the following parts: (1) basic SPARQL2Git workflow; (2) coherence with the GitHub repository contents; and (3) generating Linked Data APIs with `grlc`. In the first part, visitors to the demo will be able to interact with their GitHub repositories using their own credentials, following the workflow described in Sect. 2. A screencast of the general SPARQL2Git workflow is available online[6], and will be used as main guide for this part.

---

[6] See https://vimeo.com/207296874.

In the second part, users will check the results of the first part by exploring their modified GitHub repository, exploring the resulting annotated SPARQL queries, and whether their commit history is coherent with their previous edits in SPARQL2Git. Additionally, we will prompt users to use well-known tools, such as Git2PROV [1] and PROV-O-Viz [2], to better understand this commit history as PROV triples and visualizations. Finally, in the third part visitors turn their SPARQL queries into Linked Data APIs using grlc with no additional effort, combining different API specification values (see Fig. 1). Moreover, different Linked Data access methods other than SPARQL will be used to generate universal access APIs to Linked Data.

In the future, we will integrate additional Git features into SPARQL2Git, such as branching, specific commit SHA hash editing, etc. We will also ease access to the PROV generated by Git2PROV and visualized by PROV-O-Viz into SPARQL2Git; and we will link the PROV triples of the commit history of SPARQL queries with the PROV of grlc generated at API creation time. Finally, we will implement caching mechanisms for a more efficient synchronisation and editing of SPARQL queries and their related metadata.

Acknowledgements. This work was funded by the CLARIAH project of the Dutch Science Foundation (NWO) and by the Dutch national programme COMMIT.

References

1. De Nies, T., Magliacane, S., Verborgh, R., Coppens, S., Groth, P., Mannens, E., Van de Walle, R.: Git2PROV: exposing version control system content as W3C PROV. In: Poster and Demo Proceedings of the 12th International Semantic Web Conference, October 2013. http://www.iswc2013.semanticweb.org/sites/default/files/iswc_demo_32_0.pdf
2. Hoekstra, R., Groth, P.: PROV-O-Viz - understanding the role of activities in provenance. In: Ludäscher, B., Plale, B. (eds.) IPAW 2014. LNCS, vol. 8628, pp. 215–220. Springer, Cham (2015). https://doi.org/10.1007/978-3-319-16462-5_18
3. Hoekstra, R., Meroño-Peñuela, A., Dentler, K., Rijpma, A., Zijdeman, R., Zandhuis, I.: An ecosystem for linked humanities data. In: Sack, H., Rizzo, G., Steinmetz, N., Mladenić, D., Auer, S., Lange, C. (eds.) ESWC 2016. LNCS, vol. 9989, pp. 425–440. Springer, Cham (2016). https://doi.org/10.1007/978-3-319-47602-5_54
4. Meroño-Peñuela, A., Guéret, C., Ashkpour, A., Schlobach, S.: CEDAR: the Dutch historical censuses as linked open data. Semant. Web Interoperability Usability Appl. **8**(2), 297–310 (2015)
5. Meroño-Peñuela, A., Hoekstra, R.: grlc makes GitHub taste like Linked Data APIs. In: Sack, H., Rizzo, G., Steinmetz, N., Mladenić, D., Auer, S., Lange, C. (eds.) ESWC 2016. LNCS, vol. 9989, pp. 342–353. Springer, Cham (2016). https://doi.org/10.1007/978-3-319-47602-5_48
6. Meroño-Peñuela, A., Hoekstra, R.: The song remains the same: lossless conversion and streaming of MIDI to RDF and back. In: Sack, H., Rizzo, G., Steinmetz, N., Mladenić, D., Auer, S., Lange, C. (eds.) ESWC 2016. LNCS, vol. 9989, pp. 194–199. Springer, Cham (2016). https://doi.org/10.1007/978-3-319-47602-5_38
7. Rietveld, L., Hoekstra, R.: The YASGUI family of SPARQL clients. Semant. Web **8**(3), 373–383 (2017). http://dx.doi.org/10.3233/SW-150197

8. Saleem, M., Ali, M.I., Hogan, A., Mehmood, Q., Ngomo, A.-C.N.: LSQ: the linked SPARQL queries dataset. In: Arenas, M., Corcho, O., Simperl, E., Strohmaier, M., d'Aquin, M., Srinivas, K., Groth, P., Dumontier, M., Heflin, J., Thirunarayan, K., Staab, S. (eds.) ISWC 2015. LNCS, vol. 9367, pp. 261–269. Springer, Cham (2015). https://doi.org/10.1007/978-3-319-25010-6_15
9. Vandenbussche, P.Y., Umbrich, J., Matteis, L., Hogan, A., Buil-Aranda, C.: SPARAQLES: monitoring public SPARQL endpoints. Semant. Web J. 8(6), 1049–1065 (2017)
10. W3C: SPARQL 1.1 Overview. https://www.w3.org/TR/sparql11-overview/

Eaglet – a Named Entity Recognition and Entity Linking Gold Standard Checking Tool

Kunal Jha[1]([✉]), Michael Röder[1], and Axel-Cyrille Ngonga Ngomo[1,2]

[1] AKSW Research Group, University of Leipzig,
Augustusplatz 10, 04103 Leipzig, Germany
kunal.jha@uni-bonn.de, roeder@informatik.uni-leipzig.de
[2] Data Science Group, University of Paderborn,
Pohlweg 51, 33098 Paderborn, Germany
ngonga@upb.de

Abstract. The desideratum to bridge the unstructured and structured data on the web has lead to the advancement of a considerable number of annotation tools and the evaluation of these Named Entity Recognition and Entity Linking systems is incontrovertibly one of the primary tasks. However, these evaluations are mostly based on manually created gold standards. As much these gold standards have an upper hand of being created by a human, it also has room for major proportion of oversightedness. We will demonstrate EAGLET (Available at https://github.com/AKSW/Eaglet), a tool that supports the semi-automatic checking of a gold standard based on a set of uniform annotation rules.

Keywords: Entity Recognition · Entity Linking · Benchmarks

1 Introduction

The number of information extraction systems has grown significantly over the past few years. In particular, NER (Named Entity Recognition) frameworks aim to locate named entities in natural language documents while Entity Linking (EL) applications link the recognised entities to a given knowledge base (KB). NER and EL tools are commonly evaluated using manually created gold standards (e.g., [4]), which are partly embedded in benchmarking frameworks (e.g., [1,7]). While these gold standards have clearly spurred the development of ever better NER and EL systems, they have certain drawbacks [2]. The creation of a NER/EL gold standard is a difficult task because human annotators commonly have different interpretations of this task as shown by Ratinov et al. [6]. EAGLET provides a very generic, adaptable set of rules derived from existing benchmarks by Jha et al. [2] which allows us to check these gold standards in a semi-automatic way. EAGLET has been evaluated on 13 English gold standards and detected 38,453 errors. An evaluation of 10 tools on a subset of these datasets shows a performance difference of up to 10% micro F-measure on average [2].

© Springer International Publishing AG 2017
E. Blomqvist et al. (Eds.): ESWC 2017 Satellite Events, LNCS 10577, pp. 149–154, 2017.
https://doi.org/10.1007/978-3-319-70407-4_28

2   Architecture Overview

EAGLET works based on the architecture presented in Fig. 1. Following this architecture, we will attempt to explain the implementation. EAGLET provides a systematic classification of errors, which are in violation of the rules, with the ability
to detect and correct a significant portion of these errors with minimum human
interference. EAGLET categorises the violation of the rule set which are hard-
coded into the system. The rest of this section discusses the implementation of
each component shown in the architecture.

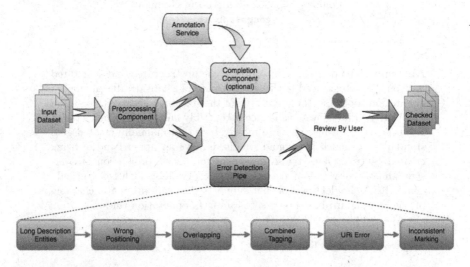

Fig. 1. EAGLET's architecture. The modules marked in purple depict the pipeline structure of EAGLET.

2.1   Input Dataset

The input of EAGLET is an annotated gold standard dataset which is primarily a
set of documents where each document is an ordered set of words $d = \{w_1, ..., w_n\}$
along with the meta information of each annotation.

2.2   Preprocessing Component

The text of each document is passed through the Stanford NLP core library [3]
to tokenise the text and lemmatise the tokens. After that, original text is coupled
with the meta-info added by the NLP module. The annotation list is extended
to the Corrected Annotation List (CAL) which contains some extra relevant
EAGLET introduced meta-information as it is passed through the pipeline.

2.3   Error Detection Pipe

The processed dataset is passed into the pipe. Every module of the pipe represents a single error type[1] and is implemented independently from the other modules. This enables the possibility to adapt the pipe by deactivating or introducing modules. An adaptation is easy since (1) the tool is available as open source project and can be adapted by the user, (2) the modules share the same API and (3) the modules act independently. Annotations, identified as faulty by each module, are marked with an error type and a suggested solution. The flow of the pipeline is as follows.

1. *Long Description Detection Component*: The module checks for the sequences of words which may describe the entity they are linked to but do only contain an indirect description of the entity instead of directly naming it. The module identifies such a description by searching for a relative clause inside an annotation.
2. *Wrong Positioning Detection Component*: This module searches for faulty annotations that do not fit to the positions of the words, e.g., an annotation that does not start with the first character. The last character of an annotation is checked in a similar way, i.e., it should be the last character of a word.
3. *Overlapping Entity Detection Component*: The module checks for annotations involving the presence of two or more annotations that share a common sub-string.
4. *Combined Tagging Detection Component*: This module searches for consecutive annotations that are separated by a white space character. Such entities are marked and a larger, combined annotation is generated and added to the CAL. This module helps in tackling a non-trivial tier of errors wherein consecutive word sequences are marked as separate entities while the word sequences, if combined, can be annotated to a more specific entity. The tool later suggests the user to review the suggested marking of this new entity and assign the new entity a URI.
5. *URI Error Detection Component*: The module verifies the URIs of all entities regarding their format. If a URI points to a set of predefined KB the module tries to dereference the URI to check whether (a) the entity exists and (b) the URI does not point to a disambiguation page. For example, if the given KB is the Wikipedia[2] or entities can be directly mapped to Wikipedia entities the module uses the Wikipedia API to determine whether the URI is outdated and derives the new URI.
6. *Inconsistent Marking Component*: This module collects all annotations in the corpus that have not been marked as faulty by one of the other modules. The lemmatized surface form of every annotation is used to search for all non-marked occurrences of the entity throughout the dataset. Since these newly

---

[1] The detailed description of each error type can be found in EAGLET research paper [2].
[2] http://wikipedia.org.

added annotations might be incorrect, e.g., because a URI that is linked to a word in one document does not need to fit to the same word in a different document, they are marked separately by the pipeline and should be checked by the user in the review module.

2.4 Completion Component

This component has been introduced as an optional module in EAGLET as the definition and requirement of the dataset completion may vary depending on the use case of the dataset. The component uses publicly available annotation services to derive a list of entity annotations on the dataset and compares it to the CAL list under consideration in the pipe, thereby generating a list of additional entities. These additional annotations support the work of a user that wants to make sure that the dataset is complete. However, since state-of-the-art annotation systems are not perfect [7], this module is based on a majority vote, i.e., the majority of the annotation systems have to contain an annotation inside their result list before it is added to the document. For this module, we relied on the open-source project GERBIL that enables the usage of up to 13 different annotation systems [5].

The components described above generated and stored a set of documents, different from the original input dataset, incorporating all the changes suggested in the pipe. This facilitates the reviewing which can be done by the user in different time duration and need not necessarily be completed in one run of EAGLET.

2.5 Review Component

This component involves at least one user reviewing all the corrections made by the pipe before they can be written to generate a final set of documents.

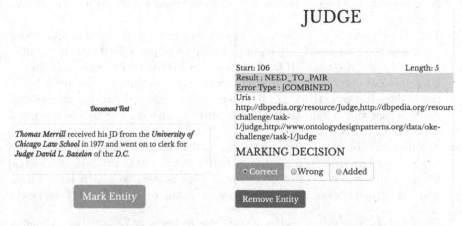

Fig. 2. Review module: document text   Fig. 3. Marking list

We implemented a user interface which allows a user to check the results in an efficient, interactive way. The user interface (see Figs. 2 and 3) of our tool allows every user to check each of the documents in the gold standards manually. Users can accept, modify or reject the suggestions of the tool as well as add new entities that have been missed by the auto-completion module. The user also has the liberty to change the URI of an entity. The review component has an auto completion module running in parallel which allows the addition made by a user in one of the documents to be automatically reflected in the other documents that have not been reviewed by the user so far reducing the redundancy in the reviewing process. The module is loaded with a login feature allowing multiple users to work on the same pipe results in order to generate a final, more accurate dataset. Each of these users can review and maintain their own versions of dataset at their own pace.

3 Conclusion

In this paper, we presented EAGLET—a tool to evaluate the gold standards used for NER and EL tasks. We described the different features of the tool which aim at correcting the existing the gold standard in order to achieve a more precise evaluation. We attempt to make this process user friendly and regard this work as a first stepping stone in a larger agenda pertaining to improving the assessment of the performance of natural language processing approaches.

Acknowledgments. This work has been supported by the H2020 project HOBBIT (GA no. 688227) as well as the EuroStars projects DIESEL (project no. 01QE1512C) and QAMEL (project no. 01QE1549C).

References

1. Cornolti, M., Ferragina, P., Ciaramita, M.: A framework for benchmarking entity-annotation systems. In: Proceedings of the 22nd International Conference on World Wide Web (WWW 2013), pp. 249–260, New York. ACM (2013)
2. Jha, K., Röder, M., Ngonga Ngomo, A.-C.: All that glitters is not gold – rule-based curation of reference datasets for named entity recognition and entity linking. In: Blomqvist, E., Maynard, D., Gangemi, A., Hoekstra, R., Hitzler, P., Hartig, O. (eds.) ESWC 2017. LNCS, vol. 10249, pp. 305–320. Springer, Cham (2017). https://doi.org/10.1007/978-3-319-58068-5_19
3. Manning, C.D., Surdeanu, M., Bauer, J., Finkel, J., Bethard, S.J., McClosky, D.: The Stanford CoreNLP natural language processing toolkit. In: Association for Computational Linguistics (ACL) System Demonstrations, pp. 55–60 (2014)
4. Mendes, P.N., Jakob, M., García-Silva, A., Bizer, C.: Dbpedia spotlight: shedding light on the web of documents. In: Proceedings of the 7th International Conference on Semantic Systems, pp. 1–8. ACM (2011)
5. Michael, R., Usbeck, R., Ngonga Ngomo, A.-C.: Techreport for GERBIL 1.2.2 - V1. Technical report, Leipzig University (2016)

6. Ratinov, L., Roth, D., Downey, D., Anderson, M.: Local and global algorithms for disambiguation to Wikipedia. In: Proceedings of the 49th Annual Meeting of the Association for Computational Linguistics: Human Language Technologies, pp. 1375–1384. ACL (2011)
7. Usbeck, R., Röder, M., Ngonga Ngomo, A.-C., Baron, C., Both, A., Brümmer, M., Ceccarelli, D., Cornolti, M., Cherix, D., Eickmann, B., Ferragina, P., Lemke, C., Moro, A., Navigli, R., Piccinno, F., Rizzo, G., Sack, H., Speck, R., Troncy, R., Waitelonis, J., Wesemann, L.: GERBIL - general entity annotation benchmark framework. In: 24th WWW Conference (2015)

Framework for Live Synchronization of RDF Views of Relational Data

Vânia M.P. Vidal[1]([⊠]), Narciso Arruda[1], Matheus Cruz[1], Marco A. Casanova[2],
Valéria M. Pequeno[3], and Ticianne Darin[1]

[1] Federal University of Ceará, Fortaleza, CE, Brazil
{vvidal,narciso}@lia.ufc.br, matheusmayron@gmail.com,
ticianne@virtual.ufc.br
[2] Department of Informatics, Pontifical Catholic University of Rio de Janeiro,
Rio de Janeiro, RJ, Brazil
casanova@inf.puc-rio.br
[3] INESC-ID, Universidade Autónoma de Lisboa, Porto Salvo, Portugal
vmp@inesc-id.pt

Abstract. This Demo presents a framework for the live synchronization of an
RDF view defined on top of relational database. In the proposed framework, rules
are responsible for computing and publishing the changeset required for the RDB-
RDF view to stay synchronized with the relational database. The computed
changesets are then used for the incremental maintenance of the RDB_RDF views
as well as application views. The Demo is based on the LinkedBrainz Live tool,
developed to validate the proposed framework.

Keywords: RDF view · View maintenance · Linked Data · Relational database

1 Introduction

There is a vast content of structured data available on the Web of Data as Linked Open
Data (LOD). In fact, a large number of LOD datasets are RDF views defined on top of
relational databases, called *RDB-RDF views*. The content of an RDB-RDF view can be
materialized to improve query performance and data availability. However, to be useful,
a materialized RDB-RDF view must be continuously maintained to reflect dynamic
source updates.

Also, Linked Data applications can fully or partially replicate the contents of a
materialized RDB-RDF view, by creating *RDF application views* defined over the RDB-
RDF view. The generation of RDF application views improves the efficiency of applications that consume data from the LOD, and increases the flexibility of sharing information. However, the generation of RDF application views raises synchronization problems, since the original datasets can be continuously updated. Thus, updates on an RDB-
RDF view must be propagated to maintain the RDF application views.

A popular strategy used by large LOD datasets to maintain RDF application views
is to compute and publish changesets, which indicate the difference between two states
of the dataset. Applications can then download the changesets and synchronize their

E. Blomqvist et al. (Eds.): ESWC 2017 Satellite Events, LNCS 10577, pp. 155–160, 2017.
https://doi.org/10.1007/978-3-319-70407-4_29

local replicas. For instance, DBpedia (http://wiki.dbpedia.org) and LinkedGeoData (http://linkedgeodata.org/About) publish their changesets in a public folder.

In this demo, we show a framework, based on rules, that provides live synchronization of RDB_RDF views. In the proposed framework (see Fig. 1), rules are responsible for computing and publishing the changeset required for the RDB-RDF view to stay in synchronization with the relational database. The computed changesets are used by the synchronization tools for the incremental maintenance of RDB_RDF views and application views. In [7] we present a formal framework for automatically generating, based on the view mappings, the rules for computing correct changesets for an RDB-RDF view. Based on the mappings, at view definition time, we are able to: (i) identify all relations that are relevant for the view; and (ii) define the rules that compute the changeset required to maintain the view w.r.t an update over a relevant relation. Our formalism allows us to precisely justify that the rules generated by the proposed approach correctly compute the changeset. The demo video is available at http://tiny.cc/ videolivesynrdbrdf (see also http://www.arida.ufc.br/livesynrdbrdf/).

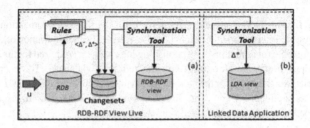

Fig. 1. Framework for live synchronization of RDB_RDF view.

The remainder of this paper is organized as follows. Section 2 describes our strategy, based on rules, for computing changesets for an RDB-RDF view. Section 3 summarizes related work. Section 4 covers an implementation and experiments. Section 5 presents the conclusions.

2   Computing Changesets for RDB-RDF Views

In our strategy, we first have to identify the relations in S that are relevant for V, that is, the relations whose updates might possibly affect the state of the view V. For each such relation R, we define triggers that are fired immediately before and after an update on R, called *before* and *after triggers*, respectively, and which are such that:

BEFORE Trigger: computes Δ^- the set of deleted triples
AFTER Trigger: computes Δ^+ the set of inserted triples

The key idea of our strategy for computing the changesets is to re-materialize only the tuples whose RDF_State (the tuple triplification) might possibly be affected by the update. Thus, using Δ^- and Δ^+, one should be able to compute the new RDF state of the tuples that are relevant to the update (formal definitions in [7]). Figure 2 shows the templates of the triggers associated with an update on a relation R.

BEFORE {UPDATE} ON R **THEN**	AFTER {UPDATE} ON R **THEN**
$\Delta^- := COMPUTE\_\ \Delta^- [R](r_{old},\ r_{new});$	$\Delta^+ := COMPUTE\_\ \Delta^+ [R](r_{old},\ r_{new});$
ADD Δ^- to changeset of V.	ADD Δ^+ to changeset of V.
(a)	(b)

Fig. 2. Triggers to compute changeset of V w.r.t. updates on R

For example, consider u, the UPDATE on R, where r_{old} and r_{new} are the old and new state of the updated tuple, respectively. Before the update, Trigger (a) is fired, and Procedure $COMPUTE\_\ \Delta^-[R]$ computes Δ^-, which contains the OLD RDF_State of the tuples that are relevant to V w.r.t update u. After the update, Trigger (b) is fired. Using the database state after the update, Procedure $COMPUTE\_\ \Delta^+[R]$ computes Δ^+, which contains the new RDF_State of the tuples that are relevant to V w.r.t update u. Note that procedures $COMPUTE\_\ \Delta^-[R]$ and $COMPUTE\_\ \Delta^+[R]$ are automatically generated, at view definition time, based on the view mappings [7]. Triggers for insertions and deletions are similarly defined and are omitted here.

Given V_{OLD}, the old state of the *RDB_RDF* view, in order to stay synchronized with the new state of database, the new state of the view is computed as

$$V_{NEW} = (V_{OLD} - \Delta^-) \cup \Delta^+$$

3   Related Work

The incremental view maintenance problem has been extensively studied in the literature for relational views [2], object-oriented views [6], semi-structured views [1], and XLM Views [3]. Despite their important contributions, none of these techniques can be directly applied to compute changesets for RDB-RDF views.

Comparatively less work addresses the problem of incremental maintenance of RDB-RDF views. Vidal et al. [8] proposed an incremental maintenance strategy, based on rules, for RDF views defined on top of relational data. Although the approach in this paper uses a similar formalism for specifying the view mappings, our strategy to compute changeset present in Sect. 2 differs considerably.

Faisal et al. [4] presented an approach to deal with co-evolution, that is, the mutual propagation of the changes between a replica and its origin dataset. Their approach relies on the assumption that either the source dataset provides a tool to compute a changeset at real-time or third party tools can be used for this purpose. Thus, the contribution of this paper is complementary and relevant to satisfy their assumption.

Konstantinou et al. [5] investigated the problem of the incremental generation and storage of the RDF graph that is the result of exporting relational database contents. In their approach, when one of the source tuples change, the whole triples map definition will be executed for all tuples in the affected table. By contrast, using our rules, we are able to identify which tuples are relevant to an update, and only the RDF_State of the relevant tuple are re-materialized.

4 Implementation and Experiments

To test our strategy, we implemented the *LinkedBrainz Live tool* (*LBL tool*), which propagates the updates over the *MusicBrainz* database (*MBD* database) to the Linked-MusicBrainz view (*LMB View*). The *LMB* View is intended to help MusicBrainz (http://musicbrainz.org/doc/about) to publish its database as Linked Data. Figure 1 depicts the general architecture of our framework, based on rules, for providing live synchronization of RDB_RDF views. The main components of the *LBL* tool are:

- **Local *MBD* database:** We installed a local copy of the *MBD* database available on March 22, 2017.
- ***LMB* View and Mappings:** We created the R2RML mapping for translating *MBD* data into the Music Ontology vocabulary (http://musicontology.com/), which is used for publishing the *LMB* view. The *LMB* view was materialized using the D2RQ tool (http://www.d2rq.org/). It took 67 min to materialize the view with approximately 41.8 GB of NTriples.
- *Triggers*: We created the triggers to implement the rules required to compute and publish the changesets, as discussed in Sect. 2.
- *LBL Synchronization tool*: This component enables the *LMB View* to stay synchronized with the *MBD* database. It is the same synchronization tool used by the DBpediaLive (http://wiki.dbpedia.org/online-access/DBpediaLive). It simply downloads the changeset files sequentially, creates the appropriate INSERT/DELETE statement and executes it against the *LMB View* triplestore.
- *LBL update extractor*: This component extracts updates from the replication file provided by MusicBrainz, every hour, which contains a sequential list of the update instructions processed by the MusicBrainz database. When there is a new replication file, the updates should be extracted and then executed against the local database

In our experiments, we used the replication file with sequential number 103114, which has 4,557 updates. Tables 1 and 2 summarize our experimental results. Due to space limitation we consider only the relevant relations (RR) *Artist* and *Track*.

- Table 1 shows: The total number of tuples in the RR and the total time (in milliseconds) spent to triplify the tuples in RR.
- Table 2 shows: the total number of updates on the RR, the average number of tuples relevant for updates on the RR, and the average time (in milliseconds) to compute the changeset $<\Delta^-, \Delta^+>$ for insertions (*i*) and updates (*u*) on RR. In the replication file, there is no deletion from relevant relations *Artist* and *Track*.

Table 1. Time spent for triplification on March 22, 2017

Relevant Relation (RR)	Number of Tuple (k)	Triplification Time (ms)
Artist	1,189	340,721
Track	22,087	435,693

Table 2. Time spent for computing changesets w.r.t replication file 103114

Relevant Relation (RR)	Number of Updates	Avg number of Relevant tuples (by update)	Δ^- (avg time) (ms)		Δ^+ (avg time) (ms)	
Artist	31	1.55	25	102	18	5
Track	397	4.05	28	39	4	3

The experiments demonstrated that the runtime for computing the changeset is negligible, when the number of relevant tuples is relatively small. This is what is expected, since the *RDB_RDF* View should be frequently updated to ensure that it remains consistent and up-to-date. Thus, we can conclude that the incremental strategy far outperforms full re-materialization, and also the re-materialization of the affected tables [5].

5   Conclusions

This Demo presented a framework for providing live synchronization of an RDF view defined on top of relational database. In the proposed framework, rules are responsible for computing and publishing the changeset required for the RDB-RDF view to stay synchronized with the relational database. The computed changesets are used for the incremental maintenance of the RDB_RDF views as well as application views.

We also implemented the *LinkedBrainz Live tool* to validate the proposed framework. We are currently working on the development of a tool to automate the generation of the rules for computing the changesets.

References

1. Abiteboul, S., McHugh, J., Rys, M., Vassalos, V., Wiener, J.L.: Incremental maintenance for materialized views over semistructured data. In: VLDB 1998, pp. 38–49 (1998)
2. Ceri, S., Widom, J.: Deriving productions rules for incremental view maintenance. In: VLDB 1991, pp. 577–589 (1991)
3. Dimitrova, K., El-Sayed, M., Rundensteiner, E.A.: Order-sensitive view maintenance of materialized XQuery views. In: ER 2003, pp. 144–157 (2003)
4. Faisal, S., Endris, K.M., Shekarpour, S., Auer, S.: Co-evolution of RDF datasets. In: 16th International Conference – ICWE 2016 (2016)
5. Konstantinou, N., Spanos, D.E., Kouis, D., Mitrou, N.: An approach for the incremental export of relational databases into RDF graphs. Int. J. Artif. Intell. Tools **24**(2), 1540013 (2015)

6. Kuno, H.A., Rundensteiner, E.A.: Incremental maintenance of materialized object-oriented views in multiview: strategies and performance evaluation. IEEE TDKE **10**(5), 768–792 (1998)
7. Vidal, V.M.P., Arruda, N., Casanova, M.A., Brito, C., Pequeno, V.M.: Computing changesets for RDF views of relational data. Technical report, Federal University of Ceara (2017). http://tiny.cc/TechnicalReportUFC2017
8. Vidal, V.M.P., Casanova, M.A., Cardoso, D.S.: Incremental maintenance of RDF views of relational data. In: ODBASE 2013, pp 572–587 (2013)

JedAI: The Force Behind Entity Resolution

George Papadakis[1]([envelope]), Leonidas Tsekouras[2], Emmanouil Thanos[3],
George Giannakopoulos[2], Themis Palpanas[4], and Manolis Koubarakis[1]

[1] University of Athens, Athens, Greece
{gpapadis,koubarak}@di.uoa.gr
[2] NCSR "Demokritos", Athens, Greece
{ltsekouras,ggianna}@iit.demokritos.gr
[3] University of Leuven, Leuven, Belgium
emmanouil.thanos@kuleuven.be
[4] Paris Descartes University, Paris, France
themis@mi.parisdescartes.fr

Abstract. We present JedAI, a toolkit for Entity Resolution that can
be used in three different ways: as an open-source Java library that
implements numerous state-of-the-art, domain-independent methods, as
a workbench that facilitates the evaluation of their relative performance
and as a desktop application that offers out-of-the-box ER solutions.
JedAI bridges the gap between the database and the Semantic Web communities, offering solutions that are applicable to both relational and
RDF data. It also conveys a modular architecture that facilitates its
extension with more methods and with more comprehensive workflows.

1 Introduction

Linked Open Data are not as linked as they have been envisaged by the Linked
Data Principles: a recent study revealed that 44% of its datasets are not connected with any other data sources [8]. To ameliorate this situation, Entity Resolution (ER) aims to interconnect the semantically equivalent resources in different
datasets with owl:sameAs relationships. ER is manifested with two sub-tasks [1]:
(i) Clean-Clean ER receives as input two overlapping data sources that are individually duplicate-free, S and T, and aims to identify all pairs $<s \in S, t \in T>$
that correspond to the same real-world object. *(ii)* Dirty ER takes as input a
single set of resources S that contains duplicates in itself and aims to detect all
pairs $\{s_i, s_j \in S : i \neq j\}$ that refer to the same real-world object.

To facilitate researchers, practitioners and simple users in applying both ER
tasks, we hereby present the *Java gEneric DAta Integration Toolkit*, JedAI for
short. JedAI offers a threefold functionality:

(1) JedAI constitutes an *open source library* that implements numerous state-of-
the-art methods for all steps of the end-to-end ER workflow of Sect. 2. This
workflow combines high time efficiency and scalability with high effectiveness [3,7]. The former aspect is accomplished by Steps 2–4, which use (meta-
)blocking to significantly reduce the search space, omitting the comparison

© Springer International Publishing AG 2017
E. Blomqvist et al. (Eds.): ESWC 2017 Satellite Events, LNCS 10577, pp. 161–166, 2017.
https://doi.org/10.1007/978-3-319-70407-4_30

of evidently irrelevant pairs of resources, while effectiveness emanates from Steps 5–6, which combine string similarity measures with advanced clustering methods that relax the transitivity of the equality relation. Every step exposes a well-defined API with detailed documentation. The code (in Java 8) is freely distributed through the Apache License V2.0, supporting both academic and commercial uses.

(2) JedAI constitutes a *desktop application* with an intuitive Graphical User Interface that can be used not only by experts in ER, but also by lay users. The user simply has to select a method for every step of the end-to-end workflow through an intuitive wizard. All methods are associated with a default configuration that has been experimentally verified to achieve the best performance on average [7], thus requiring no manual fine-tuning. All methods are also unsupervised, thus requiring no manual definition of link specifications. Finally, all methods operate in a schema-agnostic fashion, thus requiring no external domain knowledge (e.g., a training set or an ontology). As a result, the workflow that is formed by the user is carried out in a fully automatic way.

(3) JedAI can be used as a *workbench*, too. The number of methods that are available in every step yields more than 4,000 different possible workflows. JedAI facilitates users to compare in detail two or more executed workflows by reporting a large variety of performance measures in Step 7. Users can actually perform thorough experiments on top of most established benchmarks, since JedAI supports a wide variety of structured data formats (e.g., relational databases, CVS files) and semi-structured ones (e.g., RDF, XML, OWL files).

The code of the JedAI library along with several datasets for experimentation, the executable jar of the JedAI desktop application and videos presenting its features can be downloaded from https://github.com/scify/JedAIToolkit.

2   JedAI Workflow

The end-to-end ER workflow that is implemented by JedAI combines the blocking workflow proposed in [7] (Steps 2, 3 and 4) with the matching workflow used in [3] (Steps 5 and 6). In more detail, it comprises the following steps:

(1) **Data Reading** loads from the disk into main memory one (Dirty ER) or two (Clean-Clean ER) sets of resources along with the corresponding golden standard. It supports Semantic Web data contained in RDF, XML or OWL files as well as relational data contained in CSV files or SQL databases (e.g., mySQL).

(2) **Block Building** receives as input the data source(s) loaded by Data Reading and clusters their resources into a set of blocks that is returned as output. This is a mandatory step that drastically reduces the search space in order to ensure high time efficiency and scalability. At the moment, the user can select among 8 established methods. All of them use the schema-agnostic

blocking keys that were defined in [6]. Thus, they require no domain knowledge, placing every resource into multiple blocks in order to achieve high recall.

(3) **Block Cleaning** receives as input the blocks produced by Block Building. Given that they are overlapping (i.e., every resource participates in multiple blocks), they contain two types of unnecessary comparisons: the *redundant* ones, which repeat the same comparisons in different blocks, and the *superfluous* ones, which compare non-matching resources [6]. Block Cleaning discards both types of comparisons by enforcing constraints on the level of individual blocks. This results in significant gains in efficiency and scalability, though at the cost of slightly lower recall [7]. For this reason, this step is optional, yet it allows the user to choose one or more of the 4 methods that are currently available (i.e., all methods are complementary with each other).

(4) **Comparison Cleaning** receives as input a set of blocks and aims to clean it from its unnecessary comparisons, just like Block Cleaning. The difference is that Comparison Cleaning operates at a finer granularity, targeting individual comparisons. As a result, it takes more accurate decisions, but its performance is more time consuming than Block Cleaning [7]. Due to its cost in recall, it is an optional step, too. For now, the user can choose 1 out of 7 competitive methods.

(5) **Entity Matching** is a mandatory step that executes all comparisons that are contained in the set of block it receives as input. As output, it produces a *similarity graph*, with one node for every resource and one weighted edge for every compared pair of resources. The user can choose among 2 methods, which incorporate a plethora of established string similarity metrics [2].

(6) **Entity Clustering** is a mandatory step that receives as input the similarity graph of Entity Matching. Its goal is to partition its nodes into *equivalence clusters* such that every cluster contains all resources that correspond to the same real world object. At the moment, the user can select 1 out of 7 established methods, which have been experimentally evaluated in [3].

(7) **Evaluation & Storing**, the final step of our workflow, estimates the performance of the resulting set of equivalence clusters with respect to the established effectiveness measures (Precision, Recall and F-Measure). For this purpose, it relies on the golden standard that was given as input file in Step 1. This step also evaluates the time efficiency of the implemented workflow, assessing the overhead time of every individual step. Finally, the user is able to store the identified equivalence links in a variety of output formats, such as CSV. An example of this step's screen is illustrated in Fig. 2.

All methods included in every step are schema- and domain-agnostic, requiring no background knowledge from the user in order to apply them.

3   Architecture

JedAI has a *modular* architecture that is described in Sect. 2. Note that there is a separate module for every step in the workflow of Sect. 2. Each module exposes

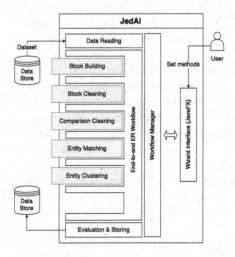

Fig. 1. JedAI architecture

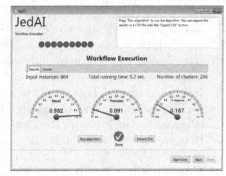

Fig. 2. Evaluation & Storing screen.

a well-defined interface so that any method that implements it can be seamlessly integrated into that module. This makes it easy to add more ER techniques in the future, as they become available. Additionally, every interface takes special care to ensure that the functionality of each method is well-documented and that its configuration parameters are associated with a short explanation of their role along with their possible values. Finally, JedAI's architecture is *extensible* with additional modules that could add more steps to the workflow of Sect. 2. This is illustrated by the empty placeholder right after the Entity Clustering module in Fig. 1; however, a new module/step could be placed anywhere in the current workflow. An example is Ontology Matching before Entity Matching or Block Building for higher effectiveness.

4   Demonstration

The goal of our demonstration is to showcase how JedAI can apply a series of ER workflows to several established benchmark datasets in a straightforward way, i.e., without requiring any manual fine-tuning or domain knowledge. To this end, we will use JedAI's desktop application to load some established CSV datasets from [4] and RDF datasets from the Ontology Alignment Evaluation Initiative (OAEI). All datasets will be loaded in their original format, without any preprocessing. Then, the user will be able to form an end-to-end ER workflow with a couple of clicks in the screen of every step. Finally, a screen similar to Fig. 2 will present the performance of the formed workflow. Different workflows or different configurations will be applied to the same dataset(s) with the same 7-step procedure in order to compare the resulting performances.

5   Related Work

Entity Resolution has been extensively studied in the literature as a special case of the more general task of Link Discovery [5]. In fact, OAEI organizes a special track for Instance Matching and several frameworks have been proposed for facilitating Link Discovery, such as RiMOM, Silk and LIMES. A recent survey can be found in [5]. These frameworks are similar to JedAI in the sense that they combine methods for high efficiency (e.g., blocking) with methods for high effectiveness (e.g., thresholds on string similarities).

However, JedAI goes beyond these frameworks in the following ways: *(i)* Most frameworks for Link Discovery focus exclusively on Clean-Clean ER, whereas JedAI covers Dirty ER, too. *(ii)* Link Discovery frameworks take as input only RDF data, while JedAI is able to process structured data, too, supporting CSV files and relational databases. *(iii)* JedAI offers out-of-the-box ER solutions, due to the schema-agnostic functionality of its methods and the default configuration that is associated with every one of them. Thus, it requires no manual fine-tuning, unlike most Link Discovery frameworks. *(iv)* JedAI is suitable for both lay and power users. The former can simply use the intuitive GUI, while the latter can use it as a library, too, through its well-defined API. In contrast, all Link Discovery frameworks require some domain knowledge from the user. *(v)* JedAI works as a workbench, too, allowing users to compare the performance of more than 4,000 different ER workflows that can be formed by combining state-of-the-art methods from every step. *(vi)* There is small overlap in the methods offered by JedAI and those offered by the Link Discovery frameworks. The former currently focuses on schema-agnostic methods, while the latter cover ontology-based methods.

6   Conclusions

We present JedAI, a toolkit that can be used as Java library, a desktop application and a workbench for domain-independent, out-of-the-box ER solutions. Its capabilities will be demonstrated by applying it to a series of established relational and RDF datasets, without requiring any manual fine-tuning or background knowledge. In the future, we plan to participate in the OAEI Instance Matching task and to integrate more methods that are based on ontologies for even better performance. We also plan to parallelize JedAI using Apache Spark.

Acknowledgments. This work has been supported by the project "Your Data Stories", which is funded by EU Horizon 2020 programme under grant agreement No. 645886. We would also like to thank Oktie Hassanzadeh for sharing with us the implementation in C of the clustering algorithms examined in [3].

References

1. Christophides, V., Efthymiou, V., Stefanidis, K.: Entity Resolution in the Web of Data. Morgan & Claypool, San Rafael (2015)
2. Cohen, W., Ravikumar, P., Fienberg, S.: A comparison of string distance metrics for name-matching tasks. In: IIWeb, pp. 73–78 (2003)
3. Hassanzadeh, O., Chiang, F., Miller, R., Lee, H.: Framework for evaluating clustering algorithms in duplicate detection. PVLDB 2(1), 1282–1293 (2009)
4. Köpcke, H., Thor, A., Rahm, E.: Evaluation of entity resolution approaches on real-world match problems. PVLDB 3(1), 484–493 (2010)
5. Nentwig, M., Hartung, M., Ngomo, A., Rahm, E.: A survey of current link discovery frameworks. Semant. Web 8(3), 419–436 (2017)
6. Papadakis, G., Alexiou, G., Papastefanatos, G., Koutrika, G.: Schema-agnostic vs schema-based configurations for blocking methods on homogeneous data. PVLDB 9(4), 312–323 (2015)
7. Papadakis, G., Svirsky, J., Gal, A., Palpanas, T.: Comparative analysis of approximate blocking techniques for entity resolution. PVLDB 9(9), 684–695 (2016)
8. Schmachtenberg, M., Bizer, C., Paulheim, H.: Adoption of the linked data best practices in different topical domains. In: Mika, P., et al. (eds.) ISWC 2014. LNCS, vol. 8796, pp. 245–260. Springer, Cham (2014). https://doi.org/10.1007/978-3-319-11964-9_16

Context-Aware and Self-learning Dynamic Transport Scheduling in Hospitals

Pieter Bonte[1]([✉]), Femke Ongenae[1], Jeroen Schaballie[1],
Wim Vancroonenburg[2], and Bert Vankeirsbilck[1], and Filip De Turck[1]

[1] IBCN Research Group, INTEC Department, Ghent University,
iGent Building, Technology Park 15, 9052 Zwijnaarde, Belgium
Pieters.Bonte@ugent.be
[2] CODeS and iMinds-ITEC, Department of Computer Science, KU Leuven,
Leuven, Belgium

Abstract. The increase in available ICT infrastructure in hospitals offers cost reduction opportunities by optimizing various workflows, while maintaining quality of care. In this demonstrator-paper, we present a self-learning dashboard, for monitoring and learning the cause of delays of hospital transports. By identifying these causes, future delays in transport time can be reduced.

1 Introduction

Due to the financial pressure on the healthcare system, many hospitals struggle to balance budgets while maintaining quality. These hospitals are therefore investigating ways to optimize care delivery processes. Since organization of logistic services in hospitals may account for more than 30% of all hospital costs [6], it is certainly an area of interest. More specifically, huge opportunities exist in the transport of logistics of patients and equipment in terms of efficiency and cost reduction.

In previous work [3,5], we introduced the AORTA project[1], where we exploit the advent of the Internet of Things and intelligent decision support systems to automatically assign the most suitable staff member to a transport based on all the available information about the context (e.g. location of staff and patients and how crowded the hospital is), the staff (e.g. competences), the patient (e.g. physical condition) and the specific transportation task (e.g. pick-up location and priority). In this work we present a self-learning dashboard that is able to monitor and learn why hospital transports were late. By identifying the cause of these delays, future delays can be avoided. To give the hospital management control over what is learned, the learned causes are presented and converted to human readable sentences. The learning is performed on the historical data from a context layer that captures all information regarding the hospital. This context layer also provides data to a dynamic scheduler, that optimally dispatched

---

[1] www.iminds.be/en/projects/2015/03/10/aorta.

E. Blomqvist et al. (Eds.): ESWC 2017 Satellite Events, LNCS 10577, pp. 167–171, 2017.
https://doi.org/10.1007/978-3-319-70407-4_31

transports to the staff-members. Once the learned delays have been inspected and approved by the management, the context layer is updated and more accurate data can be provided to the scheduler, minimizing transports delays.

2 Architecture

The overall architecture of the simulated AORTA system is visualized in Fig. 1. This work uses a *Simulator* to represent the information within the hospital, more information regarding the real components that are being simulated in this work can be found in Ongenae et al. [5]. The simulator enables easy demonstrator purposes. Note that the simulation is based on realistic data captured from two Flemish hospitals.

The **Context Layer** integrates data resulting from various sources within the hospital, such as the floor plan of the hospital, the pathology of the patients, the capabilities of the staff, their locations captured by the IoT infrastructure, information about the tasks within the hospital, etc. To integrate all this heterogeneous data, a semantic model is utilized. This allows us to perform reasoning to automatically extract implicit statements, e.g. whether staff-members can perform specific tasks based on their capabilities. Since the *Context Layer* has a view on the current context within the hospital, it can provide accurate data to the scheduler.

The **Dynamic Scheduler** constructs an optimal transports schedule such that all the requests can be handled in a timely manner with an optimal use of resources [7]. To achieve this optimal rostering, the scheduler requests the dynamic context information from the Context Layer, e.g., the locations, availability, competences, work load & average walking speed of the staff, busy areas and possible causes of delay. This allows the scheduler to take the current situation into account when scheduling tasks. It constantly maintains an overall optimal schedule and updates this schedules as new requests and status updates of on-going transports come in. When a staff member indicates that a transport has been finished, the Context Layer will communicate this to the Dynamic

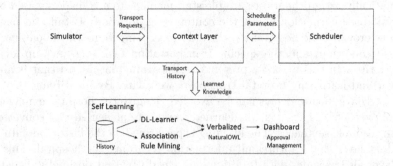

Fig. 1. The architecture of the simulation part of the AORTA system

Scheduler, which will then assign a new task to this staff member based on this overall optimized schedule.

The **Self-learning Module** keeps a historical overview of the context represented in the *Context Layer*. This information contains all the information regarding the executed transports, e.g. who executed the transport, what was the source and destination, what kind of transport mode was used, what were the pathologies of the patient, etc. Based on this historical context, the *Self-Learning Module* learns why transports in the past were delayed, such that these delays can be prevented in the future. For example, the module could learn that certain transports during the visiting hour on Friday are often late and more time should be reserved for them. The incorporation of the knowledge, modeled in the ontology, allows to learn more accurate rules. Furthermore, learning semantic rules allows to understand and validate the learned results. Once the rules have been learned, they can be inspected and approved by the management. Upon approval, the learned rules update the *Context Layer*, such that more accurate information can be provided to the *Dynamic Scheduler*.

3   Implementation

This section details the implementation of the previous presented components, with specific focus on the *Context Layer* and the *Self-Learning Module*.

To model all the hospital domain knowledge, an ontology was constructed by extending the Task Model Ontology[2], the Ambient-aware Continuous Care Ontology[3] and the Amigo Location Ontology[4]. Currently RDFox[5] is supported as triple store to capture all the context information. Semantic reasoning is implemented by defining rules. There is also support for graph databases such as Neo4j[6], however lacking the reasoning capabilities.

Two implementations [2,3] of the Self-Learning component have been researched: one utilizing Inductive Logic Programming by the use of DL-Learner [4] and one using extensions of Association Rule Mining to enable mining over semantic data. Both are capable of learning the causes of various transport delays.

Each of these techniques has its pro's and con's, e.g. by exploiting the knowledge in the ontology the ILP technique is more accurate, however the association rule mining technique scales better. The learned rules are presented to the management for final confirmation through a visual interfaces, as depicted in Fig. 2. The semantic learned rules are converted to human readable text through the use of NaturalOWL [1] that can convert OWL Axioms to sentences. By defining how the classes and properties in the ontology should be verbalized, NaturalOWL can

---

[2] www.semanticdesktop.org/ontologies/2008/05/20/tmo/.
[3] users.intec.ugent.be/pieter.bonte/ontology/accio.htm.
[4] gforge.inria.fr/projects/amigo/.
[5] www.cs.ox.ac.uk/isg/tools/RDFox/.
[6] https://neo4j.com.

Late Transports

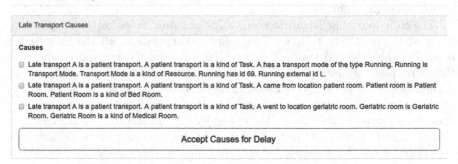

Fig. 2. An overview of the learned rules in human readable format

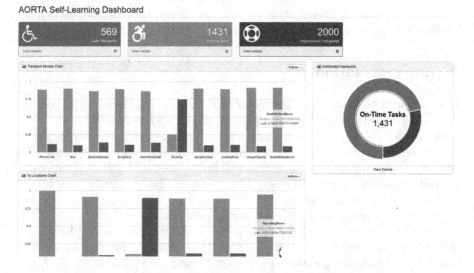

Fig. 3. The dashboard visualizing the transport distributions.

generate fluent human readable text. This makes it easier for the management to interpret the learned rules.

Once one or more learned rules are verified by management, the *Context Layer* is updated with the newly learned knowledge. This is done by calculating the average delay for the identified late transports and this delay is then added by the *Context Layer* when a new transports needs to be scheduled that adheres to the learned rule. Furthermore, a dashboard provides management a real-time overview of the distribution of transports that are on time and those that are late. As shown in Fig. 3, a few straightforward delay causes are already presented in the dashboard, i.e. the percentage of transports that are late or on time for each of the transports modes (i.e. bed, wheelchair, running,etc.), the type of room the transport came from and the type of destination.

4 Demonstrator

In the demonstrator we show a simulation of a hospital setting where a number of staff-members are dispatched to perform various transports. The dynamic scheduler will optimally schedule the transport. The simulator can be manipulated to introduce various sources of delay, allowing the self-learning module to detect these problems and update the context-layer such that more time is taken in the future for these kinds of transports and less delays occur. The demonstrator shows that after taken into account the learned rules, less transports are late. A short video presenting the described functionality can be found on http:// pbonte.github.io/aorta/.

5 Conclusions

In this paper we presented a self-learning dashboard for the AORTA system that is able to learn and optimize hospital transports. By integrating data generated in the hospital in a semantic enabled context layer, intelligent decisions can be made. Furthermore, a dynamic scheduler can optimally dispatch transports and a self-learning module can identify the delays of late transports and take steps to eliminate these delays in the future. The dashboard present the learned causes of transport delay in readable text, allowing management to easily inspect and approve the learned knowledge.

Acknowledgment. This research was partly funded by the AORTA project, co-funded by the AIO, imec, Xperthis, Televic Healthcare, AZMM and ZNA.

References

1. Androutsopoulos, I., et al.: Generating natural language descriptions from owl ontologies: the naturalowl system. J. Artif. Intell. Res. **48**, 671–715 (2013)
2. Bonte, P., Ongenae, F., Hoogstoel, E., De Turck, F.: Mining semantic rules for optimizing transport assignments in hospitals, pp. 1–6 (2016)
3. Bonte, P., Ongenae, F., De Turck, F.: Learning semantic rules for intelligent transport scheduling in hospitals. In: Know@LOD (2016)
4. Lehmann, J.: Dl-learner: learning concepts in description logics. J. Mach. Learn. Res. **10**, 2639–2642 (2009)
5. Ongenae, F., Bonte, P., Schaballie, J., Vankeirsbilck, B., De Turck, F.: Semantic context consolidation and rule learning for optimized transport assignments in hospitals. In: Sack, H., Rizzo, G., Steinmetz, N., Mladenić, D., Auer, S., Lange, C. (eds.) ESWC 2016. LNCS, vol. 9989, pp. 88–92. Springer, Cham (2016). https:// doi.org/10.1007/978-3-319-47602-5_19
6. Hastreiter, S., et al.: Benchmarking logistics services in German hospitals: a research status quo. In: ICSSSM, pp. 803–808 (2013)
7. Vancroonenburg, W., Esprit, E., Smet, P., Vanden Berghe, G.: Optimizing internal logistic flows in hospitals by dynamic pick-up and delivery models. In: Proceedings of the 11th International Conference on the Practice and Theory of Automated Timetabling (2016)

RML and FnO: Shaping DBpedia Declaratively

Ben De Meester[✉], Wouter Maroy, Anastasia Dimou,
Ruben Verborgh, and Erik Mannens

IDLab, Department of Electronics and Information Systems,
Ghent University – imec, Ghent, Belgium
{ben.demeester,wouter.maroy,anastasia.dimou,
ruben.verborgh,erik.mannens}@ugent.be

Abstract. DBpedia data is largely generated from extracting and parsing the wikitext from the infoboxes of Wikipedia. This generation process is handled by the DBpedia Extraction Framework (DBpedia EF). This framework currently consists of *data transformations*, a series of custom hard-coded steps which parse the wikitext, and *schema transformations*, which model the resulting RDF data. Therefore, applying changes to the resulting RDF data needs both Semantic Web expertise and development within the DBpedia EF. As such, the current DBpedia data is being shaped by a small amount of core developers. However, by describing both schema and data transformations declaratively, we shape and generate DBpedia data using solely declarations, splitting the concerns between implementation and modeling. The parsing functions development is decoupled from the DBpedia EF, and other data transformation functions can easily be integrated during DBpedia data generation. This demo showcases an interactive Web application that allows non-technical users to (re-)shape the DBpedia data and use external data transformation functions, solely by editing a mapping document via HTML controls.

Keywords: DBpedia · Data transformations · FnO · Linked Data generation · RML

1 Introduction

One of the most widely known Linked Datasets is DBpedia, a crowd-sourced community effort to extract structured information from Wikipedia and make this information available on the Web [1]. Data from DBpedia is generated using the DBpedia Extraction Framework (DBpedia EF) in two parts: the first part directly maps relationships from the relational database of the underlying application on which Wikipedia is built (WikiMedia), and the second part extracts and parses data from the article texts and infobox templates within the articles [2].

The successive steps of extracting the Wikipedia articles, selecting the right content, parsing the values, creating the resources and adding the relationships to generate RDF data are currently performed by the DBpedia EF in custom, hard-coded steps. For example, the founding date is extracted from the infobox

E. Blomqvist et al. (Eds.): ESWC 2017 Satellite Events, LNCS 10577, pp. 172–177, 2017.
https://doi.org/10.1007/978-3-319-70407-4_32

(e.g., 19-4-1839 for Belgium), parsed into the correct date format (a *data transformation* function generating 1839-04-19), and linked with the resource for Belgium using the correct DBpedia predicate (a *schema transformation* generating the triple dbr:Belgium dbo:foundingDate "1839-04-19"^^xsd:date).

Limited changes in the schema (e.g., adding a predicate-object pair) are currently possible using the DBpedia mapping wiki, but more extensive changes, both in the schema (e.g., using a different ontology) or in the data (e.g., using a different parsing function) involve changing the DBpedia EF source code. Thus, desired changes in the resulting RDF data currently needs both Semantic Web expertise and development within the DBpedia EF. These combined requirements are currently met by only a small amount of core developers to shape DBpedia data. As adding schema or data transformations is complex, the DBpedia EF inhibits problems that are currently not easily solved. For instance, Blake et. al. [8] unveiled quality issues in DBpedia as the current extraction framework does not support basic geographic calculations, e.g., calculating the population density. Being a custom, hard-coded framework, the DBpedia EF does not easily allow generating alternative RDF data solving these issues.

A fully declarative solution would no longer require development effort when apply changes to the DBpedia data. Instead, only editing the mapping document that shapes DBpedia is needed. This involves decoupling both the schema and data transformations from the DBpedia EF implementation. Previous work[1] has already extracted the schema transformations as RML mapping documents [5], and our recent work – which this demo accompanies – provides an approach to integrate data and schema transformations declaratively [4]. Before, changing the data transformation functions would require developers to improve the implementation of the DBpedia EF. Now, data modelers without technical background can change and replace data transformation functions or schema transformations by editing the mapping documents. Thus, the concerns between developers and modelers is decoupled. Moreover, the data transformation functions can be reused for different use cases, not only for DBpedia data.

This demo, which is available at https://fnoio.github.io/dbpedia-demo/, shows how declarative data and schema transformations make it easier to apply changes in DBpedia data. Users can alter among different data transformation functions – even functions not yet supported in the current DBpedia EF – by solely adjusting single fields within the mapping document. Using exemplary Wikipedia articles, the users can immediately verify their changes, as they are reflected at the generated Linked Data for each Wikipedia article. This Web application shows that technical knowledge about the DBpedia EF is no longer needed to make significant changes when shaping the DBpedia data.

---

[1] http://www.mail-archive.com/dbpedia-discussion@lists.sourceforge.net/msg07837.html.

2 Background: Integrated Schema and Data Transformations Using RML and FnO

Generating Linked Data involves making changes to both the schema and transforming the data values of the data sources [7]. The same is the case for DBpedia. On the one hand, schema transformations are needed to make sure the right ontologies and vocabularies are used, and that the values are related as intended, with the right data type (e.g., modeling the founding date of Belgium using the correct predicate of the DBpedia ontology and using a date as data type results in dbr:Belgium dbo:foundingDate "1839-04-19"^^xsd:date). On the other hand, very specific data transformations are required for DBpedia to parse the manually entered data in the Wikipedia infoboxes, as the input data can be inserted using *different formats* for the same data type (e.g., 04-10-1830, and October 4th 1830 denote the same date), using *different units* (e.g., entering degrees in Fahrenheit in a Celsius-valued field), or having *typos and misspellings*. In the current DBpedia EF these functions are hard-coded, thus changing these specific functions (or using different ones) entails a significant development effort.

We aligned the following technologies:

- RML [5] – a mapping language to define *schema transformations* to generate Linked Data derived from heterogeneous data, wikitext in our case; and
- FnO [3] – an ontology to describe *data transformations*, independently of their implementation and the data to which they are applied.

This way, schema transformations may be aligned with data transformations. Moreover, the aforementioned alignment does not restrict a mapping processor to support a specific set of data transformations.

This integration was kept minimal by using a single class and predicate[2]. The resulting implementation depends on the RMLProcessor[3] and a generic Function Processor[4]. We have uncoupled the DBpedia parsing functions from the DBpedia EF and re-published them as a stand-alone library[5], and allowed describing more advanced schema and data transformations declaratively [4].

3 Easily Shaping DBpedia

By decoupling the declaration from the implementation, as we explain in details at De Meester et al. [4], users without technical expertise can shape the generated DBpedia data by directly editing the DBpedia mapping document. The current DBpedia EF allows limited changes in the schema transformations without development effort using the DBpedia mapping wiki. The fully declarative solution allows more editing options: users can apply changes to both schema transformations (e.g., adding/removing types to resources and changing predicates),

---

[2] http://semweb.datasciencelab.be/ns/fnml/.
[3] https://github.com/RMLio/RML-Mapper/tree/extension-fno.
[4] https://github.com/FnOio/function-processor-java.
[5] https://github.com/FnOio/dbpedia-parsing-functions-scala.

and data transformations (e.g., changing the parameters of the parsing functions, using different parsing functions, or even using externally defined functions). The data transformation functions are no longer restricted by the DBpedia EF.

https://fnoio.github.io/dbpedia-demo/ shows an interactive Web application that allows users to easily apply changes, both for schema and data transformations, to the DBpedia mapping documents (Fig. 1). The Web application does not require users to learn a new syntax, instead, HTML form elements are used to make changes to the underlying mapping document. After the extended RMLProcessor executes the updated transformations, users can review the applied changes to the newly generated RDF data.

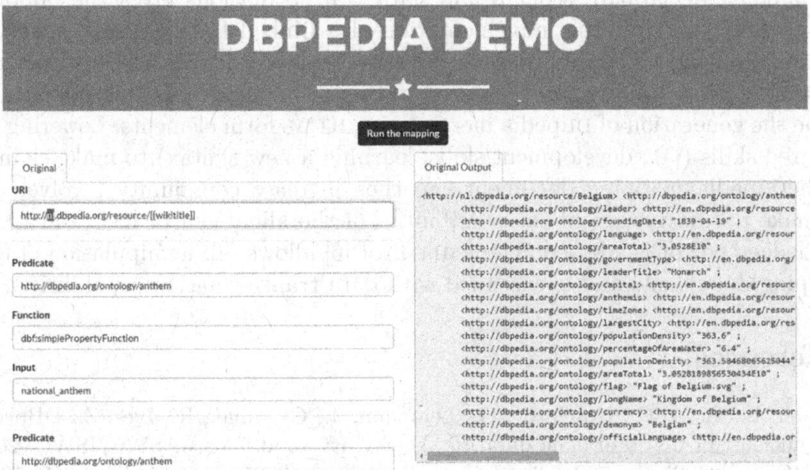

Fig. 1. When DBpedia is fully shaped declaratively, simple form controls can be used to edit the DBpedia mapping document and technical expertise about the DBpedia EF is no longer needed.

Users can generate RDF data for different types of Wikipedia infoboxes (e.g., infoboxes denoting persons or countries), using different Wikipedia articles (e.g., Belgium or The United States of America). Relying on HTML form elements, such as dropdowns and radio buttons, users can apply changes to the mapping document. Generic data transformations as defined by the popular data cleansing tool OpenRefine[6] are also selectable. This showcases that the restriction on which data transformation functions you can use is lifted. Via the *Generate* button, the updated mapping document is executed server-side. The resulting RDF data is returned to the users for inspection, together with the mapping document. The mapping documents with aligned RML and FnO statements can then be used in the updated DBpedia EF to generate the RDF data.

---

[6] https://github.com/OpenRefine/OpenRefine/wiki/GREL-Functions.

The implementation[7] shows that the Web application entirely depends on the mapping document, which contains the aligned declarative schema and data transformations. The mapping document is changed based on user interactions and saved as JSON-LD, instead of Turtle, for easier JavaScript manipulation. The server implementation is also provided, and as can be inspected, this is merely a wrapper around the extended RMLProcessor, no case specific development was needed.

4   Conclusions

Integrating data and schema transformations in mapping documents which contain aligned declarative schema and data transformations gives the opportunity to fully decouple the implementation of a Linked Data generation system without limiting its capabilities, as we show in more details at De Meester et al. [4]. The Web application presented in this demo showcases this potential to shape the generation of DBpedia merely using HTML form elements. Lowering the required skills (i.e., development skills, learning a new syntax) to make changes in theDBpedia mapping document can thus increase community involvement. To make full advantage of the possibilities of the alignment of RML and FnO, a full-fledged editor is advised. The RMLEditor [6] allows full manipulation of RML mapping documents and is extended with data transformation capabilities.

References

1. Auer, S., Bizer, C., Kobilarov, G., Lehmann, J., Cyganiak, R., Ives, Z.: DBpedia: a nucleus for a web of open data. In: Aberer, K., et al. (eds.) ASWC/ISWC -2007. LNCS, vol. 4825, pp. 722–735. Springer, Heidelberg (2007). https://doi.org/10.1007/978-3-540-76298-0_52
2. Auer, S., Lehmann, J.: What Have Innsbruck and Leipzig in Common? Extracting semantics from wiki content. In: Franconi, E., Kifer, M., May, W. (eds.) ESWC 2007. LNCS, vol. 4519, pp. 503–517. Springer, Heidelberg (2007). https://doi.org/10.1007/978-3-540-72667-8_36
3. De Meester, B., Dimou, A., Verborgh, R., Mannens, E.: An ontology to semantically declare and describe functions. In: Sack, H., Rizzo, G., Steinmetz, N., Mladenić, D., Auer, S., Lange, C. (eds.) ESWC 2016. LNCS, vol. 9989, pp. 46–49. Springer, Cham (2016). https://doi.org/10.1007/978-3-319-47602-5_10
4. De Meester, B., Maroy, W., Dimou, A., Verborgh, R., Mannens, E.: Declarative data transformations for Linked Data generation: the case of DBpedia. In: Blomqvist, E., Maynard, D., Gangemi, A., Hoekstra, R., Hitzler, P., Hartig, O. (eds.) ESWC 2017. LNCS, vol. 10250, pp. 33–48. Springer, Cham (2017). https://doi.org/10.1007/978-3-319-58451-5_3
5. Dimou, A., Vander Sande, M., Colpaert, P., Verborgh, R., Mannens, E., Van de Walle, R.: RML: a generic language for integrated RDF mappings of heterogeneous data. In: Bizer, C., Heath, T., Auer, S., Berners-Lee, T. (eds.) Proceedings of the 7th Workshop on Linked Data on the Web, CEUR Workshop Proceedings, vol. 1184, April 2014

---

[7] https://github.com/FnOio/dbpedia-demo.

6. Heyvaert, P., Dimou, A., Herregodts, A.-L., Verborgh, R., Schuurman, D., Mannens, E., Walle, R.: RMLEditor: a graph-based mapping editor for linked data mappings. In: Sack, H., Blomqvist, E., d'Aquin, M., Ghidini, C., Ponzetto, S.P., Lange, C. (eds.) ESWC 2016. LNCS, vol. 9678, pp. 709–723. Springer, Cham (2016). https://doi.org/10.1007/978-3-319-34129-3_43
7. Rahm, E., Do, H.H.: Data cleaning: problems and current approaches. IEEE Data Eng. Bull. **23**(4), 3–13 (2000)
8. Regalia, B., Janowicz, K., Gao, S.: VOLT: a provenance-producing, transparent SPARQL proxy for the on-demand computation of linked data and its application to spatiotemporally dependent data. In: The Semantic Web. Latest Advances and New Domains (2016)

Querying the Web of Data
(QuWeDa 2017)

Parallelizing Federated SPARQL Queries in Presence of Replicated Data

Thomas Minier[1]($\boxtimes$), Gabriela Montoya[2], Hala Skaf-Molli[1], and Pascal Molli[1]

[1] LS2N, Nantes University, Nantes, France
{thomas.minier,hala.skaf,pascal.molli}@univ-nantes.fr
[2] Department of Computer Science, Aalborg University, Aalborg, Denmark
gmontoya@cs.aau.dk

Abstract. Federated query engines have been enhanced to exploit new data localities created by replicated data, e.g., FEDRA. However, existing replication aware federated query engines mainly focus on pruning sources during the source selection and query decomposition in order to reduce intermediate results thanks to data locality. In this paper, we implement a replication-aware parallel join operator: PEN. This operator can be used to exploit replicated data during query execution. For existing replication-aware federated query engines, this operator exploits replicated data to parallelize the execution of joins and reduce execution time. For Triple Pattern Fragment (TPF) clients, this operator exploits the availability of several TPF servers exposing the same dataset to share the load among the servers. We implemented PEN in the federated query engine FEDX with the replicated-aware source selection FEDRA and in the reference TPF client. We empirically evaluated the performance of engines extended with the PEN operator and the experimental results suggest that our extensions outperform the existing approaches in terms of execution time and balance of load among the servers, respectively.

Keywords: Linked Data · Parallel query processing · Fragment replication · Federated SPARQL Queries Processing · Triple Pattern Fragment · Load balancing

1 Introduction

Following the Linked Data principles, billions of RDF triples are made available through SPARQL endpoints. Even if federated SPARQL query engines [1,9,17] allow to execute SPARQL queries over multiple SPARQL endpoints, data availability and reliability of SPARQL endpoints is still an issue [5].

Data replication is a common practice to overcome availability issues in distributed databases [15]. However, data replication in Linked Data is more challenging: the autonomy of data providers hosting SPARQL endpoints, and data consumers running federated query engines, prevent data replication to be designed. The fragmentation schema and the replication schema remain unknown

© Springer International Publishing AG 2017
E. Blomqvist et al. (Eds.): ESWC 2017 Satellite Events, LNCS 10577, pp. 181–196, 2017.
https://doi.org/10.1007/978-3-319-70407-4_33

until a data consumer defines a federation of SPARQL endpoints in a federated query engine.

Existing replication-aware [13,14] and duplicate-aware [16] federated query engines focus on source selection and query decomposition in order to prune redundant sources and use data-locality to reduce intermediate results. We point out that replicated data can also be used to parallelize query processing, and consequently reduce execution time.

In the previous work [12], we proposed PENELOOP, abbreviated as PEN in this paper, a replication-aware parallel join operator. More precisely, PEN solves the parallel join problem with fragment replication (PJP-FR). Given a SPARQL query and a set of data sources with replicated fragments, the problem is to use all data sources to reduce query execution time while preserving answer completeness and reducing data redundancy.

In contrast to *inter-operator parallelism* proposed in the state-of-the-art federated query engines [1,17], PEN introduces parallelization at the operator level in order to preserve properties ensured by replicated-aware source selection strategies [13] and replication-aware query decompositions [14]. PEN is based on Bound Join operator implemented in FEDX [17]. Bound joins were originally designed to reduce the number of requests sent in a nested loop join [15]. PEN extends bound joins processing to use all relevant endpoints with replicated fragments and distribute join processing among them.

In this work, we extend TPF client [18] with PEN. PEN will exploit the availability of several TPF servers exposing the same dataset to share the load among the servers. We implemented PEN in the reference TPF client. This paper presents our contribution to SPARQL federation and TPF federation: (i) We present PEN, a novel replication-aware parallel join operator that uses replicated fragments to reduce query execution time.

(ii) We extend federated query engine FEDX [17] and the source selection strategy FEDRA [13] and the TPF client with PEN.

(iii) We experiment FEDX, FEDX + FEDRA FEDX + FEDRA + PEN and TPF + PEN in different setups. We show that FEDX + FEDRA + PEN outperforms FEDX and FEDX + FEDRA in terms of execution time while preserving properties of FEDRA in terms of reduced number of transferred tuples and answer completeness. The improvements are significative for queries with a large number of intermediate results. (iv) We show that TPF + PEN does not improve execution time, however, it equally distributes the load among servers.

The paper is organized as follows: Sect. 2 provides background and motivations. Section 3 presents the PEN approach and algorithm. Section 4 presents our experimental setup and describes our results. Section 5 summarizes related works. Finally, conclusions and future works are outlined in Sect. 6.

2   Background and Motivations

For replicating data, we follow the approach of replicated fragments introduced in [13,14]. Data consumers replicate fragments composed of RDF triples

(a) Fragment description

triples(f): { dbr:A_Knight's_Tale
               dbo:director dbr:Brian_Helgeland,
               dbr:A_Thousand_Clowns
               dbo:director dbr:Fred_Coe,
               dbr:Alfie_(1966_film)
               dbo:director dbr:Lewis_Gilbert,
               dbr:A_Moody_Christmas
               dbo:director dbr:Trent_O'Donnell,
               dbr:A_Movie dbo:director
               dbr:Bruce_Conner, · · · }

fd(f): <dbpedia, ?film dbo:director ?director>

(b) Replicated fragments

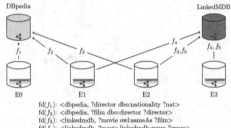

fd(f_1): <dbpedia, ?director dbo:nationality ?nat>
fd(f_2): <dbpedia, ?film dbo:director ?director>
fd(f_3): <linkedmdb, ?movie owl:sameAs ?film>
fd(f_4): <linkedmdb, ?movie linkedmdb:genre ?genre>
fd(f_5): <linkedmdb, ?genre linkedmdb:film_genre_name ?name>

(c) Federated SPARQL query $Q1$ and its relevant fragments and endpoints

```
select distinct *
where {
    ?director dbo:nationality ?nat.          (tp1)
    ?film db:director ?director.             (tp2)
    ?movie owl:sameAs ?film.                 (tp3)
    ?movie linkedmdb:genre ?genre.           (tp4)
    ?genre linkedmdb:film_genre_name ?gname. (tp5)
}
```

Triple pattern	Relevant fragment	Relevant endpoint
tp_1	f_1	E_0
tp_2	f_2	E_1, E_2
tp_3	f_3	E_2
tp_4	f_4	E_1, E_3
tp_5	f_5	E_2, E_3

Fig. 1. A federation with replicated fragments

that satisfy a given triple pattern. Figure 1a shows a fragment from DBpedia which contains RDF triples that match the triple pattern ?film dbo:director ?director. Fragments are described using a 2-tuple fd that indicates the authoritative source of the fragment, e.g. DBpedia, and the triple pattern met by the fragment's triples.

Figure 1b shows a federation with four SPARQL endpoints: E_0, E_1, E_2 and E_3. These endpoints expose replicated fragments from DBpedia and Linked-MDB. Figure 1c describes a federated SPARQL query $Q1$ executed against this federation and its relevant fragments. For instance, the triple pattern tp_4 has relevant fragment f_4 that has been replicated at E_1 and E_3.

The logical plan of Q1 produced by FEDX [17] is presented in Fig. 2a. As FEDX is not replication-aware, i.e., it does not know that the evaluation of tp_2 at E_1 or E_2 will produce the same results, query execution following this plan will retrieve redundant data from endpoints and increase significantly the query execution time.

The FEDRA [13] replication-aware source selection prunes redundant sources in order to minimize intermediate results. FEDRA selects E_2 for tp_2, tp_3 and tp_5, E_1 for tp_4 and E_0 for tp_1. Next, FEDRA lets FEDX builds the logical plan of Fig. 2b that minimizes intermediate results. Notice that this plan sends a large subquery to E_2, which can be heavy to compute, reducing the endpoint's availability. Therefore, data locality have a negative impact on load balancing by creating hotspots.

(a) FEDX Left-Linear plan for $Q1$ **(b)** FEDX + FEDRA Left-Linear plan for $Q1$

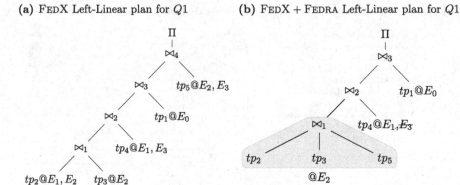

Fig. 2. Logical plans generated by FEDX and FEDX + FEDRA for $Q1$

As pointed in Fig. 2b, FEDRA has removed E_3 from selected sources of tp_4. However, it also removes an opportunity of parallelization. Indeed, it is possible to use both endpoints to perform in parallel half of the join of $\bowtie_2$ with E_1 and the other half with E_3, as they mirror each other[1].

The same parallelization principle can be applied in the context of Triple Pattern Fragments (TPF) interface [18]. Traditionally, a TPF client decompose a SPARQL query Q into simple triple patterns queries (TPQs) evaluated by a TPF server, and results are joined locally. TPQs processing can be distributed among TPF servers that replicate the same relevant data for Q.

Moreover, as TPF interfaces only accept TPQs, a TPF client cannot use data locality during query processing. This generate more remote HTTP calls, but also prevent the creation of hotspots as those seen before. Parallelization of these remote calls will then balance the load among servers and increase their availability.

Such parallelization can be obtained with a replication-aware query decomposer or with intra-operator [15] parallelism. In this paper, we focus on intra-operator parallelism because it can be easily embedded in current (federated) query engines. Consequently, the challenge is to build replication-aware parallel operators to speed-up query execution.

Parallel Join Problem with Fragment Replication (PJP-FR). Given S_1 and S_2 two disjoint sets of replicated data sources. A set of replicated data sources is a set of endpoints that replicate the same fragments. Given a join $\bowtie_i$ between O_1 and O_2 with relevant sources respectively, S_1 and S_2. The parallel join problem with fragment replication is to distribute the execution of join $\bowtie_i$ among endpoints of S_1 and S_2 in order to minimize the execution time while guaranteeing complete query answers.

---

[1] Note that joins $\bowtie_1$ and $\bowtie_3$ cannot be parallelized in this way, because $\bowtie_1$ is a local join performed at E_2, and tp_1 has only one relevant source.

3   PEN: A Replication-Aware Nested Loop Join Operator

PEN is a solution for parallel join problem with fragment replication with the following assumptions: (i) we focus on nested loop join (NLJ), (ii) we do not consider the load of different endpoints, (iii) we consider that replicated fragments are synchronized, (iv) replicated sources are determined by a replication-aware source selection algorithm, such as FEDRA before pruning.

PEN can be used for any federation of SPARQL processing services, *endpoint*, that provides access to replicated data. These services can process unrestricted SPARQL queries, e.g., SPARQL endpoints, or restricted SPARQL queries, e.g., TPF servers.

3.1   NLJ Processing

During a NLJ processing, the query engine iteratively evaluates each triple pattern, starting with a single pattern and substituting the set of mappings produced by the pattern's execution in the next evaluation step. Even if a NLJ is more efficient when the first evaluated triple pattern is more selective than the others, it still produces many remote requests in a distributed setting. For federated SPARQL queries, Schwarte et al. [17] proposed the Bound Join (BJ) operator to minimize the number of join steps and the number of requests sent in nested loop joins. A BJ consists of a nested loop join where sets of mappings are grouped in *blocks*, *i.e.*, as a single subquery using SPARQL UNION constructs. The subquery is then sent to the relevant endpoint in a single remote request. This technique acts as a distributed semijoin and allows to reduce the number of requests by a factor equivalent to the size of the *block*.

SPARQL query processing with Triple Pattern Fragments [18] (TPF) also resolves joins in a NLJ fashion and rely on dynamic iterators that optimize locally each join step. The TPF reference server provides only support for BJ with block size $b = 1$, i.e., simple nested loop (SNJ) join. In the following sections we detail a new strategy to evaluate BJs, but naturally this applies to the particular case of SNJ.

PEN proposes to parallelize the BJ operator itself. Instead of sending all blocks to the same endpoint, PEN uses the knowledge about replicated sources to further parallelize the bound join operator. When processing a join in a basic graph pattern (BGP), if the current triple pattern has N relevant sources that replicate the same fragment, PEN sends each block to a different endpoint in a Round Robin fashion, *i.e.*, the block b_i is sent to the endpoint E_k, $k = i \mod N$. Therefore, PEN does not increase the number of remote calls while increasing the parallelization during join processing.

3.2   PEN Algorithm

PEN is defined as part of a pipelining approach allowing for intermediate results to be processed by the next operator as soon as they are ready, providing higher throughput than a blocking model.

Algorithm 1. PENELOOP join algorithm

Input: $tp = <s, p, o>$: a triple pattern, $E = \{E_0, \ldots, E_{m-1}\}$: relevant endpoints of tp, $NextOp$: next operator in the pipeline, b: maximum number of mappings per block

Data: M_i: a set of mappings produced by the previous operator in the pipeline, $B = \{M_1, \ldots, M_n\}$: block of sets of mappings waiting to be sent

Init: $B = \{\}$, $k = 0$

```
1  SendBlock(block, tp):                    11 ⨽ onResults(R):
2  |  Q = GroupedSubquery(block, tp)        12 |  Send(R) to NextOp
3  |  SendQuery(Q) to E_k                    13 ⨽ onEnd():
4  |  B = {}                                 14 |  if Size(B) ≥ 0 then
5  |  k = (k + 1) mod Size(E)                15 |  |  SendBlock(B, tp)
6  ⨽ onMappings(M_i):                        16 |  end
7  |  B = B ∪ {M_i}                          17 |  Close()
8  |  if Size(B) ≥ b then
9  |  |  SendBlock(B, tp)
10 |  end
```

Algorithm 1 describes the PEN algorithm using an event driven paradigm. Sets of mappings M_i are produced by the previous operator in the pipeline and sent in continuous to PEN operator. When a set M_i arrives (Line 6), it is stored in the next block B. When B reaches its maximum size b (Line 8), PEN generates a subquery in a Bound Join fashion using B and tp (Line 2). Then, the subquery is sent to the endpoint E_k (Line 3), B is cleared and the next endpoint is selected using our Round Robin approach (Line 5).

When results, *i.e.*, new sets of mappings, arrive from the requested endpoints (Line 11), they are sent to the next operator in the pipeline. Finally, when the previous operator has completed its work and will not produce any more data (Line 13), PEN sends the last non-empty block and then close the operator.

In the following, we illustrate PEN processing for the query $Q1$ (Fig. 1c) using the query plan generated by FEDX + FEDRA (Fig. 2b). For simplicity, we fix $b = 2$.

Figure 3 illustrates a snapshot of the pipeline during the evaluation of the triple pattern tp_4 of the query $Q1$. We focus on processing of join $\bowtie_2$, performed using PEN. Two blocks $\{M_1, M_2\}$ and $\{M_3, M_4\}$ have been already sent to E_1 and E_3, respectively. A set of mappings M_5 arrived from the join $\bowtie_1$ and was placed in the next block. When another set of mappings M_6 arrives, the block will be full and sent to the next endpoint E_1. Join $\bowtie_2$ ends when no more mappings are produced by join $\bowtie_1$.

4 Experimental Study

The goal of the experimental study is to evaluate the impact of PEN parallelization on execution time. For federated SPARQL queries, such reduction is

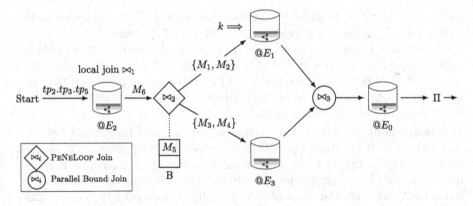

Fig. 3. Join processing of federated query $Q1$ with PEN

obtained without degrading the reduced number of transferred tuples and the answer completeness granted by FEDRA. For Triple Pattern Fragments, PEN parallelization has a positive effect on load balancing between servers.

For federated SPARQL queries, we compare the performance of the federated query engine FEDX alone, FEDX with the addition of FEDRA (FEDX + FEDRA) and FEDX with both FEDRA and PEN (FEDX + FEDRA + PEN). For TPF, we compare the performance of the reference TPF client alone and an extension with PEN (TPF + PEN). Note that combination of TPF with FEDRA is not possible because the TPF server cannot take advantage of data locality.

We expect to see that FEDX + FEDRA + PEN exhibits lower query execution time than FEDX and FEDX + FEDRA, while maintaining the same number of transferred tuples and answer completeness. We also expect to see that TPF + PENexhibits similar query execution time than the reference, but reduce the number of HTTP calls addressed per server.

Dataset and Queries: We use one instance of the Waterloo SPARQL Diversity Test Suite (WatDiv) synthetic dataset [2,3] with 10^5 triples. We generate 50,000 queries from 500 templates. Next, we unbound subjects and objects of each query. 100 queries with at least one join are then randomly picked to be executed against our federations. Generated queries are STAR, PATH and SNOWFLAKE shaped queries, we use the DISTINCT modifier.

Queries that failed to deliver an answer due to a query engine internal error are excluded from the final results.

Federations: For the SPARQL endpoints, we consider replication of dataset fragments, i.e., partial replication. We setup three federations with respectively 10, 20 and 30 SPARQL endpoints, and generate three versions of each of these federations by randomizing the fragmentation schema. Every schema is distinct from the others. Fragments are created from the 100 random queries and are replicated exactly three times to provide opportunities of parallelization. For the TPF federations we consider TPF server that provide access to the same

dataset, i.e., total replication. For experiments with TPF, we setup up to five
TPF servers, each one using four workers and a HDT backend [7].

To measure the number of transferred tuples and the repartition of HTTP
calls, query engines accesses SPARQL endpoints and TPF servers through a
proxy. All the federation endpoints and TPF servers are deployed on the same
machine, and to simulate the network latency, the proxies were configured to
add a delay of 30 ms to each request.

Hardware configuration: One machine with Intel Xeon E5-2680 v2 2.80 GHz
and 128 GB of RAM hosts the SPARQL endpoints and performs the queries.
Each SPARQL endpoint is deployed using Jena Fuseki 1.1.1[2]. Fuseki is configured to handle incoming queries on only one executing thread to increase the
stress load and study the effect of the parallelization done by the engine. Endpoints have no limitations in term of memory used.

Implementations: FEDX + FEDRA implementation[3] (in Java) has been modified to preserve the multiple sources that provide the same relevant fragments.
For TPF, PEN is implemented on top of the reference TPF client[4].

Additionally, FEDX join processing has been modified to remove some redundant synchronization barriers imposed by FEDX on the first join of a plan, *i.e.*,
the right operand can start execution before the left one has finished its evaluation, and to use PEN operator when possible[5]. Every configuration of this
experimental study has received the same modifications. Proxies used to measure results are implemented in Java 1.7, using the Apache HttpComponents
Client library 4.3.5[6].

4.1 PEN with Federated SPARQL Queries

Evaluation Metrics: (*i*) *Execution Time (ET):* is the elapsed time since the
query is posed until the complete answer is produced. We used a timeout of
1800 seconds. (*ii*) *Number of parallelized queries (NPQ):* is the number of queries
where at least one join has been parallelized by PEN. Queries marked as *improved*
have a lower execution time (*ET*) with FEDX+FEDRA+PEN than with FEDX+
FEDRA. (*iii*) *Number of Transferred Tuples (NTT):* is the number of transferred tuples from all the endpoints to the query engine during a query evaluation. This metric is only used for federated SPARQL queries. (*iv*) *Completeness
(C):* is the ratio between the answers produced by the query execution engine
and the answers produced by the evaluation of the query over the set of all triples
available in the federation; values range between 0.0 and 1.0.

Results presented for *ET*, *NTT* and *C* correspond to the average
over the three versions generated for each size of federation. In all cases,

---

[2] http://jena.apache.org/, January 2015.
[3] https://github.com/gmontoya/fedra, June 2016.
[4] https://github.com/LinkedDataFragments/Client.js, June 2017.
[5] Implementation available at: https://github.com/Callidon/peneloop-fedx.
[6] https://hc.apache.org/, October 2014.

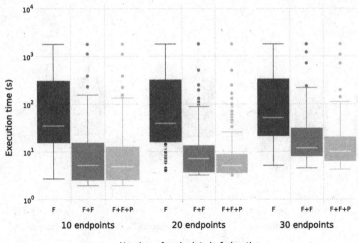

Fig. 4. Average execution time with FEDX (F), FEDX + FEDRA (F+F) and FEDX + FEDRA + PEN (F+F+P).

FEDX + FEDRA + PEN is able to produce the same answers as FEDX + FEDRA for all queries (detailed completeness (C) results are presented in [12].)

Statistical Analysis: The Wilcoxon signed rank test [19] for paired non-uniform data is used to study the significance of the improvements on performance obtained when the join execution benefits from replicated fragments.[7]

Execution Time. Figure 4 summarizes the execution time (ET) for the three federations. Execution time (ET) with FEDX + FEDRA + PEN is better for all federations than with FEDX and FEDX + FEDRA. As queries have unbounded subjects and unbounded objects, they generated more intermediate results during joins, which allow PEN to distribute more bindings between relevant sources. Figure 5 presents the execution time for queries with a large number of intermediate results (at least 1000 tuples). This represents 562 queries out of 865 for all federations. PEN is even more efficient for queries with a large number of intermediate results. This is an important result because generally the number of the intermediate results impacts negatively the query execution time.

Both FEDX + FEDRA and FEDX + FEDRA + PEN benefit from the reduction of transferred tuples granted by FEDRA, which reduce the number of mappings that PEN can distribute.

To confirm that PEN reduces the execution time of FEDX + FEDRA, a Wilcoxon signed rank test was run for results of Fig. 4 with the hypotheses:

---

[7] The Wilcoxon signed rank test was computed using the R project (http://www.r-project.org/).

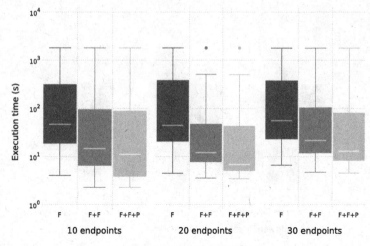

Fig. 5. Average execution time with FEDX (F), FEDX + FEDRA (F+F) and FEDX + FEDRA + PEN (F+F+P) for queries with at least 1000 intermediate results.

H0: PEN does not change the engine query execution time.
H1: PEN reduces FEDX + FEDRA's query execution time.

We obtain p-values no greater than 1.639×10^{-4} for each federation. These low p-values allow for rejecting the null hypothesis that the execution time of FEDX + FEDRA and FEDX + FEDRA + PEN are the same. Additionally, it supports the acceptance of the alternative hypothesis that FEDX + FEDRA + PEN has a lower execution time.

Number of Parallelized Queries. Figure 6 presents the number of parallelized queries (*NPQ*) in FEDX + FEDRA + PEN for the three versions of each

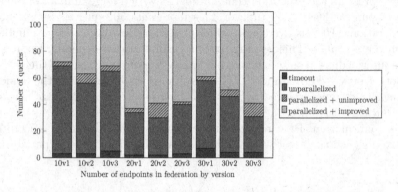

Fig. 6. Number of parallelized queries with FEDX + FEDRA + PEN.

federation. PEN increases query parallelization during join processing, especially in larger federations where fragments are more scattered across endpoints. In most cases, queries parallelized by PEN are improved, *i.e.*, they exhibit a lower execution time compared to FEDX + FEDRA. Parallelized queries with unimproved execution time are those that do not have a large number of intermediate results. Parallelization of such queries does not improve query performance, as their joins were not originally costly to evaluate.

As pointed in Figure 6, the number of parallelized queries is not constant within different versions the same federation, because the replication schema directly influences query parallelization. When this schema is not designed, as in Linked Open Data, PEN creates parallelization where locality cannot be used by FEDRA to optimize the query execution plan.

Number of Transferred Tuples. Figure 7 summarizes the number of transferred tuples (*NTT*) in different federations. FEDX + FEDRA + PEN transfers the same amount of tuples as FEDX + FEDRA. This demonstrates that PEN does not deteriorate the reduction of transferred tuples provided by FEDRA. Moreover, modifications performed on FEDX to remove some synchronisation barriers do not introduce any difference between FEDX + FEDRA and FEDX + FEDRA + PEN in terms of number of transferred tuples and do not impact FEDX + FEDRA performance.

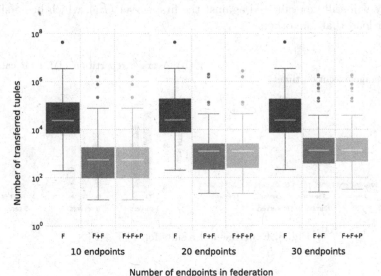

Fig. 7. Average number of transferred tuples with FEDX (F), FEDX + FEDRA (F+F) and FEDX + FEDRA + PEN (F+F+P).

4.2 PEN with Triple Pattern Fragments

Evaluation Metrics: (*i*) *Execution Time (ET):* is the elapsed time since the query is posed until the complete answer is produced. We used a timeout of 1800 s. (*ii*) *Percentage of HTTP calls per server (PHC):* is, for a given server, the ratio between the number of HTTP calls received by the server and the total number of HTTP calls produced by the query.

Results presented for *ET* correspond to the average over three consecutive executions of our random queries.

Execution Time. Figure 8a summarizes the average execution time (*ET*) with the reference TPF client (1 server) and TPF + PEN (using 2 to 5 servers). PEN does not reduce the query execution time of SPARQL queries. As we are in a context were servers are not under a heavy load, they respond quickly to TPQs issued by the client. Therefore, parallelizing these remote calls does not have an impact on the query execution as they are already very cheap to execute.

Repartition of HTTP Calls. Figure 8b summarizes the percentage of HTTP calls per server (*PHC*) with TPF + PEN using up to 5 servers. PEN is able to evenly distribute the load between servers, increasing the availability of each server. However, PEN only affects join processing, so the first triple pattern of a query will still be evaluated against the first server (E_1), which has a slightly heavier load than the others.

(b) Average repartition of HTTP calls per server

(a) Average execution time

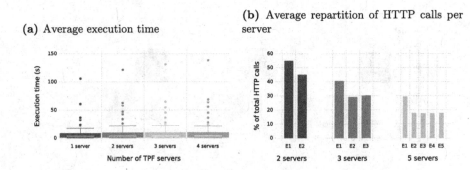

Fig. 8. Experimental results for TPF + PEN

4.3 Synthesis

Experimental study results confirm that PEN can further increase the performance of join processing in presence of replicated fragments.

For federated SPARQL queries, execution time in average is lower with FEDX + FEDRA + PEN than with FEDX or FEDX + FEDRA, and the reduced number of transferred tuples granted by FEDRA is maintained. Answer complete-ness is not degraded. PEN is able to parallelize a significant number of queries in presence of replicated fragments and shows to be more efficient on larger fed-erations. Query performance are significantly improved for queries with a large number of intermediate results, and the time to evaluate joins is reduced by taking advantage of parallel processing.

For Triple Pattern Fragments, execution time is not reduced by PEN, but the load is evenly balanced between all servers used, increasing the overall availability.

5   Related Work

FEDRA [13] is a replication-aware source selection that uses data locality pro-duced by replicated fragments to enhance federated query engines performances. FEDRA uses Union and BGP reductions to prune data sources and finds as many sub-queries that can be executed against the same endpoint as possible, lead-ing to evaluation of local joins and a reduced number of transferred tuples. PEN uses replicated fragments differently. As seen in Sect. 2, FEDRA prunes redundant endpoints that cannot be used to creates localities, whereas PEN uses these endpoints to create more opportunities of parallelization.

LILAC [14] is a replication-aware decomposer. Compared to FEDRA, LILAC is able to reduce intermediate results by allocating a triple pattern to several endpoints. As for FEDRA, PEN can reuse source selection performed by LILAC to introduce intra-operator parallelism.

Other existing sources selection techniques reduce the number of selected sources by a federated SPARQL query engine. BBQ [10] and DAW [16] use sketches to estimate the overlapping among sources, but they only operate on duplicated sources and not on replication itself. They do not provide informa-tion about replicated fragments that allow PEN to efficiently parallelize join processing.

Parallel join processing in distributed database systems has been the subject of significant investigation. Parallel nested loop algorithms have been investi-gated in [4,6], but they do not use replication for parallelization. Instead, repli-cation is mostly used for fault tolerance and to locate data closer to their access points [11,15], improving query performance by reducing communication time. PEN does not use localities created by data redundancy, but opportunities of parallelization created by this redundancy.

Parallel join processing has been also studied in federated query engines. For instance, [1,8,17] propose parallel architectures for executing queries concur-rently at different data sources. Anapsid [1] takes advantage of bushy query execution plans to create *inter-operator parallelism*. FEDX [17] implements *bound joins* in a distributed and highly parallelized environment where different subqueries can be executed at the endpoints concurrently. PEN creates intra-operator parallelism and proposes a more advanced parallel join processing using replication. Similar to FEDX, subqueries are executed concurrently, but they are distributed between endpoints, increasing parallelization.

To our knowledge, none of existing federated query engines propose to take advantage of replicated data for join processing or propose a replication-aware parallel join operator.

The Triple Pattern Fragments (TPF) [18] propose to shift complex query processing from servers to clients to improve availability and reliability of servers, at the cost of performance. A low-cost triple pattern-based interface is deployed server-side, and a client-side algorithm decomposes a SPARQL query into triple patterns that are evaluated against this interface. Compared to TPF, PEN allows for the execution of a single query over different TPF servers that replicate the same dataset. This improves the load balancing by distributing the query processing over several servers instead of one.

6   Conclusions and Future Works

In this paper, we extended a replication-aware federated query engine and the reference TPF client with a new replication-aware parallel join operator PEN. PEN provides intra-operator parallelism relying on replicated data. In this way, PEN preserves properties of source-selection and query decomposition replication-aware federated query engines. We implemented PEN in both FEDX and TPF. Evaluation results demonstrates that PEN improves significantly query performance, in terms of execution time for FEDX and in terms of load balancing for TPF.

PEN is the first attempt to use replicated data to parallelize query processing in Linked Open Data and opens several perspectives.

First, we made the assumption that the load of the endpoints is uniform during query execution. We can leverage this hypothesis by making PEN adaptive to the performances of endpoints.

Second, we focused on a Nested Loop Join operator, we can also parallelize others operators such as Symmetric Hash-Join [20] used in Anapsid.

Acknowledgments. This work is partially supported through the FaBuLA project, part of the AtlanSTIC 2020 program.

References

1. Acosta, M., Vidal, M.-E., Lampo, T., Castillo, J., Ruckhaus, E.: ANAPSID: an adaptive query processing engine for SPARQL endpoints. In: Aroyo, L., Welty, C., Alani, H., Taylor, J., Bernstein, A., Kagal, L., Noy, N., Blomqvist, E. (eds.) ISWC 2011. LNCS, vol. 7031, pp. 18–34. Springer, Heidelberg (2011). https://doi.org/10.1007/978-3-642-25073-6_2
2. Aluç, G., Hartig, O., Özsu, M.T., Daudjee, K.: Diversified stress testing of RDF data management systems. In: Mika, P., Tudorache, T., Bernstein, A., Welty, C., Knoblock, C., Vrandečić, D., Groth, P., Noy, N., Janowicz, K., Goble, C. (eds.) ISWC 2014. LNCS, vol. 8796, pp. 197–212. Springer, Cham (2014). https://doi.org/10.1007/978-3-319-11964-9_13

3. Aluç, G., Ozsu, M., Daudjee, K., Hartig, O.: chameleon-db: a workload-aware robust RDF data management system. University of waterloo. Technical report, CS-2013-10 (2013)

4. Bitton, D., Boral, H., DeWitt, D.J., Wilkinson, W.K.: Parallel algorithms for the execution of relational database operations. ACM Trans. Database Syst. (TODS) **8**(3), 324–353 (1983)

5. Buil-Aranda, C., Hogan, A., Umbrich, J., Vandenbussche, P.-Y.: SPARQL web-querying infrastructure: ready for action? In: Alani, H., Kagal, L., Fokoue, A., Groth, P., Biemann, C., Parreira, J.X., Aroyo, L., Noy, N., Welty, C., Janowicz, K. (eds.) ISWC 2013. LNCS, vol. 8219, pp. 277–293. Springer, Heidelberg (2013). https://doi.org/10.1007/978-3-642-41338-4_18

6. DeWitt, D.J., Naughton, J.F., Burger, J.: Proceedings of the Second International Conference on Nested loops revisited. In: Parallel and Distributed Information Systems, 1993, pp. 230–242. IEEE (1993)

7. Fernández, J.D., Martínez-Prieto, M.A., Gutiérrez, C., Polleres, A., Arias, M.: Binary RDF representation for publication and exchange (HDT). Web Semant. Sci. Serv. Agents World Wide Web **19**, 22–41 (2013)

8. Görlitz, O., Staab, S.: SPLENDID: SPARQL endpoint federation exploiting void descriptions. In: Proceedings of the Second International Conference on Consuming Linked Data, COLD 2011, vol. 782, pp. 13–24, Aachen, Germany (2010). CEUR-WS.org, http://dl.acm.org/citation.cfm?id=2887352.2887354

9. Görlitz, O., Staab, S.: Federated data management and query optimization for linked open data. In: Vakali, A., Jain, L.C. (eds.) New Directions in Web Data Management 1. SCI, vol. 331, pp. 109–137. Springer, Heidelberg (2011). https://doi.org/10.1007/978-3-642-17551-0_5

10. Hose, K., Schenkel, R.: Towards benefit-based RDF source selection for SPARQL queries. In: Proceedings of the 4th International Workshop on Semantic Web Information Management, p. 2. ACM (2012)

11. Kossmann, D.: The state of the art in distributed query processing. ACM Comput. Surv. (CSUR) **32**(4), 422–469 (2000)

12. Minier, T., Montoya, G., Skaf-Molli, H., Molli, P.: PeNeLoop: Parallelizing federated SPARQL queries in presence of replicated fragments. In: Joint Proceedings of the 2nd RDF Stream Processing (RSP 2017) and the Querying the Web of Data (QuWeDa 2017) workshops, CEUR Workshop Proceedings, pp. 37–50 (2017)

13. Montoya, G., Skaf-Molli, H., Molli, P., Vidal, M.-E.: Federated SPARQL queries processing with replicated fragments. In: Arenas, M., Corcho, O., Simperl, E., Strohmaier, M., d'Aquin, M., Srinivas, K., Groth, P., Dumontier, M., Heflin, J., Thirunarayan, K., Staab, S. (eds.) ISWC 2015. LNCS, vol. 9366, pp. 36–51. Springer, Cham (2015). https://doi.org/10.1007/978-3-319-25007-6_3

14. Montoya, G., Skaf-Molli, H., Molli, P., Vidal, M.E.: Decomposing federated queries in presence of replicated fragments. Web Semant. Sci. Serv. Agents World Wide Web **42**, 1–18 (2017)

15. Özsu, M.T., Valduriez, P.: Principles of Distributed Database Systems. Springer Science & Business Media, New York (2011). https://doi.org/10.1007/978-1-4419-8834-8

16. Saleem, M., Ngonga Ngomo, A.-C., Xavier Parreira, J., Deus, H.F., Hauswirth, M.: DAW: Duplicate-AWare federated query processing over the web of data. In: Alani, H., Kagal, L., Fokoue, A., Groth, P., Biemann, C., Parreira, J.X., Aroyo, L., Noy, N., Welty, C., Janowicz, K. (eds.) ISWC 2013. LNCS, vol. 8218, pp. 574–590. Springer, Heidelberg (2013). https://doi.org/10.1007/978-3-642-41335-3_36

17. Schwarte, A., Haase, P., Hose, K., Schenkel, R., Schmidt, M.: FedX: optimization techniques for federated query processing on linked data. In: Aroyo, L., Welty, C., Alani, H., Taylor, J., Bernstein, A., Kagal, L., Noy, N., Blomqvist, E. (eds.) ISWC 2011. LNCS, vol. 7031, pp. 601–616. Springer, Heidelberg (2011). https://doi.org/10.1007/978-3-642-25073-6_38

18. Verborgh, R., Vander Sande, M., Hartig, O., Van Herwegen, J., De Vocht, L., De Meester, B., Haesendonck, G., Colpaert, P.: Triple pattern fragments: a low-cost knowledge graph interface for the web. Web Semant. Sci. Serv. Agents World Wide Web 37, 184–206 (2016)

19. Wilcoxon, F., Kotz, S.: Individual comparisons by ranking methods. In: Kotz, S., Johnson, N.L. (eds.) Breakthroughs in Statistics. Statistics (Perspectives in Statistics), pp. 196–202. Springer, New York (1992). https://doi.org/10.1007/978-1-4612-4380-9_16

20. Wilschut, A.N., Apers, P.M.: Dataflow query execution in a parallel main-memory environment. Distrib. Parallel Databases 1(1), 103–128 (1993)

Semantic Web Solutions for Large-Scale Biomedical Data Analytics (SeWeBMeDA)

Biomedical Semantic Resources for Drug Discovery Platforms

Ali Hasnain[✉] and Dietrich Rebholz-Schuhmann

Insight Centre for Data Analytics, National University of Ireland, Galway, Ireland
{Ali.Hasnain,Dietrich.Rebholz-Schuhmann}@insight-centre.org

Abstract. The biomedical research community is providing large-scale data sources to enable knowledge discovery from the data alone, or from novel scientific experiments in combination with the existing knowledge. Increasingly semantic Web technologies are being developed and used including ontologies, triple stores and combinations thereof. The amount of data is constantly increasing as well as the complexity of data. Since the data sources are publicly available, the amount of content can be measured giving an overview on the accessible content but also on the state of the data representation in comparison to the existing content. For a better understanding of the existing data resources, i.e. judgements on the distribution of data triples across concepts, data types and primary providers, we have performed a comprehensive analysis which delivers an overview on the accessible content for semantic Web solutions (from publicly accessible data servers). It can be derived that the information related to genes, proteins and chemical entities form the core, whereas the content related to diseases and pathways forms a smaller portion. As a result, any approach for drug discovery would profit from the data on molecular entities, but would lack content from data resources that represent disease pathomechanisms.

Keywords: Biomedical Ontologies and Databases · Life Sciences Linked Open Data (LSLOD)

1 Introduction

The deluge of biomedical data in the last few years, partially caused by the advent of high-throughput gene sequencing technologies, has been a primary motivation for efforts related to curating, integrating, publishing, querying and visualising biomedical data [7,12]. The biomedical research domain encompasses a wide range of spatial and temporal scales, from genes to organism through protein, cell, tissue, and organ, as well as from molecular events to human lifetime through cell signalling, diffusion, motility, mitosis and protein turnover. Information available at those different scales is organised in data resources where each data resource mainly specialises in a particular type of data [8]. The result is a large number of established online datasets that describe human biology.

© Springer International Publishing AG 2017
E. Blomqvist et al. (Eds.): ESWC 2017 Satellite Events, LNCS 10577, pp. 199–218, 2017.
https://doi.org/10.1007/978-3-319-70407-4_34

Nevertheless an efficient and comprehensive search activity across these datasets can become quite problematic since similar data is located in many distributed datasets and is usually available in different data models and formats [9–11,25]. As a result an individual scientist could perform manual search in several databases, take the results returned, change their format and paste them to the next database in search for an answer. Such a procedure would be very cumbersome and does not contribute to efficient scientific workflows.

The semantic connectivity between biomedical data constitutes a critical issue of biomedical scientific research and has been successfully exploited in a number of research projects for transitional medicine and drug discovery [17]. Moreover the adoption of linked data technologies will allow the integration of biomedical datasets provided by different and heterogeneous data sources (i.e. research groups, libraries, databases), as well as the provision of an aggregated view of the biomedical data in a machine-readable and semantically-enriched way that will facilitate reuse [21].

At the schema level, these resources mainly consist of both domain ontologies and terminological resources [15,23]. Jimeno-Yepes et al. [16], propose a loose coupling between the domain ontologies and lexicon that cannot be treated with the same techniques nor simply merged into a single resource [20]. Term vocabularies, Dictionaries and Lexicon are used interchangeably and consist of a compendium of words enriched with information of its usage [14]. Whereas a domain ontology is an explicit specialisation of a conceptualisation.

In a recent study, the scope and the size of the terminological resources have been estimated taking into consideration the semantic domain covered by a specific resource [22]. This analysis – for the first time – quantified the "Lexeome", i.e. the full range of terms provided from the terminological (and ontological) resources to give an upper estimate of entities captured in semantic resources.

In this paper the focus lies on introducing biomedical resources especially ontologies, repositories, and other data resources relevant in the context of *Drug Discovery* and *Cancer Chemoprevention*. We monitor the transformation of content into the triple representation and quantify the available content. The analysis gives an overview of which resources have to be considered, what amount of data requires integration and provides the opportunity to tailor semantic solutions to specific needs in terms of size and performance.

2   Biomedical Ontologies

There are several initiatives that address the need to standardise biomedical data. The first standard terminology, namely the International Classification of Diseases (ICD), was created in 1893[1]. Since then several terminologies have been created. However, emphasis was given only to ensure that there are enough terms to cover the domain of focus. Over the period of time, terminologies have advanced from simple lists and hierarchies of terms to formal representations of

---

[1] http://www.who.int/classifications/icd/en/HistoryOfICD.pdf (retr.10/02/2017).

concepts in a semantically standardised structure. Terminologies that use formal representations and usable by computers are often called "ontologies" [6,18].

In contrast to manually-created hierarchical organisations of terms (referred to as taxonomies), ontologies make use of formal structures, relations and definitions to provide a conceptualisation of domain knowledge. A large collection of biomedical ontologies or bio-ontologies are available nowadays through services e.g. Bioportal[2] and OBO foundry[3]. These have mostly been developed as joint efforts by communities to enable easy integration of biomedical data from both the literature and publicly-available biomedical databases. This section highlight the most well-studied and prominent ontologies applicable to biomedical research and especially relevant for Drug Discovery and other scenarios. Furthermore, several general ontologies used for medical and clinical terms are also investigated in order to provide insights into how data can be represented.

These ontologies can fall into three main categories, namely (1) biomedical Ontologies, (2) drugs and chemical compound ontologies and (3) upper level ontologies. The biomedical ontologies are mainly used by biomedical applications and define the basic biological structures (e.g. genes, pathways etc.). The Drugs and Chemical Compound Ontologies are related to the clinical drugs and their active ingredients. Finally, the upper level ontologies describe general concepts that many biomedical ontologies share.

Biomedical Ontologies cover (amongst others): (1) Advancing Clinico-Genomic Trials on Cancer (ACGT) Master Ontology (MO)[4], (2) Biological Pathway Exchange (BioPAX)[5], (3) Experimental Factor Ontology (EFO)[6], (4) Gene Ontology (GO)[7], (5) Medical Subject Headings (MeSH)[8], (6) Microarray Gene Expression Data Ontology (MGED)[9], (7) National Cancer Institute (NCI) Thesaurus[10], (8) Ontology for biomedical Investigations (OBI)[11], (9) Unified Medical Language System (UMLS)[12].

Drugs and Chemical Compound Ontologies would mainly comprise RxNorm[13], and Generic and Upper Ontologies would consider: (1) Basic Formal Ontology (BFO)[14], (2) OBO Relation Ontology (RO)[15], (3) Provenance Ontology (PROVO)[16].

---

[2] https://bioportal.bioontology.org/ (retr.10/04/2017).
[3] http://www.obofoundry.org/ (retr.10/04/2017).
[4] http://bioportal.bioontology.org/ontologies/ACGT-MO (retr.10/02/2017).
[5] http://www.biopax.org/ (retr.10/02/2017).
[6] http://www.ebi.ac.uk/efo/ (retr.10/02/2017).
[7] http://www.geneontology.org/ (retr.10/02/2017).
[8] http://www.nlm.nih.gov/mesh/ (retr.10/02/2017).
[9] http://bioportal.bioontology.org/ontologies/MO (retr.10/02/2017).
[10] http://ncit.nci.nih.gov (retr.10/02/2017).
[11] http://obi-ontology.org/page/Main_Page (retr. 31/01/2017).
[12] http://www.nlm.nih.gov/research/umls/about_umls.html (retr. 10/02/2017).
[13] http://www.nlm.nih.gov/research/umls/rxnorm (retr. 22/02/2017).
[14] http://ontology.buffalo.edu/bfo/ (retr. 10/03/2017).
[15] http://obo.sourceforge.net/relationship/ (retr. 10/03/2017).
[16] http://bioportal.bioontology.org/ontologies/PROVO/ (retr. 25/01/2017).

Table 1 provides implementation details and quantitative overview of ontologies that are listed in Sect. 2, year of release (as per listed at Bioportal), the visibility (public/private) and implementation details (language and type of data) of different ontologies. Size and coverage of these ontologies in terms of total triples, number of entries/entities, dependency/or reuse of any ontology on others, sub-classification and brief description are also presented in the table. We also present the quantitative comparison of different ontologies in terms of *total number of classes, total number of properties, total number of individuals* and *maximum depth.*

3   Public Data Repositories for Drug Discovery

In this section, we analyse a comprehensive list of biomedical libraries and databases closely related to drug discovery that have been provided from the biomedical community. Since drug discovery has a focus to a specific disease domain, we have chosen to focus on cancer chemoprevention as a use case and thus list data resources relevant for this domain.

The databases are separated into the following categories:

- *Gene, Gene Expression and Protein Databases* for gene and protein annotations as well as the expression levels and related clinical data,
- *Pathway databases* denoting the protein interactions and the overall functional outcomes,
- *Chemical and Structure Databases including Biological Activities* for the information related to drugs and other chemicals including also toxicity observations and clinical trials,
- *Disease Specific Databases for Prevention* which deliver content specific to the prevention of cancer,
- *Literature databases.*

Table 2 provides implementation details and quantitative overview of the Life Sciences related databases presented in Sect. 3. In addition, it lays out information regarding the year of release, accessibility (public, private) and implementation details (language and type of data) of different databases. Size and coverage of these databases in terms of total triples, number of entries/entities, sub-classification and brief description are also presented in the table.

3.1   Gene, Gene Expression and Protein Databases

For the complete understanding of the molecular processes, e.g., in cancer, it is highly relevant to be able to analyse the molecular processes. Such processes leads into the need to decompose functional processes into molecular processes and to predict the outcomes of such processes from the genetic background. Although cancer genomics tends to be complex due to the fact that cancer cells deviate from regular process, the genomics information – in particular the data

Table 1. Quantitative overview of implementation details of public ontologies (selected). (**BO**:biomedical Ontologies, **DCCO**:Drugs and Chemical Compound Ontologies, **GUO**: Generic and Upper Ontologies, **T/C**: Type/Category, **Y**: Year (acc. to Bioportal), Individuals, Classes/Concepts, Properties, Depth Public, "_" = N/A.)

Ontology	T/C	Y	Topic	Implementation	Dependency	C	P	I	D	Sub classification/ Description
ACGT-MO	BO	2008	Cancer	OWL,CSV,RDF/XML, Diff	BFO/OBO	1'769	260	61	18	data exchange in oncology, integration of clinical and molecular data
BioPAX	BO	2010	Pathways	OWL,CSV,RDF/XML	-	68	96	0	4	metabolic, biochemical, transcription regulation, protein synthesis and signal transduction pathways
EFO	BO	2015	Modelling Experimental Factors	OWL,CSV,RDF/XML,Diff	-	18'596	35	0	14	enhance and promote consistent annotation, facilitate automatic annotation to integrate external data
GO	BO	2016	Genomic and Proteomic	OWL,CSV,RDF/XML,Diff	MOD	44'195	9	0	16	for describing biological processes, molecular functions and cellular components of gene products
MeSH	BO	2009	Health	RDF/TTL,CSV	GO	252'375	38	0	15	hierarchical structure for indexing, cataloguing, and searching for biomedical and health-related information
MGED	BO	2009	microarray experiment	OWL,CSV,RDF/XML	-	233	121	698	8	describes the biological sample, the treatment regarding sample and the micro-array chip technology used in the experiment
NCIT	BO	2007	Clinical care, translational research	OWL,CSV,RDF/XML,Diff	-	118'167	173	457'715	16	integrates molecular and clinical cancer-related information enabling researchers to integrate, retrieve and relate relevant concepts
OBI	BO	2008	integration of experimental data	OWL,CSV,RDF/XML,Diff	-	2'932	106	178	16	designs, protocols, instrumentation, materials, processes, data and types of analysis in biological and biomedical investigations
UMLS	BO	1993	Medical terms & concepts	RRF	-	3'221'702	-	-	-	meta-terminology that summarise the terminologies about biomedical and health related concepts in enable interoperability
RxNorm	DCCO	1993	clinical drugs	CSV,HDF/XML,Diff	-	118'555	46	0	0	contains standard names for clinical drugs (active drug ingredient, dosage strength, physical form) and links
BFO	GUO	2003	Genuine upper level ontology	OWL,CSV,RDF/XML,Diff	-	35	0	0	5	formalise entities such as 3D enduring objects and comprehending processes conceived as extended through time
RO	GUO	2005	Core relations for OBO ontologies	OWL,CSV,RDF/XML,Diff	-	-	-	-	-	provides methodology for providing formal definitions of the basic relations that cross-cut the biomedical domain
PROVO	GUO	2012	Provenance Data Model	OWL,CSV,RDF/XML,Diff	-	30	50	4	3	provides classes, properties and restrictions to represent provenance information

with regards to the function of genes, their expression and transformation into proteins – is a major source for the understanding of molecular processes.

The following data sources have to be considered for a complete and coherent representation of such molecular processes.

GenBank[17] is an open-access annotated collection of all publicly available nucleotide sequences and their protein translations. GenBank and its collaborators receive sequences produced in laboratories throughout the world from more than 380'000 distinct organisms.

ArrayExpress[18] archive is a database of functional genomics experiments including gene expression where one can query and download data collected to Minimum Information about a Microarray Experiment (MIAME) and Minimum Information about a high-throughput SeQuencing Experiment (MINSEQE).

Gene Expression Omnibus (GEO)[19] is a public repository that archives and freely distributes microarray, next-generation sequencing and other forms of high-throughput functional genomic data submitted by the scientific community.

Cancer Gene Expression Database (CGED)[20] is a database of gene expression profile and accompanying clinical information. This database offers graphical presentation of expression and clinical data with similarity search and sorting functions. CGED includes data on breast (prognosis and docetaxel datasets), colorectal, hepatocellular, esophageal, thyroid, and gastric cancers [4].

Universal Protein Resource (UniProt)[21] is a comprehensive resource for protein sequence and annotation data. The UniProt Knowledgebase (UniProtKB) is the central hub for the collection of functional information on proteins, with accurate consistent and rich annotation [4]. This includes widely accepted biological ontologies, classifications and cross-references, as well as clear indications of the quality of annotation in the form of evidence attribution of experimental and computational data.

Protein Database[22] is a collection of sequences from several sources, including translations from annotated coding regions in GenBank and TPA (Tissue plasminogen activator) as well as records from SwissProt, Protein Information Resource (PIR), Protein Research Foundation (PRF), UniProt and PDB. Protein sequences are the determinants of biological structure and function.

Protein Data Bank (PDB)[23] is a repository for the 3D structural data of large biological molecules, such as proteins and nucleic acids. The data, typically obtained by X-ray crystallography or NMR (Nuclear Magnetic Resonance) spectroscopy and submitted by biologists and biochemists from around the world, is

---

[17] http://www.ncbi.nlm.nih.gov/genbank/ (retr. 10/01/2017).
[18] http://www.ebi.ac.uk/arrayexpress/ (retr. 12/01/2017).
[19] http://www.ncbi.nlm.nih.gov/geo/ (retr. 12/01/2017).
[20] http://lifesciencedb.jp/cged/ (retr. 12/01/2017).
[21] http://www.uniprot.org/ (retr. biomedical researchers can utilise cPath).
[22] http://www.hprd.org/ (retr. 20/08/2015).
[23] http://www.pdb.org (retr. 20/08/2015).

freely accessible on the Internet. Most major scientific journals and some funding agencies require scientists to submit their structure data to the PDB [4].

3.2 Pathway Databases

Modelling of pathways provides the crucial information to understand functional states in the cells. Different sources are available which partially overlap. The richest source is KEGG with about 50 M triples provided.

Kyoto Encyclopedia of Genes and Genomes (KEGG)[24] is a database resource that integrates genomic, chemical, and systemic functional information. In particular, gene catalogues are linked to higher-level systemic functions of the cell, the organism, and the ecosystem. KEGG is further expanded towards more practical applications with molecular network-based views of diseases, drugs, and environmental compounds [4].

Reactome[25] is an open-source, open access, manually curated and peer-reviewed pathway database. The rationale behind Reactome is to convey the rich information in the visual representations of biological pathways familiar from textbooks and articles in a detailed, computationally accessible format. Entities (nucleic acids, proteins, complexes and small molecules), participating in reactions form a network of biological interactions, are grouped into pathways. Examples of biological pathways in Reactome include signalling, innate and acquired immune function, transcriptional regulation, translation, apoptosis and classical intermediary metabolism [4].

Wikipathways [19] is an open, collaborative platform dedicated to the curation of biological pathways. WikiPathways thus presents a model for pathway databases that enhance and complement ongoing efforts, such as KEGG, Reactome and Pathway Commons.

cPath: Pathway Database Software[26] is a software platform for collecting/-querying biological pathways. It can serve as the core data handling component in information systems for pathway visualisation, analysis and modelling. cPath can be used for content aggregation, query and analysis. More specifically, its main features include: (i) Aggregate pathway data from multiple sources (e.g. BioCyc, KEGG, Reactome), (ii) Import/Export support with different formats PSI-MI (Proteomics Standards Initiative Molecular Interaction) and BioPAX, (iii) Data visualisation using Cytoscape and (iv) Simple web service.

3.3 Chemical and Structure Databases Including Biological Activities

The treatment of any disease and cancer in particular is based on chemical entities with a defined biological activity. Several data sources provide information

---

[24] http://www.genome.jp/kegg/ (retr. 12/01/2017).
[25] http://www.reactome.org (retr. 12/01/2017).
[26] http://cbio.mskcc.org/software/cpath/ (retr. 12/01/2017).

on the chemical compound, on its relevance to specific treatments and the side effects that they may induce. The amount of data (i.e. triples) with regards to the different data sources is large and data integration is an ongoing difficult task (see OpenPhacts project). The following data sources are publicly available.

Chemical Compounds Database (Chembase)[27] collects and provides information on chemical compounds and their physical and chemical properties, NMR (Nuclear Magnetic Resonance) spectra, mass spectra, UV/Vis (Ultra-violet-Visible Spectroscopy) absorption and IR data.

Sigma-Aldrich[28] product database includes datasheets for commercially available compounds including solubility.

ChemDB[29] is a public database of small molecules available on the Web. The database contains approximately 4.1 million commercially available compounds and 8.2 million isomers. It includes a user-friendly graphical interface, chemical reactions capabilities as well as unique search capabilities.

Chemical Entities of Biological Interest (ChEBI)[30] is a database and ontology of small molecular entities. The term *'molecular entity'* refers to any isotopically distinct atom, molecule, ion, ion pair, radical, radical ion, complex, conformer etc. that is identifiable as a separately distinguishable entity. Molecules directly encoded by the genome, such as nucleic acids, proteins and peptides derived from proteins by proteolysis cleavage, are not included.

DrugBank database [24] is a bioinformatics and cheminformatics resource that combines detailed drug (i.e. chemical, pharmacological and pharmaceutical) data with comprehensive drug target (i.e. sequence, structure, and pathway) information. The database contains 6826 drug entries including 1431 Food and Drug Administration (FDA)-approved small molecule drugs, 133 FDA-approved biotech (protein/peptide) drugs, 83 nutraceuticals and 5211 experimental drugs. Additionally 4435 non-redundant protein (i.e. drug target/enzyme/transporter/-carrier) sequences are linked to these drug entries.

PubChem[31] provides information on the biological activities of small molecules including substance information, compound structures, and BioActivity data in three primary databases. PubChem is integrated with Entrez, NCBI's (National Center for Biotechnology Information) primary search engine, and also provides compound neighbouring, sub/superstructure, similarity structure, BioActivity data, and other searching features [4]. PubChem contains substance descriptions and small molecules with fewer than 1000 atoms and 1000 bonds.

Aggregated Computational Toxicology Resource (ACToR)[32] is an online warehouse of all publicly available chemical toxicity data and can be used to find data about potential chemical risks to human health and the environment.

---

[27] http://urlm.co/www.chembase.com#web (retr. 12/07/2017).
[28] https://www.sigmaaldrich.com/catalog/ (retr. 18/04/2017).
[29] http://cdb.ics.uci.edu/ (retr. 12/05/2017).
[30] http://www.ebi.ac.uk/chebi/ (retr. 12/01/2017).
[31] http://pubchem.ncbi.nlm.nih.gov/ (retr. 12/01/2017).
[32] http://actor.epa.gov/actor/faces/ACToRHome.jsp (retr. 12/01/2017).

ACToR aggregates data from over 500 public sources on over 500'000 environmental chemicals searchable by chemical name and by chemical structure [4]. It
allows users to search and query data from chemical toxicity databases including: (1) ToxRefDB for animal toxicity studies, (2) ToxCastDB covering data
from 1'000 chemicals in over 500 assays, (3) ExpoCastDB consolidating human
exposure and exposure factor data, and (4) Distributed Structure-Searchable
Toxicity (DSSTox) for high quality chemical structures and annotations.

ClinicalTrials[33] is an up-to-date registry and results database of federally and
privately supported clinical trials conducted in the United States and around
the world [4].

TOXicology Data NETwork (TOXNET)[34] provides access to full-text and
bibliographic databases oriented to toxicology, hazardous chemicals, environmental health and related areas.

3.4   Disease Specific Databases for Prevention

More of such databases will arise, once the data becomes available but currently
it is limited to a smaller number of data resources with limited data contained.

Colon Chemoprevention Agents Database (CCAD) [3] contains results
from a systematic review of the literature of Colon Chemoprevention in human,
rats and mice. Target cancers are colorectal adenoma and adenocarcinoma, aberrant crypt foci (ACF) (a preneoplasic lesion), and Min mice polyp (adenomas
in Apc+/− mutant mice). The Chemopreventive agents are ranked by efficacy
(potency against carcinogenesis).

Dietary Supplements Labels Database[35] offers information on label ingredients in more than 5'000 selected brands of dietary supplements to compare label
ingredients in different brands. Information is also provided on the "structure/-
function" claims made by manufacturers and can therefore be used to narrow
down active ingredients in different types of food which may be applicable as
Chemoprevention agents. Ingredients of dietary supplements in this database are
linked to other databases such as MedlinePlus and PubMed [4].

REPAIRtoire Database[36] is a database resource for systems biology of DNA
damage/repair. It collects and organises the information including: (i) DNA
damage linked to environmental mutagenic and cytotoxic agents, (ii) pathways
comprising individual processes and enzymatic reactions involved in the removal
of damage, (iii) proteins participating in DNA repair and (iv) diseases correlated
with mutations in genes encoding DNA repair proteins. It also provides links to
publications and external databases. REPAIRtoire can be queried by the name
of pathway, protein, enzymatic complex, damage and disease.

---

[33] http://clinicaltrials.gov/ (retr. 10/01/2017).
[34] http://toxnet.nlm.nih.gov/ (retr. 12/01/2017).
[35] http://www.dsld.nlm.nih.gov/dsld/ (retr. 20/03/2017).
[36] http://repairtoire.genesilico.pl/ (retr. 14/01/2017).

3.5 Literature Databases

The scientific literature is still one of the most comprehensive data sources for experimental findings. The content is provided in an unstructured way and some of its content is delivered through data curation into the data sources above. The most relevant data sources are listed below.

Pubmed[37] is the most widely used source for biomedical literature. PubMed provides access to citations from the MEDLINE database and additional Life Science journals including links to many full-text articles at journal Web sites and other related Web resources. PubMed was first released in January 1996. The knowledge regarding Chemoprevention agents available as publications makes Pubmed a primary source of biomedical information [4].

PubMed Dietary Supplement Subset[38] is designed to limit search results to citations from a broad spectrum of dietary supplement literature including vitamin, mineral, phytochemical, ergogenic, botanical and herbal supplements in human nutrition and animal models. It retrieves citations on topics including: chemical composition; biochemical role and function - both in vitro and in vivo; clinical trials; health and adverse effects; fortification; traditional Chinese medicine and other folk/ethnic supplement practices. [13].

4 Biomedical Services for Semantic Resources

The increase in the number of ontologies and databases creates new needs in the community of ontology users to find, reconcile and relate own data to the growing number of biomedical ontologies, thus requiring access to the full body of biomedical ontologies. A number of tools and services for this purpose have already been developed which facilitate the biomedical community locating ontologies, drugs, proteins and publications. More specifically, this section reviews the following biomedical services [13]:

- BioPortal[39]
- Open biomedical Ontology (OBO)[40]
- Ontobee[41]
- Ontology Lookup Service[42]
- AmiGO[43]
- Entrez[44]
- e-meducation[45]

---

[37] http://www.ncbi.nlm.nih.gov/pubmed (retr. 22/02/2017).
[38] http://ods.od.nih.gov/research/PubMed_Dietary_Supplement_Subset.aspx (retr. 12/03/2017).
[39] http://bioportal.bioontology.org/ retr. 20/02/2016.
[40] http://www.obofoundry.org/ retr. 22/02/2016.
[41] http://www.ontobee.org/.
[42] http://www.ebi.ac.uk/ontology-lookup/ retr. 22/02/2016.
[43] http://amigo.geneontology.org/cgi-bin/amigo/go.cgi retr. 22/02/2016.
[44] http://www.ncbi.nlm.nih.gov/sites/gquery retr. 18/02/2016.
[45] http://www.e-meducation.org retr. 18/02/2016.

Table 2. Quantitative overview of implementation details of public libraries and databases (selected) (LD: Literature Databases, T/C: Type/ Category, Public, Visibility, "-" = N/A)

Database	T/C	Year	Topic	Implementation	Content
GenBank	GDD	1982	nucleotide sequences & translations	WebBased	more than 193'739'511 sequences; over 65 B nucleotide bases in more than 61 M sequences
UniProt	PD	2002	protein sequence and annotation data	WebBased/LOD	63'686'057 sequences, 21'364'768'379 amino acids
PDB	PD	1971	3D structural data of proteins	WebBased/LOD	classifications, cross-references, annotation of proteins; 118280 Biological Structures
PDBe	PD	2009	3D Protein sequences	WebBased	evidence of experimentally validated protein structures; 30'047Protein Entries, 41'327PPIs
GEO	GED	2011	microarray, NGS	WebBased	translated coding regions from GenBank, TPA, SwissProt, PIR, PRF, UniProt and PDB. 3'848 datasets; gene expression for specific studies
ArrayExpress	GED	2011	genomics experiments	WebBased	65060 experiments 1973'776 assays; annotated data for gene expression from biological experiments
OGED	GED	-	gene expression & clinical data	-	cancer of breast, colorectal, hepatocellular, esophageal, thyroid, gastric cancers
KEGG	PAD	1995	genomic, chemical, systemic info	WebBased/ LOD	432'883PathwayMaps, 133'776hierarchies
Reactome	PAD	2003	pathways	WebBased	genome sequencing and high-throughput experimental technologies; 9'386 Proteins
Wikipathways	PAD	2007	biological pathways	WebBased	pathway data for signalling, transcriptional regulation, translation, apoptosis; 2'475 pathways
cPath	PAD	2005	biological pathways	Desktop/ WebBased	pathway database complementing e.g. KEGG, Reactome, Pathway Commons; 31'698 pathways, 1'151'476 interactions; pathway visualisation, analysis and modelling
Chembase	CPSD	-	chemical compounds	WebBased	150'000 pages; compounds, their physical and chemical properties, mass spectra
Sigma-Aldrich	CPSD	1975	compounds datasheets	WebBased	20000+ products, 500+ services; data for commercial compounds
ChemDB	CPSD	1989	small molecules	WebBased	more than 4.1 M compounds; 4.1 M commercial compounds, 8.2 M counting isomers
CCAD	DSCD	2002	colon-chemoprevention	WebBased	1,137 agents; literature data for colon chemoprevention in human, rats, mice
DrugBank	BACD	2008	drug data	WebBased/LOD	8,261 drugs, 4,164 targets, 243 Enzymes, 118 Transporters, drug (chemical, pharmaceutical), drug target (sequence, structure, pathway)
ChEBI	BACD	-	small molecules	WebBased/LOD	48'296 compounds; natural and synthetic atom, molecule, ion, radical, conformer
PubChem	BACD	2004	compound structures, bioactivity data	WebBased/LOD	89'124'401 Compounds; compound neighbouring, sub/superstructure, bioactivity data
TOXNET	TED	1987	toxicology database	WebBased	toxicology, hazardous chemicals, environmental health and related areas
ACToR	BACD	2008	chemical toxicity data	WebBased	more than 500 public source; environmental chemicals searchable by name and structure
REPAIRtoire	BACD	2019	DNA damage & repair	WebBased	DNA damage links, pathways, proteins for DNA re-pair, diseases related to mutations; 213'868 studies
ClinicalTrials	TED	2000	clinical trial data	WebBased	offers information for locating clinical trials for diseases and conditions
Pubmed	LD	1996	biomedical Literature	WebBased/Excel	11 M + journal citations; Primary source of information for bio-medical researchers
PDSS	LD	1999	citations of dietary supplement	WebBased	dietary supplement literature including vitamin, mineral, botanical/herbal supplements; more than 5'000 selected brands
DSLD	NSCAD	2013	label Ingredients of dietary supplements	WebBased	Ingredients of dietary supplements linked to MedlinePlus and PubMed

4.1 BioPortal

BioPortal, created by the NCBO (National Centre for biomedical Ontology), is the Web interface that provides access to the full body of ontologies from the biomedical research community. They can be accessed in a variety of standard ontology formats. BioPortal organises ontologies according to a set of categories (such as anatomy, genomics, development etc.) enabling users to find groups of ontologies of interest as well as to visualise their content. BioPortal users will be able to rate ontologies, comment on how appropriate ontologies are for specific tasks and how well they cover their target domain (Table 3).

Table 3. Quantitative overview of ontologies listed at bioportal (as of June 2017).

Ontologies	Classes	ResourcesIndexed	IndexedRecords	DirectAnnotation	ExpandedAnnotation
566	8,152,116	48	39,537,360	95,468,433,792	144,789,582,932

4.2 Open Biomedical Ontology (OBO)

The OBO project is a repository with a Web portal containing ontologies as well as links to controlled vocabularies for shared use between medical and biological domains. The ontologies found in the OBO library are partially overlapped since they can be combined between themselves adding relations and giving rise to new ontologies. Researchers in the OBO project have also developed the OBO language for representing biomedical ontologies.

4.3 Ontobee

Ontobee is a linked data server designed for ontologies that aim to facilitate ontology data sharing, visualisation, query, integration and analysis. This service dynamically de-references and presents individual ontology term URIs to:

– HTML based web pages for user-friendly web browsing and navigation.
– RDF source code for Semantic Web applications.

Ontobee is the default linked data server for most OBO Foundry library ontologies as well as for many ontologies not registered at OBO (stats Table 4).

Table 4. Quantitative overview of ontologies listed at Ontobee (as of June 2017).

Ontologies	Classes	Object Property	Datatype Property	Annotation Property	Instances
187	3,856,631	9,322	638	8,6372	667,618

4.4 Ontology Lookup Service

The Ontology Lookup Service from the European Bioinformatics Institute provides a centralised query interface for ontologies in the OBO format. All ontologies are indexed and the user can query the content of the integrated ontologies with search terms to retrieve the most relevant related concept label and ontological definition. The service provides the best benefits to curators who have to explore the existence of a specific concept for their daily work (stats Table: 5).

Table 5. Quantitative overview of ontologies listed at Ontology Lookup Service (as of June 2017).

Ontologies	Terms	Properties	Individuals
191	4,891,249	15,572	474,090

4.5 AmiGO

AmiGO, built by Gene Ontology Consortium, gives efficient access to the Gene Ontology and annotations stored in a specialist GO database. This solution is focused to only one ontology, but this ontology forms an over-arching role in the biomedical domain, since it encodes the key findings from biomolecular research: molecular function, biological process and cellular location. Again, this solution is mainly relevant to curation teams.

4.6 Entrez

Entrez [5] is a Web-based search and retrieval engine developed by the NCBI. It is capable of searching multiple NCBI databases through a single query. Entrez returns search results that can include a combination of many types of data on the query, such as nucleotide sequences, protein sequences, macro-molecular structures and related articles in the literature. The search engine forms a powerful means to oversee the collected information from different sources for a specific entity, e.g., a gene or a pathway.

4.7 E-Meducation

The Alfa Institute of Biomedical Sciences (AIBS) has created a medical portal providing a selection of open access Internet links in several medical fields, including internal medicine, infectious diseases, dermatology, nosocomial infections, antimicrobial resistance, Hepatitis B virus, general surgery and surgical infections. A feature of the e-meducation is the custom-built medical search engine that permits the tracking of medical information without having to filter for hours. The custom search engine generates results from professional oriented sites for Healthcare providers.

5   Linked Data

In March 2007 the W3C Semantic Web Education and Outreach (SWEO) Interest Group announced a new Community Project called *"Interlinking Open Data"*[46] that was subsequently shortened to *"Linking Open Data" (LOD)*. The goal of the Linked Open Data project is twofold: (i) to bootstrap the Semantic Web by creating, publishing and interlinking RDF exports from open datasets, and, (ii) introduce the benefits of Semantic Web technologies to the broader Open Data community [2]. Linked Data aims to make data available on the Web in an inter-operate-able format so that agents can discover, access, combine and consume content from different sources with higher levels of automation than would otherwise be possible. The result is a *"Web of Data"*, a Web of structured data with rich semantic links where agents can query in a unified manner, across sources, using standard languages and protocols. Over the past few years, hundreds of knowledge-bases with billions of facts have been published according to the Semantic Web standards (using RDF as a data model and RDFS and OWL for explicit semantics) following the Linked Data principles.

5.1   Life Sciences Linked Open Data Cloud

This section reviews the linked biomedical datasets relevant in a Cancer Chemoprevention and drug discovery scenario, three significant providers are as follow: (1) Linked Open Drug Data (LODD), (2) Bio2RDF, and (3) LinkedLifeData.

Linked Open Drug Data (LODD)[47] is a set of linked datasets relevant to Drug Discovery. It includes data from several datasets including Drugbank, LinkedCT, DailyMed, Diseasome, SIDER, STITCH, Medicare, RxNorm, ClinicalTrials.gov, NCBI Entrez Gene and OMIM. The LODD datasets have been crawled by the Semantic Web Search Engine (SWSE)[48] that can be accessed via a faceted browsing interface.

Bio2RDF[49] constitutes a project that contains multiple linked biological databases including pathways databases such as KEGG, PDB and several NCBIs databases [1]. Bio2RDF is an open-source project that uses Semantic Web technologies to build and provide the largest network of Linked Data for the Life Sciences. Bio2RDF defines a set of simple conventions to create RDF(s) compatible Linked Data from a diverse set of heterogeneously formatted sources obtained from multiple data providers.

As of July 2014, Bio2RDF Release 3 contains[50] about 11 billion triples across 35 datasets (based on Virtuoso 7.1.0 as the SPARQL 1.1 endpoint). The new types of data have been included for example from OrphaNet,

---

[46] http://www.w3.org/blog/SWEO/page-2 retr. 05/02/2017.
[47] http://www.w3.org/wiki/HCLSIG/LODD (retr: 05/02/2017).
[48] http://swse.deri.org/ (retr. 27-04-2016).
[49] http://bio2rdf.org (retr: 05/02/2017).
[50] https://github.com/bio2rdf/bio2rdf-scripts/wiki (retr: 05/02/2017).

PubMed, SIDER, GenDR, and LSR. Further local endpoints have been integrated: Chembl, LinkedSPL, PathwayCommons, and Reactome. In the current version, every URI is an instance of an `owl:Class`, `owl:ObjectProperty`, or `owl:DatatypeProperty`.

LinkedLifeData (LLD)[51] is a semantic data integration platform for the biomedical domain containing 5 billion RDF statements from various sources including UniProt, PubMed, EntrezGene and 20 more. LDD allows writing complex data analytical queries, answering complex bioinformatics questions, helps navigate through the information or export results subsets. LDD offers two different access levels: (1) LLD Public – completely free anonymous access; and (2) LLD Enterprise – premium service access with extra features.

5.2   Quantitative Overview of Datasets

Table 6 provides implementation details and quantitative overview of dataset listed in Sect. 5.1, but also information regarding the year of release (as per reported at http://www.datahub.io, http://www.bio2rdf.org, http://www.linkedlifedata.com), the visibility (public/ private) and the implementation details (language and type of data) provided by different datasets. Size and coverage of these datasets in terms of total triples, number of entries/entities, link of SPARQL endpoint, sub-classification and brief description is also presented in the table. Quantitative comparison of datasets in terms of combination of information including *total number of classes*, *total number of properties*, *total number of Instances*, *total number of triples* and *total number of entities* is presented.

Table 6 shows that the largest triple store collections (2 to 10 B triples) have been from genes or proteins data and branch out to the reference information after data integration.

These triple stores will serve as a reference data resource, since the data integration is performed by providers of several of the integrated databases.

The next collection of triple stores (200 to 500 M triples; PubMed, ChEMBL, CTD, PharmGKB) are primary data resources that cover individual observations, where a scientific publication is categorized similarly. All these data resources are growing at a rate that is linked to ongoing research in this domain, in contrast to a data resource that would report on scientific entities that can only be discovered once, e.g. a specific protein in a given species.

The following two fields of data resources (50 to 100 M triples; 12 to 50 M triples) contain different types of resources. The data in the resource from the first group correlates with experiments that are performed according to discovery needs and may lose relevance over time (see Affymetrix data). The second group contains reference data resources for species (Wormbase, SGD), pathways (KEGG, Reactome, iRefIndex), but also large-scale resources with a very specific purpose, such as Taxonomy, BioPortal, and SIDER.

For the remaining resources, it can be expected that they will be developing into large-scale resources as seen above (MGI, dbSNP, BioModels) whereas

---

[51] http://linkedlifedata.com (retr: 05/02/2017).

Table 6. Counts of triples (:T) and entities :E across the most relevant datasets across LSLOD, Bio2RDF and LLD (T/C: Type/-Category, Y/D:Year/Date, E/F: Environmental Factors, SPLs: Structured Product Labels, DIKB: Drug Interaction Knowledge Base, LLD: Linked Life Data) "_" = N/A)

Dataset	T/C	Y/D	Topic	Size/ Coverage	Description
LLD	LLD	2014-06-04	Drugs, Chromosomes etc	10'192'641'644:T, 15'536'206'391:E	25 public biomedical databases with access to complex bioinformatics
iProClass	Bio2RDF	2014-06-09	Proteins, pathways, genes	3'306'107'223:T, 364'255'265:E	UniProtKB and UniParc proteins, with links to biological databases
NCBI Gene	Bio2RDF	2014-09-20	Genes	2'010'283'833:T, 189'594'629:E	nomenclature, RefSeqs, maps, pathways, variations, phenotypes, locus-specific
PubMed	Bio2RDF	2014-06-27	Citations	500'5343'905:T, 412'593'720:E	citations from MEDLINE and LS journals for biomedical articles after 1950s
ChEMBL	Bio2RDF	-	bioactive compounds,bioactivities	409'942'525:T, 50'061'452:E	bioactive compounds, quantitative properties and bioactivities)
CTD	Bio2RDF	2014-06-09	Chemical-gene/protein interactions	326'720'894:T, 19'768'641:E	cross-species chemical-gene/protein interactions, chemical-gene-disease
PharmGKB	Bio2RDF	2014-06-27	genotype/phenotype	278'049'209:T, 25'325'504:E	genotype/phenotype data, gene variants, gene-drug-disease relationships
ClinicalTrials	Bio2RDF	2014-09-25	Clinical Trials	98'835'804:T, 7'337'123:E	publicly and privately supported clinical studies
GOA	Bio2RDF	2014-06-05	Gene Ontology Annotations	97'520'151:T, 5'950'074:E	Gene Ontology(GO) annotations to proteins in UniProtKB and IPI
Affymetrix	Bio2RDF	2014-08-01	Microarrays	86'942'371:T, 6'679'943:E	probesets used in the Affymetrix microarrays
KEGG	Bio2RDF	2014-08-13	Genes	50'197'150:T, 6'533'307:E	16 databases of biological, genomic, and chemical information
iRefIndex	Bio2RDF	2014-06-22	Proteins, pathways, genes	48'781'511:T, 3'110'993:E	protein interactions in BIND/BioGRID/DIP/HPRD/MPPI/OPHID
WormBase	Bio2RDF	2014-06-04	Genome	22'682'002:T, 1'840'311:E	genome of the Caenorhabditis elegans
Taxonomy	Bio2RDF	2014-05-27	Taxonomy	21'310'356:T, 1'147'211:E	organisms in the genetic databases with one nucleotide or protein sequence
BioPortal	Bio2RDF	2014-07-20	Biological/biomedical ontologies	19'920'395:T, 2'199'594:E	an open repository of biomedical ontologies
SIDER	Bio2RDF	2014-07-22	Drugs	17'627'864:T, 1'222'429:E	medicines and adverse drug reactions, side effect frequency/ classifications
SGD	Bio2RDF	2014-08-07	Biochemical reactions	12'494'945:T, 9'57'558:E	molecular biology and genetics of the yeast Saccharomyces cerevisiae
Reactome	Bio2RDF	-	Pathways	12'487'446:T, 2'461'010:E	core pathways and reactions in human biology
dbSNP	Bio2RDF	2014-07-15	Nucleotide substitutions	8'801'487:T, 530'538:E	single nucleotide substitutions, deletion insertion polymorphisms
OMIM	Bio2RDF	2014-09-19	Mendelian disorders, Genes	87'507'774:T, 1'013'389:E	human genes and genetic phenotypes
MGI	Bio2RDF	2014-06-05	Genes	8'206'813:T, 924'257:E	gene, nomenclature, mapping, homologies, sequence links, phenotypes, allelic's
MeSH	Bio2RDF	2014-05-27	terms and terminologies	7'323'864:T, 305'401:E	naming descriptors in hierarchical structure for searching specificity
HomoloGene	Bio2RDF	2014-07-04	Annotated Gene	7'189'769:T, 869'985:E	automated detection of homologs among the annotated genes
NDC	Bio2RDF	2014-08-02	Drugs Identifies	6'199'488:T, 488'146:E	UPI used in the USA for drugs intended for human use
PC	Bio2RDF	-	Pathways	5'700'724:T, 1'024'572:E	biological pathway information collected from public pathway databases
DrugBank	Bio2RDF	2014-07-25	Drugs	3'672'531:T, 316'950:E	detailed drug data with comprehensive drug target
HGNC	Bio2RDF	2014-07-04	Human Gene	3'628'205:T, 372'136:E	gives unique and meaningful names to every human gene
SABIO-RK	Bio2RDF	2014-06-05	Biochemical reactions	2'716'421:T, 448'248:E	biochemical reactions, kinetic equations, parameters, conditions
BioModels	Bio2RDF	2014-06-05	Biological/mathematical models	2'380'009:T, 188'380:E	store, search, retrieve published mathematical models of biological interests
InterPro	Bio2RDF	2014-06-02	Proteins and Genomes	2'323'345:T, 176'579:E	predictive protein "signatures"/ annotation of proteins and genomes
LinkedSPL	Bio2RDF	-	Drugs	2'174'579:T, 59'776:E	Linked Data version of DailyMed
WikiPathways	Bio2RDF	-	Pathway maps	514'397:T, 71'879:E	open and public collection of pathway maps
Orphanet	Bio2RDF	2014-06-02	Rare diseases/Orphan drugs	377'947:T, 28'871:E	rare diseases and orphan drugs. Diagnosis, care and treatment of rare diseases
GenAge	Bio2RDF	2014-06-03	Genes	73'048:T, 6'995:E	human and model organism genes related to longevity and ageing
LSr	Bio2RDF	2014-07-16	LS terminologies	55'914:T, 5'032:E	datasets and terminologies used in the Life Sciences
GenDR	Bio2RDF	2014-06-03	Genes	11'663:T, 1'129:E	genes associated with dietary restriction (DR)

Table 7. Quantitative overview of datasets involving LODD only without judgement on the number of entries versus triples. (**T/C**: Type/Category, **Y/D**: Year/Date, **SPLs**: Structured Product Labels, **DDIs**: Drug Drug Interactions, "-": N/A)

Dataset	T/C	Y/D	Topic	Size/Coverage	Description
DBpedia	LODD	2009	Drugs/Diseases/ Proteins	218 M:**T**; 2'300 drugs; 2'200 proteins	2.49 M wikipedia things
ChEMBL	LODD	2010	Assays(Proteins, Organisms)	130 M :**T**	trial drugs and activity against targets
LinkedCT	LODD	–	Clinical Trials	25 M :**T**, 106'000 trials	trials from ClinicalTrials.gov
RxNorm	LODD	2011	Drugs	> 7.7 M :**T**	connects drugs, ingredients and NDC
GHO	LODD	2011	Infectious Diseases	3 M :**T**	infectious diseases demographically
DailyMed	LODD	2010	Drugs	1'604'893:**T**, 36'000+ product	all FDA-approved SPLs and NDF-RT
DrugBank	LODD	2010	Drugs	766'920:**T**, 4'800 drugs	drug data with drug target info
SIDER	LODD	2010	Diseases/Side Effects	192'515:**T**; 63'000 effect, 1'737 genes	marketed drugs/ their adverse effects
RDF-TCM	LODD	2009	Genes/Diseases/ Medicine	117'643:**T**	Chinese medicine, gene, disease association
Diseasome	LODD	2010	Diseases/ Genes	91'182:**T**; 2'600 genes	disorders and disease genes links
DIKB	LODD	2011	Drugs/ (DDIs)	> 41 k :**T**	Drugs and DDIs Claims
STITCH	LODD	2010	Chemicals/ Proteins	7'500'000 chemicals; 500'000 proteins	chemicals, proteins, and their interactions
UPNR	LODD	–	Drugs/Procedures/ Diagnoses	38'664	800 full-text clinical notes of Univ of Pittsburgh
Medicare	LODD	2010	Medicare Formulary	–	doctors, healthcare professionals, services

others by the nature of their content, would show only very limited growth, such as HGNC, DrugBank, Orphanet, and also possibly InterPro. Further resources have been considered (ref. Table 7), but could not be analysed to the degree of detail as for the data resources given in Table 6.

As a conclusion, the life science research community has to determine, which technological solutions allow the delivery of the large-scale semantic Web triple stores to the general public. Other data resources may well be replicated at different sites for local integration work.

6   Conclusion

In this paper we analysed (and quantified) different tiers of biomedical data relevant to the *Cancer Chemoprevention* and *Drug Discovery* domain. This involves ontologies, libraries and databases in healthcare and the biomedical domain, Linked Data and Life Science Linked Open Data.

We classify ontologies into three main classes: (i) biomedical Ontologies (e.g. EFO, OBI, GO etc.), (ii) Drugs and Chemical Compound Ontologies (e.g. RxNorm) and (iii) Generic and Upper Ontologies (e.g. BFO, RO, PROV). Similarly we categorise libraries and databases in five categories that comprise (i) *Gene, Gene Expression and Protein Databases*, (ii) *Pathway databases*, (iii) *Chemical and Structure Databases including Biological Activities*, (iv) *Disease Specific Databases for Prevention*, and the (v) *Literature databases*. This paper also highlights biomedical services that provide ontologies and databases resources relevant for drug discovery.

Access to the data repositories

Affymetrix (http://cu.affymetrix.bio2rdf.org/sparql), **BioModels** (http://cu.biomodels.bio2rdf.org/sparql), **BioPortal** (http://cu.bioportal.bio2rdf.org/sparql), **ChEMBL** (http://cu.chembl.bio2rdf.org/sparql, http://rdf.farmbio.uu.se/chembl/sparql), **ClinicalTrials** (http://cu.clinicaltrials.bio2rdf.org/sparql), **CTD** (http://cu.ctd.bio2rdf.org/sparql), **DailyMed** (http://purl.org/net/nlprepository/linkedSPLs), **DBpedia** (http://dbpedia.org/sparql), **dbSNP** (http://cu.dbsnp.bio2rdf.org/sparql), **DIKB** (http://dbmi-icode-01.dbmi.pitt.edu:2020/), **Diseasome** (http://www4.wiwiss.fu-berlin.de/diseasome/sparql), **DrugBank** (http://cu.drugbank.bio2rdf.org/sparql, http://www4.wiwiss.fu-berlin.de/drugbank/sparql), **GenAge** (http://cu.genage.bio2rdf.org/sparql), **GenDR** (http://cu.gendr.bio2rdf.org/sparql), **GHO** (http://gho.aksw.org), **GOA** (http://cu.goa.bio2rdf.org/sparql), **HGNC** (http://cu.hgnc.bio2rdf.org/sparql), **HomoloGene** (http://cu.homologene.bio2rdf.org/sparql), **InterPro** (http://cu.interpro.bio2rdf.org/sparql), **iProClass** (http://cu.iproclass.bio2rdf.org/sparql), **iRefIndex** (http://cu.irefindex.bio2rdf.org/sparql), **KEGG** (http://cu.kegg.bio2rdf.org/sparql), **LinkedCT** (http://data.linkedct.org/sparql), **LinkedLifeData** (http://linkedlifedata.com/sparql), **LinkedSPL** (http://cu.linkedspl.bio2rdf.org/sparql), **LSR** (http://cu.lsr.bio2rdf.org/sparql), **Medicare** (http://www4.wiwiss.fu-berlin.de/medicare/sparql), **MeSH** (http://cu.mesh.bio2rdf.org/sparql), **MGI** (http://cu.mgi.bio2rdf.org/sparql), **NCBI Gene** (http://cu.ncbigene.bio2rdf.org/sparql), **NDC** (http://cu.ndc.bio2rdf.org/sparql), **OMIM** (http://cu.omim.bio2rdf.org/sparql), **Orphanet** (http://cu.orphanet.bio2rdf.org/sparql), **PathwayCommons** (http://cu.pathwaycommons.bio2rdf.org/sparql), **PharmGKB** (http://cu.pharmgkb.bio2rdf.org/sparql), **PubMed** (http://cu.pharmgkb.bio2rdf.org/sparql), **RDF-TCM** (http://www.open-biomed.org.uk/sparql/endpoint/tcm), **Reactome** (http://cu.reactome.bio2rdf.org/sparql), **RxNorm** (http://link.informatics.stonybrook.edu/sparql/), **SABIO-RK** (http://cu.sabiork.bio2rdf.org/sparql), **SGD** (http://cu.sgd.bio2rdf.org/sparql), **SIDER** (http://cu.sider.bio2rdf.org/sparql, http://www4.wiwiss.fu-berlin.de/sider/sparql), **STITCH** (http://www4.wiwiss.fu-berlin.de/stitch/sparql), **Taxonomy** (http://cu.taxonomy.bio2rdf.org/sparql), **UPNR** (http://dbmi-icode-01.dbmi.pitt.edu:8080/sparql), **WikiPathways** (http://cu.wikipathways.bio2rdf.org/sparql), **WormBase** (http://cu.wormbase.bio2rdf.org/sparql).

Acknowledgements. The work presented in this paper has been partly funded by EU FP7 GRANATUM project (project number 270139) and Science Foundation Ireland under Grant No. SFI/12/RC/2289.

References

1. Belleau, F., Nolin, M.A., Tourigny, N., Rigault, P., Morissette, J.: Bio2RDF: towards a mashup to build bioinformatics knowledge systems. J. Biomed. Inform. **41**(5), 706–716 (2008)
2. Berners-Lee, T., Bizer, C., Heath, T.: Linked data-the story so far. Int. J. Semant. Web Inform. Syst. **5**(3), 1–22 (2009)
3. Corpet, D.E., Taché, S.: Most effective colon cancer chemopreventive agents in rats: a systematic review of aberrant crypt foci and tumor data, ranked by potency. Nutr. Cancer **43**(1), 1–21 (2002)
4. Deus, K.T.W.P.C.N.T.B.C.G.C.K.H.F.: D1.1 – requirements analysis. Technical report, CERTH, NUIG-DERI, FIT, CYBION, UCY, and DKFZ (2011)
5. Doolittle, R., Abelson, J., Simon, M.: Computer methods for macromolecular sequence analysis. In: Methods in Enzymology, vol. 266 (1996)
6. Greenes, R.A., McClure, R.C., Pattison-Gordon, E., Sato, L.: The findings-diagnosis continuum: implications for image descriptions and clinical databases. In: Proceedings of the Annual Symposium on Computer Application in Medical Care, p. 383. American Medical Informatics Association (1992)
7. Hasnain, A., Fox, R., Decker, S., Deus, H.F.: Cataloguing and linking life sciences LOD Cloud. In: 1st International Workshop on Ontology Engineering in a Data-driven World collocated with EKAW12 (2012)
8. Hasnain, A., et al.: Linked biomedical dataspace: lessons learned integrating data for drug discovery. In: Mika, P., et al. (eds.) ISWC 2014. LNCS, vol. 8796, pp. 114–130. Springer, Cham (2014). https://doi.org/10.1007/978-3-319-11964-9_8
9. Hasnain, A., Mehmood, Q., e Zainab, S.S., Saleem, M., Warren, C., Zehra, D., Decker, S., Rebholz-Schuhmann, D.: BioFed: federated query processing over life sciences linked open data. J. Biomed. Semant. **8**(1), 13 (2017). http://dx.doi.org/10.1186/s13326-017-0118-0
10. Hasnain, A., Mehmood, Q., e Zainab, S.S., Hogan, A.: SPORTAL: profiling the content of public SPARQL endpoints. Int. J. Semant. Web Inform. Syst. (IJSWIS) **12**(3), 134–163 (2016). http://www.igi-global.com/article/sportal/160175
11. Hasnain, A., Mehmood, Q., e Zainab, S.S., Hogan, A.: SPORTAL: searching for public SPARQL endpoints. In: Proceedings of the ISWC 2016 Posters & Demonstrations Track co-located with 15th International Semantic Web Conference (ISWC 2016), Kobe, Japan, 19 October 2016 (2016). http://ceur-ws.org/Vol-1690/paper78.pdf
12. Hasnain, A., et al.: A roadmap for navigating the life sciences linked open data cloud. In: Supnithi, T., Yamaguchi, T., Pan, J.Z., Wuwongse, V., Buranarach, M. (eds.) JIST 2014. LNCS, vol. 8943, pp. 97–112. Springer, Cham (2015). https://doi.org/10.1007/978-3-319-15615-6_8
13. Hasnain, S.M.A.: Cataloguing and linking publicly available biomedical SPARQL endpoints for federation-addressing aPosteriori data integration. Ph.D. thesis (2017)
14. Hirst, G.: Ontology and the lexicon. In: Staab, S., Studer, R. (eds.) andbook on Ontologies: International Handbooks on Information Systems, pp. 269–292. Springer, Heidelberg (2004). https://doi.org/10.1007/978-3-540-92673-3_12
15. Hoehndorf, R., Dumontier, M., Gkoutos, G.V.: Evaluation of research in biomedical ontologies. Brief. Bioinform. **14**(6), 696–712 (2012)

16. Jimeno-Yepes, A., Jiménez-Ruiz, E., Berlanga, R., Rebholz-Schuhmann, D.: Use of shared lexical resources for efficient ontological engineering. In: Semantic Web Applications and Tools for Life Sciences Workshop (SWAT4LS), CEUR WS Proceedings, vol. 435, pp. 93–136 (2008)
17. Machado, C.M., Rebholz-Schuhmann, D., Freitas, A.T., Couto, F.M.: The semantic web in translational medicine: current applications and future directions. Brief Bioinform., bbt079 (2013)
18. Musen, M.A.: Dimensions of knowledge sharing and reuse. Comput. Biomed. Res. **25**(5), 435–467 (1992)
19. Pico, A.R., Kelder, T., Iersel, M.P., Hanspers, K., Conklin, B.R., Evelo, C.: WikiPathways: pathway editing for the people. PLoS Biol. **6**(7), e184 (2008)
20. Rebholz-Schuhmann, D., Oellrich, A., Hoehndorf, R.: Text-mining solutions for biomedical research: enabling integrative biology. Nat. Rev. Genet. **13**(12), 829–839 (2012)
21. Rebholz-Schuhmann, D., Grabmuller, C., Kavaliauskas, S., Harrow, I., Kapushevsky, M., Westaway, M., Woollard, P., Wilkinson, N., Strutt, P., Braxtenthaler, M., Hoole, D., Wilson, J., O'Beirne, R., Kidd, R.R., Filsell, W., Marshall, C., Backofen, R., Clark, D.: Semantic integration of gene-disease associations for diabetes type II from literature and biomedical data resources. Drug Discov. Today **19**(7), 882–889 (2014)
22. Rebholz-Schuhmann, D., Kim, J.H., Yan, Y., Dixit, A., Friteyere, C., Backofen, R., Lewin, I.: Evaluation and cross-comparison of Lexical Entities of Biological Interest (LexEBI). PLoS One **8**(10), e75185 (2013)
23. Splendiani, A., Gundel, M., Austyn, J.M., Cavalieri, D., Scognamiglio, C., Brandizi, M.: Knowledge sharing and collaboration in translational research, and the DC-THERA Directory. Brief. Bioinform. **12**(6), 562–575 (2011)
24. Wishart, D.S., Knox, C., Guo, A.C., Cheng, D., Shrivastava, S., Tzur, D., Gautam, B., Hassanali, M.: DrugBank: a knowledgebase for drugs, drug actions and drug targets. Nucleic Acids Res. **36**(suppl 1), D901–D906 (2008)
25. e Zainab, S.S., Hasnain, A., Saleem, M., Mehmood, Q., Zehra, D., Decker, S.: FedViz: a visual interface for SPARQL queries formulation and execution. In: Visualizations and User Interfaces for Ontologies and Linked Data (VOILA 2015), Bethlehem, Pennsylvania, USA (2015)

SHARP: Harmonizing and Bridging Cross-Workflow Provenance

Alban Gaignard[1](✉), Khalid Belhajjame[2], and Hala Skaf-Molli[3]

[1] l'institut du thorax, INSERM, CNRS, UNIV Nantes, Nantes, France
alban.gaignard@univ-nantes.fr
[2] Université de Paris-Dauphine, LAMSADE, Paris, France
kbelhajj@googlemail.com
[3] Université de Nantes, LS2N, Nantes, France
hala.skaf@univ-nantes.fr

Abstract. PROV has been adopted by a number of workflow systems for encoding the traces of workflow executions. Exploiting these provenance traces is hampered by two main impediments. Firstly, workflow systems extend PROV differently to cater for system-specific constructs. The difference between the adopted PROV extensions yields heterogeneity in the generated provenance traces. This heterogeneity diminishes the value of such traces, *e.g.* when combining and querying provenance traces of different workflow systems. Secondly, the provenance recorded by workflow systems tends to be large, and as such difficult to browse and understand by a human user. In this paper (extending [14], initially published at SeWeBMeDA'17), we propose SHARP, a Linked Data approach for harmonizing cross-workflow provenance. The harmonization is performed by chasing tuple-generating and equality-generating dependencies defined for workflow provenance. This results in a provenance graph that can be summarized using domain-specific vocabularies. We experimentally evaluate SHARP (i) on publicly available provenance documents and (ii) using a real-world omic experiment involving workflow traces generated by the Taverna and Galaxy systems.

Keywords: Reproducibility · Scientific workflows · Provenance · Prov constraints

1 Introduction

Reproducibility has recently gained momentum in (computational) sciences as a means for promoting the understanding, transparency and ultimately the reuse of experiments. This is particularly true in life sciences where Next Generation Sequencing (NGS) equipments produce tremendous amounts of omics data, and lead to massive computational analysis (aligning, filtering, etc.). Life scientists urgently need for reproducibility and reuse to avoid duplication of storage and computing efforts.

E. Blomqvist et al. (Eds.): ESWC 2017 Satellite Events, LNCS 10577, pp. 219–234, 2017.
https://doi.org/10.1007/978-3-319-70407-4_35

Workflows have been used for almost two decades as a means for specifying, enacting and sharing scientific experiments. To tackle reproducibility challenges, major workflow systems have been instrumented to automatically track provenance information. Such information specifies, among other things, the data products (entities) that were used and generated by the operations of the experiments and their derivation paths. Workflow provenance has several applications since it can be utilized for debugging workflows, tracing the lineage of workflow results, as well as understanding the workflow and enabling its reuse and reproducibility [4,6,17,21].

Despite the fact that workflow systems are currently adopting extensions of the PROV recommendation [18], the extensions they adopt use different constructs of PROV. An increasing number of provenance-producing environments adopt semantic web technologies and propose/use extensions of the PROV-O ontology [16]. Because of this, exploiting the provenance traces of multiple workflows, enacted by different workflow systems, is hindered by their heterogeneity.

We present in this paper SHARP, a solution that we investigated for harmonizing and linking the provenance traces produced by different workflow systems.

Specifically, we make the following contributions:

- An approach for interlinking and harmonizing provenance traces recorded by different workflow systems based on PROV inferences.
- An application of provenance harmonization towards Linked Experiment Reports by using domain-specific annotations as in [15].
- An evaluation with public PROV documents and a real-world omic use case.

The paper is organized as follows. Section 2 describes motivations and problem statement. Section 3 presents the harmonization of multiple PROV Graphs and its application towards Linked Experiment Reports. Sections 4 and 5 report our implementation and experimental results. Section 6 summarizes related works. Finally, conclusions and future works are outlined in Sect. 7.

2   Motivations and Problem Statement

Due to costly equipments and massively produced data, DNA sequencing is generally outsourced to third-party facilities. Therefore, one part of the experiments is conducted by the sequencing facility requiring dedicated computing infrastructures, and a second part is conducted by the scientists themselves to analyze and interpret the results based on traditional computing resources. Figure 1 illustrates a concrete example of two workflows enacted by different workflow systems, namely Galaxy [2] and Taverna [20].

The first workflow (WF1), in blue in Fig. 1, is implemented in Galaxy and addresses common DNA data pre-processing. Such workflow takes as input two DNA sequences from two biological samples s1 and s2, represented in green. For each sample, the sequence data is stored in forward[1] (.R1) and reverse (.R2) files.

---

[1] DNA sequencers can decode genomic sequences in both forward and reverse directions which improves the accuracy of alignment to reference genomes.

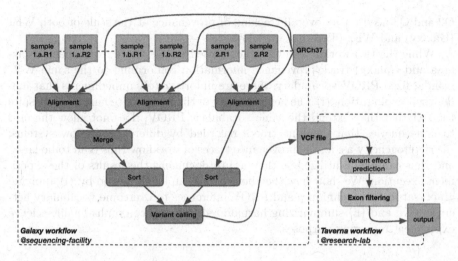

Fig. 1. A multi-site genomics workflow, involving Galaxy and Taverna workflow environments. (Color figure online)

The first sample has been split by the sequencer in two parts, (.a) and (.b). The very first processing step consists in aligning (`Alignment`[2]) short sequence reads onto a reference human genome (`GRCh37`). Then the two parts a and b are merged[3] into a single file. Then the aligned reads are sorted[4] prior to genetic variant identification[5] (`Variant Calling`). This primary analysis workflow finally produces a VCF[6] file which lists all known genetics variations compared to the `GCRh37` reference genome.

The second workflow (WF2) is implemented with Taverna, and highly depends on scientific questions. It is generally conducted by life scientists possibly from different research labs and with less computational needs. Such workflow proceeds as follows. It first queries a database of known effects to associate a predicted effect[7] (`Variant effect prediction`). Then all these predictions are filtered to select only those applying to the exon parts of genes (`Exon filtering`). The results obtained by the executions of such workflows allow the scientists to have answers for questions such as Q1: *"From a set of gene mutations, which are common variants, and which are rare variants?"*, Q2: *"Which alignment algorithm was used when predicting these effects?"*, or Q3: *"A new version of a reference genome is available, which genome was used when predicting these effects?"*. While Q1 can be answered based on provenance tracking from WF1,

---

[2] BWA-mem: http://bio-bwa.sourceforge.net.
[3] PICARD: https://broadinstitute.github.io/picard/.
[4] SAMtools sort: http://www.htslib.org.
[5] SAMtools mpileup.
[6] Variant Call Format.
[7] SnpEff tool: http://snpeff.sourceforge.net.

Q2 and Q3 need for an overall tracking of provenance at the scale of both WF1 (Galaxy) and WF2 (Taverna) workflows.

While the two workflow environments used in the above experiments (Taverna and Galaxy) track provenance information conforming to the same W3C standardized PROV vocabulary, there are unfortunately impediments that hinder their exploitation. (i) The heterogeneity of the provenance languages, despite the fact that they extend the same vocabulary PROV, does not allow the user to issue queries that combine traces recorded by different workflow systems. (ii) Heterogeneity aside, the provenance traces of workflow runs tend to be large, and thus cannot be utilized as they are to document the results of the experiment execution. We show how the above issues can be addressed by, (i) applying graph saturation techniques and PROV inferences to overcome vocabulary heterogeneity, and (ii) summarizing harmonized provenance graphs for life-science experiment reporting purposes.

3   Harmonizing Multiple PROV Graphs

Faced with the heterogeneity in the provenance vocabularies, we can use classical data integration approaches such as peer-to-peer data integration or mediator-based data integration [11]. Both options are expensive since they require the specification of schema mappings that often require heavy human inputs. In this paper, we explore a third and cheaper approach that exploits the fact that many of the provenance vocabularies used by workflow systems extend the W3C PROV-O ontology. This means that such vocabularies already come with implicit mappings between the concepts and relationships they used and those of the W3C PROV-O. Of course, not all the concepts and relationships used by individual mappings will be catered for in PROV. Still this solution remains attractive because it does not require any human inputs, since the constraints (mappings) are readily available. We show in this section how the different provenance traces can be harmonized by capitalizing on such constraints.

3.1   Tuple-Generating Dependencies

Central to our approach to harmonizing provenance traces is the saturation operation. Given a possibly disconnected provenance RDF graph G, the saturation process generates a saturated graph G^∞ obtained by repeatedly applying some rules to G until no new triple can be inferred. We distinguish between two kinds of rules. **OWL entailment rules** includes, among other things, rules for deriving new RDF statements through the transitivity of class and property relationships. **Prov constraints** [8], these are of interest to us as they encode inferences and constraints that need to be satisfied by provenance traces, and can as a such be used for deriving new RDF provenance triples.

In this section, we examine such constraints by identifying those that are of interest when harmonizing the provenance traces of workflow executions, and show (when deemed useful) how they can be translated into SPARQL queries for saturation purposes. It is worth noting that the W3C Provenance constraint document presents the inferences and constraints assuming a relational-like model with possibly relations of arity greater than 2. We adapt these rules to the context of RDF where properties (relations) are binary. For space limitations, we do not show all the inferences rules that can be implemented in SPARQL, we focus instead on representative ones. We identify three categories of rules with respect to expressiveness (i) rules that contain only universal variables, (ii) rules that contain existential variables, (iii) rules making use of n-array relations (with $n \geqslant 3$). The latter is interesting, since RDF reification is needed to represent such relations. For exemplary rule, we present the rules using tuple-generating dependencies TGDs [1], and then show how we encode it in SPARQL. A TGD is a first order logic formula $\forall \bar{x}\bar{y} \ \phi(\bar{x}, \bar{y}) \rightarrow \exists \bar{z} \ \psi(\bar{y}, \bar{z})$, where $\phi(\bar{x}, \bar{y})$ and $\psi(\bar{y}, \bar{z})$ are conjunctions of atomic formulas.

Transitivity of alternateOf. Alternate-Of is a binary relation that associates two entities e_1 and e_2 to specify that the two entities present aspects of the same thing. The following rule states that such a relation is transitive, and it can be encoded using a SPARQL construct query, in a straightforward manner.

$$\text{alternateOf}(e_1, e_2), \ \text{alternateOf}(e_2, e_3) \ \rightarrow \ \text{alternateOf}(e_1, e_3).$$

Inference of Usage and Generation from Derivation. The following rule states that if an entity e_2 was derived from an entity e_1, then there exists an activity a, such that a used e_1 and generated e_2.

$$\text{wasDerivedFrom}(e_2, e_1) \ \rightarrow \ \exists \ a \ \text{used}(a, e_1), \ \text{wasGeneratedFrom}(e_2, a).$$

Notice that unlike the previous rule, the head of the above rule contains an existential variable, namely the activity a. To encode such a rule in SPARQL, we make use of blank nodes[8] for existential variables as illustrated below.

```
CONSTRUCT {
    ?e_2 prov:wasGeneratedBy _:blank_node .
    _:blank_node prov:used ?e_1
} WHERE { ?e_2 prov:wasDerivedFrom ?e_1 }
```

Using the Qualification Patterns. In the previous rule, derivation, usage and generation are represented using binary relationships, which do not pose any problem to be encoded in RDF. Note, however, that PROV-DM allows such relationships to be augmented with optional attributes. For example, usage can be associated with a timestamp specifying the time at which the activity used the entity. The presence of extra optional attributes increases the arity of the relations that can no longer be represented using an RDF property. As a solution, the PROV-O opts for qualification patterns[9] introduced in [12].

The following rule shows how the inference of usage and generation from derivation can be expressed when such relationships are qualified. It can also be encoded using a SPARQL Construct query with blank nodes.

---

[8] https://www.w3.org/TR/rdf11-concepts/#dfn-blank-node.
[9] https://www.w3.org/TR/prov-o/.

$$\begin{aligned}
\texttt{qualifiedDerivation}(e_2, d), \texttt{provEntity}(d, e_1) \\
\rightarrow \exists\, a, u, g\; \texttt{qualifiedUsage}(a, u), \\
\texttt{provEntity}(u, e_1), \texttt{qualifiedGeneration}(e_2, g), \texttt{provActivity}(g, a).
\end{aligned}$$

Figure 2 presents inferred statements in dashed arrows resulting from the application of this rule.

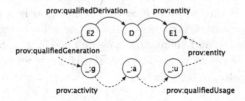

Fig. 2. Inferred qualified usage and generation relationships.

3.2   Equality-Generating Dependencies

As well as the tuple-generating dependencies, we need to consider equality-generating dependencies (EGDs), which are induced by uniqueness constraints. An EGD is a first order formula: $\forall \bar{x} \phi(\bar{x}) \rightarrow (x_1 = x_2)$, where $\phi(\bar{x})$ is a conjunction of atomic formulas, and x_1 and x_2 are among the variables in $\bar{x}$. We give below an example of an EGD, that is implied by the uniqueness of the generation that associates a given activity a with a given entity e.

$$\begin{aligned}
\texttt{wasGeneratedBy}(gen_1, e, a, attrs_1), \texttt{wasGeneratedBy}(gen_2, e, a, attrs_2) \\
\rightarrow (gen_1 = gen_2)
\end{aligned}$$

Having defined an example EGD, we need to specify what it means to apply it (or chase it [13]) when we are dealing with RDF data. The application of an EGD has three possible outcomes. To illustrate them, we will work on the above example EGD. Typically, the generations gen_1 and gen_2 will be represented by two RDF resources. We distinguish the following cases:

(i) **gen_1 is a non blank RDF resource and gen_2 is a blank node.** In this case, we add to gen_1 the properties that are associated with the blank node gen_2, and remove gen_2. (ii) **gen_1 and gen_2 are two blank nodes.** In this case, we create a single blank node gen to which we associate the properties obtained by unionizing the properties of gen_1 and gen_2, and we remove the two initial blank nodes. (iii) **gen_1 and gen_2 are non blank nodes that are different.** In this case, the application of the EGD (as well as the whole saturation) fails. In general, we would not have this case, if the initial workflows runs that we use as input are valid (i.e., they respect the constraints defined in the W3C Prov Constraint recommendation [8]).

Algorithm 1. EGD pseudo-code for merging blank nodes produced by PROV inference rules with existential variables.

Input   : G' : the provenance graph resulting from the application of TGD on G
Output: G'': the provenance graph with substituted blank nodes, when possible.

```
1  begin
2      G'' ← G'
3      substitutions ← new List < Pair < Node, Node >> ()
4      repeat
5          S ← findSubstitutions(G')
6          foreach (s ∈ S) do
7              source ← s[0]
8              target ← s[1]
9              foreach (in ∈ G'.listStatements(*, *, source)) do
10                 G'' ← G''.add(in.getSubject(), in.getPredicate(), target)
11                 G'' ← G''.del(in)
12             foreach (out ∈ G'.listStatements(source, *, *)) do
13                 G'' ← G''.add(target, out.getPredicate(), out.getObject())
14                 G'' ← G''.del(out)
15     until (S.size() = 0)
```

To select the candidate substitutions (line 5 of Algorithm 1), we express the graph patterns illustrated in the previous cases 1 and 2 as a SPARQL query. This query retrieves candidate substitutions as blank nodes coupled to their substitute, *i.e.*, another blank node or a URI.

For each of the found substitution (line 6), we merge the incoming and outgoing relations between the source node and the target node. This operation is done in two steps. First, we navigate through the incoming relations of the source node (line 9), we copy them as incoming relations of the target node (line 10), and finally remove them from the source node (line 11). Second, we repeat this operation for the outgoing relations (lines 12 to 14). We repeat this process until we can't find any candidate substitutions.

3.3 Full Provenance Harmonization Process

The full provenance harmonization workflow is sketched in Fig. 3.

❶ **Multi-provenance Linking.** This process starts by first linking the traces of the different workflow runs. Typically, the outputs produced by a run of a given workflow are used to feed the execution of a run of another workflow as depicted in Fig. 1.

The main idea consists in providing an *owl:sameAs* property between the PROV entities associated with the same physical files. The production of *owl:sameAs* can be automated as follows: (i) generate a fingerprint of the files (SHA-512 is one of the recommended hashing functions), (ii) produce the PROV annotation associated the fingerprint to the PROV entities, (iii) generate, through a SPARQL CONSTRUCT query, the *owl:sameAs* relationships when fingerprints are matched. When applied to our motivating example (Fig. 1), the PROV entity

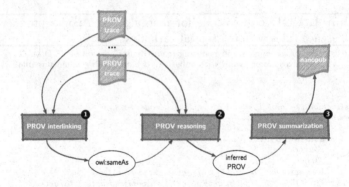

Fig. 3. From multiple PROV traces to linked experiment summaries.

annotating the *VCFFile* produced by the Galaxy workflow becomes equivalent to the one as input of Taverna workflow. A PROV example associating a file name and its fingerprint is reported below:

```
<http://fr.symetric#c583bef6-de69-4caa-bc3a-00000000>
        a            prov:Entity ;
        rdfs:label   "my-variants.vcf"^^xsd:String ;
        crypto:sha512  "1d305986330304378f82b938d776ea0be48eda8210f7af6c
        152e8562cf6393b2f5edd452c22ef6fe8c729cb01eb3687ac35f1c5e57ddefc4
        6276e9c60409276a"^^xsd:String .
```

The following SPARQL Construct query can be used to produce owl:sameAs relationships:

```
CONSTRUCT { ?x owl:sameAs ?y }
WHERE {
    ?x a prov:Entity .
    ?x crypto:sha512 ?x_sha512 .
    ?y a prov:Entity .
    ?y crypto:sha512 ?y_sha512 .
    FILTER( ?x_sha512 = ?y_sha512 ) }
```

❷ **Multi-provenance Reasoning.** Once the traces of the workflow runs have been linked, we saturate the graph obtained using OWL entailment rules. This operation can be performed using an existing OWL reasoner[10] (e.g., [7]). We then start by repeatedly applying the TGDs and EGDs derived from the W3C PROV constraint document, as illustrated in Sects. 3.1 and 3.2. The harmonization process terminates when we can no longer apply any existing TGD or EGD. This harmonization process raises the question as to whether such process will terminate. The answer is affirmative. Indeed, it has been shown in the W3C PROV Constraint document that the constraints are weakly acyclic, which guarantees the termination of the chasing process in polynomial time (see Fagin *et al.* [13] for more details).

---

[10] Apache Jena - Reasoners and rule engines: Jena inference support. The Apache Software Foundation (2013)

❸ Harmonized Provenance Summarization. The previously described reasoning step may lead to intractable provenance graphs from a human perspective, both in terms of size and lack of domain-specificity. We propose in this last step to make sense of the harmonized provenance through domain-specific provenance summaries. This application is described in the following section.

3.4 Application of Provenance Harmonization: Domain-Specific Experiment Reports

In this section we propose to exploit harmonized provenance graphs by transforming them into *Linked Experiment Reports*. These reports are no longer machine-only-oriented and benefit from a humanly tractable size, and domain-specific concepts.

Domain-Specific Vocabularies. *Workflow annotations.* P-Plan[11] is an ontology aimed at representing the plans followed during a computational experiment. *Plans* can be atomic or composite and are a made by a sequence of processing *Steps*. Each *Step* represents an executable activity, and involves input and output *Variables*. P-Plan fits well in the context of multi-site workflows since it allows to work at the scale of a site-specific workflow as well as at the scale of the global workflow.

Domain-Specific Concepts and Relations. To capture knowledge associated to the data processing steps, we rely on EDAM[12] which is actively developed in the context of the Bio.Tools bioinformatics registry. However these annotations on processing tools do not capture the scientific context in which a workflow takes place. SIO[13], the Semantic science Integrated Ontology, has been proposed as a comprehensive and consistent knowledge representation framework to model and exchange physical, informational and processual entities. Since SIO has been initially focusing on Life Sciences, and is reused in several Linked Data repositories, it provides a way to link the data routinely produced by PROV-enabled workflow environment to major linked open data repositories, such as Bio2RDF.

NanoPublications[14] are minimal sets of information to publish data as citable artifacts while taking into account the attribution and authorship. NanoPublications provide named graphs mechanisms to link *Assertion*, *Provenance*, and *Publishing* statements. In the remainder of this section, we show how fine-grained and machine-oriented provenance graphs can be summarized into NanoPublications.

Linked Experiment Reports. Based on harmonized multi-provenance graphs, we show how to produce NanoPublications as exchangeable and citeable scientific experiment reports. Figure 4 drafts how data artifacts and scientific

---

[11] http://purl.org/net/p-plan.
[12] http://edamontology.org.
[13] http://sio.semanticscience.org.
[14] http://nanopub.org.

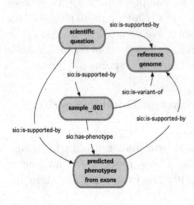

```
:head {
    ex:pub1 a np:Nanopublication .
    ex:pub1 np:hasAssertion :assertion1 ;
        np:hasAssertion :assertion2 .
    ex:pub1 np:hasProvenance :provenance .
    ex:pub1 np:hasPublicationInfo :pubInfo .}
:assertion1 {
    ex:question a sio:Question ;
        sio:has-value "What are the effects of SNPs
        located in exons for study-Y samples"  ;
        sio:is-supported-by ex:referenceGenome ;
        sio:is-supported-by ex:sample_001 ;
        sio:is-supported-by ex:annotatedVariants .}
:assertion2 {
    ex:referenceGenome a sio:Genome .
    ex:sample_001 a sio:Sample ;
        sio:is-variant-of ex:referenceGenome ;
        sio:has-phenotype ex:annotatedVariants .}
:provenance { :assertion2 prov:wasDerivedFrom
    :harmonizedProvBundle .}
:pubInfo { ex:pub1 prov:wasAttributedTo ex:MyLab .}
```

Fig. 4. Graphical and RDF representation of an experiment report, providing context and linking the most relevant multi-site workflow artifacts to domain specific statements.

context can be related to each other into a NanoPublication, for the motivating scenario introduced in Sect. 2. For the sake of simplicity we omitted the definition of namespaces, and we used the labels of SIO predicates instead of their identifiers.

To produce this NanoPublication, we identify a data lineage path in multiple PROV graphs, beforehand harmonized (as proposed in Sect. 3). Since we identified the *prov:wasInfluencedBy* as the most commonly inferred lineage relationship, we search for all connected data entities through this relationship. Then, when connected data entities are identified, we extract the relevant ones so that they can be later on incorporated and annotated through new statements in the NanoPublication. The following SPARQL query illustrates how `:assertion2` can be assembled from a matched path in harmonized provenance graphs. The key point consists in relying on SPARQL property path expressions (`prov:wasInfluencedBy`)+ to identify all paths connecting data artifacts composed by one or more occurrences of the *prov:wasInfluencedBy* predicate. Such SPARQL queries could be programmatically generated based on P-Plan templates as it has been proposed in our previous work [15].

```
CONSTRUCT {
    GRAPH :assertion {
        ?ref_genome a sio:Genome .
        ?sample a sio:Sample ;
            sio:is-variant-of ?ref_genome ;
            sio:has-phenotype ?out .
        ?out rdfs:label ?out_label .
        ?out sio:is-supported-by ?ref_genome . }
} WHERE {
    ?sample rdfs:label ?sample_label.
    FILTER (contains(lcase(str(?sample_label)), lcase("fastq"))) .
    ?ref_genome rdfs:label ?ref_genome_label.
    FILTER (contains(lcase(str(?ref_genome_label)), lcase("GRCh"))) .
```

```
?out ( prov:wasInfluencedBy )+ ?sample
?out tavernaprov:content ?out_label .
FILTER (contains(lcase(str(?out_label)), lcase("exons"))) . }
```

4 Implementation

Although Taverna allows to export PROV traces, this is not yet the case for
the Galaxy workbench[15]. We thus developed an open-source provenance capture
tool[16] for Galaxy. Users provide the URL of their Galaxy workflow portal, and
their private API key. Then, the tool communicates with the Galaxy REST API
to produce PROV RDF triples. We implemented the full PROV harmonization
process (Fig. 3) in the sharp-prov-toolbox[17]. This open-source tool has been
implemented in Java and is supported by Jena[18] for RDF data management and
reasoning. PROV Constraints[19] inference rules have been implemented in the
Jena syntax[20]. HTML and JavaScript code templates have been used to generate
harmonized provenance visualization. Figure 5 shows the resulting data lineage
graph associated with the two workflow traces of our motivating use case (Fig. 1).
While the left part of the graphs represents the Galaxy workflow invocation, the
right part represents the Taverna one.

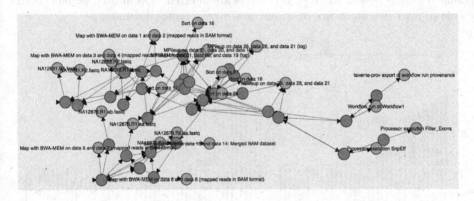

Fig. 5. *prov:wasInfluencedBy* properties between Galaxy and Taverna.

---

[15] https://usegalaxy.org.
[16] galaxy-PROV: https://github.com/albangaignard/galaxy-PROV.
[17] sharp-prov-toolbox: https://github.com/albangaignard/sharp-prov-toolbox.
[18] Jena: https://jena.apache.org.
[19] https://www.w3.org/TR/prov-constraints/.
[20] https://github.com/albangaignard/sharp-prov-toolbox/blob/master/
     SharpProvToolbox/src/main/resources/provRules_all.jena.

5   Experimental Results and Discussion

As a first evaluation, we ran two experiments. The first one evaluates the harmonization process at large scale. In a second experiment, we evaluated the ability of the system to answer the domain-specific questions of our motivating scenario.

5.1   Harmonization of Heterogeneous PROV Traces at Large Scale

In this experiment, we used provenance documents from ProvStore[21]. We selected the 369 public documents of 2016. These documents have different sizes from 1 to 58572 triples and use different PROV concepts and relations. We ran the provenance harmonization process as described in this paper on a classical desktop computer (4-cores CPU, 16 GB of memory). From the initial 217165 PROV triples, it took 38 min to infer 1291549 triples. Each provenance document has been uploaded as a named graph to a Jena Fuseki endpoint. The two histograms of Fig. 6 show the number of named graphs in which PROV predicates are present. We filtered the predicates to show only predicates using the PROV prefix. Figure 6 shows that we have been able to harmonize (right histogram, in orange) the provenance documents since we increase the number of named graphs in which PROV predicates are inferred. Specifically, we have been able to infer new *influence* relations in 318 provenance documents.

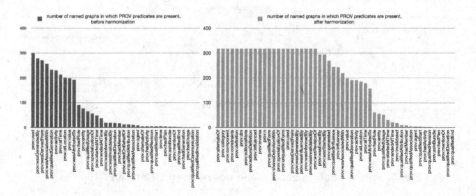

Fig. 6. Distribution of asserted (blue) and inferred (orange) PROV predicates in the public ProvStore documents for year 2016, before and after the proposed harmonization process. (Color figure online)

5.2   Usage of Semi-automatically Produced NanoPublications

We run the multi-site experiment of Sect. 2 using Galaxy and Taverna workflow management systems. The Galaxy workflow has been designed in the context of the SyMeTRIC systems medicine project, and was run on the production Galaxy

---

[21] https://provenance.ecs.soton.ac.uk/store/.

instance[22] of the BiRD bioinformatics infrastructure. The Taverna workflow was run on a desktop computer. Provenance graphs were produced by the Taverna built-in PROV feature, and by a Galaxy dedicated provenance capture tool[23], based on the Galaxy API, the later transforms a user history of actions into PROV RDF triples.

Table 1 presents a sorted count of the top-ten predicates in (i) the Galaxy and Taverna provenance traces without harmonization, (ii) these provenance traces after the first iteration of the harmonization process:

Table 1. Most prominent predicates when considering the initial two PROV graphs and their harmonization (*PROV++*)

Galaxy PROV		Taverna PROV		Harmonized PROV++	
predicates	counts	predicates	counts	predicates	counts
prov:wasDerivedFrom	118	rdf:type	54	owl:differentFrom	3617
rdf:type	76	rdfs:label	13	rdf:type	958
rdfs:label	62	prov:atTime	8	prov:wasInfluencedBy	515
prov:used	61	wfprov:descByParameter	6	prov:influenced	291
prov:wasAttributedTo	34	rdfs:comment	6	rdfs:seeAlso	268
prov:wasGeneratedBy	33	prov:hadRole	6	rdfs:subClassOf	223
prov:endedAtTime	26	prov:activity	5	owl:disjointWith	218
prov:startedAtTime	26	purl:hasPart	4	rdfs:range	208
prov:wasAssociatedWith	26	prov:agent	4	rdfs:domain	199
prov:generatedAtTime	1	prov:endedAtTime	4	prov:wasGeneratedBy	172
all	463	*all*	177	*all*	8654

We executed the summarization query proposed in Sect. 3.4 on the harmonized provenance graph. The resulting NanoPublication (*assertion* named graph) represents the input DNA sequences aligned to the GRCh37 human reference genome through an *sio:is-variant-of* predicate. It also links the annotated variants (Taverna WF output) with the preprossessed DNA sequences (Galaxy WF inputs). Related to the Q3 life-science question highlighted in Sect. 2, this NanoPublication can be queried to retrieve for instance the reference genome used to select and annotate the resulting genetic variants.

6 Related Works

Data integration [11] and summarization [3] have been largely studied in different research domains. Our objective is not to invent yet another technique for integrating and/or summarizing data. Instead, we show how provenance constraint rules, domain annotations, and Semantic Web techniques can be combined to harmonize and summarize provenance data into linked experiment reports.

---

[22] https://galaxy-bird.univ-nantes.fr/galaxy/.
[23] https://github.com/albangaignard/sharp-prov-toolbox.

Several proposals tackle scientific reproducibility[24]. For example, Reprozip [9] captures operating system events that are then utilized to generate a workflow illustrating the events that happened and their sequences. While valuable, such proposals neither address the harmonization of multi-systems and heterogeneous provenance traces nor machine- and human-tractable experiment reports, as proposed in SHARP.

Datanode ontology [10] proposes to harmonize data by describing relationships between data artifacts. Datanode allows to present in a simple way dataflows that focus on the fundamental relationships that exist between original, intermediary, and final datasets. Contrary to Datanode, SHARP uses existing PROV vocabularies and constraints to harmonize provenance traces, thereby reducing harmonization efforts.

LabelFlow [5] proposes a semi-automated approach for labeling data artifacts generated from workflow runs. Compared to LabelFlow, SHARP uses existing PROV ontology and Semantic Web technology to harmonize dataflows. Moreover, *LabelFlow* is confined to single workflows, whereas SHARP targets a collection of workflow runs that are produced by different workflow systems.

In previous work [15], we proposed *PoeM* to produce linked in silico experiment reports based on workflow runs. As SHARP, *PoeM* leverages Semantic Web technologies and reference vocabularies (PROV-O, P-Plan) to generate provenance mining rules and finally assemble linked scientific experiment reports (Micropublications, Experimental Factor Ontology). SHARP goes steps forward by proposing the harmonization of multi-systems provenance traces.

7 Conclusions

In this paper, we presented SHARP, a Linked Data approach for harmonizing cross-workflow provenance. The resulting harmonized provenance graph can be exploited to run cross-workflow queries and to produce provenance summaries, targeting human-oriented interpretation and sharing. Our ongoing work includes deploying SHARP to be used by scientists to process their provenance traces or those associated with provenance repositories, such as ProvStore. For now, we work on multi-site provenance graphs with centralized inferences. Another exciting research direction would be to consider low-cost highly decentralized infrastructure for publishing NanoPublication as proposed in [19].

References

1. Abiteboul, S., Hull, R., Vianu, V.: Foundations of Databases. Addison-Wesley, Reading (1995)
2. Afgan, E., Baker, D., van den Beek, M., et al.: The galaxy platform for accessible, reproducible and collaborative biomedical analyses: 2016 update. Nucl. Acids Res. **44**(W1), W3–W10 (2016)

---

24 http://www.refinery-platform.org.

3. Aggarwal, C.C., Wang, H.: Graph data management and mining: a survey of algorithms and applications. In: Aggarwal, C., Wang, H. (eds.) Managing and Mining Graph Data. Advances in Database Systems, vol. 40, pp. 13–68. Springer, Boston (2010). https://doi.org/10.1007/978-1-4419-6045-0_2

4. Alper, P., Belhajjame, K., Goble, C.A., Karagoz, P.: Enhancing and abstracting scientific workflow provenance for data publishing. In: Proceedings of the Joint EDBT/ICDT 2013 Workshops, pp. 313–318. ACM (2013)

5. Alper, P., Belhajjame, K., Goble, C.A., Karagoz, P.: LabelFlow: exploiting workflow provenance to surface scientific data provenance. In: Ludäscher, B., Plale, B. (eds.) IPAW 2014. LNCS, vol. 8628, pp. 84–96. Springer, Cham (2015). https://doi.org/10.1007/978-3-319-16462-5_7

6. Altintas, I., Barney, O., Jaeger-Frank, E.: Provenance collection support in the kepler scientific workflow system. In: Moreau, L., Foster, I. (eds.) IPAW 2006. LNCS, vol. 4145, pp. 118–132. Springer, Heidelberg (2006). https://doi.org/10.1007/11890850_14

7. Carroll, J.J., Dickinson, I., et al.: Jena: implementing the semantic web recommendations. In: Proceedings of the 13th International World Wide Web Conference on Alternate Track Papers & Posters, pp. 74–83. ACM (2004)

8. Cheney, J., Missier, P., Moreau, L.: Constraints of the provenance data model. Technical report (2012)

9. Chirigati, F., Shasha, D., Freire, J.: ReproZip: using provenance to support computational reproducibility. In: 5th USENIX Workshop on the Theory and Practice of Provenance, Berkeley (2013)

10. Daga, E., d'Aquin, M., et al.: Describing semantic web applications through relations between data nodes (2014)

11. Doan, A., Halevy, A., Ives, Z.: Principles of Data Integration, 1st edn. Morgan Kaufmann Publishers Inc., San Francisco (2012)

12. Dodds, L., Davis, I.: Linked Data patterns: a pattern catalogue for modelling, publishing, and consuming Linked Data, May 2012

13. Fagin, R., Kolaitis, P.G., Miller, R.J., Popa, L.: Data exchange: semantics and query answering. Theor. Comput. Sci. **336**(1), 89–124 (2005)

14. Gaignard, A., Belhajjame, K., Skaf-Molli, H.: Sharp: harmonizing cross-workflow provenance. In: SeWeBMeDA Workshop on Semantic Web Solutions for Large-Scale Biomedical Data Analytics (2016)

15. Gaignard, A., Skaf-Molli, H., Bihouée, A.: From scientific workflow patterns to 5-star linked open data. In: 8th USENIX Workshop on the Theory and Practice of Provenance (2016)

16. Lebo, T., Sahoo, S., McGuinness, D., et al.: PROV-O: the PROV ontology. W3C Recommendation, 30 April 2013

17. Miles, S., Groth, P., Branco, M., Moreau, L.: The requirements of using provenance in E-science experiments. J. Grid Comput. **5**(1), 1–25 (2007)

18. Missier, P., Belhajjame, K., Cheney, J.: The W3C PROV family of specifications for modelling provenance metadata. In: Proceedings of the 16th International Conference on Extending Database Technology, pp. 773–776. ACM (2013)

19. Kuhn, T., Chichester, C., Krauthammer, M., et al.: Decentralized provenance-aware publishing with nanopublications. PeerJ Comput. Sci. **2**, e78 (2016). https://doi.org/10.7717/peerj-cs.78

20. Wolstencroft, K., Haines, R., Fellows, D., et al.: The taverna workflow suite: designing and executing workflows of web services on the desktop, web or in the cloud. Nucl. Acids Res. **41**(Webserver–Issue), 557–561 (2013)
21. Zhao, J., Wroe, C., Goble, C., Stevens, R., Quan, D., Greenwood, M.: Using semantic web technologies for representing E-science provenance. In: McIlraith, S.A., Plexousakis, D., Harmelen, F. (eds.) ISWC 2004. LNCS, vol. 3298, pp. 92–106. Springer, Heidelberg (2004). https://doi.org/10.1007/978-3-540-30475-3_8

Scientometrics Workshop

Scholia, Scientometrics and Wikidata

Finn Årup Nielsen[1(✉)], Daniel Mietchen[2], and Egon Willighagen[3]

[1] Cognitive Systems, DTU Compute, Technical University of Denmark,
Lyngby, Denmark
faan@dtu.dk
[2] EvoMRI Communications, Jena, Germany
[3] Department of Bioinformatics - BiGCaT, NUTRIM, Maastricht University,
Maastricht, The Netherlands

Abstract. Scholia is a tool to handle scientific bibliographic information
through Wikidata. The Scholia Web service creates on-the-fly scholarly
profiles for researchers, organizations, journals, publishers, individual
scholarly works, and for research topics. To collect the data, it queries the
SPARQL-based Wikidata Query Service. Among several display formats
available in Scholia are lists of publications for individual researchers and
organizations, plots of publications per year, employment timelines, as
well as co-author and topic networks and citation graphs. The Python
package implementing the Web service is also able to format Wikidata
bibliographic entries for use in LaTeX/BIBTeX. Apart from detailing
Scholia, we describe how Wikidata has been used for bibliographic information and we also provide some scientometric statistics on this information.

1 Introduction

Wikipedia contains significant amounts of data relevant for scientometrics, and
it has formed the basis for several scientometric studies [4,14,15,17,18,20,21,
28,29,34,39]. Such studies can use the structured references found in Wikipedia
articles or use the intrawiki hyperlinks, e.g., to compare citations from Wikipedia
to scholarly journals with Thomson Reuters journal citation statistics as in [20]
or to rank universities as in [39].

While many Wikipedia pages have numerous references to scientific articles,
the current Wikipedias have very few entries *about* specific scientific articles. This
is most evident when browsing the *Academic journal articles* category on the
English Wikipedia.[1] Among the few items in that category are famed papers such
as the 1948 physics paper *The Origin of Chemical Elements* [2] – described in
the English Wikipedia article *Alpher–Bethe–Gamow paper*[2] – as well as the 1953
article *Molecular Structure of Nucleic Acids: A Structure for Deoxyribose Nucleic*

---

[1] https://en.wikipedia.org/wiki/Category:Academic_journal_articles.
[2] https://en.wikipedia.org/wiki/Alpher%E2%80%93Bethe%E2%80%93Gamow_paper.

© The Author(s) 2017
E. Blomqvist et al. (Eds.): ESWC 2017 Satellite Events, LNCS 10577, pp. 237–259, 2017.
https://doi.org/10.1007/978-3-319-70407-4_36

Acid [37] on eight Wikipedias. Another scientific article is Hillary Putnam's *Is Semantics Possible?* [31][3] from 1970 on the Estonian Wikipedia.

References in Wikipedia are often formatted in templates, and it takes some effort to extract and match information in the template fields. For instance, in a study of journals cited on Wikipedia, a database was built containing journal name variations to match the many different variations that Wikipedia editors used when citing scientific articles [20]. The use of standard identifiers — such as the Digital Object Identifier (DOI) — in citations on Wikipedia can help to some extent to uniquely identify works and journals.

Several other wikis have been set up to describe scientific articles, such as WikiPapers, AcaWiki, Wikilit [25] and Brede Wiki [22].[4] They are all examples of MediaWiki-based wikis that primarily describe scientific articles. Three of them use the Semantic MediaWiki extension [16], while the fourth uses MediaWiki's template functionality[5] to structure bibliographic information.

Since the launch of Wikidata[6] [36], the Wikimedia family includes a platform to better handle structured data such as bibliographic data and to enforce input validation to a greater degree than Wikipedia. Wikidata data can be reified to triples [5,9], and RDF/graph-oriented databases, including SPARQL databases, can represent Wikidata data [10]. The Wikidata Query Service (WDQS)[7] is an extended SPARQL endpoint that exposes the Wikidata data. Apart from offering a SPARQL endpoint, it also features an editor and a variety of frontend result display options. It may render the SPARQL query result as, e.g., bubble charts, line charts, graphs, timelines, list of images, points on a geographical map, or just provide the result as a table. These results can also be embedded on other Web pages via an HTML iframe element. We note that Wikidata is open data published under the Public Domain Dedication and Waiver (CC0),[8] and that it is available not only through the SPARQL endpoint, but also as Linked Data Fragments[9] [35] and—like any other project of the Wikimedia family—through an API and dump files.[10]

In the following sections, we describe how Wikidata has been used for bibliographic information, some statistics on it and present Scholia, our website built to expose such information. We furthermore show how Scholia can be used for bibliography generation and discuss limitations and advantages with Wikidata and Scholia.

---

[3] https://et.wikipedia.org/wiki/Is_Semantics_Possible%3F.
[4] http://wikipapers.referata.com/, https://acawiki.org/, http://wikilit.referata.com/ and http://neuro.compute.dtu.dk/wiki/.
[5] https://www.mediawiki.org/wiki/Help:Templates.
[6] https://www.wikidata.org.
[7] https://query.wikidata.org.
[8] https://creativecommons.org/publicdomain/zero/1.0/deed.en.
[9] https://query.wikidata.org/bigdata/ldf.
[10] The API is at https://www.wikidata.org/w/api.php, and the dump files are available at https://www.wikidata.org/w/api.php.

Table 1. Summary of Wikidata as a digital library. This table is directly inspired by
[11, Table 1]. Note that the size has grown considerably in August 2017. The value of
2.3 million is per 2 August 2017. A week later the number of scientific articles had
passed 3 million.

Dimension	Description
Domain	Broad coverage
Size	$>2,300,000$ scientific articles
Style of Metadata	Export via, e.g., Lars Willighagen's citation.js[a]
Persistent Inbound Links?	Yes, with the Q identifiers
Persistent Outbound Links	Yes, with identifiers like DOI, PMID, PMCID, arXiv
Full Text?	Via identifiers like DOI or PMCID; dedicated property for 'full text URL'
Access	Free access

[a]https://github.com/larsgw/citation.js

2   Bibliographic Information on Wikidata

Wikidata editors have begun to systematically add scientific bibliographic data
to Wikidata across a broad range of scientific domains — see Table 1 for a summary of Wikidata as a digital library. Individual researchers and scientific articles not described by their own Wikipedia article in any language are routinely
added to Wikidata, and we have so far experienced very few deletions of such
data in reference to a notability criterion. The current interest in expanding bibliographic information on Wikidata has been boosted by the WikiCite project,
which aims at collecting bibliographic information in Wikidata and held its first
workshop in 2016 [33].

The bibliographic information collected on Wikidata is about books, articles (including preprints), authors, organizations, journals, publishers and more.
These items (corresponding to *subject* in Semantic Web parlance) can be interlinked through Wikidata properties (corresponding to the *predicate*), such as
author (P50),[11] published in (P1433), publisher (P123), series (P179), main
theme (P921), educated at (P69), employer (P108), part of (P361), sponsor
(P859, can be used for funding), cites (P2860) and several other properties.[12]

Numerous properties exist on Wikidata for deep linking to external resources,
e.g., for DOI, PMID, PMCID, arXiv, ORCID, Google Scholar, VIAF, Crossref
funder ID, ZooBank and Twitter. With these many identifiers, Wikidata can act
as a hub for scientometrics studies between resources. If no dedicated Wikidata
property exists for a resource, one of the URL properties can work as a substitute for creating a deep link to a resource. For instance, P1325 (*external data*

---

[11] The URI for Wikidata property P50 is http://www.wikidata.org/prop/direct/P50
or with the conventional prefix wdt:P50. Similarly for any other Wikidata property.
[12] A Wikidata table lists properties that are commonly used in bibliographic contexts:
https://www.wikidata.org/wiki/Template:Bibliographical_properties.

Table 2. Statistics on bibliographic information in Wikidata on 2 August 2017.

Count	Description
2,380,009	Scientific articles
93,518	Scientific articles linked to one or more author items
5,562	Scientific articles linked to one or more author items and no author name string (indicating that the author linking may be complete)
3,379,786	Citations, i.e., number of uses of the P2860 property
16,327	Distinct authors (author items) having written a scientific article
13,332	Distinct authors having written a scientific article with author gender indicated

available at) can point to raw or supplementary data associated with a paper. We have used this scheme for scientific articles associated with datasets stored in OpenfMRI [27], an online database with raw brain measurements, mostly from functional magnetic resonance imaging studies. Using WDQS, we query the set of OpenfMRI-linked items using the following query:

```
?item wdt:P1325 ?resource .
filter strstarts(str(?resource),
                 "https://openfmri.org/dataset/")
```

A similar scheme is used for a few of the scientific articles associated with data in the neuroinformatics databases Neurosynth [38] and NeuroVault [6].

When bibliographic items exist in Wikidata, they can be used as references to support claims (corresponding to *triplets* with extra qualifiers) in other items of Wikidata, e.g., a biological claim can be linked to the Wikidata item for a scientific journal.

By using these properties systematically according to an emerging data model,[13] editors have extended the bibliographic information in Wikidata. Particularly instrumental in this process was a set of tools built by Magnus Manske, *QuickStatements*[14] and *Source MetaData,*[15] including the latter's associated *Resolve authors* tool[16] as well as the *WikidataIntegrator*[17] associated with the Gene Wiki project [30] and the *fatameh* tool[18] based on it. Information can be extracted from, e.g., PubMed, PubMed Central and arXiv and added to Wikidata.

---

[13] https://www.wikidata.org/wiki/Wikidata:WikiProject_Source_MetaData/ Bibliographic_metadata_for_scholarly_articles_in_Wikidata.

[14] https://tools.wmflabs.org/wikidata-todo/quick_statements.php.

[15] https://tools.wmflabs.org/sourcemd/.

[16] https://tools.wmflabs.org/sourcemd/new_resolve_authors.php.

[17] https://github.com/SuLab/WikidataIntegrator/.

[18] https://tools.wmflabs.org/fatameh/ with documentation available at https://www.wikidata.org/wiki/Wikidata:WikiProject_Source_MetaData/fatameh.

How complete is Wikidata in relation to scientific bibliographic information? Journals and universities are well represented. For instance, 31,902 Wikidata items are linked with their identifier for the Collections of the National Library of Medicine (P1055). This number can be obtained with the following WDQS SPARQL query:

```
SELECT (COUNT(?item) AS ?count) WHERE {
    ?item wdt:P1055 ?nlm .
}
```

Far less covered are individual articles, individual researchers, university departments and citations between scientific articles. Most of the scientific articles in Wikidata are claimed to be an *instance of* (P31) the Wikidata item *scientific article* (Q13442814). With a WDQS query, we can count the number of Wikidata items linked this way to *scientific article*:

```
SELECT (COUNT(?work) AS ?count) WHERE {
    ?work wdt:P31 wd:Q13442814 .
}
```

As of 2 August 2017, the query returned the result 2,380,009, see also Tables 1 and 2 (the number of scientific articles has grown considerable since the end of July 2017). In comparison, arXiv states having 1,289,564 e-prints and ACM Digital Library states having 24,668 proceedings.[19] In 2014, a capture/recapture method estimated the number of scholarly English-language documents on the public web to be "at least 114 million" [13], while researchers found 87,542,370 DOIs in the Crossref database as of 21 March 2017 [32], thus Wikidata currently records only a minor part of all scientific articles. There were 16,327 authors associated with Wikidata items linked through the *author* property (P50) to items that are *instance of scientific article*:

```
SELECT (COUNT(DISTINCT ?author) AS ?count) WHERE {
    ?work wdt:P50 ?author .
    ?work wdt:P31 wd:Q13442814 .
}
```

The number of citations as counted by triples using the P2860 (*cites*) property stood at 3,379,786:

```
SELECT (COUNT(?citedwork) AS ?count) WHERE {
    ?work wdt:P2860 ?citedwork .
}
```

The completeness can be fairly uneven. Articles from Public Library of Science (PLOS) journals are much better represented than articles from the journals of IEEE. On 9 August 2017, we counted 160,676 works published in PLOS journals with this WDQS query,

---

[19] As of 2 August 2017 according to https://arxiv.org/ and https://dl.acm.org/contents_guide.cfm.

```
SELECT (COUNT(?work) AS ?count) WHERE {
  ?work wdt:P1433 ?venue .
  ?venue wdt:P123 wd:Q233358 .
}
```

while the equivalent for IEEE (Q131566) only returns 4,595. Note that 160,676 PLOS articles are far more than the 4,553 PLOS articles reported back in 2014 as cited from the 25 largest Wikipedias [17], thus Wikidata has a much better coverage here than Wikipedia.

Table 3. h-indices for three researchers whose publications are well-covered in Wikidata. For Web of Science, we searched its core collection with "Nielsen FÅ", "Willighagen E" and "Jensen LJ".

Service	Finn Årup Nielsen	Egon Willighagen	Lars Juhl Jensen
Google Scholar	28	24	72
ResearchGate	28	23	–
Scopus	22	22	60
Web of Science	18	20	57
Wikidata	9	12	21

Given that Wikidata only has around 3.4 million P2860-citations, it is no surprise that the current number of citations is considerable less than the citation counts one finds in other web services, — even for authors with a large part of their published scientific articles listed in Wikidata. Table 3 shows h-index statistics for three such authors. The Wikidata count has been established by WDQS queries similar to the following:

```
SELECT ?work (COUNT(?citing_work) AS ?count) WHERE {
  ?work wdt:P50 wd:Q20980928 .
  ?citing_work wdt:P2860 ?work .
}
GROUP BY ?work
ORDER BY DESC(?count)
```

Even for these well-covered researchers, the h-index based on P2860-citations in Wikidata is around two to three times lower than the h-indices obtained with other services.

The sponsor property (P859) has been used extensively for research funded by the *National Institute for Occupational Safety and Health* (NIOSH), with 52,852 works linking to the organization, 18,135 of which are *instance of scientific articles*, but apart from NIOSH, the use of the property has been very limited for scientific articles.[20]

---

[20] National Institute for Occupational Safety and Health has a Wikimedian-in-Residence program, through which James Hare has added many of the NIOSH works.

3   Scholia

Scholia provides both a Python package and a Web service for presenting and interacting with scientific information from Wikidata. The code is available via https://github.com/fnielsen/scholia, and a first release has been archived in Zenodo [23].

As a Web service, its canonical site runs from the Wikimedia Foundation-provided service *Wikimedia Toolforge* (formerly called *Wikimedia Tool Labs*) at https://tools.wmflabs.org/scholia/, but the Scholia package may be downloaded and run from a local server as well. Scholia uses the Flask Python Web framework [7].

The current Web service relies almost entirely on Wikidata for its presented data. The frontend consists mostly of HTML iframe elements for embedding the on-the-fly-generated WDQS results and uses many of the different output formats from this service: bubble charts, bar charts, line charts, graphs and image lists.

Initially, we used the table output from WDQS to render tables in Scholia, but as links in WDQS tables link back to Wikidata items — and not Scholia items — we have switched to using the DataTables[21] Javascript library.

Through a JavaScript-based query to the MediaWiki API, an excerpt from the English Wikipedia is shown on the top of each Scholia page if the corresponding Wikidata item is associated with an article in the English Wikipedia. The label for the item is fetched via Wikidata's MediaWiki API. While some other information can be fetched this way, Scholia's many aggregation queries are better handled through SPARQL.

Scholia uses the Wikidata item identifier as its identifier rather than author

---

[21] https://datatables.net/.

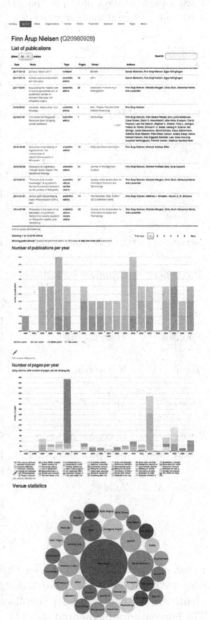

Fig. 1. Overview screenshot of part of the Scholia Web page for an author: https://tools.wmflabs.org/scholia/author/Q20980928. Fig. 2 zooms in on one panel.

Table 4. Aspects in Scholia: Each Wikidata item can be viewed in one or more aspects. Each aspect displays multiple "panels", which may be, e.g., a table of publications or a bar chart of citations per year.

Aspect	Example	Example panels
Author	Scientists	List of publications, publications per year, co-authors, topics, timelines, map, citations, academic tree
Work	Papers, books	Recent citations, citations in the work, statements supported in Wikidata
Organization	Universities	Affiliated authors, co-author graph, recent publications, page production, co-author-normalized citations per year
Venue	Journals, proceedings	Recent publications, topics in the publications, author images, prolific authors, most cited works, most cited authors, most cited venues
Series	Proceedings series	Items (venues) in the series, published works from venues in the series
Publishers	Commercial publisher	Journals and other publications published, associated editors, most cited papers, number of citations as a function of number of published works
Sponsor	Foundations	List of publications funded, sponsored authors, co-sponsors
Topic	Keywords	Recent publication on the topic, co-occurring topics
Disease	Mental disorders	Genetically associated diseases, publications per year
Protein	Receptor proteins	Cofunctional proteins, publications per year
Pathway	Receptor pathways	Participants, recently published works, publications per year
Chemical	Acids	Identifiers, related compounds, physchem properties, recently published works on the chemical, publications per year

name, journal titles, etc. A search field on the front page provides a Scholia user with the ability to search for a name to retrieve the relevant Wikidata identifier. To display items, Scholia sets up a number of what we call "aspects". The currently implemented aspects (see Table 4) are author, work, organization, venue, series, publisher, sponsor, award, topic, disease, protein, chemical and (biological) pathway.

The present selection was motivated by the possibilities inherent in the Wikidata items and properties. We plan to extend this to further aspects. A URL scheme distinguishes the different aspects, so the URL path

/scholia/author/Q6365492 will show the author aspect of the statistician Kanti V. Mardia, while /scholia/topic/Q6365492 will show the topic aspect of the person, i.e., articles about Mardia.

Likewise, universities can be viewed, for instance, as organizations or as sponsors. Indeed, any Wikidata item can be viewed in any Scholia aspect, but Scholia can show no data if the user selects a "wrong" aspect, i.e. one for which no relevant data is available in Wikidata.

For each aspect, we make multiple WDQS queries based on the Wikidata item for which the results in the panels are displayed. Plots are embedded with HTML iframes. For the author aspect, Scholia queries WDQS for the list of publications, showing the result in a table, displaying a bar chart of the number of publications per year, number of pages per year, venue statistics, co-author graph, topics of the published works (based on the "main theme" property), associated images, education and employment history as timelines, academic tree, map with locations associated with the author, and citation statistics – see Fig. 1 for an example of part of an author aspect page. The citation statistics displays the most cited work, citations by year and citing authors. For the academic tree, we make use of Blazegraph's graph analytics RDF GAS API[22] that is available in WDQS.

The embedded WDQS results link back to WDQS, where a user can modify the query. The interactive editor of WDQS allows users not familiar with SPARQL to make simple modifications without directly editing the SPARQL code.

Related to their work on quantifying conceptual novelty in the biomedical literature [19], Shubhanshu Mishra and Vetle Torvik have set up a website profiling authors in PubMed datasets: LEGOLAS.[23] Among other information, the website shows the number of articles per year, the number of citations per year, the number of self-citations per year, unique collaborations per year and NIH grants per year as bar charts that are color-coded according to, e.g., author role (first, solo, middle or last author). Scholia uses WDQS for LEGOLAS-like plots. Figure 2 displays one such example for the number of published items as a function of year of publication on an author aspect page, where the components of the bars are color-coded according to author role.

For the organization aspect, Scholia uses the employer and affiliated Wikidata properties to identify associated authors, and combines this with the author query for works. Scholia formulates SPARQL queries with property paths to identify suborganizations of the queried organization, such that authors affiliated with a suborganization are associated with the queried organization. Figure 3 shows a corresponding bar chart, again inspired by the LEGOLAS style. Here, the Cognitive Systems section at the Technical University of Denmark is displayed with the organization aspect. It combines work and author data. The bar chart uses the P1104 (number of pages) Wikidata property together with a normalization based on the number of authors on each of the work items. The

[22] https://wiki.blazegraph.com/wiki/index.php/RDF_GAS_API.
[23] http://abel.lis.illinois.edu/legolas/.

Number of publications per year

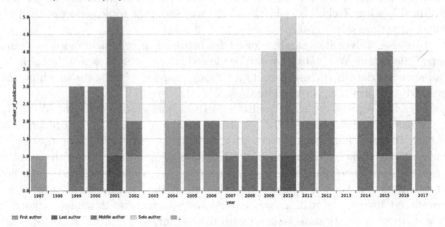

Fig. 2. Screenshot of Scholia Web page with the number of papers published per year for Finn Århup Nielsen: https://tools.wmflabs.org/scholia/author/Q20980928. Inspired by LEGOLAS. Colors indicate author role: first, middle, last or solo author. (Color figure online)

Page production

Scientific article page production per year per author. The number of pages for a multiple-author paper is distributed among the authors. The statistics is only for papers where the "number of pages" property has been set.

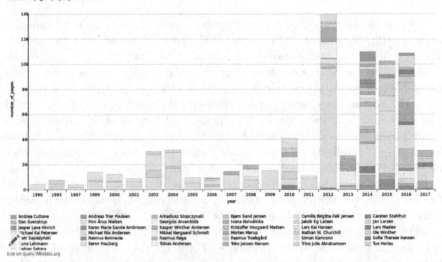

Fig. 3. Scholia screenshot with page production for a research section (Cognitive Systems at the Technical University of Denmark), where the number of pages per paper has been normalized by the number of authors. The bars are color-coded according to author. The plot is heavily biased, as only a very limited subset of papers from the section is available in Wikidata, and the property for the number of pages is set for only a subset of these papers. From https://tools.wmflabs.org/scholia/organization/Q24283660. (Color figure online)

bars are color-coded according to individual authors associated with the organization. In this case, the plot is heavily biased, as only a very limited subset of publications from the organization is currently present in Wikidata, and even the available publications may not have the P1104 property set. Other panels shown in the organization aspect are a co-author graph, a list of recent publications formatted in a table, a bubble chart with most cited papers with affiliated first author and a bar chart with co-author-normalized citations per year. This last panel counts the number of citations to each work and divides it by the number of authors on the cited work, then groups the publications according to year and color-codes the bars according to author.

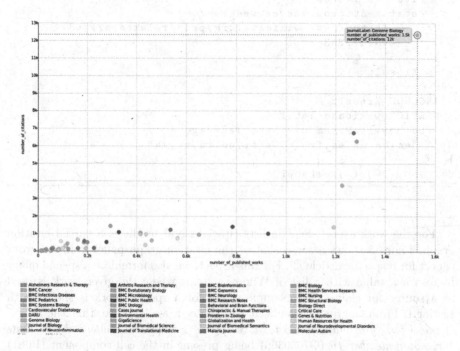

Fig. 4. Screenshot from Scholia's publisher aspect with number of publications versus number of citations for works published by BioMed Central. The upper right point with many citations and many published works is the journal *Genome Biology*. From https://tools.wmflabs.org/scholia/publisher/Q463494.

For the publisher aspect, Scholia queries all items where the P123 property (publisher) has been set. With these items at hand, Scholia can create lists of venues (journals or proceedings) ordered according to the number of works (papers) published in each of them, as well as lists of works ordered according to citations. Figure 4 shows an example of a panel on the publisher aspect page with a scatter plot detailing journals from *BioMed Central*. The position of each journal in the plot reveals impact factor-like information.

248   F.Å. Nielsen et al.

Listing 1. SPARQL query on the work aspect page for claims supported by a work,
— in this case Q22253877 [1].

```
SELECT ?item ?itemLabel ?property ?propertyLabel
        ?value ?valueLabel
WITH {
  SELECT distinct ?item ?property ?value
  WHERE {
    ?item ?p ?statement .
    ?property wikibase:claim ?p .
    ?statement ?a ?value .
    ?item ?b ?value .
    ?statement prov:wasDerivedFrom/
        <http://www.wikidata.org/prop/reference/P248>
        wd:Q22253877 .
  }
} AS %result
WHERE {
  INCLUDE %result
  SERVICE wikibase:label {
    bd:serviceParam wikibase:language
    "en,da,de,es,fr,it,jp,nl,no,ru,sv,zh" . }
}
ORDER BY DESC(?itemLabel)
```

For the work aspect, Scholia lists citations and produces a partial citation graph. Figure 5 shows a screenshot of the citation graph panel from the work aspect for a specific article [3]. For this aspect, we also formulate a special query to return a table with a list of Wikidata items where the given work is used as a source for claims. An example query for a specific work is shown with Listing 1. From the query results, it can be seen, for instance, that the article *A novel family of mammalian taste receptors* [1] supports a claim about *Taste 2 receptor member 16* (Q7669366) being present in the cell component (P681) *integral component of membrane* (Q14327652). For the topic aspect, Scholia uses a property path SPARQL query to identify subtopics.

For a given item where the aspect is not known in advance, Scholia tries to guess the relevant aspect by looking at the *instance of* property. The Scholia Web service uses that guess for redirecting, so for instance, /scholia/Q8219 will redirect to /scholia/author/Q8219, the author aspect for the psychologist Uta Frith. This is achieved by first making a server site query to establish that Uta Frith is a human and then using that information to choose the author aspect as the most relevant aspect to show information about Uta Frith.

We have implemented a few aspects that are able to display information from two or more specified Wikidata items. For instance, /scholia/organizations/Q1269766,Q193196 displays information from University College London and Technical University of Denmark. One panel lists coauthorships between

Citation graph

Partial citation graph

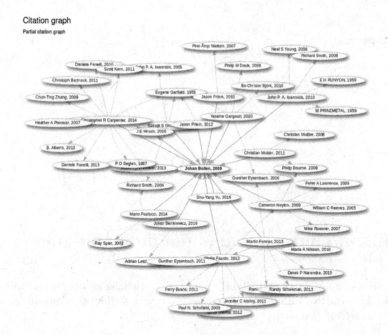

Fig. 5. Screenshot of part of a Scholia Web page at https://tools.wmflabs.org/scholia/ work/Q21143764 with the partial citation graph panel of the work aspect for Johan Bollen's article from 2009 [3].

authors affiliated with the two organizations. Another panel shows a "Works per year" plot for the specified organizations, see Fig. 6. Likewise, an address such as /scholia/authors/Q20980928,Q24290415,Q24390693,Q26720269 displays panels for 4 different authors. With the graph queries in BlazeGraph, Scholia shows co-author paths between multiple authors in a graph plot. Figure 7 shows the co-author path between Paul Erdős and Natalie Portman, which can give an estimate of Portman's Erdős-number (i.e., the number of coauthorships between a given author and Erdős).

A few redirects for external identifiers are also implemented. For instance, with Uta Frith's Twitter name 'utafrith', /scholia/twitter/utafrith will redirect to /scholia/Q8219, which in turn will redirect to /scholia/author/Q8219. Scholia implements similar functionality for DOI, ORCID, GitHub user identifier as well as for the InChIKey [8] and CAS chemical identifiers.

For the index page for the award aspect, we have an aggregated plot for all science awards with respect to gender, see Fig. 8. The plot gives an overview of awards predominantly given to men (awards close to the x-axis) or predominantly given to women (awards close to the y-axis).

Works per year

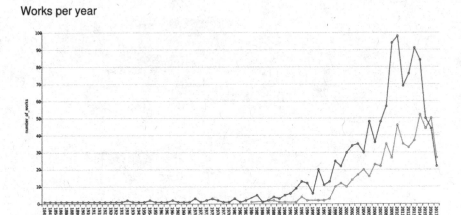

Fig. 6. Screenshot of panel with "Works per year" on Scholia aspect for multiple organizations, here the two European universities *University College London* and the *Technical University of Denmark*.

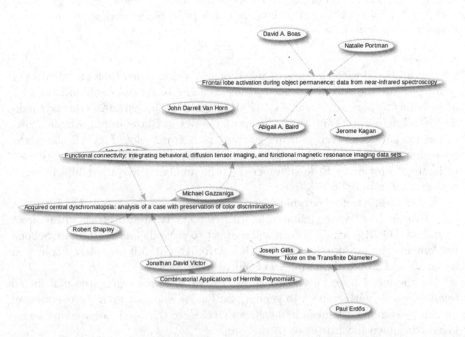

Fig. 7. A co-author path between Paul Erdős and Natalie Portman (Natalie Hershlag) on the page for multiple authors https://tools.wmflabs.org/scholia/authors/Q37876, Q173746.

Male-female statistics

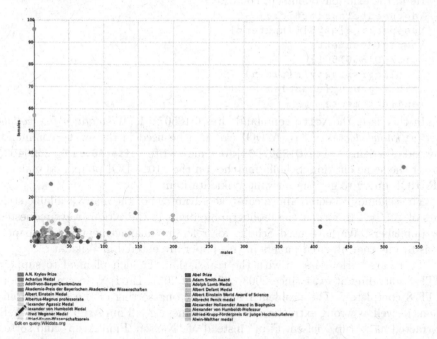

Fig. 8. Aggregation on science awards with respect to gender from the award aspect index page at https://tools.wmflabs.org/scholia/award/ with number of male recipients on the x-axis and number of female recipients on the y-axis.

4   Using Wikidata as a Bibliographic Resource

As a command-line tool, Scholia provides a prototype tool that uses Wikidata and its bibliographic data in a LaTeX and BIBTEX environment. The current implementation looks up citations in the LaTeX-generated .aux file and queries Wikidata's MediaWiki API to get cited Wikidata items. The retrieved items are formatted and written to a .bib that bibtex can use to format the bibliographic items for inclusion in the LaTeX document. The workflow for a LaTeX document with the filename example.tex is

```
latex example
python -m scholia.tex write-bib-from-aux example.aux
bibtex example
latex example
latex example
```

Here, the example document could read

```
\documentclass{article}
\usepackage[utf8]{inputenc}
\begin{document}
\cite{Q18507561}
\bibliographystyle{plain}
\bibliography{example}
\end{document}
```

In this case, the `\cite` command cites Q18507561 (*Wikidata: a free collaborative knowledgebase* [36]). A DOI can also be used in the `\cite` command: instead of writing `\cite{Q18507561}`, one may write `\cite{10.1145/2629489}` to get the same citation. Scholia matches on the "10." DOI prefix and makes a SPARQL query to get the relevant Wikidata item.

The scheme presented above can take advantage of the many available style files of BibTeX to format the bibliographic items in the various ways requested by publishers. We have used Scholia for reference management in this paper. This means that all cited papers in this paper are entered in Wikidata.

There are various issues with the translation. Though planned to support UTF-8 encoding at least since 2003 [26], as of 2017, BibTeX does not support UTF-8 completely. The problem results in wrong sorting of the bibliographic items as well as wrong extraction of the surname, e.g., "Finn Årup Nielsen" gets extracted as "Årup Nielsen, Finn" instead of "Nielsen, Finn Årup" and sorted among the last items in the bibliography rather than under "N". A workaround could convert UTF-8 encoded characters to LaTeX escapes. A small translation table can handle accented characters, but miss, e.g., non-ASCII non-accented characters like ø, æ, å, ð and Ð. The combination of Biblatex/Biber can handle UTF-8, but required style files might not be available. The current Scholia implementation has a very small translation table to handle a couple of non-ASCII UTF-8 characters that occur in names.

5 Discussion

WDQS and Scholia can provide many different scientometrics views of the data available in Wikidata. The bibliographic data in Wikidata are still quite limited, but the number of scientometrically relevant items will likely continue to grow considerably in the coming months and years.

The continued growth of science data on Wikidata can have negative impact on Scholia, making the on-the-fly queries too resource demanding. In the current version, there are already a few queries that run into WDQS's time out, e.g., it happens for the view of co-author-normalized citations per year for Harvard University. If this becomes a general problem, we will need to redefine the queries. Indeed, the WDQS time out will be a general problem if we want to perform large-scale scientometrics studies. An alternative to using live queries would be to use dumps, which are available in several formats on a weekly basis, with daily increments in between.[24] The problem is not a limitation of SPARQL,

---

[24] https://www.wikidata.org/wiki/Wikidata:Database_download.

but a limitation set by the server resources. Some queries may be optimized, especially around the item labeling.

Working with Scholia has made us aware of several issues. Some of these are minor limitations in the Wikidata and WDQS systems. The Wikidata label length is limited to 250 characters, whereas the 'monolingual text' datatype used for the 'title' property (P1476) is limited to 400 characters. There are scholarly articles with titles longer than those limits.

Wikidata fields cannot directly handle subscripts and superscripts, which commonly appear in titles of articles about chemical compounds, elementary particles or mathematical formulas. Other formatting in titles cannot directly be handled in Wikidata's title property,[25] and recording a date such as "Summer 2011" is difficult.

Title and names of items can change. Authors can change name, e.g. due to marriage, and journals can change titles, e.g. due to a change of scope or transfer of ownership. For instance, the *Journal of the Association for Information Science and Technology* has changed name several times over the years.[26] Wikidata can handle multiple titles in a single Wikidata item and with qualifiers describe the dates of changes in title. For scientometrics, this ability is an advantage in principle, but multiple titles can make it cumbersome to handle when Wikidata is used as a bibliographic resource in document preparation, particularly for articles published near the time when the journal changed its name. One way to alleviate this problem would be to split the journal's Wikidata item into several, but this is not current practice.

In Wikidata, papers are usually not described to be affiliated with organizations. Scholia's ability to make statistics on scientific articles published by an organization is facilitated by the fact that items about scientific articles can link to items about authors, which can link to items about organizations. It is possible to link scientific articles to organization directly by using Wikidata qualifiers in connection with the author property. However, this scheme is currently in limited use. This scarcity of direct affiliation annotation on Wikidata items about articles means that scientometrics on the organizational level are unlikely to be precise at present. In the current version, Scholia even ignores any temporal qualifier for the affiliation and employer property, meaning that a researcher moving between several organization gets his/her articles counted under multiple organizations.

---

[25] By way of an example, consider the article "A library of 7TM receptor C-terminal tails. Interactions with the proposed post-endocytic sorting proteins ERM-binding phosphoprotein 50 (EBP50), N-ethylmaleimide-sensitive factor (NSF), sorting nexin 1 (SNX1), and G protein-coupled receptor-associated sorting protein (GASP)", another article with the title "Cerebral 5-HT$_{2A}$ receptor binding is increased in patients with Tourette's syndrome", where "2A" is subscripted, and "User's Guide to the amsrefs Package", where the "amsrefs" is set in monospaced font.

[26] http://onlinelibrary.wiley.com/journal/10.1002/(ISSN)2330-1643/issues records these former titles: *Journal of the American Society for Information Science and Technology, Journal of the American Society for Information Science,* and *American Documentation.*

Data modeling on Wikidata gives rise to reflections on what precisely a "publisher" and a "work" is. A user can set the *publisher* Wikidata property of a work to a corporate group, a subsidiary or possibly an imprint. For instance, how should we handle *Springer Nature, BioMed Central* and *Humana Press*?

Functional Requirements for Bibliographic Records (FRBR) [12] suggests a scheme for works, expressions, manifestations and "items". In Wikipedia, most items are described on the work level as opposed to the manifestation level (e.g., book edition), while citations should usually go to the manifestation level. How should one deal with scientific articles that have slightly different "manifestations", such as preprint, electronic journal edition, paper edition and postprint, or editorials that were co-published in multiple journals with identical texts? An electronic and a paper edition may differ in their dates of publication, but otherwise have the same bibliographic data, while a preprint and its journal edition usually have different identifiers and may also differ in content. From a scientometrics point of view, these difference in manifestation may not matter in some cases, but could be the focus of others. Splitting a scientific article as a work (in the FRBR sense) over multiple Wikidata items seems only to complicate matters.

The initial idea for Scholia was to create a researcher profile based on Wikidata data with list of publications, picture and CV-like information. The inspiration came from a blog post by Lambert Heller: *What will the scholarly profile page of the future look like? Provision of metadata is enabling experimentation.*[27] In this blog post, he discussed the different features of several scholarly Web services: ORCID, ResearchGate, Mendeley, Pure, VIVO, Google Scholar and ImpactStory. In Table 5, we have set up a table listing Heller's features for the Wikidata–Scholia combination. Wikidata–Scholia performs well in most aspects, but in the current version, Scholia has no backend for storing user data, and user features such as forum, Q&A and followers are not available.

Beyond the features listed by Heller, which features set Wikidata–Scholia apart from other scholarly Web services? The collaborative nature of Wikidata means that Wikidata users can create items for authors that do not have an account on Wikidata. In most other systems, the researcher as a user of the system has control over his/her scholarly profile and other researchers/users cannot make amendment or corrections. Likewise, when one user changes an existing item, this change will be reflected in subsequent live queries of that item, and it may still be in future dumps if not reverted or otherwise modified before the dump creation.

With WDQS queries, Scholia can combine data from different types of items in Wikidata in a way that is not usually possible with other scholarly profile Web services. For instance, Scholia generates lists of publications for an organization by combining items for works and authors and can show co-author graphs restricted by affiliation. Similarly, the co-author graph can be restricted to authors publishing works annotated with a specific main theme. Authors

---

[27] http://blogs.lse.ac.uk/impactofsocialsciences/2015/07/16/scholarly-profile-of-the-future/.

Table 5. Overview of Wikidata and Scholia features in terms of a scholarly profile. Directly inspired by a blog post by Lambert Heller (see text).

Feature		Description
Business model	Y	Community donations and funding from foundations to Wikimedia Foundation and affiliated chapters
Portrait picture	Y	The P18 property can record Wikimedia Commons images related to a researcher
Alternative names	Y	Aliases for all items, not just researchers
IDs/profiles in other systems	Y	Numerous links to external identifiers: ORCID, Scopus, Google Scholar, etc.
Papers and similar	Y	Papers and books are individual Wikidata items
Uncommon research products	Y	For instance, software can be associated with a developer
Grants, third party funding	(N)	Currently no property for grant holders and probably no individual grants in Wikidata. The sponsor property can be used to indicate the funding of a paper
Current institution	Y	Affiliation and employer can be recorded in Wikidata
Former employers, education	Y	Education, academic degree can be specified, and former employers can be set by way of qualifiers
Self-assigned keywords	(Y)	The main theme of a work can be specified, interests or field of work can be set for a person. The values must be items in Wikidata. Users can create items
Concepts from controlled vocabulary	Y	See above
Social graph of followers/friends	N	There are no user accounts on the current version of Scholia
Social graph of co-authors	Y	
Citation/attention metadata from platform itself	Y	Citations between scientific articles are recorded with a property that can be used to count citations. Citation/reference between Wikidata items
Citation/attention metadata from other source	(N)	Deep links to other citation resources like Google Scholar and Scopus
Comprehensive search to match/include papers	(N)	Several tools like Magnus Manske's *Source MetaData* that look up bibliographic metadata based on DOI, PMID or PMCID
Forums, Q&A etc	N	
Deposit own papers	(Y)	Appropriately licensed papers can be uploaded to Wikimedia Commons or Wikisource
Research administration tools	N	
Reuse of data from outside of the service	Y	API, WDQS, XML dump, third-party services

are typically annotated with gender in Wikidata, so Scholia can show gender color-coding of co-author graphs. On the topic aspect page, the Scholia panel that shows the most cited works that are cited from works around the topic can point to an important paper for a topic – even if the paper has not been annotated with the topic – by combining the citations data and topic annotation. References for claims are an important part of Wikidata and also singles Wikidata out among other scholarly profile Web service, and it acts as an extra scientometrics dimension. The current version of Scholia has only a few panels where the query uses references, e.g., the "Supports the following statement(s)" on the work aspect page, but it is possible to extend the use of this scientometrics dimension.

Acknowledgements. This work was supported by Innovationsfonden through the DABAI project. The work on Scholia was spawned by the WikiCite project [33]. We would like to thank the organizers of the workshop, particularly Dario Taraborelli. Finn Årup Nielsen's participation in the workshop was sponsored by an award from the Reinholdt W. Jorck og Hustrus Fund. We would also like to thank Magnus Manske, James Hare, Tom Arrow, Andra Waagmeester, and Sebastian Burgstaller-Muehlbacher for considerable work with Wikidata tools and data in the context of WikiCite. This paper was extended from another paper [24]. We thank Chiara Ghidini and the two other reviewers for providing suggestions for the improvement of that manuscript.

References

1. Adler, E., Hoon, M.A., Mueller, K.L., Chandrashekar, J., Ryba, N.J., Zuker, C.S.: A novel family of mammalian taste receptors. Cell **100**, 693–702 (2000)
2. Alpher, R.A., Bethe, H., Gamow, G.: The origin of chemical elements. Phys. Rev. **73**, 803–804 (1948)
3. Bollen, J., de Sompel, H.V., Hagberg, A., Chute, R.: A principal component analysis of 39 scientific impact measures. PLOS ONE **4**, e6022 (2009)
4. Eom, Y.H., Frahm, K.M., Benczúr, A., Shepelyansky, D.L.: Time evolution of Wikipedia network ranking. Eur. Phys. J. B **86** (2013). Article ID 492
5. Erxleben, F., Günther, M., Krötzsch, M., Mendez, J., Vrandečić, D.: Introducing Wikidata to the Linked Data web. In: Mika, P., et al. (eds.) ISWC 2014. LNCS, vol. 8796, pp. 50–65. Springer, Cham (2014). https://doi.org/10.1007/978-3-319-11964-9_4
6. Gorgolewski, K.J., Varoquaux, G., Rivera, G., Schwarz, Y., Ghosh, S.S., Maumet, C., Sochat, V.V., Nichols, T.E., Poldrack, R., Poline, J.B., Yarkoni, T., Margulies, D.S.: NeuroVault.org: a web-based repository for collecting and sharing unthresholded statistical maps of the human brain. Front. Neuroinformatics **9**, 8 (2015)
7. Grinberg, M.: Flask Web Development, April 2014
8. Heller, S.R., McNaught, A., Stein, S., Tchekhovskoi, D., Pletnev, I.: InChI - the worldwide chemical structure identifier standard. J. Cheminformatics **5**, 7 (2013)
9. Hernández, D., Hogan, A., Krötzsch, M.: Reifying RDF: what works well with Wikidata? In: Proceedings of the 11th International Workshop on Scalable Semantic Web Knowledge Base Systems, September 2015. http://users.dcc.uchile.cl/~dhernand/research/ssws-2015-reifying.pdf

10. Hernández, D., Hogan, A., Riveros, C., Rojas, C., Zerega, E.: Querying Wikidata: comparing SPARQL, relational and graph databases. In: Groth, P., et al. (eds.) ISWC 2016. LNCS, vol. 9982, pp. 88–103. Springer, Cham (2016). https://doi.org/10.1007/978-3-319-46547-0_10

11. Hull, D., Pettifer, S., Kell, D.: Defrosting the digital library: bibliographic tools for the next generation web. PLOS Comput. Biol. **4**, e1000204 (2008)

12. IFLA Study Group on the Functional Requirements for Bibliographic Records: Functional Requirements for Bibliographic Records, February 2009. http://www.ifla.org/files/assets/cataloguing/frbr/frbr_2008.pdf

13. Khabsa, M., Giles, C.L.: The number of scholarly documents on the public web. PLOS ONE **9**, e93949 (2014)

14. Kikkawa, J., Takaku, M., Yoshikane, F.: DOI links on Wikipedia. In: Morishima, A., Rauber, A., Liew, C.L. (eds.) ICADL 2016. LNCS, vol. 10075, pp. 369–380. Springer, Cham (2016). https://doi.org/10.1007/978-3-319-49304-6_40

15. Kousha, K., Thelwall, M.: Are Wikipedia citations important evidence of the impact of scholarly articles and books? J. Am. Soc. Inf. Sci. **68**, 762–779 (2016)

16. Krötzsch, M., Vrandečić, D., Völkel, M.: Semantic MediaWiki. In: Cruz, I., et al. (eds.) ISWC 2006. LNCS, vol. 4273, pp. 935–942. Springer, Heidelberg (2006). https://doi.org/10.1007/11926078_68

17. Lin, J., Fenner, M.: An analysis of Wikipedia references across PLOS publications, December 2014. https://figshare.com/articles/An_analysis_of_Wikipedia_references_across_PLOS_publications/1048991/files/1546358.pdf

18. Maggio, L.A., Willinsky, J., Steinberg, R., Mietchen, D., Wass, J., Dong, T.: Wikipedia as a gateway to biomedical research: the relative distribution and use of citations in the English Wikipedia. bioRxiv.org: the preprint server for biology, July 2017

19. Mishra, S., Torvik, V.I.: Quantifying conceptual novelty in the biomedical literature. DLib Mag. **22**(9/10) (2016). https://doi.org/10.1045/september2016-mishra

20. Nielsen, F.Å.: Scientific citations in Wikipedia. First Monday **12** (2007). http://firstmonday.org/article/view/1997/1872

21. Nielsen, F.Å.: Clustering of scientific citations in Wikipedia, December 2008. http://www2.imm.dtu.dk/pubdb/views/edoc_download.php/5666/pdf/imm5666.pdf

22. Nielsen, F.Å.: Brede Wiki: a neuroinformatics web service with structured information. Front. Neur. Conference Abstract: Neuroinformatics (2009). https://doi.org/10.3389/conf.neuro.11.2009.08.072

23. Nielsen, F.Å., Mietchen, D., Willighagen, E.: Scholia, March 2017

24. Nielsen, F.Å., Mietchen, D., Willighagen, E.: Scholia and scientometrics with Wikidata, March 2017. https://arxiv.org/pdf/1703.04222.pdf

25. Okoli, C., Mehdi, M., Mesgari, M., Nielsen, F.Å., Lanamäki, A.: The people's encyclopedia under the gaze of the sages: a systematic review of scholarly research on Wikipedia, March 2012. https://papers.ssrn.com/sol3/papers.cfm?abstract_id=2021326

26. Patashnik, O.: BIBTEX yesterday, today, and tomorrow. TUGboat **24**, 25–30 (2003). https://www.tug.org/TUGboat/Articles/tb24-1/patashnik.pdf

27. Poldrack, R., Barch, D.M., Mitchell, J.P., Wager, T.D., Wagner, A.D., Devlin, J.T., Cumba, C., Koyejo, O., Milham, M.P.: Toward open sharing of task-based fMRI data: the OpenfMRI project. Front. Neuroinformatics **7**, 12 (2013)

28. Pooladian, A., Borrego, Á.: Methodological issues in measuring citations in Wikipedia: a case study in Library and Information Science. Scientometrics **113**, 455–464 (2017)

29. Priem, J., Piwowar, H.A., Hemminger, B.M.: Altmetrics in the wild: using social media to explore scholarly impact, March 2012. https://arxiv.org/html/1203.4745

30. Putman, T.E., Lelong, S., Burgstaller-Muehlbacher, S., Waagmeester, A., Diesh, C., Dunn, N., Munoz-Torres, M., Stupp, G., Wu, C., Su, A.I., Good, B.M.: WikiGenomes: an open web application for community consumption and curation of gene annotation data in Wikidata. In: Database 2017, March 2017. http://biorxiv.org/content/biorxiv/early/2017/01/21/102046.full.pdf

31. Putnam, H.: Is semantics possible? Metaphilosophy 1, 187–201 (1970)

32. Romero, A.R., Tzovaras, B.G., Greene, C.S., Himmelstein, D.S., McLaughlin, S.R.: Sci-Hub provides access to nearly all scholarly literature. PeerJ preprints, July 2017

33. Taraborelli, D., Dugan, J.M., Pintscher, L., Mietchen, D., Neylon, C.: WikiCite 2016 report, November 2016. https://upload.wikimedia.org/wikipedia/commons/2/2b/WikiCite_2016_report.pdf

34. Teplitskiy, M., Lu, G., Duede, E.: Amplifying the impact of open access: Wikipedia and the diffusion of science. J. Am. Soc. Inf. Sci. 68(9), 2116–2127 (2017)

35. Verborgh, R., Sande, M.V., Colpaert, P., Coppens, S., Mannens, E., de Walle, R.V.: Web-scale querying through linked data fragments. In: Proceedings of the Workshop on Linked Data on the Web, July 2014. http://ceur-ws.org/Vol-1184/ldow2014_paper_04.pdf

36. Vrandečić, D., Krötzsch, M.: Wikidata: a free collaborative knowledgebase. Commun. ACM 57, 78–85 (2014). http://cacm.acm.org/magazines/2014/10/178785-wikidata/fulltext

37. Watson, J.D., Crick, F.: Molecular structure of nucleic acids: a structure for deoxyribose nucleic acid. Nature 171, 737–738 (1953). http://www.nature.com/nature/dna50/watsoncrick.pdf

38. Yarkoni, T., Poldrack, R., Nichols, T.E., Essen, D.C.V., Wager, T.D.: Large-scale automated synthesis of human functional neuroimaging data. Nat. Methods 8, 665–670 (2011)

39. Zhirov, A.O., Zhirov, O.V., Shepelyansky, D.L.: Two-dimensional ranking of Wikipedia articles. Eur. Phys. J. B 77, 523–531 (2010)

2nd RDF Stream Processing Workshop (RSP 2017)

SLD Revolution: A Cheaper, Faster yet More Accurate Streaming Linked Data Framework

Marco Balduini, Emanuele Della Valle, and Riccardo Tommasini[✉]

DEIB, Politecnico of Milano, Milano, Italy
{marco.balduini,emanuele.dellavalle,riccardo.tommasini}@polimi.it

Abstract. The RDF Stream Processing (RSP) is gaining momentum. The RDF stream data model is progressively adopted and many SPARQL extensions for continuous querying are converging to a unified RSP query language. However, the RSP community still has to investigate when transforming data streams in RDF streams pays off. In this paper, we report on several experiments on a revolutionized version of our Streaming Linked Data framework (namely, SLD Revolution). SLD Revolution (i) operates on time-stamped generic data items (events, tuples, trees and graphs), and (ii) it applies a lazy-transformation approach, i.e. it processes data according to their nature as long as possible. SLD Revolution results to be a cheaper (it uses less memory and has a smaller CPU load), faster (it reaches higher maximum input throughput), yet more accurate (it provides a smaller error rate in the results) solution than its ancestor SLD.

1 Introduction

RDF Stream Processing (RSP) is gaining momentum. The RSP W3C community group[1] has just reached 100 members. It is actively working on a report that will present the RDF Stream data model, the possible RDF Stream serializations and the syntax and semantics of the RSP-QL query language.

We started using RSP in 2011, when we won the Semantic Web Challenge with Bottari [1]. A key ingredient of our solution was the Streaming Linked Data framework [2] (SLD). SLD is a middleware that extends RSP engines with adapters, decorators and publishers. All these components observe and push RDF streams to a central RDF stream bus. The adapters are able to ingest any kind of external data, transforming them into RDF streams modeled as time-stamped RDF Graphs and push them to the bus. A network of C-SPARQL queries [3] analyzes the RDF streams in the bus, elaborate them, and push the results to other internal streams. Decorators can semantically enrich RDF streams using user defined functions (e.g., in Bottari to add the opinion that a social media user expresses about a given named entity in a micro-post). Publishers push data to the bus encoded in the Streaming Linked Data format [4].

---

[1] https://www.w3.org/community/rsp/.

© Springer International Publishing AG 2017
E. Blomqvist et al. (Eds.): ESWC 2017 Satellite Events, LNCS 10577, pp. 263–279, 2017.
https://doi.org/10.1007/978-3-319-70407-4_37

SLD it is currently a key component of Fluxedo[2], i.e. a commercial solution for monitoring topics on social media. A typical deployment of SLD in Fluxedo processes in real-time thousands of micro-posts per minute on a 50 e/month machine in the cloud (8 GB of RAM and 4 cores), providing semantic analysis and sophisticated visualizations.

In five years of SLD usage, we learned that using RDF streams is valuable when (i) data are naturally represented as graphs, i.e. micro-posts in the larger social graph, and when (ii) the availability of popular vocabularies makes easy writing adapters that semantically annotate the incoming data, e.g. we wrote adapters that annotated streams from the major social networks using SIOC [5].

However, we have also found out several weaknesses of the approach:

- RDF streams cannot be found in the wild, yet. JSON is largely used in practice (e.g., Twitter Streaming APIs[3] and W3C activity stream 2.0 working draft[4]).
- The results of C-SPARQL queries are often relational and forcing them into an RDF streams is not natural, i.e., a user would naturally use the REGISTER QUERY ... AS SELECT ... form instead of REGISTER STREAM ... AS CONSTRUCT ... one. It takes three triples to state how many times a hashtag appears in the micro-posts observed in 1 min, while the tuple ⟨timestamp, hashtag, count⟩ is more succinct.
- It is harder to express some computation using C-SPARQL over RDF streams and graphs than writing a path expression over JSON; or writing an SQL query over relations; or writing an EPL statement over events.
- SLD builds on the C-SPARQL engine and, thus, shares with it some shortcomings, i.e. it gives incorrect answers when it is overloaded engine [6,7].

In this paper, we challenge the hypothesis that RDF streams should play such a central role in SLD. We investigate if (i) using time-stamped generic data items (instead of focusing only time-stamped RDF graphs) and (ii) processing them according to their event-, tuple-, tree- and graph-based nature, offer the opportunity to engineer a cheaper (uses less memory and CPU), faster (it reaches higher maximum input throughput) yet more accurate (i.t. with a smaller error in the results) version of SLD that we called SLD Revolution. We bring experimental evidence that supports the design decision of revolutionizing SLD in those two directions. Using our experience on social media monitoring, we design a set of experiments to evaluate our hypothesis: we chose the expected maximum rate of micro-posts per minute and the machine to deal with the worst-case scenario; by reducing the available memory and processor time requirement we push the overload status to an higher input rate.

The remainder of the paper is organized as follows. Section 2 introduces the state-of-the-art in stream processing with a focus on RSP. Section 3 presents SLD Revolution and its new processing model. Sections 4 and 5, respectively, describe

---

the settings and the results of the experiments we run. Finally, in Sect. 6, we conclude and present our future work.

2   State of the Art

Data model. RSP extends the RDF data model and the SPARQL query model in order to take into account the streaming nature of the data.

A **relational data stream** [9] S is defined as an unbounded sequence of time-stamped data items (d_i, t_i): $S = (d_1, t_1), (d_2, t_2), \ldots, (d_n, t_n), \ldots$, where d_i is a relation and $t_i \in \mathbb{N}$ the associated time instant. Different approaches constrain t_i so that it holds either $t_i \leq t_{i+1}$, i.e. stream items are in a non-decreasing time order, or $t_i < t_{i+1}$, i.e. stream items are in strictly increasing time order.

An **RDF Stream** is defined in the same way, but d_i is either an RDF statement (as done in most of the RSP approaches [3, 10–12]) or an RDF graph (as done in SLD [2] and proposed by the RSP W3C community). An RDF statement is a triple $(s, p, o) \in (I \cup B) \times (I) \times (I \cup B \cup L)$, where I is the set of IRIs, B is the set of blank nodes and L is the set of literals. An RDF graph is a set of RDF statements.

Processing Model. Also the processing model of RSP [3, 10, 11] inherits from the work done in the database community. In particular, it is inspired by the CQL stream processing model (proposed by the DB group of the Stanford University [8]) which defines three classes of operators (Fig. 1.a):

- **stream-to-relation** operators are able to transform streams in relations. Since a stream is a potentially infinite bag of time-stamped data items, those operators extract finite bags of data enabling query answering. One of the most studied operator of this class is the *sliding window* that chunks the incoming streams into portions of length ω and slides of a length β
- **relation-to-relation** operators transform relations in other relations. Relational algebraic expressions are a well-known cases of this class of operators.
- **relation-to-stream** operators are optional and allow to output the results as a part of a stream. Alternatively, a time-varying relation is provided.

Figure 1.b presents the CQL model adapted to the RSP case. The stream and the relation concepts are mapped to RDF streams and to set of mappings (using

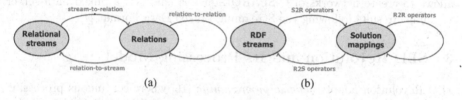

(a)   (b)

Fig. 1. The CQL model, cf. [8], and its adaptation for RDF stream processing

the SPARQL algebra terminology), respectively. To highlight the similarity of the RSP operators [12] to the CQL ones, similar names are used: **S2R**, **R2R** and **R2S** to indicate the operators respectively analogous to stream-to-relation, relation-to-relation and relation-to-stream operators.

RSP Middlewares. In order to ease the task of deploying the RSP Engine in real-world applications, three middleware were designed: the Linked Stream Middleware [13], a semantically enabled service architecture for mashups over streaming and stored data [14] and our SLD [2].

The three approaches fulfill similar requirements for the end user. They offer extensible means for real-time data collection, for publishing and querying collected information as Linked Data, and for visualizing data and query results. They differ in the approach. Our SLD and the Linked Stream Middleware take both a data driven approach, but they address in a different way the non-functional requirements; while SLD is an in-memory solution for stream processing of RDF streams with limited support for static information, the Linked Stream Middleware is a cloud-based infrastructure to integrate time-dependent data with other Linked Data sources. The middleware described in [14], instead, takes a service oriented approach, thus it also includes service discovery and service composition among its features.

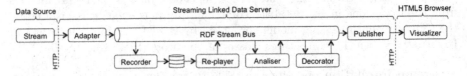

Fig. 2. The architecture of the streaming linked data framework [2].

Figure 2 illustrates the architecture of SLD that offers: (i) a set of adapters that transforms heterogeneous data streams in RDF streams attaching to each received element a time-stamp that identifies the ingestion time (e.g., a stream of micro-posts in JSON as an RDF stream using the SIOC vocabulary [5] or a stream of weather sensor observations in XML using the Semantic Sensor Network vocabulary [15]); (ii) a publish/subscribe bus to internally manage RDF streams, (iii) some facilities to record and replay RDF streams; (iv) a set of user defined components to decorate an RDF stream (e.g., adding sentiment annotations to micro-posts); (v) a wrapper for the C-SPARQL Engine [3] that allows to create networks of C-SPARQL queries, and (vi) a linked data server to publish results following the Streaming Linked Data Format [4].

3   SLD Revolution and Its Processing Model

SLD Revolution adopts *generic programming* [16] where continuous processing operators are expressed in terms of types *to-be-specified-later*. This idea - which was pioneered in [17] - can be adapted to stream processing by choosing to model the element d_i in the stream S as time-stamped generic data items that are instantiated when needed for specific types provided as parameters.

Figure 3 illustrates the SLD Revolution processing model. The stream and the relation concepts of CQL are mapped to **generic data streams** $S\langle T \rangle$ and to **instantaneous generic data items** $I\langle T \rangle$.

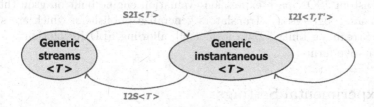

Fig. 3. The processing model of the SLD revolution framework.

In line with CQL and RSP-QL, SLD Revolution proposes three classes of operators:

- The **stream-to-instantaneous S2I** $\langle T \rangle$ operators transform the infinite generic data stream $S\langle T \rangle$ in to a finite bag of **instantaneous generic data items** $I\langle T \rangle$.
- The **instantaneous-to-instantaneous I2I** $\langle T, T' \rangle$ operators transform instantaneous generic data items $I\langle T \rangle$ into other **instantaneous generic data items** $I\langle T' \rangle$, where T and T' can be of the same type or of different types. For instance, a C-SPARQL query of the type REGISTER QUERY ... AS SELECT ... takes in input time-stamped RDF graphs and generates as output time-stamped relations.
- The **instantaneous-to-stream I2S** $\langle T \rangle$ operators transform **instantaneous generic data items** $I\langle T \rangle$ into a **generic data stream** $S\langle T \rangle$.

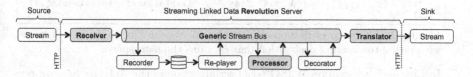

Fig. 4. The architecture of the SLD revolution framework. In gray the components that were redesign to adopt the generic programming approach.

SLD Revolution generalizes SLD architecture (cf. Fig. 4 with Fig. 2). The Generic Stream Bus replace of the RDF stream bus. The receivers replace the adapters. As the adapters they allow to ingest external data streams, but they no longer transform the received events in time-stamped RDF graphs. Data items remain in their original form, only the ingestion time is added, postponing the transformation to the moment when it is required (we name this approach *lazy transformation*). The processors substitute the C-SPARQL-based analyzers. The C-SPARQL engine remains as one of the possible processors, but SLD Revolution can be extended with any continuous processing engine. The current implementation includes the Complex Event Processor Esper, the SPARQL Engine Jena-ARQ that operates on time-stamped RDF graphs one at a time, and a custom JSON path expression evaluation engine built on gson (https://github.com/google/gson). Translators generalize publishers, which are specific for the Streaming Linked Data format [4], allowing SLD Revolution to output in alternative formats.

4   Experimental Settings

In this Section, we present the experimental settings of this work. As domain we chose Social Network analysis as done by the Linked Data Benchmark Council (LDBC) in the SNBench[5]. We first explain the type of data we used for our experiments. Then, we explain how the data were sent to SLD and SLD Revolution. We describe the two continuous processing pipelines that we registered in SLD and in SLD Revolution. Finally, we state which key performance indicators (KPIs) we measure and how.

Input Data. SLD and SLD Revolution receive information in the same way, they both connect to a web socket server and handle JSON-LD files.

```
 1  {"@context": { ... }, "@type": "Collection", "totalItems": 1,
 2      "prov:wasAssociatedWith": "sr:Twitter",
 3   "items":[{
 4    "@type":"Post",
 5    "published":"2016-04-26T15:40:03.054+02:00",
 6    "actor":{"@type":"Account", "@id":"user:1", "sioc:name":"
            @streamreasoning"},
 7    "object":{
 8     "@type":"Content", "@id":"post:2", "alias":"http://.../2",
 9     "prov:wasAssociatedWith":"sr:Twitter",
10     "sioc:content":"You ARE the #socialmedia!",
11     "dct:language":"en",
12     "tag":[{ "@type":"Tag", "@id":"tag:3", "displayName":"socialmedia"}]}
13    }]}
```

Listing 1. JSON representation of a Twitter micro-post. Due to the lack of space we omitted the context declaration that contains the namespace.

In Listing 1, we propose a JSON-LD serialization of the Activity Stream representation of a tweet as it was injected during the experiments in both systems. The JSON-LD representation of an Activity Stream is a *Collection* (specified by *@type* property) composed by one or more social media items. The *Collection* is described with two properties, i.e., *totalItems* and *prov:wasAssociatedWith*, which tell respectively the number of items and the provenance of the items. The collection in the example contains a *Post* created on *2016-04-26* (*published* property) by an *actor* (Line 6) that produce the *object* (Lines 7-13). The *Actor*

---

[5] http://www.ldbcouncil.org/benchmarks/snb.

has a unique identifier *@id*, a *displayName*, a *sioc:name* and a *alias*. The *Object* has a *sioc:content*, a *dct:language*, zero or more *tags*, and optionally a *url* and a *to* to represent, respectively, links to web pages and mentions of other actors.

```
1  <post:2> a sma:Tweet ;
2      dcterms:created "2016-04-26T15:40:03.054+02:00"^^xsd:dateTime ;
3      dcterms:language "en"^^xsd:string ;
4      sioc:content "You ARE the #socialmedia!"^^xsd:string ;
5      sioc:has_container "Twitter"^^xsd:string ;
6      sioc:has_creator <user:1> ;
7      sioc:id "2"^^xsd:string ;
8      sioc:link "http://.../status/2"^^xsd:string ;
9      sioc:topic <tag:3> .
10 <tag:3> a sioct:Tag ;
11     rdfs:label "socialmedia"^^xsd:string .
12 <user:1> a sioc:UserAccount ;
13     sioc:account_of "StreamReasoning"^^xsd:string ;
14     sioc:creator_of <post:2> ;
15     sioc:id "1"^^xsd:string ;
16     sioc:name "@streamreasoning"^^xsd:string .
```

Listing 2. RDF N3 representation of a Twitter micro-post

Listing 2 shows the RDF produced by the SLD adapter in transforming the JSON-LD in Listing 1. The translation operation exploits well known vocabularies, in particular *sioc* to represent the online community information, *prov* to track the provenance of an item and *dcterms* to represents information about the *object*.

Sending data. A test consists of sending a constant amount of synthetic data using the JSON-LD serialization presented in Listing 1. The data is sent in chunks three times per minute (i.e. at the 10th, the 30th and the 50th seconds of the minute). Each chunk contains the same amount of posts. We tested the configuration for different rates: 1500 posts per minute (i.e., three chunks of 500 posts), 3000 posts per minute, 6000 posts per minute, 9000 posts per minute, 12000 posts per minute and 18000 posts per minute.

The rates and and the input methodology were chosen based on our experiences on social monitoring (see Sect. 1). They test a normal situation for SLD (1500 and 3000 posts per minutes) as well as situations that we know to overload SLD (more than 6000 posts per minute).

Pipelines. We tested SLD and SLD revolution with different pipelines:

- the *area chart* pipeline computes the number of tweets observed over time. It uses a 15 min long window that slides every minute. The results can be continuously computed *(i)* using a generic sliding window operator, which works looking only to the time-stamps of the data items in the generic stream, and *(ii)* accessing with a path expression the *totalItems* property in the JSON-LD file, i.e., the number of items in the collection.
- the *bar chart* pipeline counts how often hashtags appear in the tweets received in the last 15 min. As the area chart pipeline, the window slides every minute. In this second pipeline, RDF streams are adequate and it is convenient to write a C-SPARQL query that counts the number of times each hashtag appears.

The two pipelines are coded in SLD and SLD Revolution in two different ways. SLD performs the transformations of JSON-LD in RDF by default, on all the input data, independently from the task to perform. SLD Revolution keeps the data in its original format as much as possible, i.e., it performs *lazy transformations*.

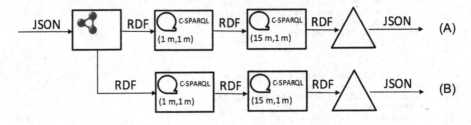

Fig. 5. SLD pipeline

SLD Pipelines. Figure 5 presents the two pipelines in SLD. The input data are translated in RDF as soon as they enter the pipelines. The computations for the area chart and for the bar chart (see the part marked with **A** and **B**) are composed by the same type of components and share the new RDF stream translated by the *Adapter*.

The pipeline **A** uses two C-SPARQL queries. The first (see Listing 3) applies a tumbling window of 1 min[6] and counts the tweets.

The second aggregates the results from the first query using a 15 min time window that slides every minute (see Listing 4).

```
1  REGISTER STREAM presocialstr AS
2  CONSTRUCT { ?id sma:twitterCount ?twitterC }
3  FROM STREAM <http://.../socialstr> [RANGE 1m STEP 1m]
4  WHERE { SELECT (uuid() AS ?id) ?twitterC
5          WHERE { SELECT (COUNT (DISTINCT ?mp) AS ?twitterC)
6                  WHERE { ?mp a sma:Tweet } } }
```

Listing 3. C-SPARQL pre-query for the area chart that applies a tumbling window of 1 min and counts the tweets.

```
1  REGISTER STREAM ac AS
2  CONSTRUCT { ?uid sma:twitterCount ?totTwitter ; sma:created_during ?
       unixTimeFrame }
3  FROM STREAM <http://.../presocialstr> [RANGE 15m STEP 1m]
4  WHERE {
5    SELECT (uuid() AS ?uid) ?unixTimeFrame (SUM(?twitter) AS ?totTwitter)
6    WHERE { ?id sma:twitterCount ?twitter ; sma:created_during ?timeFrame .
7            ?timeFrame a sma:15mTimeFrame ; sma:inUnixTime ?unixTimeFrame
       }
8    GROUP BY ?unixTimeFrame }
```

Listing 4. C-SPARQL query for the area chart that aggregates the results from the query in Listing 3 using a 15 min time window that slides every minute.

---

[6] A tumbling window is a sliding window that slides for its length.

It is worth to note that the first query is an important optimization in terms of memory consumption. It avoids the engine to keep 15 min of tweets to only count them. In SLD we often use this design pattern, we call this first query a *pre-query*.

Pipeline **B** also exploits this design; it applies a pre-query to reduce the amount of data and then a query to produce the final result.

It is also worth to note that all the C-SPARQL queries use the form REGISTER STREAM ... AS CONSTRUCT ..., because RDF streams are the only means of communication between SLD components.

The last components of both pipelines are publishers that make the results available to external process outside SLD. In this case, the publisher writes JSON files on disk.

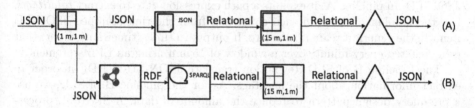

Fig. 6. SLD revolution pipeline

SLD Revolution Pipelines. Figure 6 presents the pipelines in SLD Revolution. As for SLD, the pipeline **A** is for the area chart, while **B** is for the bar chart. The first component is no longer an adapter. The data directly enter SLD revolution in JSON-LD format. The first query is a generic 1 min long tumbling window implemented with the EPL statement in Listing 5. FORCE_UPDATE and START_EAGER tells the stream processing engine, respectively, to emit also empty reports and to start processing the window as soon as the query is registered (i.e., without waiting for the first time-stamped data item to arrive). It is worth to note that this query exploits the event-based nature of the generic stream it is observing; it does not inspect the payload of the events, it only uses their time-stamps.

```
select * from GenericEvent.win:time_batch(1\,min, "FORCE_UPDATE,
    START_EAGER")
```

Listing 5. The generic window query in common to both the pipelines in SLD Revolution

The FORCE_UPDATE flow control keyword instructs the view to post an empty result set to listeners if there is no data to post for an interval. When using this keyword the irstream keyword should be used in the select clause to ensure the remove stream is also output. Note that FORCE_UPDATE is for use with listeners to the same statement and not for use with named windows. Consider output rate limiting instead.

The START_EAGER flow control keyword instructs the view to post empty result sets even before the first event arrives, starting a time interval at statement creation time. As when using FORCE_UPDATE, the view also posts an empty result set to listeners if there is no data to post for an interval, however it starts doing so at time of statement creation rather then at the time of arrival of the first event.

As explained in Sect. 3, processors are the central components of SLD Revolution. They can listen to one or more generic streams, compute different operations and push out a generic streams. The type of the input and output streams can be different. The two pipelines uses different processors (e.g. RDF translator, windower and SPARQL).

SLD Revolution maintains the data format as long as possible in order to reduce the overhead of the translations. It can exploit the tree-based nature of JSON-LD. In pipeline **A**, it exploits a path expression data to extract *totalItems*, i.e., the number of items in each collection, from the time-stamped JSON-LD items in the generic stream it listens to. It outputs a tuple ⟨timeframe,count⟩ that is aggregated every minute over a window of 15 min using an EPL statement.

The Pipeline **B** of SLD Revolution translate JSON-LD in RDF in order to extract information about the hashtags. As for the pipeline **B** of SLD, we use a pre-query design pattern to reduce the amount of data. A SPARQL processor applies the SELECT query in Listing 6 to every data-item in the generic stream it listens to and pushes out a stream of tuples ⟨hashtagLabel,count⟩. The relational stream is then aggregated with an esper processor with a 15 min time window that slides every 1 min (see Listing 7).

```
1  SELECT ?htlabel (COUNT(DISTINCT(?mpTweet)) AS ?htTweetCount)
2  WHERE { ?mpTweet a sma:Tweet ; sioc:topic ?tweetTopic .
3          ?tweetTopic a sioctypes:Tag ; rdfs:label ?htlabel }
4  GROUP BY ?htlabel
5  ORDER BY desc(?htTweetCount)
```

Listing 6. SPARQL pre-query for the bar chart

```
select htlabel, sum(count) as sumHt from HTCountEvent.win:time(15\,min)
group by htlabel output snapshot every 1\,min
```

Listing 7. EPL query for the bar chart

KPIs. As key performance indicators (KPIs), we measure the resources consumption of the two systems and the correctness of the results. For the resource consumption we measure every 10 seconds: *(i)* the CPU load of the system thread in percent, *(ii)* the memory consumption of the thread in megabytes and *(iii)* the memory consumption of the Java Virtual Machine (JVM). For the correctness, we compared the computed results with the expected results. Being the input a constant flows of tweets that only differ for the ID, the area chart is expected to be flat and the bar chart is expected to count exactly the same number of hashtags every minute.

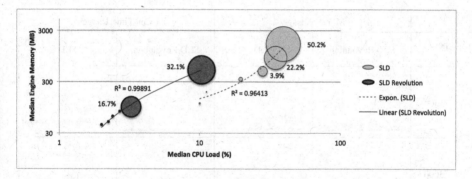

Fig. 7. An overview of the experimental results; larger bubbles means greater % errors.

5   Evaluation Results

Figure 7 offers an overview of the results of the experiments. The full results are reported at the end of this section in Fig. 10. On the X axis we plot the median of the CPU load in percent, while on the Y axis we plot the memory allocated by the engine thread. The size of the bubble maps the median of the error of the area chart. Bubbles in the lower left corner correspond to the experiment where we sent 1500 tweets per minute.

Increasing the throughput results in more memory consumption and CPU load for both systems. However, not SLD Revolution consumes less memory than SLD and occupies less CPU. Moreover, SLD Revolution presents a linear increment for both these KPIs, while the resource usage for SLD grows exponentially with the throughput. Also the error in the results increases with the throughput: SLD already shows an error greater than 3% in the bar chart at 3000 tweets per minutes and in the area chart at 9000 tweets per minute; SLD Revolution is faster - i.e. it reaches higher maximum input throughput - and more accurate – i.e. it reaches 3% error level only for 18000 tweets per minutes, providing more precise results than SLD.

Figure 8 presents the recorded time-series for CPU load and memory usage in both systems. The memory usage graphs contains two different time series. The blue one represents the memory usage of the system thread, while the orange one shows the total memory usage for the JVM.

The memory usage of the system thread accounts for all the components and data in the pipeline. Notably, when the system under testing is not overloaded, the memory usage is constant over time, while when the system is overloaded it grows until the system crashes. The total memory usage of the JVM shows, instead, the typical pattern of the garbage collector that lets the JVM memory grow before freeing it. Also in this case, when the system it is overloaded, the garbage collector fails to free the memory.

During the experiments the median of the memory used by SLD spans from 115 MB, when loaded with at 1500 posts/min, to 1.6 GB, when loaded with 18000 posts/min. For SLD Revolution, instead, it spans from 44 MB to 511.5 MB

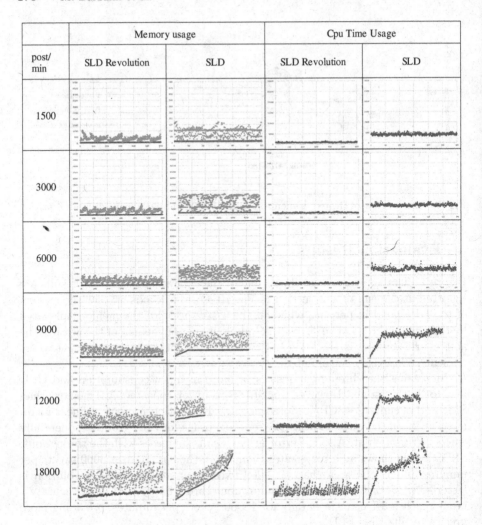

Fig. 8. Memory and CPU usage over time

in the same load conditions. The experimental results clearly shows that SLD Revolution consumes (in average) three times less memory than its ancestor.

The same considerations can be proposed for the CPU load. The median of the CPU load spans from 2% to 10% for SLD Revolution, while it spans from 10% to 39.5% for SLD. SLD Revolution consumes in average 4 time less CPU time than SLD. Moreover, offers higher level of stability for both the parameters in all the experiments. The memory usage and the CPU loads clearly explode at higher input rate and allow the machine to produce results for a higher load in input.

The correctness results are summarized in Fig. 9. As explained in Sect. 4, the percentage of errors is computed by comparing the results for each time interval

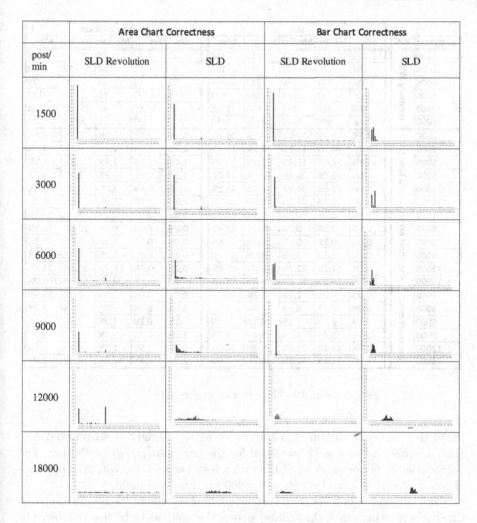

Fig. 9. Area chart and bar chart errors distributions

with the expected ones. The X axis of each plot shows the percentage of error; it ranges from 0% to 100%. The Y axis is the percentage of results with that error; it also ranges from 0% to 100%. A bar as tall as the Y axis in the left side of the graph means that all results where correct. The smaller that bar is and the greater the number of bars to the right is, the more errors were observed.

In general, the results shows that SLD Revolution is more accurate (the result error is smaller) than SLD. For the area chart the distribution shows that SLD Revolution percentage of error is very low when the input throughput is between 1500 posts/min and 9000 posts/min. When it is higher (i.e., 12000 and 18000 posts/min) also SLD Revolution starts suffering and percentage of errors starts growing. For SLD, errors are present even at lower input rate, the graph

post/min	KPI	SLD					SLD Revolution				
		Min.	1st Qu.	Median	3rd Qu.	Max.	Min.	1st Qu.	Median	3rd Qu.	Max.
1500	memory (MB)	112	114	115	115	116	42	43	44	45	48
3000		188	190	191	192	193	45	48	50	52	58
6000		330	337	340	342	353	52	61	64	67	78
9000		n.a.	481	485	488	504	59	73	80	84	102
12000		684	783	888	956	1015	66	88	97	107	144
18000		n.a.	919	1652	2565	4451	212	392	511,5	597,2	774
1500	CPU load (%)	7,3%	9,3%	10,0%	10,8%	14,1%	1,3%	1,8%	2,0%	2,2%	3,4%
3000		8,3%	10,5%	11,2%	12,1%	16,2%	1,3%	2,0%	2,2%	2,5%	3,8%
6000		16,1%	18,6%	19,7%	21,0%	29,5%	1,4%	2,1%	2,4%	2,8%	4,5%
9000		n.a.	26,3%	28,3%	30,4%	37,0%	1,5%	2,3%	2,7%	3,2%	5,1%
12000		n.a.	32,6%	34,9%	36,9%	43,3%	1,3%	2,6%	3,2%	4,2%	8,9%
18000		n.a.	35,2%	39,6%	46,1%	72,5%	2,8%	7,2%	10,3%	13,8%	26,2%
1500	area chart error	0,0%	0,0%	0,0%	0,1%	66,7%	0,0%	0,0%	0,0%	0,0%	33,3%
3000		0,0%	0,0%	0,0%	0,1%	33,4%	0,0%	0,0%	0,0%	0,0%	33,3%
6000		0,0%	0,1%	0,6%	8,1%	61,8%	0,0%	0,0%	0,0%	0,0%	33,3%
9000		0,1%	1,2%	3,9%	9,5%	30,2%	0,0%	0,0%	0,0%	0,0%	33,3%
12000		0,1%	14,1%	22,2%	26,0%	82,4%	0,0%	0,0%	16,7%	33,3%	33,3%
18000		38,2%	44,8%	50,2%	59,5%	93,1%	0,0%	16,9%	32,1%	53,7%	100,0%
1500	bar chart error	0,0%	0,0%	2,2%	2,3%	6,7%	0,0%	0,0%	0,0%	0,0%	93,3%
3000		0,0%	0,1%	4,5%	4,5%	4,5%	0,0%	0,0%	0,0%	0,1%	2,2%
6000		0,1%	2,3%	2,3%	4,1%	5,7%	0,1%	0,1%	2,3%	2,3%	2,3%
9000		1,8%	3,4%	4,2%	5,4%	7,5%	1,6%	2,4%	2,4%	2,4%	3,2%
12000		13,6%	19,4%	21,0%	25,0%	28,0%	0,2%	1,5%	2,5%	4,7%	6,1%
18000		49,5%	51,1%	52,6%	54,7%	57,9%	2,9%	9,4%	12,6%	16,3%	22,4%

Fig. 10. The experimental results.

shows that the error distribution starts moving to the right at 6000 posts/min. Similar consideration can be proposed for the bar chart error distribution. The degradation of performance of SLD starts a very low rate, a substantial presence of errors around 7% can be seen with 6000 posts/min in input.

Figures 8 and 9 show the deep correlation between resources usage and errors. Clearly, a growing input throughput drives the systems to be less reliable. For both the versions of the SLD framework (SLD Revolution and SLD) the correctness of the results decreases as soon as the machine is overloaded and the resources usage starts rising out of control.

6   Conclusions and Future Works

In our future work, we intend: *(i)* to empirically demonstrate the value of using SLD Revolution for all our deployments of Fluxedo, and *(ii)* to investigate if SLD Revolution can be the target platform for a new generation of Ontology Based Data Integration [18] system for Stream Reasoning [19]. This system could have the potential to tame the velocity and variety dimension of Big Data simultaneously.

As for the former, we first intend to stress test SLD Revolution using workloads that resemble reality. Then, we aim at putting it at work in parallel to

SLD in real-world deployments. Once we will have collected enough evidence that SLD Revolution is always cheaper faster yet more accurate than SLD, we will start using it for all our deployments.

As for the latter, we aim at further investigating the generic processing model presented in Sect. 3. We are defining an algebra able to capture the semantics of complex stream processing applications that need to integrate a variety of data sources. The current sketch of this algebra uses **S2I** and **I2S** operators from CQL [8] but keeping them generic w.r.t. the payloads. It uses SPARQL 1.1 algebra as **I2I** operators that take in input graph-based payloads and generate in output either graph-based or tuple-based payloads. The relational algebra will cover the **I2I** transformations of tuple-based payloads. We are studying the application of R2RML [20] for formulating mappings that works as **I2I** operators. Indeed, R2RML allows to write mapping from relational data to RDF; more generally, **I2I** operators takes in input tuple-based payloads and output graph-based ones. We still need to choose an algebra for transforming tree-based payloads.

In our opinion, the grand challenge is how to fit all those formal elements in a coherent framework that allows a system to automatically decide which is the latest moment for transforming data (i.e., introducing the concept of *lazy transformation*) and to perform optimization such as introducing the pre-query that we put in all the pipelines illustrated in Sect. 4.

When the work on this formally defined generic stream processing model will be completed, we will be able to start investigating how to extend mapping languages like R2RML[7] and, potentially, also ontological languages in order to make them time-aware [21] while keeping the whole computational problem tractable.

Acknowledgement. We thank the reviewers of the 2nd RDF Stream Processing Workshop co-located with ESWC 2017 for their valuable comments. They allowed us to refine this version of [22] for the ESWC 2017 workshops post-proceedings.

References

1. Balduini, M., Celino, I., Dell'Aglio, D., Della Valle, E., Huang, Y., Lee, T.K., Kim, S., Tresp, V.: BOTTARI: an augmented reality mobile application to deliver personalized and location-based recommendations by continuous analysis of social media streams. J. Web Sem. **16**, 33–41 (2012)
2. Balduini, M., Della Valle, E., Dell'Aglio, D., Tsytsarau, M., Palpanas, T., Confalonieri, C.:Social listening of city scale events using the streaming linked data framework. In: [23], pp. 1-16
3. Barbieri, D.F., Braga, D., Ceri, S., Della Valle, E., Grossniklaus, M.: Querying RDF streams with C-SPARQL. SIGMOD Record **39**(1), 20–26 (2010)
4. Barbieri, D.F., Della Valle, E.: A proposal for publishing data streams as linked data - a position paper. In: Bizer, C., Heath, T., Berners-Lee, T., Hausenblas, M. (eds.): Proceedings of the WWW2010 Workshop on Linked Data on the Web, LDOW 2010, Raleigh, 27 April 2010, Vol. 628 of CEUR Workshop Proceedings. CEUR-WS.org (2010)

---

[7] https://www.w3.org/TR/r2rml/.

5. Breslin, J.G., Decker, S., Harth, A., Bojars, U.: Sioc: an approach to connect web-based communities. IJWBC **2**(2), 133–142 (2006)
6. Le-Phuoc, D., Dao-Tran, M., Pham, M.-D., Boncz, P., Eiter, T., Fink, M.: Linked stream data processing engines: facts and figures. In: Cudré-Mauroux, P., Heflin, J., Sirin, E., Tudorache, T., Euzenat, J., Hauswirth, M., Parreira, J.X., Hendler, J., Schreiber, G., Bernstein, A., Blomqvist, E. (eds.) ISWC 2012. LNCS, vol. 7650, pp. 300–312. Springer, Heidelberg (2012). doi:10.1007/978-3-642-35173-0_20
7. Dell'Aglio, D., Calbimonte, J.-P., Balduini, M., Corcho, O., Della Valle, E.: On correctness in RDF stream processor benchmarking. In: [23], pp. 326-342
8. Arasu, A., Babu, S., Widom, J.: The cql continuous query language: semantic foundations and query execution. VLDB J. **15**(2), 121–142 (2006)
9. Garofalakis, M., Gehrke, J., Rastogi, R.: Data Stream Management: Processing High-Speed Data Streams (Data-Centric Systems and Applications). Springer-Verlag, New York (2007)
10. Le-Phuoc, D., Dao-Tran, M., Xavier Parreira, J., Hauswirth, M.: A native and adaptive approach for unified processing of linked streams and linked data. In: Aroyo, L., Welty, C., Alani, H., Taylor, J., Bernstein, A., Kagal, L., Noy, N., Blomqvist, E. (eds.) ISWC 2011. LNCS, vol. 7031, pp. 370–388. Springer, Heidelberg (2011). doi:10.1007/978-3-642-25073-6_24
11. Calbimonte, J.-P., Corcho, O., Gray, A.J.G.: Enabling ontology-based access to streaming data sources. In: Patel-Schneider, P.F., Pan, Y., Hitzler, P., Mika, P., Zhang, L., Pan, J.Z., Horrocks, I., Glimm, B. (eds.) ISWC 2010. LNCS, vol. 6496, pp. 96–111. Springer, Heidelberg (2010). doi:10.1007/978-3-642-17746-0_7
12. DellAglio, D., Della Valle, E., Calbimonte, J., Corcho, Ó.: RSP-QL semantics: a unifying query model to explain heterogeneity of RDF stream processing systems. Int. J. Semantic Web Inf. Syst. **10**(4), 17–44 (2014)
13. Le Phuoc, D., Nguyen-Mau, H.Q., Parreira, J.X., Hauswirth, M.: A middleware framework for scalable management of linked streams. J. Web Sem. **16**, 42–51 (2012)
14. Gray, A.J.G., García-Castro, R., Kyzirakos, K., Karpathiotakis, M., Calbimonte, J.-P., Page, K., Sadler, J., Frazer, A., Galpin, I., Fernandes, A.A.A., Paton, N.W., Corcho, O., Koubarakis, M., Roure, D., Martinez, K., Gómez-Pérez, A.: A semantically enabled service architecture for mashups over streaming and stored data. In: Antoniou, G., Grobelnik, M., Simperl, E., Parsia, B., Plexousakis, D., Leenheer, P., Pan, J. (eds.) ESWC 2011. LNCS, vol. 6644, pp. 300–314. Springer, Heidelberg (2011). doi:10.1007/978-3-642-21064-8_21
15. Compton, M., Barnaghi, P.M., Bermudez, L., Garcia-Castro, R., Corcho, Ó., Cox, S., Graybeal, J., Hauswirth, M., Henson, C.A., Herzog, A., Huang, V.A., Janowicz, K., Kelsey, W.D., Le Phuoc, D., Lefort, L., Leggieri, M., Neuhaus, H., Nikolov, A., Page, K.R., Passant, A., Sheth, A.P., Taylor, K.: The ssn ontology of the w3c semantic sensor network incubator group. J. Web Sem. **17**, 25–32 (2012)
16. Jazayeri, M., Loos, R., Musser, D.R. (eds.): Generic Programming. Springer, Heidelberg (2000). doi:10.1007/3-540-39953-4
17. Milner, R., Morris, L., Newey, M.: A logic for computable functions with reflexive and polymorphic types. University of Edinburgh, Department of Computer Science (1975)
18. Lenzerini, M.: Data integration: a theoretical perspective. In: Proceedings of the Twenty-first ACM SIGACT-SIGMOD-SIGART Symposium on Principles of Database Systems, pp. 233–246. Madison, 3–5 June 2002
19. Della Valle, E., Ceri, S., van Harmelen, F., Fensel, D.: It's a streaming world! reasoning upon rapidly changing information. IEEE Intell. Syst. **24**(6), 83–89 (2009)

20. Priyatna, F., Corcho, Ó., Sequeda, J.: Formalisation and experiences of r2rml-based SPARQL to SQL query translation using morph. In: Chung, C., Broder, A.Z., Shim, K., Suel, T. (eds.) 23rd International World Wide Web Conference WWW 2014, pp. 479–490. Seoul, 7–11 April 2014. ACM (2014)
21. Artale, A., Kontchakov, R., Ryzhikov, V., Zakharyaschev, M.: A cookbook for temporal conceptual data modelling with description logics. ACM Trans. Comput. Log. **15**(3), 25:1–25:50 (2014)
22. Balduini, M., Della Valle, E., Tommasini, R.: SLD revolution: a cheaper, faster yet more accurate streaming linked data framework. In: Joint Proceedings of the 2nd RDF Stream Processing (RSP 2017) and the Querying the Web of Data (QuWeDa 2017) Workshops Co-located with 14th ESWC 2017, pp. 1–15. ESWC (2017)
23. Alani, H., Kagal, L., Fokoue, A., Groth, P.T., Biemann, C., Parreira, J.X., Aroyo, L., Noy, N.F., Welty, C., Janowicz, K. (eds.): The Semantic Web - ISWC 2013. Springer, Heidelberg (2013). doi:10.1007/978-3-642-41338-4

3rd International Workshop on Emotions, Modality, Sentiment Analysis and the Semantic Web (EMSASW 2017)

From Conditional Random Field (CRF) to Rhetorical Structure Theory(RST): Incorporating Context Information in Sentiment Analysis

Aggeliki Vlachostergiou[1](✉), George Marandianos[1], and Stefanos Kollias[2]

[1] National Technical University of Athens,
Iroon Polytexneiou 9, 15780 Zografou, Greece
{aggelikivl,Gmarandianos}@image.ntua.gr
[2] University of Lincoln, Brayford Pool, Lincoln, UK
skollias@lincoln.ac.uk

Abstract. This paper investigates a method based on Conditional Random Fields (CRFs) to incorporate sentence structure (syntax and semantics) and context information to identify sentiments of sentences. It also demonstrates the usefulness of the Rhetorical Structure Theory (RST) taking into consideration the discourse role of text segments. Thus, this paper's aim is to reconsider the effectiveness of CRF and RST methods in incorporating the contextual information into Sentiment Analysis systems. Both methods are evaluated on two, different in size and genre of information sources, the Movie Review Dataset and the Finegrained Sentiment Dataset (FSD). Finally, we discuss the lessons learned from these experimental settings w.r.t. addressing the following key research questions such as whether there is an appropriate type of social media repository to incorporate contextual information, whether extending the pool of the selected features could improve context incorporation into SA systems and which is the best performing feature combination to achieve such improved performance.

Keywords: HCI · Sentiment analysis · Context · RST · Context-aware sentiment analysis systems · Movie reviews dataset · FSD collection

1 Introduction

Incorporating context information to improve Sentiment Analysis (SA) is an emerging research area due to the clear benefits of context-aware applications, including: the detection of important events in news [14], consumers' opinions on products [18], extraction of the sentiment orientation (i.e. positive or negative) of opinionated text [25], etc. Recently, it has been shown that it can yield competitive advantages for businesses [3], as extracting sentiment at the fine-grained level [2,8,9,11,26–28] (e.g. at the sentence- or phrase-level) has received increasing attention due to its challenging nature [24]. It can be thus inferred

© Springer International Publishing AG 2017
E. Blomqvist et al. (Eds.): ESWC 2017 Satellite Events, LNCS 10577, pp. 283–295, 2017.
https://doi.org/10.1007/978-3-319-70407-4_38

that, the performance of context-aware SA systems strongly depends on a number of predefined parameters during the experimental setting [10,24]. Particular interest revolves round the SA when it is performed in the domain of movies and general product reviews [25].

Previous studies have proposed various approaches to increase the robustness of context-aware SA systems: Understanding the sentiment of sentences allows us to summarize online opinions which could make informed decisions. Automated sentiment incorporation has seen great research efforts for many years and has achieved some promising results [24]. On one hand, different machine learning techniques, exploit patterns in vector representations of text and lexicon-based methods [31] account for semantic orientation in individual words, while on the other hand, some researchers have proposed rule-based (and unsupervised) methods to improve SA. Still, even though the current insight is that all of the state-of-the-art algorithms perform well on individual sentences without considering any context information, their accuracy is dramatically lower on the document level, due to the fact that they fail to consider context.

Hence, recent studies on context-aware SA have started to consider methods that provide more control, e.g. [5] uses CRFs to tackle opinion source identification as a sequential tagging task, whereas [15] identifies the target of the opinion with CRF to further incorporate the context information into SA systems. In addition to this research direction, discourse analysis has also been employed to adjust prior polarity of terms. Further improvements were reported when a more sophisticated weighting approach based on RST [20] was introduced.

Therefore, it is time to reconsider the effectiveness of these methods for incorporating context information into SA. The contribution of this paper is to present an approach of combining CRF and RST methods with SA to effectively analyze context. Particularly, compared to existing algorithms of sentiment analysis both on sentence and document levels, our proposed approach attempts to improve SA by taking full advantage of the sentence structure, by using context information to capture the relationship among sentences and to improve document-level SA, by taking into consideration the Internet language word set and emoticons and finally by extending the pool of the contextual features used with semantic, syntactic, structural and context-aware RST features. So far, a wide range of features has been independently tested by a large number of research teams, mostly in constrained settings. Table 1 summarizes the main characteristics of some of the studies performed in this area. There is no clear picture of the impact of every feature set and there is little evidence regarding how some features behave with information sources different in size and genre. Thus, there is a need of systematic studies that compare the most meaningful features under uniform conditions.

The structure of the paper is as follows: in Sect. 2 we present related work along with our incorporation method; the experimental settings and the evaluation are described in Sect. 3 in detail. Finally, we report on lessons learned in Sect. 4 and propose directions for future research in Sect. 5.

2   Background and Resources

2.1   Relation to Prior Work

An important research direction in context-aware SA is improving the robustness of SA systems after incorporating context. The state-of-the-art in automated SA has been reviewed extensively [1, 24]. Existing methods rely on sentiment lexicons, which are enumerative lists of sentiment terms that indicate the sentiment changes. Popular examples include General Inquirer [30], Subjectivity Lexicon and Subjectivity Sense Annotations and SentiWordNet. Additionally, domain knowledge plays a key role, since a sentiment term's linguistic context often impacts its sentiment charge. Early work on SA used syntactic relations to identify new sentiment terms, which can be considered as an early form of context exploitation [12]. Sentiment is often expressed in a subtle manner, which makes it difficult to identify when processing sentences or paragraphs in isolation. Thus, context remains an essential ingredient to further improve SA.

On the whole, research in SA can be organized into two broad methods: Machine Learning and Lexicon-Based. With Machine learning approaches, an algorithm is trained with sentiment labeled data and the learnt model is used to classify new documents. This method requires the initial labeled data, which is typically generated through labor-intensive human annotation. As far as the Lexicon-based method concerns, the former involves the extraction and aggregation of terms' sentiment scores offered by a lexicon (i.e. prior polarities) to make sentiment prediction. Nevertheless, it is observed that the main strength of the lexicon-based approaches is at the same time also their weakness. Considering that the lexicons are predefined, they are unable to adapt to novel or domain specific forms of expressions. In addition, lexicon-based approaches do not naturally produce the level of confidence during the analysis, which is automatically provided by machine-learning approaches.

Table 1. Main characteristics of some publicly available datasets. The table reports the type of data, the level of analysis, the size of the collection, the type of classification (task) and the features considered. The feature sets are labeled as follows: vocabulary: unigrams and bigrams (voc), Part-Of-Speech (pos), sentiment words (sw), syntactic patterns (sp), position (p) and discourse (d).

Work	Type of data	Level of analysis	Size	Task	Features used
Pang et al. [25]	Movie reviews	Docs.	1400	pos/neg	voc, pos, p
Turney [33]	Reviews	Docs.	410	pos/neg	sp
Pang and Lee [23]	Movie reviews	Docs.	2000	pos/neg	voc, p
Beineke et al. [4]	Movie reviews	Sents.	2500	Summarization	voc, l
Wiebe and Riloff [34]	Press articles	Sents.	9289	subj/obj	pos, sp
Taboada et al. [31]	Reviews	Docs.	400	pos/neg	pos, sw, d
Heerschop et al. [13]	Movie reviews	Docs.	1000	pos/neg	sw, d
Katz et al. [17]	Hotel reviews	Docs.	30.000	pos/neg	voc, pos, sp, p
Katz et al. [17]	Movie reviews	Docs.	2000	pos/neg	voc, pos, sp, p

2.2   Incorporation Method

Understanding the sentiment of sentences allows us to summarize opinions which could help people make informed decisions. All of the state-of-the-art algorithms perform well on individual sentences without considering any context information, but their accuracy is dramatically lower on the document level because they fail to consider context. There are many difficulties due to the special characteristics and diversity in sentence structure in the way people express their opinions (e.g. opinions expressed indirectly through comparison etc.). In addition, complicated sentence structure and emoticons make sentiment analysis even more challenging.

In this work, we do not only consider syntax that may influence the sentiment, including newly emerged Internet language, emoticons, positive and negative words and negation words, but also incorporate information about sentence structure, like conjunction words and comparisons, the position of positive and negative words and the context-aware RST features. Therefore, we employ a CRF [19] model to capture syntactic, semantic and contextual features of sentences and the RST to unfold the rhetorical relations for SA.

Conditional Random Fields(CRF) method: '
CRF is well known for sequence labeling tasks [19]. CRFs are a class of discriminative undirected probabilistic graphical model generally applied in pattern recognition and machine learning, where they are specifically designed to optimize structure prediction. A "generic" classifier predicts a label for a single sample without regarding to "neighboring/connected" samples, however a (linear-chain) CRF can take context into account.

Hence, in the case we want to capture the context information (e.g. neighboring sentences or sentences connected by transition words), the procedure of sentiment identification becomes a kind of sequence labeling. Particularly, CRFs provide a probabilistic framework for calculating the probability of Y globally conditioned on X, where X is a random variable/vector over sequence data to be labeled, and Y is a random variable/vector over corresponding label sequences. X and Y could have a natural and/or complicated graph structure.

So far, the CRF model, in its simplest form, has been widely used in the text labeling domain [22]. CRF examples given in seminal works such as [19] and [22] assumed linear chain structure as well. A further observation reveals that there is a one-to-one correspondence between states and labels. Figure 1a gives a simple visualization of how a CRF model looks like.

Rhetorical Structure method in SA:
Within a natural language text, rhetorical relations that hold between parts of the text, unfold and are typically used to distinguish important text segments from less important ones in terms of their contribution to a text's overall sentiment. Within a discourse structure, the former is an important part of what makes a text coherent. Thus, the analysis of the discourse structure is divided into two tasks: discourse segmentation and discourse parsing. Discourse segmentation is the task of taking a sequence of word and punctuation tokens as input

and identifying boundaries where new discourse units begin. Discourse parsing is the task of taking a sequence of discourse units and identifying relationships, such as causality, contrast and specification between them. In our case, the set of these relationships form a tree. The leaves of the Discourse Tree (DT) representation correspond to contiguous atomic text spans, also called Elementary Discourse Units (EDUs). The adjacent EDUs are connected by a rhetorical relation (e.g. elaboration), and the resulting larger text spans are recursively also subject to this relation linking. A span linked by a rhetorical relation can be either a nucleus or a satellite depending on how central the message is to the author.

Previous studies on discourse analysis have been quite successful in identifying what machine learning approaches and what features are more useful for automatic discourse segmentation and parsing [29]. However, one of the reported downsides of SA guided w.r.t. RST is the high processing time required for analyzing discourse in natural language text [13]. This problem seems to obstruct the applicability of such methods in large-scale scenarios.

2.3 Datasets

We evaluate our incorporation method on two types of datasets[1] from different domains and different length: on the Movie Reviews Dataset [23] and on the FSD collection [32].

Movie Review Dataset: From our point of view, it seems adequate to use the Movie Review Dataset provided by Pang and Lee that is freely available[2]. The fact that many articles in SA discuss this dataset and have used it to validate their own methods and approaches makes it an ideal candidate from the benchmarking angle. Aligned with this approach, a recent work [7] presents the DRANZIERA evaluation protocol composed of a multi-domain dataset and guidelines, which allows both to evaluate opinion mining systems in different contexts and to compare them to each other and to a number of baselines.

Finegrained Sentiment Dataset (FSD) collection: This dataset contains 294 product reviews from various online sources. The reviews are approximately balanced with respect to domain (covering books, DVDs, electronics, music and videogames) and overall review sentiment (positive, negative and neutral). The main statistics of the collections are reported in Table 2.

We did some preprocessing tasks on the original data, including tokenization and sentence splitting, part-of-speech (POS) tagging, lemmatization, NER, parsing, and coreference resolution based on the Stanford CoreNLP annotation pipeline framework [21]. A representative example of a sentence after the preprocessing is presented in ConNLL format in Fig. 1b.

---

[1] For our experimental setting, we randomly split each collection into a training and a test set of 75% and 25% respectively.
[2] http://www.cs.cornell.edu/people/pabo/movie-review-data.

Table 2. Test collections for experimentation in two-class categorization analysis problem. The table also includes the number of unigrams and bigrams after preprocessing.

Datasets	Subj./Pos. sent	Obj./Neg. sent	Unigrams	Bigrams
Movie reviews [23]	5000	5000	4948	9103
FSD [32]	923	1320	1275	1996

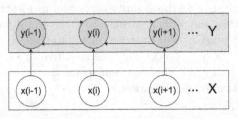

(a) $x_i's$ corresponds to the sentences in a document and $y_i's$ correspond to the sentiment label for each x_i.

(b) Representation of the CoNLL format.

Fig. 1. (a) Graphical representation of a linear-chain of a simple CRF model [19]. (b) Part of the movies review dataset sentence "the movie begins in the past where a young boy named sam attempts to save celebi from a hunter." in the CoNLL format.

3 Experiments

In this section, we describe our proposed method to explore the optimum size and type of the data used for context incorporation, the nature of the training data, the ideal candidates, if possible, for the selection of sentence features and the best performing features to incorporate new context information using the feature set we created, presented in Table 3.

3.1 Classification Problem and Experimental Settings

Considering that different subjectivity may generate different or even reversed sentiments for sentences, we set our experimental procedure as follows: we assume that the input is a set of m document: $\{d_1, d_2, ..., d_m\}$ along with the specified subject: $\{sub_1, sub_2, ...sub_m\}$. Each d_i contains n_i sentences S^i: $\{s^{i1}, s^{i2}, ..., s^i_{n_i}\}$. The output for all documents is that for the jth sentence in the ith document s^i_j, it will assign a sentiment $o^{ij} \in \{P : positive, N : negative\}$ and a sentiment $o^{ij} \in \{S : subjective, O : objective\}$ respectively.

Conditional Random Fields (CRF) provides a probabilistic framework for calculating the probability of label sequences Y globally conditioned on sequences data X to be labeled.

Parameters $\Theta = \lambda_k, \mu_l$ are estimated by maximizing the conditional log-likelihood function $\mathcal{L}(\Theta)$ of the training data [19].

$$P(Y|X) = \frac{1}{Z_X} exp(\sum_{i,k} \lambda_k f_k(y_{i-1}, y_i, X) + \sum_{i,l} \mu_l g_l(y_i, X))$$

where Z_X is the normalization constant.

$$\mathcal{L}(\Theta) = \sum_{j=1\ldots M} log(P(Y^j|X^j; \Theta)) - \sum_k \frac{\lambda_k^2}{2\sigma_k^2} - \sum_l \frac{\mu_l^2}{2\sigma_l^2}.$$

So far, a wide variety of features has been widely extracted from sentences for sentiment analysis and can be leveraged through CRF model. In this work, we use the features listed in Table 3. Particularly, we have used the CRF++ 0.58[3], which is an open source tool for implementing the machine learning framework to build our linear CRF chain, with a one-to-one correspondence between states and labels. Our aim is to capture the context information (e.g. neighboring sentences or sentences connected by transition words) among sentences in a document. The procedure of sentiment incorporation therefore becomes a kind of sequence labeling. The goal of the model is to give a label to each sentence corresponding to the sentence sequence.

As far as the RST method concerns, it has been introduced successfully at the review level [13] and sub-sentence level [36] and has shown its capability of using discourse relations in the text to compute sentiment values. Specifically, our approach uses a parser that implements the Rhetorical Structure Theory (RST) [20] to find discourse elements in the text. Particularly, we convert the produced XML files into CoNLL-like format using the Stanford CoreNLP annotation pipeline framework [21]. After we complete the preprocessing of our data, we segment it into EDUs and finally we use a tool for parsing of discourse (DPLP) [16], to create the RST trees for the individual sentences based on the suggested given feature set. Finally, with the use of the RST parser, we further generate the bracketing file for each document, which we use for evaluation.

The nature of the training data: It is also important to note that the evaluated datasets vary in the length of the analyzed text and also that the categorization problem in the FSD collection is unbalanced. This diversity enables us to evaluate the robustness of our proposed approach in different experimental settings. With this in mind, we test asymmetric misclassification costs so that positive sentences classified as negative will be penalized more strongly.

Adaptation schemes: We experiment with the linear classifiers of the Liblinear Library, which supports classification by means of Support Vector Machines(SVMs) and Logistic Regression (LR). We extensively test these classifiers against the training collection to select the best classifier. We optimize the classifiers using 5-fold cross-validation against the training data. For each collection, we further validate with the test set, the classifier that performed the best at training time (in terms of F_1). By that, we reduce the variance of the

---

[3] https://taku910.github.io/crfpp/.

Table 3. Features used for this sequence labeling problem.

Set	Features
vocabulary	Unigrams and Bigrams (binary)
num_pos_words	A positive word list of 1948 words [35]
num_neg_words	A negative word list of 4550 words [35]
exist_pos_emotic	A positive emoticon list of 52 emoticons. For example "=)" represents smiling
exist_neg_emotic	A negative emoticon list of 35 emoticons. For example "v_v" represents sadness
exist_comp_sent	Existence of comparative adjectives, adverbs, superlative adjectives and adverbs or phrases ("compare to", "in contrast", etc.)
conjunction_words	Subordinating, coordinating, and correlative conjunctions words
sent_post	Sentence position. if the sentence is within first 20% of the sentences, it's a beginning sentence; an end sentence if within the last 20%, and middle for all others.
post_pos_words	Position of positive words occurring. 0: no positive words occur; 1: only exist in the first part of a sentence; 2: only exist in the second part; -1: exist in both parts (mixed)
post_neg_words	Position of negative words
post_negation_words	Position of negation words
comp_sub	Comparison subject: If the subjectivity is the same as the input subjectivity.
cos_sim_neigh_sent	cosine similarity score to neighboring sentences (previous sentence and next sentence)[a]
LSI_sim_neigh_sent	LSI similarity score to neighboring sentences (previous sentence and next sentence)[b]
context-aware RST	binary feature for each type of RST relationships. Every sentence has only one of these features set to 1

[a]We use cosine similarity to capture the word-level similarity.
[b]We use the dimension reduction method of Latent Semantic Indexing [6] to measure the semantic similarity.

performance results and make the comparison less dependent on the specific test set. We repeat this process ten times and we average the performance over these ten folds. Finally, we measure the statistical significance with a paired, two-sided micro sign test. Instead of using the paired F_1 values, we compare the two systems based on all their binary decisions and we apply the Binomial distribution to compute the p-values under the null hypothesis of equal performance.

4   Results

Table 4 gives the classification results across settings. We present our results as average value of F_1 score for both positive, negative, subjective and objective categories to quantify classification quality. We also report precision (Pr) and recall (R) for completeness. Moreover, we discuss our research questions. We

Table 4. 2-class categorization problem for the Movie Review (MR) [23] and the Finegrained Sentiment (FSD) [32] datasets in terms of precision, recall and F_1. For every vocabulary representation (i.e. unigrams, or unigrams and bigrams), the best performance for each metric is bolded.

Features (MR)	Subjective			Objective			Microavg
	Prec.	Rec.	F_1	Prec.	Rec.	F_1	F_1
Unigrams	0.8939	0.8910	0.8924	0.8916	**0.8944**	0.8930	0.8927
Length	0.8614	**0.8940**	0.8774	0.8901	0.8565	0.8730	0.8752
Positional	-	-	-	-	-	-	-
Sentiment-carrying words	0.8926	**0.8995**	0.8960	0.8989	0.8920	0.8954	0.8958
RST	0.8934	0.8910	0.8922	0.8915	**0.8939**	0.8927	0.8924
All	0.8876	**0.9005**	0.8940	0.8993	0.8862	0.8927	0.8934
Uni+Bigrams	0.9043	0.8942	0.8992	0.8956	**0.9055**	0.9005	0.8999
Length	0.8829	0.8811	0.8820	0.8816	**0.8834**	0.8825	0.8822
Positional	-	-	-	-	-	-	-
Sentiment-carrying words	**0.9016**	0.8964	0.899	0.8973	0.9024	0.8998	0.8994
RST	0.9054	0.8888	0.8970	0.8910	**0.9073**	0.8991	0.8980
All	0.8999	**0.9026**	0.9012	0.9025	0.8999	0.9012	0.9012
Features (FSD)	Positive			Negative			Microavg
	Prec.	Rec.	F_1	Prec.	Rec.	F_1	F_1
Unigrams	0.6596	0.6175	0.6379	0.7302	**0.7647**	0.7471	0.7021
Length	0.6451	0.5195	0.5755	0.6897	**0.7889**	0.7360	0.6745
Positional	0.6720	0.6217	0.6459	0.7352	**0.7758**	0.7550	0.7104
Sentiment-carrying words	0.6936	0.6117	0.6825	0.7630	0.7808	**0.7718**	0.7345
RST	0.6690	0.6074	0.6367	0.7285	**0.7780**	0.7524	0.7055
All	0.6245	0.7348	0.6752	**0.7747**	0.6737	0.7207	0.6996
Uni+Bigrams	0.6801	0.5872	0.6302	0.7231	**0.7960**	0.7578	0.7073
Length	0.6618	0.4590	0.5421	0.6742	**0.8268**	0.7427	0.6705
Positional	0.6958	0.5855	0.6359	0.7260	**0.8109**	0.7661	0.7152
Sentiment-carrying words	0.7149	0.6578	0.6852	0.7614	0.8063	**0.7832**	0.7432
RST	0.6878	0.5734	0.6254	0.7194	0.8078	0.7610	0.7082
All	0.6297	0.7385	0.6798	**0.7786**	0.6793	0.7256	0.7045

consider the unigrams and the unigrams combined with bigrams as baselines, and we further incorporate the feature set presented in Table 3 into our baseline classifiers.

4.1 Is This Type of Social Media in Terms of Size and Source of Repository Appropriate to Incorporate Context?

According to our results, features such as word/sentence length, sentiment carrying words and word/sentence position could be indicative of subjectivity of objectivity respectively. We observe that such features affect the performance analysis of both type repositories and combined with our proposed approach, we can correctly infer the context.

4.2 Is It Important to Extend the Pool of the Selected Features to Incorporate Context into SA Systems?

Overall, classifying sentences based on unigrams-bigrams is an effective and safe choice. **Length features** do not contribute to discriminate between objective and subjective sentences. **Positional features** seem to work particular well for discovering subjective content. Even thought we do not have **positional features** in the MR collection, we suspect that their ability to classify objective sentences seems to be limited[4] Additionally, incorporating **Context-aware RST features** did not work well as expected. Apparently, the presence of particular rhetorical relations per sentence does not convey much more robust classifiers than those constructed from unigrams and bigrams. Finally, when combining **all features** into a single classifier we obtained a good classifier in terms of recall of subjective sentences but recall of objective sentences tended to fall. This led to classification performance that was sometimes worse than the baseline's performance.

In a similar way, we report the classification performance on the FSD collection respectively. One main observation is that the presence of the **length, positional** and **context-aware RST** features do not convey much more information to the overall classification performance in terms of polarity, while appeared to have much more power in indicating subjective sentences. Finally, the combination of **all features** worked well, but was inferior to **sentiment word features**.

4.3 Which Is the Best Performing Feature Combination to Identify and Incorporate Context Information?

The best performing combination was the one that included the **sentiment-word features**. It was the only feature set able to statistically improve the baselines in all situations across different test sets. Combining unigrams or bigrams with sentiment-word features is a way to account for both general purpose opinion expressions and domain-specific opinion expressions. This led to robust subjectivity classifiers. In a same manner, as far as the FSD classification performance's results, one of the best performing combinations is once again the one that includes the **sentiment-carrying words** features.

5   Conclusions and Future Work

We have thoroughly studied the usefulness of the CRF model and the RST discourse theory to incorporate sentence structure and context information into

---

[4] This could be explained by the fact that we tend to use subjective sentences in specific parts of the document e.g. in the beginning or at the end of the document.

context-aware Sentiment Analysis systems, in two information sources which are different in size and genre. First, we have shown how to improve SA by taking full advantage of the sentences structure, using context information to capture the relationship among sentences and to improve document-level SA. The reason of this success lies in extending the pool of the contextual features used with semantic, syntactic and context-aware RST features rather than repeating the already existing approaches.

Our experimental results show that to classify the FSD collection, the combination of sentiment-carrying words combined with unigrams/bigrams provides also quite accurate results. Moreover, it is indeed only when we combine context-aware RST features with unigrams/bigrams, we can obtain clear polarity classification performance improvements at the sentence level. The most valuable features of the polarity classifiers essentially capture the way in which polar terms are used in a sentence. With this in mind, one possible way of further exploiting would be the sentence's discourse units and their rhetorical roles within the sentence (inter-sentence analysis).

For future work, we plan to develop additional features for our methods according to the type of the data examined, to consider additional evaluation measures and finally to compare our proposed context incorporation method with deep neural network approaches.

References

1. Appel, O., Chiclana, F., Carter, J.: Main concepts, state of the art and future research questions in sentiment analysis. Acta Polytech. Hung. **12**(3), 87–108 (2015)
2. Palmero Aprosio, A., Corcoglioniti, F., Dragoni, M., Rospocher, M.: Supervised opinion frames detection with RAID. In: Gandon, F., Cabrio, E., Stankovic, M., Zimmermann, A. (eds.) SemWebEval 2015. CCIS, vol. 548, pp. 251–263. Springer, Cham (2015). https://doi.org/10.1007/978-3-319-25518-7_22
3. Bal, D., Bal, M., Bunningen, A., Hogenboom, A., Hogenboom, F., Frasincar, F.: Sentiment analysis with a multilingual pipeline. In: Bouguettaya, A., Hauswirth, M., Liu, L. (eds.) WISE 2011. LNCS, vol. 6997, pp. 129–142. Springer, Heidelberg (2011). https://doi.org/10.1007/978-3-642-24434-6_10
4. Beineke, P., Hastie, T., Manning, C., Vaithyanathan, S.: Exploring sentiment summarization. In: Proceedings of the AAAI Spring Symposium on Exploring Attitude and Affect in Text: Theories and Applications, vol. 39 (2004)
5. Choi, Y., Cardie, C., Riloff, E., Patwardhan, S.: Identifying sources of opinions with conditional random fields and extraction patterns. In: Proceedings of the Conference on Human Language Technology and Empirical Methods in Natural Language Processing, pp. 355–362. Association for Computational Linguistics (2005)
6. Deerwester, S., Dumais, S.T., Furnas, G.W., Landauer, T.K., Harshman, R.: Indexing by latent semantic analysis. J. Am. Soc. Inf. Sci. **41**(6), 391 (1990)
7. Dragoni, M., Tettamanzi, A.G., Pereira, C.D.C.: Dranziera: an evaluation protocol for multi-domain opinion mining. In: 10th International Conference on Language Resources and Evaluation (LREC 2016), pp. 267–272. European Language Resources Association (ELRA) (2016)

8. Federici, M., Dragoni, M.: Towards unsupervised approaches for aspects extraction
9. Federici, M., Dragoni, M.: A knowledge-based approach for aspect-based opinion mining. In: Sack, H., Dietze, S., Tordai, A., Lange, C. (eds.) SemWebEval 2016. CCIS, vol. 641, pp. 141–152. Springer, Cham (2016). https://doi.org/10.1007/978-3-319-46565-4_11
10. Feldman, R.: Techniques and applications for sentiment analysis. Commun. ACM **56**(4), 82–89 (2013)
11. Gangemi, A., Presutti, V., Recupero, D.R.: Frame-based detection of opinion holders and topics: a model and a tool. IEEE Comput. Intell. Mag. **9**(1), 20–30 (2014)
12. Hatzivassiloglou, V., McKeown, K.R.: Predicting the semantic orientation of adjectives. In: 35th Annual Meeting of the Association for Computational Linguistics and 8th Conference of the European Chapter of the Association for Computational Linguistics, pp. 174–181. ACL (1997)
13. Heerschop, B., Goossen, F., Hogenboom, A., Frasincar, F., Kaymak, U., de Jong, F.: Polarity analysis of texts using discourse structure. In: 20th International Conference on Information and Knowledge Management, pp. 1061–1070. ACM (2011)
14. Hogenboom, A., Hogenboom, F., Frasincar, F., Schouten, K., van der Meer, O.: Semantics-based information extraction for detecting economic events. Multimedia Tools Appl. **64**(1), 27–52 (2013)
15. Jakob, N., Gurevych, I.: Extracting opinion targets in a single-and cross-domain setting with conditional random fields. In: Proceedings of the Conference on Empirical Methods in Natural Language Processing, pp. 1035–1045. Association for Computational Linguistics (2010)
16. Ji, Y., Eisenstein, J.: Representation learning for text-level discourse parsing. In: ACL (1), pp. 13–24 (2014)
17. Katz, G., Ofek, N., Shapira, B.: Consent: context-based sentiment analysis. Knowl. Based Syst. **84**, 162–178 (2015)
18. Kim, S.M., Hovy, E.: Automatic identification of pro and con reasons in online reviews. In: Proceedings of the COLING/ACL on Main Conference Poster Sessions, pp. 483–490. Association for Computational Linguistics (2006)
19. Lafferty, J., McCallum, A., Pereira, F.: Conditional random fields: probabilistic models for segmenting and labeling sequence data. In: Proceedings of the Eighteenth International Conference on Machine Learning ICML, vol. 1, pp. 282–289 (2001)
20. Mann, W.C., Thompson, S.A.: Rhetorical structure theory: toward a functional theory of text organization. Text-Interdisc. J. Study Discourse **8**(3), 243–281 (1988)
21. Manning, C.D., Surdeanu, M., Bauer, J., Finkel, J.R., Bethard, S., McClosky, D.: The stanford corenlp natural language processing toolkit. In: ACL (System Demonstrations), pp. 55–60 (2014)
22. McCallum, A.: Efficiently inducing features of conditional random fields. In: Proceedings of the Nineteenth Conference on Uncertainty in Artificial Intelligence, pp. 403–410. Morgan Kaufmann Publishers Inc. (2002)
23. Pang, B., Lee, L.: A sentimental education: sentiment analysis using subjectivity summarization based on minimum cuts. In: Proceedings of the 42nd Annual Meeting on Association for Computational Linguistics, p. 271. Association for Computational Linguistics (2004)
24. Pang, B., Lee, L.: Opinion mining and sentiment analysis. Found. Trends Inf. Retrieval **2**(1–2), 1–135 (2008)

25. Pang, B., Lee, L., Vaithyanathan, S.: Thumbs up?: sentiment classification using machine learning techniques. In: Proceedings of the ACL 2002 Conference on Empirical Methods in Natural Language Processing, vol. 10, pp. 79–86. Association for Computational Linguistics (2002)

26. Recupero, D.R., Presutti, V., Consoli, S., Gangemi, A., Nuzzolese, A.G.: Sentilo: frame-based sentiment analysis. Cognitive Comput. **7**(2), 211–225 (2015)

27. Rexha, A., Kröll, M., Dragoni, M., Kern, R.: Exploiting propositions for opinion mining. In: Sack, H., Dietze, S., Tordai, A., Lange, C. (eds.) SemWebEval 2016. CCIS, vol. 641, pp. 121–125. Springer, Cham (2016). https://doi.org/10.1007/978-3-319-46565-4_9

28. Rexha, A., Kröll, M., Dragoni, M., Kern, R.: Polarity classification for target phrases in tweets: a word2Vec approach. In: Sack, H., Rizzo, G., Steinmetz, N., Mladenić, D., Auer, S., Lange, C. (eds.) ESWC 2016. LNCS, vol. 9989, pp. 217–223. Springer, Cham (2016). https://doi.org/10.1007/978-3-319-47602-5_40

29. Soricut, R., Marcu, D.: Sentence level discourse parsing using syntactic and lexical information. In: Proceedings of the 2003 Conference of the North American Chapter of the Association for Computational Linguistics on Human Language Technology, vol. 1, pp. 149–156. Association for Computational Linguistics (2003)

30. Stone, P.J., Dunphy, D.C., Smith, M.S.: The General Inquirer: A Computer Approach to Content Analysis. MIT Press, Cambridge (1966)

31. Taboada, M., Voll, K., Brooke, J.: Extracting sentiment as a function of discourse structure and topicality. Simon Fraser Univeristy School of Computing Science Technical Report (2008)

32. Täckström, O., McDonald, R.: Discovering fine-grained sentiment with latent variable structured prediction models. In: Clough, P., Foley, C., Gurrin, C., Jones, G.J.F., Kraaij, W., Lee, H., Mudoch, V. (eds.) ECIR 2011. LNCS, vol. 6611, pp. 368–374. Springer, Heidelberg (2011). https://doi.org/10.1007/978-3-642-20161-5_37

33. Turney, P.D.: Thumbs up or thumbs down?: semantic orientation applied to unsupervised classification of reviews. In: Proceedings of the 40th Annual Meeting on Association for Computational Linguistics, pp. 417–424. Association for Computational Linguistics (2002)

34. Wiebe, J., Riloff, E.: Creating subjective and objective sentence classifiers from unannotated texts. In: Gelbukh, A. (ed.) CICLing 2005. LNCS, vol. 3406, pp. 486–497. Springer, Heidelberg (2005). https://doi.org/10.1007/978-3-540-30586-6_53

35. Wiebe, J., Wilson, T., Cardie, C.: Annotating expressions of opinions and emotions in language. Lang. Resour. Eval. **39**(2–3), 165–210 (2005)

36. Zirn, C., Niepert, M., Stuckenschmidt, H., Strube, M.: Fine-grained sentiment analysis with structural features. In: IJCNLP, pp. 336–344 (2011)

1st International Workshop on Applications of Semantic Web Technologies in Robotics (ANSWER 2017)

Making Sense of Indoor Spaces Using Semantic Web Mining and Situated Robot Perception

Jay Young[1]([✉]), Valerio Basile[2], Markus Suchi[3], Lars Kunze[4], Nick Hawes[1], Markus Vincze[3], and Barbara Caputo[5]

[1] The University of Birmingham, Birmingham, UK
j.young@cs.bham.ac.uk
[2] Université Côte d'Azur, Inria, CNRS, I3S, Sophia Antipolis, France
[3] Technische Universität Wien, Vienna, Austria
[4] Oxford Robotics Institute, Department of Engineering Science,
University of Oxford, Oxford, UK
[5] Università di Roma - Sapienza, Rome, Italy

Abstract. Intelligent Autonomous Robots deployed in human environments must have understanding of the wide range of possible semantic identities associated with the spaces they inhabit – kitchens, living rooms, bathrooms, offices, garages, etc. We believe robots should learn this information through their own exploration and situated perception in order to uncover and exploit structure in their environments – structure that may not be apparent to human engineers, or that may emerge over time during a deployment. In this work, we combine semantic web-mining and situated robot perception to develop a system capable of assigning semantic categories to regions of space. This is accomplished by looking at web-mined relationships between room categories and objects identified by a Convolutional Neural Network trained on 1000 categories. Evaluated on real-world data, we show that our system exhibits several conceptual and technical advantages over similar systems, and uncovers semantic structure in the environment overlooked by ground-truth annotators.

Keywords: Robotics · Artificial intelligence · Semantic web-mining · Deep vision · Service robots · Machine learning · Space classification · Semantic mapping · Imagenet · Convolutional Neural Networks

1 Introduction

Many tasks in Human-Robot Interaction (HRI) scenarios require autonomous mobile service robots to relate to objects and places (or rooms) in their environment at a semantic level. This capability is essential for interpreting task instructions such as "Get me a mug from the kitchen" and for generating referring expressions in real-world scenes such as "I found a red and a blue mug in the kitchen, which one should I get?" However, in dynamic, open-world environments such as human environments, it is simply impossible to pre-program

© Springer International Publishing AG 2017
E. Blomqvist et al. (Eds.): ESWC 2017 Satellite Events, LNCS 10577, pp. 299–313, 2017.
https://doi.org/10.1007/978-3-319-70407-4_39

robots with the required knowledge about task-related objects and places in advance. Hence, they need to be equipped with learning capabilities that allow them to acquire knowledge of previously unknown objects and places online. In previous work, we demonstrated how knowledge about perceived objects can be acquired by mining textual resources [9] and image databases on the Semantic Web [10]. In this work, we focus on *knowledge about places* and investigate ways of acquiring it using web mining and situated robot perception. In particular, we aim to learn the semantic categories of places observed by an autonomous mobile robot in real-world office environments.[1]

When mobile service robots are deployed in human-inhabited locations such as offices, homes, industrial workplaces and similar locations, we wish them to be equipped with ways of learning and the ability to extend their own knowledge on-line using information about the environment they gather through *situated experiences*. This too is a difficult task, and is much more than just a matter of data collection. Some form of *semantic* information is desirable too. We expect that structured and semi-structured Web knowledge sources such as DBPedia and WordNet [2] to answer some of these questions. By linking robot knowledge to entries in semantic ontologies, we can begin to exploit rich knowledge-bases to facilitate better robot understanding of the world (Fig. 1).

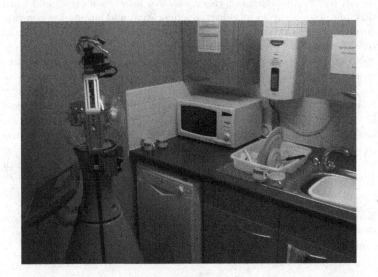

Fig. 1. A mobile robot learning about objects in a kitchen setting.

One data source of interest to us is ImageNet, which is a large database of categorised images organised using the WordNet lexical ontology.

---

[1] A version of this paper first appeared in the 1st International Workshop on Application of Semantic Web technologies in Robotics (AnSWeR 2017). After winning the best paper prize, the authors were invited to submit a special extended version to be included in the proceedings of the 14th Extended Semantic Web Conference 2017.

The ImageNet Large Scale Visual Recognition Challenge (ILSVRC) [3] has in recent years produced machine learning tools trained on ImageNet for object detection and image classification. Of particular interest to us are *deep learning* based approaches using Convolutional Neural Networks, trained on potentially thousands of object categories [4]. This approach raises the question of how well such predictors perform when queried with the challenging image data endemic to mobile robot platforms, as opposed to the cleaner, and higher-resolution, data they are typically trained and evaluated on. This domain adaptation problem is a major difficulty in using these state-of-the-art vision techniques on robots. Using vision techniques with (ever-growing) training sets the size of ImageNet, will allow us to extend a robot's knowledge base far beyond what it can be manually equipped with in advance of a deployment.

In this paper we document our work using the technologies mentioned so far towards enabling a mobile robot to learn the semantic categories associated with different regions of space in its environment. To do this, we employ large-scale object recognition systems to generate semantic label hypotheses for objects detected by robots in real-world environments. These hypotheses are linked to *structured, semantic knowledge bases* such as DBPedia and WordNet, allowing us to link a robot's situated experiences with higher-level knowledge. We then use these object hypotheses to perform text-mining of the semantic web to produce further hypotheses over the semantic category of particular regions of space.

To summarise, this paper makes the following contributions:

- an unsupervised approach for learning semantic categories of indoor spaces using deep vision and semantic web mining;
- an evaluation of our approach on real-world robot perception data; and
- a proof-of-concept demonstration of how knowledge about semantic categories can be transferred to novel environments.

2   Previous Work

Space categorisation for mobile robots is an extensive, well-studied topic, and one which it would be impossible to provide an in-depth review of in the space available. For this, we would reccomend the work of [16], which provides a thorough survey of the wider field of robot semantic mapping to-date. The majority of work in the area of space categorisation utilises *semantic cues* to identify and label regions of space such as offices, hallways, kitchens, bathrooms, laboratories, and the partitions between them. One of the most commonly used semantic cues is the presence of objects, and as this is also the semantic cue we use, we will focus on this area of the work.

The work of [13] realises a Bayesian approach to room categorisation, and builds a hierarchical representation of space. This hierarchy is encoded by the authors, who admit that their own views and experiences in regards to the composition of these concepts could bias the system. In further work, the same authors [14] provide a more object-focused approach to space classification, however this again required the development and evaluation of a knowledge base linking objects to room types. The work of Pronobis and Jensfelt [15] is significant in this area in that it integrates heterogeneous semantic cues, such as the shape, size and appearance of rooms, with object observations. However, their system was only capable of recognising 6 object types and 11 room categories, which again required the gathering and annotation of much training data, and it is unclear how well this generalises to new environments and how much retraining would be required. Similar systems [17] exhibit the same pitfalls. The work of Hanheide [18] on the Dora platform realises a robot system capable of exploiting knowledge about the co-occurence of objects and rooms. This is facilitated by linkage to the *Open Mind Indoor Common Sense* database, and is used for space categorisation and to speed up object search by exploiting semantic relations between objects and rooms.

We argue that our approach exhibits several technical and conceptual advantages over other pieces of work in this area:

- The categorisation module requires no robot perceptual data collection or training, and works fully on-line.
- The system is domain agnostic, not fitted to particular types of environments, room structures or organisations.
- We use existing, mature, tried-and-tested semantic ontologies, and as such there is no knowledge-engineering required by the system designer to use this information.
- The use of large-scale object recognition tools mean we are not limited to a small number of objects, and the use of text-mining means we are not limited to a small number of room categories.
- The relations between objects and room categories are derived *statistically* from text mining, rather than being encoded by the developer or given by an ontology (Fig. 2).

These key points lead to a novel way of solving the problem of space classification on mobile robots.

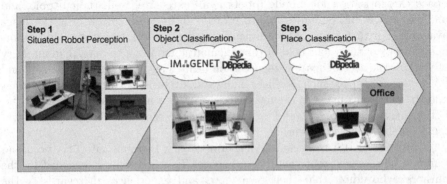

Fig. 2. Overview.

3   Approach Overview

We use a robot platform (a modified Scitos A5) to observe the world at various waypoints specified in its environment. The robot is provided with a SLAM map of its environment, and a set of waypoints within this map. At each of these places the robot perceives its surroundings by rotating its camera (an ASUS Xtion RGB-D camera mounted on the head), taking a sequence of views at different angles from its starting orientation, such that it eventually rotates 360°. The different views taken by the robot are aligned and integrated into a consistent environment model in which object candidates are identified and clustered into groups according to their proximity. For each object candidate, we predict its class by using its visual appearance as an input to classifiers trained on a large-scale object database, namely ImageNet. Based on the set of labelled (or classified) object candidates which are in the same group, we perform a web-based text-mining step to classify the region of space constrained by a bounding polygon of the group of objects. Semantic labels like "kitchen" or "office" or "garage" etc. can then be attached to these polygons and fed back into the robot's internal representation of the world.

In the following, we describe the individual components in more detail.

4   Object Category Recognition

Our aim is to identify the semantic labels most strongly associated with a particular point in a robot's environment by looking at the kinds of objects that are visible from that point. As such, it is crucial for a robot to be able to recognise the objects that inhabit its environment. It is typical in robotics that object recognition is facilitated by a training step prior to deployment [15,18] (though unsupervised approaches do exist [1]) whereby selected objects from the robot's environment are learned and later re-recognised and used for space categorisation. The advantage of this is that the robot learns to recognise objects using models trained using its own sensors and situated conditions, however it also means that we must anticipate which objects a robot is likely to encounter so as to determine which ones to learn and which to ignore. This process can also be very time-consuming and error-prone.

Previous work [10] has used Convolutional Neural Networks (CNNs) trained on large image databases such as ImageNet, which provide databases of several million images, for object recognition on a mobile robot. Results can vary, and this is because the images used to train ImageNet-sourced CNNs possess very different characteristics to those images observed by robots – robot data is often noisy, grainy and typically low-resolution, and is exasperated by the difficulties robots have in getting close to objects, especially small ones. One cause of this is what is known as the *domain adaptation problem*, where the features learning mechanisms discover from their high-resolution training data do not robustly and reliably map on to lower-resolution, noise-prone spaces. This is an active, ongoing area of research in the computer vision community, the solution to which holds the key to generic, off-the-shelf object recognition for mobile robots.

We evaluated a set of state-of-the-art CNNs trained on ImageNet on a sample (1000 object images) from one of our robot datasets. We measure our accuracy using a WUP similarity score [5], which calculates the semantic relatedness of the ground-truth concept types against the concept predicted by the CNN by considering their depth of their lowest common super-concept in the WordNet ontology. A WUP score of 1.0 means two concepts are identical. The concepts *Dog* and *cat*, for instance, have a WUP relatedness score of 0.86. To compare, we also built a wrapper for the Google Web Vision API, that mapped its output to the WordNet ontology. We evaluated against Google Web Vision, the GoogleNet CNN, and the AlexNet and ResNet-152 CNNs. Our results were 0.392, 0.594, 0.590 and 0.681 respectively, given as average WUP score over a randomly sampled 1000 images from our labelled robot dataset. As such, we chose the ResNet152 model to work with [20].

This result raises interesting questions regarding the use of such techniques to mobile robot platforms, where typical object observations will be subject to sensor noise and the dynamics of the real world. Our own robots are fitted with head-mounted cameras, meaning that the ability of the robot to move close to an object in order to obtain a more detailed image is limited, and as such larger objects are more reliably segmented and identified. Despite this, there are clear differences between the performance of various CNNs – all of which are trained on the same ILSVRC15 dataset, and all of which are evaluated against the same robot dataset. The ImageNet data is largely collated from contributed images taken on high-resolution digital cameras, so typically features very clear images. The key challenge for these vision systems is to robustly learn features from the high-resolution data that map well on to the lower-resolution, noise-prone data from robot sensors. An example of this disparity is shown in Fig. 3. That improvements can be found by modifying the *architecture* of the

Fig. 3. Left: Examples of "Mug" found in ImageNet training data set. Right: Examples of "Mug" observed in the real-world by a mobile robot, annotated by a human.

networks presents much room for future work, and hand-in-hand with improving the quality of mobile robot sensors suggests exciting new capabilities for robot object recognition and understanding in the near future.

4.1 Scene Segmentation

In order to identify objects we must first have an idea about where they are in the environment, this is the task of *object proposal generation*. To generate these hypotheses we make use of our own implementation of the RGB-D depth segmentation algorithm of [19]. This is a patch-based approach, which clusters locally co-planar surfaces in RGB-D point clouds. These initial surfaces are geometrically modeled into planes and non-uniform rational B-splines using a best fit approach. The adjacency relation between those models yield a graph and by applying a graph-cut algorithm we refine the segmentation further. Given an observation of a scene from the robot – as a RGB-D point cloud – this algorithm returns a set of segmented candidate objects from the scene as smaller, segmented RGB-D point clouds. From there, we perform basic filtering for instance to filter out objects that are too small, too large or too dark, as these characteristics are likely to be representative of errors or noise. For instance, since we are mainly interested in *human-manipulable objects*, if the robot segments out a large portion of a wall or a desk, or floor, we would rather ignore this. These step filters are hand-tuned based on the results of previous robot deployments, and are typically very sensitive to environmental changes and sensor noise. This filtering process improves the results of object proposal generation greatly, but it is still unreliable and so noise, badly segmented objects and other errors may still slip through. However, after this process we can then extract 2D boundingboxes around the objects detected in a scene to be passed directly to the object recognition system. Noise or badly segmented objects will result in erroneous detections.

5 Text Mining

At the end of the object recognition step of the pipeline, the robot is equipped with knowledge about the objects observed at the scene. This knowledge comes in the form of a set of labels each indicating an object, and additional information regarding their size, distance, etc. In order to improve the performance of tasks such as room detection, the knowledge about the objects must be enriched, in particular by exploiting their mutual relationships. This is the core goal of the module described in this section, that is, to provide new knowledge starting from a *set* of objects, rather than each of them individually.

There has been recent work towards developing a Semantic Web-Mining component for mobile robot systems [9,10] which we make use of. The system computes the aggregate of the relatedness of a candidate unknown object to each of the scene objects contained in the query, returning a ranked list of object label candidates based on relatedness. With this approach, the system is capable of improving the accuracy of the identification of unknown objects found at the scene.

We re-work the same approach to instead return ranked relatedness distributions over *room categories* given a *set of observed objects*. Given a set of room categories (Kitchen, Office, Eating Area, Garage, Bathroom), the system provides a distribution over these categories for input sets of objects. We then use this ranking to select the most suitable room for the set of objects found at the scene.

5.1   Room Detection Web Service

We implemented the module as a RESTful Web service, so that is can be queried by multiple robots independently. The structure of a request to the system describes the objects that were observed in a scene, encoded as a JSON structure. Each entry in this structure describes an set of objects that were observed at the scene, along with additional information about their position. An example query is shown in Fig. 4, and the results of the query are shown in Fig. 4.

```
1  {
2    "bounding_box": [],
3    "centroid": [-3.21, 7.14, 0.0],
4    "co_occurrences": [],
5    "context_history": [],
6    "context_room_label": "UNKNOWN",
7    "context_surface_label": "UNKNOWN",
8    "local_id": 86,
9      "local_objects": [
10         [ "Microwave",  "1","small","near_2"],
11         [ "Refrigerator",  "1",  "small",  "near_2"],
12         [ "Bottle",  "1",  "small",  "near_2"]
13     ],
14
15    "query_ground_truth": "UNKNOWN"
16    "size": ""
17  }
```

Fig. 4. An example data fragment taken from a series of observations from the robot. This structure is used to query the room detection Web service.

Upon receiving a query, the service computes the *semantic relatedness* between each object included in the co-occurrence structure and a fixed list of candidate rooms. We discuss the details of the semantic relatedness in Sect. 5.2. Using relatedness to score the likely categories of a room follows from the intuition that objects and rooms tend to be semantically related when a prototypical relation *locatedAt* holds between them. This principle, called *distributional*

Table 1. Table showing the results of the query from Fig. 4, with the top result identifying this cluster of objects as most likely belonging to a Kitchen.

Label	Relatedness
Kitchen	0.71
Bathroom	0.64
Dining Room	0.56
Bedroom	0.49
Office	0.35
Garage	0.21

relational hypothesis has been used to build knowledge bases of prototypical knowledge in [6].

Formally, given n observed objects in the query $q_1, ..., q_n$, and m rooms in the universe under consideration $r_1, ..., r_m \in O$, each r_i is given a score that indicates its likelihood of being the correct room by aggregating its relatedness across all observed objects. The aggregation function can be as simple as the arithmetic mean of the relatedness scores, or a more complex function. For instance, if the aggregation function is the product, the likelihood of a room r_i is given by:

$$likelihood(o_i) = \prod_{j=1}^{n} relatedness(r_i, q_j)$$

We experimented with the product as aggregating function. This way of aggregating similarity scores gives higher weight to highly related pairs, as opposed to the arithmetic mean, where each query object contributes equally to the final score. The idea behind this choice is that if an object is highly related to the target room it should be regarded as more informative.

5.2 Semantic Relatedness

The module described in this section is based on the computation of the *semantic relatedness* between each object included in the co-occurrence structure and every room in a fixed set of candidate rooms.

This pairwise semantic relatedness is computed by leveraging the vectorial representation of the DBpedia concepts provided by the NASARI resource [7]. In NASARI each concept contained in the multilingual resource BabelNet [11] is represented as a vector in a high-dimensional geometric space. The vector components are computed with the *word2vec* [12] tool, based on the co-occurrence of the mentions of each concept, in this case using Wikipedia as source corpus.

Since the vectors are based on distributional semantic knowledge (based on the *distributional hypothesis*: words that occurr together often are likely semantically related.), vectors that represent related entities end up close in the vector space. We are able to measure such relatedness by computing the inverse of the cosine distance between two vectors. For instance, the NASARI vectors for Fork and Kitchen have relatedness 0.69 (on a continuous scale from 0 to 1), while Fork and Bathroom are 0.52 related. Similarly, Towel and Kitchen have relatedness 0.58, less than the 0.65 of Towel and Bathroom. From this simple example, we can clearly state that, according to the vector-based model, forks belong to the kitchen and towels to the bathroom.

6   Experiments and Results

We employ two datasets of observations taken by our robot during two long-term (3 months) deployments in two separate office environments a year apart. The first dataset was labelled by a human to produce 3800 views of various objects, with the data collection methodology following the approach of Ambruş et al. [8]. The robot is provided with a map, and a set of waypoints in the map that it visits several times per day, performing full 360° RGB-D scans of the environment at those points. The second dataset is as-yet unlabelled (Fig. 5).

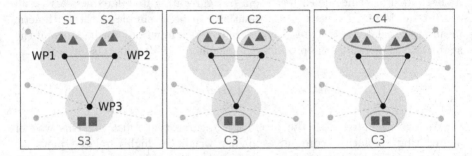

Fig. 5. Experimental Setup. **Left:** A robot makes 360° scans (S1–S3) at several predefined waypoints (WP1–WP3) in its environment whereby it observes several objects (△, □). **Middle:** Objects (△, □) are clustered into regions (C1–C3) and classified. **Right:** Nearby clusters are merged (C4).

We perform two main experiments – first, we demonstrate the results of our approach on the first, human-labelled dataset gathered from site 1 (dataset G). Since this is hand-labelled it gives us access to a representation of the objects encountered by the robot under ideal conditions – assuming no segmentation errors, and perfect object recognition. First, we sample the objects observed at each waypoint over the period of the deployment by selecting the top-n occurring objects, here using $n == 30$. From here we perform Euclidean Clustering to group objects together, producing clusters of those objects that appear within 0.5 m of one-another.

Each of these clusters is then incrementally sent to our text-mining module. In return, we receive a distribution over room categories at those points in space. After all clusters have been processed we perform a round of merging, coalescing any clusters that possess centroids within a 1.5 m of one-another, and which share the same top-ranked category. From here, we can use these new clusters to calculate bounding polygons to produce larger, categorised spatial regions. For a more intuitive representation, we found it helpful to include an inflation parameter for this – because we would like to categorise the area *around* an object or set of objects, which we expect is better served by a geometrical bounding area around objects rather than treating them as points. We apply a bounding area of 1.5 m around objects (Fig. 6).

Fig. 6. Experimental Setup at G. **Left:** A robot makes 360° scans at several predefined waypoints in its environment. **Right:** robot plans views to investigate parts of the mapped environment.

In our second experiment, we perform the exact procedure as described above on data gathered from site 2 (dataset T), however the input to the system takes the form of dynamically segmented objects using the segmentation procedure described previously, and using object hypotheses from the ImageNet-based CNN approach. Since this dataset is significantly larger, we sampled from it an equal number of observations per waypoint (4), providing us with roughly 2800 individual RGB-D clouds of scenes of the environment. Segmenting these resulted in 85,000 segments, however we applied a standard filtering by ignoring any segments that were more than 2 m away from the robot base, which filtered the set of segments down to roughly 24,000 (Fig. 7).

To evaluate our results, we provided each of the clusters of objects to five human annotators, and asked them to identify the room categories they believed to be most closely related to the set of objects. This was done without visual information on the appearance of the objects or the environment in which they were found, in the first experiment at site 1 we achieved an agreement between the annotators and the system of 74%. In the second experiment at site 2, we achieved an agreement of 80% between annotators and our system. In a second round of evaluation, a different set of seven annotators were provided images observed by the robot at each waypoint, and asked to identify the likely room categories displayed in the images from the same set of candidate rooms provided to the robot. We apply these ground-truth labels to the areas of space around each waypoint. This allows us to compare these ground-truth category labels with the labels suggested by our system. The results are shown in Table 1. On the map, dark blue polygons represent regions learned by our system, red squares indicate the waypoints where the robot took observations, and light coloured

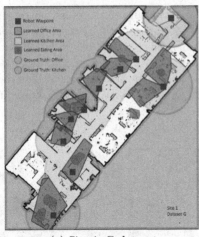

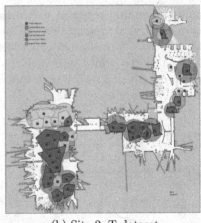

(a) Site 1, G dataset   (b) Site 2, T dataset

Fig. 7. Space categorisation results from both sites, showing learned and categorised regions and ground-truth annotations. A zoomed view is recommended. (Color figure online)

circles indicate the ground-truth label of the space around each waypoint – human annotators agreed on labels for these areas, so there is no variance.

7   Discussion

In our results from site 1, the system categorised three region types – kitchen, office and eating area. Our ground-truth labellers, given the same list of candidate rooms as the robot, only labelled kitchen and office areas. All of the office and kitchen areas learned by the system fall into the corresponding areas labelled by the human annotators, and represent a sub-section of that space. These were labelled by detecting objects such as filing cabinets, computer equipment, printers, telephones and whiteboards, which all ultimately most strongly correlated with the office room category. But where do the eating areas come from? These areas were labelled by detecting objects such as water bottles, coffee cups and mugs on the desks and cabinets of workers in the deployment environment. These objects were typically *surrounded* by office equipment. While comparing these region labels to our ground-truth data would suggest the answer is wrong, we believe that this captures a more finely-grained semantic structure in the environment that does in fact make sense. While the regions themselves may not, to a human, meet the requirements for a dining area, the objects encompassed within them are far more closely linked in the data with eating areas and kitchens than they are with computer equipment and stationary, and so the system annotates these regions differently.

At site 2 we see that the robot did not learn these characteristic eating area regions. While inspection of the data shows that many desks do exhibit the same structure of having mugs, cups and bottles on them in certain areas, the object recognition system used in the second set of experiments failed to correctly identify them. These objects are typically small, and difficult for a mobile robot to get close to. The results for the second dataset are also more noisy – there are misclassified regions. These were caused primarily by object recognition errors, themselves compounded by segmentation errors and sensor noise. To filter these out, we included a filter on system that ignored any classification result that came back with a confidence below 0.1 – ignoring those objects completely filtered out around 18, 000 segments.

There are many different possible representations for the data our system generates. We opted for a clustering and bounding-polygon based approach in order to most clearly visualise our results, but other approaches could be used such as flood-fill algorithms, heat-maps or potential fields. Choice of representation should be informed by the task that is intended to make use of the information.

Our system is ultimately limited by its reliance on objects to generate hypotheses for space classification. This means that our approach is unable to categorise areas of space such as corridoors or hallways. However it is intended to work as a component of object-search systems, so this is not necessary at this stage. To illustrate this, we built a query interface for the system which takes an arbitrary object label and suggests an area of space where the object can be found, ranking results using the semantic relations of the object with the categories learned at each region. This allows a robot to generate priors over possible locations of objects it has never seen before, and we view as the first step towards *unknown object search*, and is one of our avenues for future work. In this task, a lifelong-learning robot will be asked to locate specific items in its environment, and may be asked to locate objects it may have not seen before. A knowledge of the semantics of objects and locations present in the environment is therefore crucial in order to formulate a sensible search plan, and a self-extending vision system is needed to acquire training data (from web-based sources) and re-train any on-board object recognisers to identify the new object. This is a challenging, integrated problem of which the systems presented in this work are a component.

8   Conclusion

In this work we presented a robot system capable of categorising regions of space in real-world, noisy human-inhabited environments. The system used concepts in a lexical ontology to represent object labels, and harnessed this representation to mine relations between observed objects and room categories from corpora of text. Transferring these relations back to the real-world, we used them to annotate the robot's world with polygons indicating specific semantic categories. We found that the system was largely able to discover and categorise regions similar in area to human annotators, but was also able to discover some structure overlooked by those annotators. Our future work in this area will aim to extend the system with the ability to learn visual features from non-object environmental structure – such as particular types of walls, windows, tiles, ceilings etc. – and use the system presented here as a labelling signal to associate those visual features with room categories. In such a way we hope to classify areas in greater detail and to extend our system to work in situations where objects are not present.

Acknowledgments. The research leading to these results has received funding from EU FP7 grant agreement No. 600623, STRANDS, and CHIST-ERA Project ALOOF.

The authors also wish to thank Daniel Hayes for his careful and attentive contributions upon which this work depends.

References

1. Faeulhammer, T., et al.: Autonomous learning of object models on a mobile robot. IEEE RAL **PP**(99), 1 (2016)
2. Kilgarriff, A., Fellbaum, C.: Wordnet: An electronic lexical database (2000)
3. Russakovsky, O., et al.: ImageNet large scale visual recognition challenge. Int. J. Comput. Vis. (IJCV) **115**(3), 211–252 (2015)
4. Krizhevsky, A., et al.: Imagenet classification with deep convolutional neural networks. In: Pereira, F., Burges, C.J.C., Bottou, L., Weinberger, K.Q. (eds.) Advances in Neural Information Processing Systems 25, pp. 1097–1105. Curran Associates Inc. (2012)
5. Wu, Z., Palmer, M.: Verbs semantics and lexical selection. In: ACL. ser. ACL 1994, pp. 133–138. Association for Computational Linguistics, Stroudsburg (1994)
6. Basile, V., Jebbara, S., Cabrio, E., Cimiano, P.: Populating a knowledge base with object-location relations using distributional semantics. In: Blomqvist, E., Ciancarini, P., Poggi, F., Vitali, F. (eds.) EKAW 2016. LNCS (LNAI), vol. 10024, pp. 34–50. Springer, Cham (2016). https://doi.org/10.1007/978-3-319-49004-5_3
7. Camacho-Collados, J., et al.: Nasari: a novel approach to a semantically-aware representation of items. In: Mihalcea, R., Chai, J.Y., Sarkar, A. (eds.) HLT-NAACL, pp. 567–577. The Association for Computational Linguistics (2015)
8. Ambruş, R., et al.: Meta-rooms: building and maintaining long term spatial models in a dynamic world. In: 2014 IEEE/RSJ International Conference on Intelligent Robots and Systems, pp. 1854–1861. IEEE (2014)
9. Young, J., et al.: Towards lifelong object learning by integrating situated robot perception and semantic web mining. In: Proceedings of the European Conference on Artificial Intelligence (ECAI) (2016)
10. Young, J., et al.: Semantic web-mining and deep vision for lifelong object discovery. In: Proceedings of the IEEE International Conference on Robotics and Automation (ICRA) (2017)
11. Navigli, R., Ponzetto, S.P.: Babelnet: the automatic construction, evaluation and application of a wide-coverage multilingual semantic network. Artif. Intell. **193**, 217–250 (2012)
12. Mikolov, T., Chen, K., Corrado, G., Dean, J.: Efficient estimation of word representations in vector space. arXiv preprint arXiv:1301.3781 (2013)
13. Vasudevan, S., Siegwart, R.: Bayesian space conceptualization and place classification for semantic maps in mobile robotics. Robot. Auton. Syst. **56**(6), 522–537 (2008)
14. Vasudevan, S., et al.: Cognitive maps for mobile robotsan object based approach. Robot. Auton. Syst. **55**(5), 359–371 (2007)

15. Pronobis, A., Jensfelt, P.: Large-scale semantic mapping and reasoning with heterogeneous modalities. In: IEEE International Conference on Robotics and Automation (2012)

16. Kostavelis, I., Gasteratos, A.: Semantic mapping for mobile robotics tasks: a survey. Robot. Auton. Syst. **66**, 86–103 (2015)

17. Zender, H., et al.: Conceptual spatial representations for indoor mobile robots. Robot. Auton. Syst. **56**(6), 493–502 (2008)

18. Hanheide, M., et al.: Dora, a robot exploiting probabilistic knowledge under uncertain sensing for efficient object search. In: Proceedings of Systems Demonstration of the 21st International Conference on Automated Planning and Scheduling (ICAPS), Freiburg, Germany (2011)

19. Potapova, E., et al.: Attention-driven object detection and segmentation of cluttered table scenes using 2.5 d symmetry. In: 2014 IEEE International Conference on Robotics and Automation (ICRA), pp. 4946–4952. IEEE (2014)

20. He, K., et al.: Deep residual learning for image recognition. In: Proceedings of the IEEE Conference on Computer Vision and Pattern Recognition, pp. 770–778 (2016)

2nd International Workshop on Linked Data and Distributed Ledgers (LD-DL 2017)

TRiC: Terms, RIghts and Conditions Semantic Descriptors for Smart Contracts

Luis-Daniel Ibáñez$^{(\boxtimes)}$ ⓘ and Elena Simperl ⓘ

University of Southampton, Southampton, UK
{l.d.ibanez,e.simperl}@soton.ac.uk

Abstract. Smart Contracts have emerged as a novel way to auto-mate the execution of contracts in a decentralised and secure environment, minimising the risk of breach or non-compliance. However, recent research points out that the same measures that secure Smart Contracts against disruption with the purpose of breach makes altering the terms, rights and conditions of contracts difficult. The same research proposes a set of standards inspired in paper-contract law that Smart Contract platforms should implement to enable Smart Contract Undo and Alteration. This paper is about preliminary work on describing terms, rights, and conditions of Smart Contracts as RDF documents linked to them, levering Semantic Web tools enabling: (i) Definition and checking of complex rights and conditions (ii) Separation of the terms of the contract from its execution logic. (iii) Querying and Updating via SPARQL (iv) Alteration of terms that were not initially considered as modifiable.

Keywords: Smart Contracts · Semantic Web · Smart contract update

1 Introduction

Distributed Ledger Technologies (DLTs) have emerged as a novel way to implement decentralised, disintermediated and tamper-free *transactions* of value. After their success as a mean to implement *digital currencies* [9] that do not require a bank or intermediate to secure transactions made with them, efforts were focused to generalise such an approach to the state transitions of programs written in Turing-Complete languages. Such generalisation would enable the secure, decentralised and disintermediated execution of arbitrarily complex interactions between agents. Following the analogy of a *contract* between agents, programs executed in such an environment are known as *Smart Contracts*. Researchers have already started to study the applicability of Smart Contracts for online identity and reputation [10], define interactions between IoT devices [4] and re-imagining several types of financial services and contracts [6].

A recent work by Marino and Juels [7] highlights an important shortcoming of Smart Contracts when used to replace paper-based contracts deposited with a legal intermediary: the improved security and tamper-free properties obstruct the application of desirable undoes and alterations in response to unforeseen or

© Springer International Publishing AG 2017
E. Blomqvist et al. (Eds.): ESWC 2017 Satellite Events, LNCS 10577, pp. 317–326, 2017.
https://doi.org/10.1007/978-3-319-70407-4_40

changing circumstances, raising the following issue: *How to undo or alter terms of Smart Contracts?* In the same paper, they propose a set of standards to bring existing tools for paper-based contracts to the Smart Contract realm, and show how to implement them as part of their code for the particular case of the Ethereum platform [1] and its Solidity language [2].

We argue that *metadata* about the terms, rights and conditions (that we abbreviate as *TRiCs*) of Smart Contracts should be separated from their logic in the same way runtime parameters are separated from the logic of traditional programs. We propose to encode TRiCs as RDF documents *linked* to Smart Contracts that we call *TRiC descriptors*. Such a decoupling and the use of RDF and related Semantic Web technologies enables the following desirable properties:

- Improve readability by avoiding boilerplate code
- Reduce the number of re-factorisation and re-deployment cycles. Redeployment can be expensive in some Smart Contract platforms (e.g., Ethereum)
- Reasoning capabilities that enable the definition and checking of complex rights and conditions
- Query and Update of TRiCs via SPARQL, opening the door to mashing and integration with other contracts, their TRiCs, and the Web of Data

In this paper we describe preliminary work towards the definition and implementation of TRiC descriptors. Section 2 provides a brief overview of Smart Contracts and the definitions we will be using throughout the paper. Section 3 gives an overview of the requirements defined by [7] for undoing and altering Smart Contracts, and describes our running example. Section 4 details the TRiC descriptor proposed approach. Finally, Sect. 5 concludes the paper and provides an overview of the research questions stemming from the future realisation of our approach.

2   Smart Contracts Preliminaries

The first definition of Smart Contract was given by Nick Szabo in [8].

Definition 1 (Smart Contract (from [8])). Smart contracts are a combination of protocols, users interfaces, and promises expressed via those interfaces, to formalize and secure relationships over public networks.

Smart Contracts enable better ways to formalize digital relationships than paper-based contracts, reducing costs imposed by either principals or third parties. The advent of Distributed Ledger Technologies made possible the development of platforms to code and execute decentralised applications, *i.e.*, parties wanting to execute a program do not need to trust each other or an external partner to execute it. Smart Contracts are a natural use case for these platforms, and many of them were designed with them in mind. We adopt the definition of Smart Contract given in the White Paper of the Ethereum platform [1].

Definition 2 (Smart Contract (from [1])). *A Smart Contract is a computer program code that is capable of facilitating, executing, and enforcing the negotiation or performance of an agreement (i.e. contract) using blockchain (Distributed Ledger) technology.*

We will also adopt the programming language of Ethereum, Solidity [2], for our code examples. Further required definitions are below.

Definition 3 (Smart Contract Platform). *A Smart Contract Platform (In short, Platform) is the infrastructure and machinery required to store and execute Smart Contracts.*

We abstract from the particular implementation of the platform, but we assume it implements the following affordances: (i) Has in place a system for agents to get *pseudonyms* and send messages under these pseudonyms to trigger, halt or alter contracts. Note that we allow an agent to have as many pseudonyms as it wants (ii) Each pseudonym has an *account* that holds cryptocurrency that may be transferred to contracts to trigger their functions (iii) A function (or a Smart Contract) that allows several pseudonyms to agree in a certain action, *e.g.*, invoke a function of a Smart Contract with the approval of all of them. Every time we say that pseudonyms or agents *agree*, we assume they did it through this function.

Definition 4 (Signatories). *Given a Smart Contract, we call* signatories *to the set of pseudonyms that have the right to alter it.*

Definition 5 (Variable terms). *Given a Smart Contract, we call its* variable terms *to the subset of its variables agreed by all signatories that can be altered.*

Definition 6 (Functional terms). *Given a Smart Contract, we call its* functional terms *to the subset of its functions agreed by all signatories that can be altered*[1].

Example 1.1 shows a simplified Smart Contract for a Crowdraise[2]. We will use it as a running example for the remainder of the paper. The example defines a funding goal and two beneficiaries. The *contribute* function increments the amount raised in one unit every time is called. The *payable* keyword enables the handling by the platform of the transfer of *msg.value* (*i.e.*, the amount specified by the caller) units of cryptocurrency from the account of the caller of the function to the Smart Contract. Once the contract is deployed in the platform, agents wanting to collaborate can transfer funds to the contract by calling the *contribute* function. The withdrawal function checks that the funding goal has been achieved and that the caller is the first beneficiary, before sending half of the raised funds to each beneficiary[3]. We assume that both beneficiaries are also signatories of the Smart Contract.

---

[1] Functional and variable terms are referred in [7] as *Variable-Captured* and *Function-Captured* terms but not defined.

[2] Loosely based on the example in https://www.ethereum.org/crowdsale.

[3] For the sake of brevity, we omit the definition of the *FundTransfer* function.

320   L.-D. Ibáñez and E. Simperl

Example 1.1. Simplified Smart Contract for Crowdraising

```
contract Crowdraise {
  uint amountRaised;
  uint fundingGoal = 500;
  address[] benefs = {beneficiary1, beneficiary2}

  function contribute() payable
  {
    amountRaised = amountRaised + msg.value;  }

  function withdrawal()
  {
    if (amountRaised >= fundingGoal &&
            msg.sender == beneficiary1) {
      FundTransfer(beneficiary1, amountRaised/2);
      FundTransfer(beneficiary2, amountRaised/2);
    } }
}
```

Note that a simplistic way[4] to see a Smart Contract like our example is as a cryptographic safe box that contains value and only unlocks it if certain conditions are met. Note also that the Smart Contract executes a specific piece of code (one of its functions) whenever a message or transaction invokes it.

After a Smart Contract is deployed, it might be necessary to alter or undo some terms. Smart Contracts in platforms like Ethereum cannot be modified after being deployed, and redeployment of contracts may incur in high cryptocurrency fees. Based on our running example, we aim at providing a solution for the following alterations: (1) Modify the *fundingGoal* variable term (2) Temporarily stop receiving contributions or *disabling* the *contribute* function. (3) Change who has the right to call the withdrawal function (4) Change how the funds are transferred (e.g. 1/4th for one beneficiary and 3/4th for the other), *i.e.*, modify the *withdrawal* functional term.

3 Undo and Alteration of Smart Contracts

The work in [7] classifies undo and alteration of Smart Contracts according to the agent that solicits it. *By Right* means that one or more signatories have the right to undo or alter the Smart Contract unilaterally. *By Agreement* means that all signatories agree on undo or altering the contract. *By Court* means that a court mandated the undo or alteration. The implementation of all types can be summarized as the execution of the following steps:

---

[4] Though used in the live version of Ethereum's white paper https://github.com/ethereum/wiki/wiki/White-Paper#ethereum.

1. Check the rights of the soliciting signatory, court or that the agreement is valid.
2. Check that further termination or alteration conditions beyond pseudonym rights are met
3. Halt the execution of the Smart Contract
4. If altering the Smart Contract, delete/add/edit terms
5. Compensate partial performance of all terms of the Smart Contract if undoing, if altering, compensate deleted/added/edited terms
6. If altering, start execution of modified Smart Contract

In this paper we focus on steps 1, 2 and 4, mapping to the following research questions: *How to model and check arbitrarily complex rights and termination conditions?* and *How to delete/add/edit terms while avoiding re-deployment.* In [7], these are implemented *into* the code of the Smart Contract using Solidity constructs available at their time. Based on their work, we rewrote them currently available Solidity constructs. Example 1.2 shows the final result.

To implement rights checking, we use a special function called *modifier*[5], that can be used to check conditions before executing other functions. In our example, we use the *rightscheck* modifier to check if *beneficiary1* is the pseudonym calling the function, stopping the execution otherwise. To modify the *fundingGoal* variable, we use the *setFundingGoal* function (a simple setter method), together with the *rightscheck* modifier. For disabling/enabling the *contribute* function, we use a combination of a *halt* boolean variable that is switched through the *fliphalt* function, and the *haltcheck* modifier, that simply aborts execution if *halt* is set to *true*. Note that with this pattern, the deletion of a function term is implemented as "disabling forever". Finally, for altering the *withdrawal*, we declare the address of a so-called *satellite* contract that can be set like any other variable term, the withdrawal function in the *master* contract is simply a wrapper to the function in the satellite contract. Note that the Satellite contract pattern naturally induces a *link* between both Smart Contracts.

We note several drawbacks of this approach: (i) It requires prognostication of which terms will be altered to place the appropriate modifier calls or setter methods. What if we need to add a new beneficiary? Or disable the withdrawal function following a court mandate? If the setter method was omitted before deploying, refactorization and redeployment is the only solution. (ii) It increases the number of lines of code not related to the logic of the contract. This becomes more evident if the contract requires complex rules, in our running example, what happens if each function needs to be called by a different beneficiary? What if there are other raising campaigns running in parallel and the right to withdraw funds from this campaign depends on the results of the others? (iii) It is not straight forward to alter the rights and conditions themselves. In our example, what happens if after a certain time both beneficiaries agree that both need to approve withdrawal of funds?

We argue that terms, rights and conditions in Smart Contracts are similar to *runtime parameters* in traditional programming. As such, we propose to separate

---

[5] https://solidity.readthedocs.io/en/develop/contracts.html#function-modifiers.

Example 1.2. CrowdFunding Smart Contract with in-place code for alteration management

```
contract Crowdraise {

  uint amountRaised;
  uint fundingGoal = 500;
  address[] benefs = {beneficiary1, beneficiary2}

  bool halt = false;
  address satelliteContract;

  modifier rightscheck(){
    if (msg.sender != beneficiary1) throw;
    _; }

  modifier haltcheck(){
    if (halt) throw;
    _; }

  function setFundingGoal() {
    rightscheck
    amountRaised = msg.value;  }

  function flipHalt() {
    rightscheck
    halt = !halt;       }

  function setSatellite(){
    rightscheck
    satelliteContract = msg.value;    }

  function contribute() payable{
    haltcheck
    amountRaised = amountRaised + msg.value;  }

  function withdrawal(){
    Satellite sat = Satellite(satelliteAddress);
    sat.withdrawal();  }

  /* This function gets moved to a satellite contract
  function withdrawal(){
    if (amountRaised >= fundingGoal) {
        FundTransfer(beneficiary1, amountRaised/2);
        FundTransfer(beneficiary2, amountRaised/2);  }
  }
  */
}
```

them from their logic, in a similar way to configuration files. We propose to use RDF to encode these configuration files, in order to leverage the power of Semantic Web tools like inferencing and linking to external sources for enabling complex rights and conditions.

4 TRiC Descriptors

In this section, we describe our approach of Terms, RIghts and Conditions (TRiC) descriptors. A TRiC descriptor is an RDF document that encodes that describes the terms, rights and conditions of a Smart Contract. We assume that the platform is extended with the following capabilities: (i) A domain name and an URI minting machine under bespoke domain name. Each pseudonym and each Smart Contract in the platform have an IRI under the platform's domain name. We also assign an IRI to each variable and each function of each deployed Smart Contract (ii) Storage of RDF-Documents in a Distributed Ledger. Updates in these documents are treated as transactions in a Distributed Ledger, therefore, guaranteeing that they are tamper-free. (iii) A Graph Store to load RDF-Documents and execute SPARQL queries

Definition 7 (TRiC descriptor). *Given a Smart Contract S, its TRiC descriptor is an RDF document that contains data about its signatories, functional and variable terms, and rights and conditions*

A minimal TRiC descriptor contains one RDF triple stating a single signatory. A TRiC descriptor can be arbitrarily large, depending on the complexity of the rights and conditions that it encodes. The only modification that our approach requires to the Smart Contract code in Example 1.1 is the addition of a link to a TRiC descriptor. This should be done in a way that guarantees it can be changed afterwards, for example, with a special variable that has a default setter that can be triggered upon agreement of all signatories. Compare this with the amount of code that had to be introduced in Example 1.2.

It is out of the scope of this paper to discuss the most appropriate vocabularies to describe Smart Contracts and model rights. For the latter, we expect that work on general ontology-based access control like [3] could be adapted for this purpose. For the former, [5] presents MiniBlockVoc, a minimal vocabulary for Distributed Ledgers, including a *Smart Contract* class and property for declaring *signatories*. Following the requirements of our running example, we extend MiniBlockVoc with the following properties:

- A class *Term* and a property *hasTerm* with domain *Smart Contract* and range *Term*
- A Class *variableTerm*, having the property *value*, that represents the value of a variable term
- A Class functional term, having the properties *enabled*, with range *xsd:boolean*, representing if the function is enabled or not; *authorizedCaller* with range *Member*, representing Members with the right to call the function; and *replacedBy*, with range *functionalTerm* that represents when a functional term has been replaced by other term

Figure 1 shows a diagram of our extension to MiniBlockVoc.

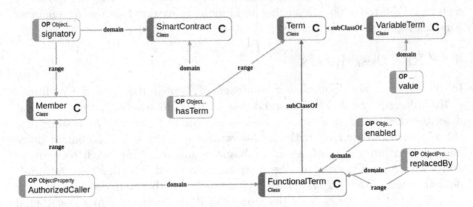

Fig. 1. Extension of the MiniBlockVoc vocabulary [5] for including terms and authorized callers

Example 1.2 shows the TRiC descriptor corresponding to our running example. Lines 4–5 state that *beneficiary1* and *beneficiary2* (here shortened to b1 and b2) are the signatories of the contract linked to this descriptor. Lines 7–9 state that *fundingGoal* is a variable term and sets its value (600) different from declaration. Lines 11–13 declare *contribute* as a function, the *active* property set to false indicates that it has been disabled. Lines 15–18 state that *withdrawal* is an active function and that its authorized caller is the agent identified with the pseudonym *b1* of this platform. Finally, line 20 states that the *withdrawal* function has been replaced by the *new-withdrawal* function on the *alt-contract* contract.

Example 1.2. TRiC descriptor corresponding to our running example

```
1    PREFIX plat:  <http://platform-domain.org/>
2    PREFIX mbv:  <https://github.com/ldibanyez/miniblockvoc/MinimalBlockChain.owl>
3
4    plat:Crowdraise mbv:signatory platform/pseudonym/b1
5    plat:Crowdraise mbv:signatory platform/pseudonym/b2
6
7    plat:Crowdraise mbv:hasTerm plat:fundingGoal
8    plat:fundingGoal rdf:type mbv:variableTerm
9    plat:fundingGoal mbv:value 600
10
11   plat:Crowdraise mbv:function plat:contribute
12   plat:Crowdraise/contribute rdf:type mbv:functionalTerm
13   plat:Crowdraise/contribute mbv:enabled 'False'^^xsd:boolean
14
15   plat:Crowdraise mbv:function plat:withdrawal
16   plat:withdrawal rdf:type function
17   plat:withdrawal mbv:active 'True'^^xsd:boolean
18   plat:withdrawal mbv:authorizedCaller plat:pseudo/b1
19
20   plat:Crowdraise/withdrawal mbv:replacedBy
21                        plat:alt-contract/new-withdrawal
```

When a function of the Smart Contract is invoked, the platform executes the following algorithm:

1. Dereference the descriptor and load it into its Graph Store.
2. Ask if the function is active or not. If so, continue, else, return.
3. Ask if the caller of the function has the right to do so according to the descriptor. If so, continue, else, return.
4. Override the values of all variables with new values according to the descriptor.
5. Ask if the function has been *replaced* by another one. If so, delegate the call to it. If not, execute the function as described in the contract.

To modify any term, right or condition, signatories agree[6] on a SPARQL Update query to be applied to the TRiC descriptor. In our running example, if signatories want to re-enable the *contribute* function, they agree in executing the SPARQL Update shown in Listing 1.3.

Example 1.3. SPARQL Update over TRiC descriptor

```
PREFIX plat: <http://platform-domain.org/>
PREFIX mbv: <https://github.com/ldibanyez/miniblockvoc/MinimalBlockChain.owl>

DELETE { plat:Crowdraise/contribute mbv:enabled "false"^xsd:boolean }
INSERT { plat:Crowdraise/contribute mbv:enabled "true"^xsd:boolean }
WHERE
  { plat:Crowdraise/contribute mbv:enabled "false"^xsd:boolean }
```

5 Conclusion and Outlook

In this paper we presented preliminary work on TRiC descriptors, RDF documents describing Terms, RIghts and Conditions linked to Smart Contracts. TRiC descriptors enable a subset of the conditions proposed by Marino and Juels [7] for undo and alteration of Smart Contracts. The advantages of using TRiC descriptors over expressing TRiCs into Smart Contracts are numerous: (i) Separates the definition of rights and conditions from the Smart Contract logic, improving readability. (ii) Enables the querying, inference and update of terms, rights and conditions (via SPARQL) (iii) Allows the alteration of terms that were not identified as *modifiable* at deployment time

Our next steps are to develop an ontology for expressing the alteration requirements that could be shared among several Smart Contract platforms, and to implement TRiC descriptors into an existing Smart Contract platform to test their feasibility and performance. We believe that in this endeavour there are several challenges that need to be tackled:

– How to integrate a Graph Store into a Smart Contract Platform? Is it relevant for the TRiC descriptor context to execute SPARQL queries in a Smart Contract Platform as if they were code? If so, how to do it?

---

[6] Except if the alteration is by court.

- How to efficiently store TRiC descriptors? Note that our approach implies replacing re-factorisation and re-deployment with data updates, therefore, optimisation of said updates in a Distributed Ledger Environments environment is crucial
- How to check the validity of alterations made via TRiC descriptors from an execution and legal point of view? The question becomes more challenging in the presence of dependencies to other contracts.
- In our current definition, one TRiC descriptor is associated with one Smart Contract, is it possible to improve the approach to enable the re-use of descriptors (or parts of them) across several contracts?

References

1. A next-generation smart contract and decentralized application platform. https://github.com/ethereum/wiki/wiki/White-Paper
2. Solidity 0.4.10 documentation. https://solidity.readthedocs.io/en/develop/contracts.html
3. Buffa, M., Faron-Zucker, C.: Ontology-based access rights management. In: Guillet, F., Ritschard, G., Zighed, D. (eds.) Advances in Knowledge Discovery and Management. SCI, vol. 398, pp. 49–61. Springer, Heidelberg (2012). https://doi.org/10.1007/978-3-642-25838-1_3
4. Christidis, K., Devetsikiotis, M.: Blockchains and smart contracts for the internet of things. IEEE Access **4**, 2292–2303 (2016)
5. Ibáñez, L.D., Simperl, E., Gandon, F., Story, H.: Redecentralising the web with distributed ledgers. IEEE Intell. Syst. **32**(1), 92–95 (2017)
6. MacDonald, T.J., Allen, D.W.E., Potts, J.: Blockchains and the boundaries of self-organized economies: predictions for the future of banking. In: Tasca, P., Aste, T., Pelizzon, L., Perony, N. (eds.) Banking Beyond Banks and Money. NEW, pp. 279–296. Springer, Cham (2016). https://doi.org/10.1007/978-3-319-42448-4_14
7. Marino, B., Juels, A.: Setting standards for altering and undoing smart contracts. In: Alferes, J.J.J., Bertossi, L., Governatori, G., Fodor, P., Roman, D. (eds.) RuleML 2016. LNCS, vol. 9718, pp. 151–166. Springer, Cham (2016). https://doi.org/10.1007/978-3-319-42019-6_10
8. Szabo, N.: Formalizing and securing relationships on public networks. First Monday **2**(9) (1997)
9. Tschorsch, F., Scheuermann, B.: Bitcoin and beyond: a technical survey on decentralized digital currencies. IEEE Commun. Surv. Tutorials **18**(3), 2084–2123 (2015)
10. Yasin, A., Liu, L.: An online identity and smart contract management system. In: 40th Annual Computer Software and Applications Conference (COMPSAC), vol. 2, pp. 192–198. IEEE (2016)

Towards the Temporal Streaming of Graph Data on Distributed Ledgers

Allan Third[(✉)], Ilaria Tiddi, Emanuele Bastianelli, Chris Valentine,
and John Domingue

Knowledge Media Institute, The Open University,
Walton Hall, Milton Keynes MK7 6AA, UK
{allan.third,ilaria.tiddi,emanuele.bastianelli,chris.valentine,
john.domingue}@open.ac.uk

Abstract. We present our work-in-progress on handling temporal RDF graph data using the Ethereum distributed ledger. The motivation for this work are scenarios where multiple distributed consumers of streamed data may need or wish to verify that data has not been tampered with since it was generated – for example, if the data describes something which can be or has been sold, such as domestically-generated electricity. We describe a system in which temporal annotations, and information suitable to validate a given dataset, are stored on a distributed ledger, alongside the results of fixed SPARQL queries executed at the time of data storage. The model adopted implements a graph-based form of temporal RDF, in which time intervals are represented by named graphs corresponding to ledger entries. We conclude by discussing evaluation, what remains to be implemented, and future directions.

1 Introduction

This paper presents ongoing work in the use of distributed ledgers to provide validation for temporal graph-based data collected from sensor hardware. In particular, we use smart contracts executing on the Ethereum [16] distributed ledger to implement a named-graph-based temporal model for RDF data streams.

There are a number of motivating scenarios in which this can prove useful. [5] outlines criteria for the meaningful use of blockchain technologies. Among these are the requirements that data must be interacted with by multiple parties, who do not necessarily trust each other. We have identified two such scenarios among our current projects, relating to the collection of environmental data.

The GreenDATA project [11] focuses on gathering energy generation data from domestic generation systems. We collect this data from volunteers among colleagues, students, and other interested parties across the UK and elsewhere in order to make these datasets available to our students of sustainable energy modules, both to provide access to real system properties and also to encourage the development of data handling and analysis skills. One of the potential uses of distributed ledgers for renewable energy is to enable a disintermediated market: domestic producers could potentially sell surplus energy directly to domestic

E. Blomqvist et al. (Eds.): ESWC 2017 Satellite Events, LNCS 10577, pp. 327–332, 2017.
https://doi.org/10.1007/978-3-319-70407-4_41

consumers using cryptocurrency transactions on a blockchain. In such a scenario, with money changing hands, there would of course be a need for verification of data on behalf of both parties to a transaction. We therefore seek to allow students to model this scenario using a private distributed ledger in order to provide them with a way to explore how it might work.

The second scenario we are considering involves the collection of sensor data from moving vehicles, with limited network connectivity and computational power. Real-world situations where this might occur with a need for verification of data include the transport of environmentally-sensitive materials, such as food or medicines, disaster relief, or in long-distance motor racing, both of which can have financial or health consequences in the case of invalid data. We are planning to carry out a number of experiments in this setting over the next year, as two of the authors take part in the Mongol Rally [2] using a car equipped with a wide range of sensors and communication equipment to travel from Milton Keynes in the UK through Mongolia to Ulan Ude in Russia. The data gathered, with sub-second resolution on some sensors, and data gathered continuously while driving, will be streamed as RDF, network permitting, for on-the-fly and later analysis, including event detection. We intend to take this opportunity to experiment with the use of Ethereum light clients in a resource-limited setting and incorporating spatial data in our blockchain data handling.

2   Temporal Graphs and RDF Streams

The Resource Description Framework (RDF) [14] is a flexible semantic model for representing data, in the form of *triples* – "subject predicate object" sentences, with terms in each position represented by a (generally dereferencable) URL or, in the "object" position, a literal data value. One of the aims of RDF is to permit the easy linking and integration of data by means of URL matching and inference, for which use it has been highly successful [1]. The usual language for querying RDF data is SPARQL [13], although other approaches, such as Linked Data Fragments [12], are also used.

The typical use of RDF has been for the publication of datasets which are relatively static, with variability in the range of SPARQL queries used to extract information from them, severally or in combination. The "facts" represented by RDF triples are, in some sense, timeless, with issues about their lifespan or validity left outside the RDF model. In recent years, there has been increasing interest in the use of RDF to represent *streams* of temporally-annotated data, permitting explicit timestamps or time intervals to be associated with (sets of) RDF triples. This temporal aspect is essential for streaming data, as often the facts represented by the triples will only have limited temporal validity. It has been argued [15] that the approach to querying streams is the inverse to the usual querying model: highly volatile data with a small number of relatively static queries to extract information from them.

3   Distributed Ledgers and Smart Contracts

The Ethereum blockchain platform is a distributed ledger designed not just for cryptocurrency use but also as a decentraised computing platform. A *blockchain* is a data structure, duplicated on every node of a blockchain network, consisting of *blocks*, which are collections of *transactions* – records of transfers of cryptocurrency – between *accounts*. The creation of blocks – *mining* – is carried out by nodes, which compete for the opportunity to mine the next block at any given time. The choice as to which node may mine a block is made by consensus by some particular protocol, meaning that anyone seeking to insert a block containing an incorrect or fraudulent transaction must control or convince more than 50% of the nodes on the whole blockchain network to agree, and anyone seeking to alter an established transaction record must convince more than 50% of the nodes to roll back all transactions which have been recorded since the target record. In this way, in a large enough and diverse enough network, transactions on a blockchain can be trusted and effectively immutable. By encoding non-financial information in the transaction record, blockchains can be used to record trustworthy permanent records of other forms of data.

Ethereum specialises the blockchain concept further, by adding account types and addressing for *smart contracts*. A smart contract is a compiled unit of executable code which is stored on Ethereum and can be executed on all nodes via transactions involving the relevant account. As the compiled code is stored on the blockchain, it is possible to be assured that a particular contract has not been tampered with since it was compiled and deployed. In this way, Ethereum is intended to serve as a decentralised distributed computing platform.

Smart contracts have *state*, which can be updated by a contract when it is executed. The blockchain maintains a record of all previous states of a contract – inevitably, as to overwrite previous state would involve overwriting records earlier in the blockchain. Smart contracts can thus be used to implement a form of dynamic data storage with history in the Ethereum environment.

4   Use Cases in Detail

4.1   GreenDATA

The GreenDATA project [11] aims to collect data from domestic energy generation, from solar, wind and geothermal sources, with the purposes of making it available for students of sustainable energy, so that they might be able to study the behaviour of real systems in practice, in different locations and of different generation modalities. Contributors to GreenData have energy generating installations across the UK, and beyond, with participants in Austria and Crete.

Data is collected using either contributors' own hardware, or, more usually, using an OpenEnergyMonitor emonPi [8], a Raspberry Pi [9] based device which can be clamped to the appropriate cables of, for example, a solar photovoltaic system, and which then analyses the performance and behaviour of the system. The collected data can be stored locally to the emonPi, or, as in the GreenData installations, transmitted over a domestic WiFi connection or a GSM signal to a remote data store. Types of data collected include grid supply voltage, power imported or exported, indoor and outdoor temperature, among others. The temporal resolution of the data is 10 s and data collection is continuous, 24 h a day. The timestamp of each data point is taken from GPS.

A modification to the emonPi software means that data is lifted to RDF on each device, before being sent to an RDF store hosted centrally, via an Ethereum light client [4] installed on the emonPi. The motivation behind having a blockchain infrastructure to verify the gathered data is twofold. Firstly, to serve as an experiment in the validation of data using blockchains in general, and secondly, to allow students to explore the potential role of blockchains in simulated disintermediated energy markets, in which consumer-producers of energy can trade energy surpluses directly with each other.

4.2   MK2MG – Milton Keynes to Mongolia

From mid-2017, two of the authors will be taking part in the Mongol Rally [2], driving an old car from Milton Keynes in the UK to a point near the border between Mongolia and Russia. The primary purpose of taking part is to raise money for charity, but we intend to use their journey to carry out a number of experiments using sensors attached to the car and both participants. Data relating to speed, location, temperature, humidity, heart rate and physical activity will be collected at a sub-second resolution, and both stored as RDF locally in on-car hardware and transmitted to a central server via a GSM connection. Event detection will be applied to the data in both locations. We aim to run an Ethereum light client on the in-car hardware in order to handle blockchain communications. In particular, we are interested in the results of streaming large quantities of data with blockchain-based recording in a scenario with connectivity and computational power limited by space, energy and cost.

The applications of the lessons we hope to learn from this exercise are in situations where there is a need for validated and trustworthy data in low power, intermittently connected settings, such as medication transport or disaster relief.

5   Temporal Graphs on the Ethereum Distributed Ledger

The Ethereum blockchain is not suited to storing large amounts of data – the speed of execution is unlikely to be fast enough to support high volume data streams. However, in order to achieve the goal of validation of data integrity, it is not necessary to store the data itself on the blockchain; all we need is to store sufficient metadata to allow anyone who does possess a chunk of the data to verify that its contents are intact. We need, therefore, a canonical representation of the data which can be hashed reproducibly to provide a verification – for example, the RDF serialisation of the source – and a reliable form of "punctuation" in the data stream, to identify complete chunks of data to be used for the hash.

The form of punctuation used depends on the temporal model used in the data. Multiple approaches have been taken to the representation of temporal

RDF streams. Broadly, they vary as to whether temporal information is associated with each triple individually ("triple-based") or with RDF graphs, where the triples in an individual graph share the same temporal information. In the latter approach, a graph usually corresponds to a time *interval*. In the former, the temporal information attached to a triple may either be an interval or a timestamp representing an instant. [3,6,7,10] The difference between interval and timestamp is not deeply relevant; with an interval representation, one can always simulate a timestamp by setting the start and end points of the interval to be identical, with no loss of information. For the purposes of this work, given the requirement to group sections of the data stream in order to implement what is needed for verification, it seems most appropriate to use the graph approach.

We therefore ensure that the data streams generated from sensors are segmented, at source, into named graphs corresponding to time intervals, with the length of intervals to be determined also at the source, and indicated within the data itself. Variable rather than static intervals provide more flexibility.

Smart contracts running on (a private instance of) the Ethereum blockchain have been written to receive the data, with each remote client provided with the address of the relevant contract(s). Each time data is sent, the contract identifies graphs specified by the source, and calculates a verification hash, extracting the start and end times of the interval covered by each graph. Four items – graph URI, hash, start and end time – are stored in the state of a new smart contract, the address of which is stored in a "master" contract and which, along with the original data, is forwarded onto a traditional RDF store.

At the same time, clients performing event detection construct an RDF representation of each event detected, and send it to a separate smart contract, along with the names and hashes of the relevant temporal graphs. The duplication of hashes provides a separate source of validity information for each graph.

In order to support the verification of data in standard SPARQL querying scenarios, a custom SPARQL endpoint, running off-blockchain, is being written to respond to federated SPARQL requests using the SERVICE keyword. Any triple patterns passed to this endpoint specified to be in a temporal graph known to be hashed on the blockchain are queried from the full dataset, and each relevant graph is hashed, and compared to the entries stored in the blockchain both from the streaming data contracts, and any relevant contracts from event detection. The custom endpoint returns a triple stating whether verification succeeded, allowing at least a base level of verification within SPARQL.

6 Conclusion and Future Plans

As stated at the outset, this paper presents a work-in-progress in the use of distributed ledger technology to provide a layer of verifiability to temporal RDF graphs containing streaming data. What we have achieved so far indicates that the approach proposed is practical to implement and flexible enough to cover the use cases proposed without limiting scope for further extension.

In practice, there are a number of parameters in this approach with which we can experiment to test their effects on performance, reliability and suitability for the goals. These include, among others, the sizes of data batching, the use of on-chain vs. off-chain hashing and any compression approaches we can use with the data streams. Data we collect about the behaviour of, in particular, the MK2MG interactions with the blockchain will inform how best to handle limited connectivity and computational power systems.

In future work, we would like to explore the performance and execution cost implications of implementing at least some aspects of SPARQL directly inside smart contracts, to evaluate the possibility of having some limited temporal reasoning performed within a trusted context on the distributed ledger. We also intend to explore the use of distributed file systems to store the full data. It would be interesting, too, to explore how doing so might enable more Linked Data application scenarios to be implemented in a fully distributed, decentralised setting, with less reliance on external datastores as we do now, and following more closely the distributed ledger philosophy.

References

1. Abele, A., McCrae, J.P., Buitelaar, P., Jentzsch, A., Cyganiak, R.: Linking open data cloud diagram 2017 (2017). http://lod-cloud.net/
2. The Adventurists. Mongol Rally (2017). http://bit.ly/1gSXyjx
3. Bereta, K., Smeros, P., Koubarakis, M.: Representation and querying of valid time of triples in linked geospatial data. In: Cimiano, P., Corcho, O., Presutti, V., Hollink, L., Rudolph, S. (eds.) ESWC 2013. LNCS, vol. 7882, pp. 259–274. Springer, Heidelberg (2013). doi:10.1007/978-3-642-38288-8_18
4. EthereumWiki. Ethereum light client protocol (2017). http://bit.ly/2qbOqmL
5. Greenspan, G.: Avoiding the pointless blockchain project, November 2015. http://bit.ly/2pfT43Z
6. Kietz, J.U., Scharrenbach, T., Fischer, L., Bernstein, A., Nguyen, K.: TEF-SPARQL: The DDIS query-language for time annotated event and fact triple-streams. Technical report, University of Zurich, Department of Informatics (2013)
7. Le-Phuoc, D., Dao-Tran, M., Xavier Parreira, J., Hauswirth, M.: A native and adaptive approach for unified processing of linked streams and linked data. In: Aroyo, L., Welty, C., Alani, H., Taylor, J., Bernstein, A., Kagal, L., Noy, N., Blomqvist, E. (eds.) ISWC 2011. LNCS, vol. 7031, pp. 370–388. Springer, Heidelberg (2011). doi:10.1007/978-3-642-25073-6_24
8. OpenEnergyMonitor. OpenEnergyMonitor (2017). http://openenergymonitor.org
9. The Raspberry Pi Foundation. Raspberry pi (2017). http://raspberrypi.org
10. Tappolet, J., Bernstein, A.: Applied temporal RDF: efficient temporal querying of RDF data with SPARQL. In: Aroyo, L., et al. (eds.) ESWC 2009. LNCS, vol. 5554, pp. 308–322. Springer, Heidelberg (2009). doi:10.1007/978-3-642-02121-3_25
11. Valentine, C.: GreenDATA (2016). http://projects.kmi.open.ac.uk/greendata
12. Verborgh, R., Vander Sande, M., Colpaert, P., Coppens, S., Mannens, E., Van de Walle, R.: Web-scale querying through Linked Data Fragments. In: LDOW (2014)
13. W3C. SPARQL (2008). https://www.w3.org/TR/rdf-sparql-query/
14. W3C. Resource Description Framework (2014). https://www.w3.org/RDF/
15. W3C. RDF stream models (2017). http://bit.ly/2pwWTFb
16. Wood, G.: Ethereum: a secure decentralised generalised transaction ledger. Ethereum Project Yellow Paper (2014)

4th Workshop on Linked Data Quality (LDQ 2017)

A Linked Data Profiling Service for Quality Assessment

Nandana Mihindukulasooriya[1]([✉]) [iD], Raúl García-Castro[1], Freddy Priyatna[1],
Edna Ruckhaus[1], and Nelson Saturno[2]

[1] Ontology Engineering Group, Universidad Politécnica de Madrid, Madrid, Spain
{nmihindu,rgarcia,fpriyatna,eruckhaus}@fi.upm.es
[2] Universidad Simón Bolívar, Caracas, Venezuela

Abstract. The Linked (Open) Data cloud has been growing at a rapid
rate in recent years. However, the large variance of quality in its datasets
is a key obstacle that hinders their use, so quality assessment has become
an important aspect. Data profiling is one of the widely used techniques
for data quality assessment in domains such as relational data; nevertheless, it is not so widely used in Linked Data. We argue that one reason for
this is the lack of Linked Data profiling tools that are configurable in a
declarative manner, and that produce comprehensive profiling information with the level of detail required by quality assessment techniques.
To this end, this demo paper presents the Loupe API, a RESTful web
service that profiles Linked Data based on user requirements and produces comprehensive profiling information on explicit RDF general data,
class, property and vocabulary usage, and implicit data patterns such as
cardinalities, instance ratios, value distributions, and multilingualism.
Profiling results can be used to assess quality either by manual inspection, or automatically using data validation languages such as SHACL,
ShEX, or SPIN.

Keywords: Linked Data · Quality · Data profiling · Services

1 Introduction

The Linked (Open) Data cloud has been growing at a rapid rate in recent years.
Some portions of it come from crowd-sourced knowledge bases such as Wikipedia,
while others come from government administrations, research publishers, and
other organizations. These datasets have different levels of quality [1] such that
for most practical use cases, they need to be assessed to get an indication of
their quality.

Juran and Godfrey describe quality using multiple views [2]. On the one hand,
quality can be seen as "fit for intended use in operations, decision-making, and

N. Mihindukulasooriya—This research is partially supported by the 4V (TIN2013-
46238-C4-2-R) and MobileAge (H2020/693319) projects and the FPI grant (BES-
2014-068449.).

© Springer International Publishing AG 2017
E. Blomqvist et al. (Eds.): ESWC 2017 Satellite Events, LNCS 10577, pp. 335–340, 2017.
https://doi.org/10.1007/978-3-319-70407-4_42

planning", i.e., relevance, recency, completeness, and precision. On the other hand, quality is also viewed as "freedom from deficiencies", i.e., correctness and consistency. In either case, quality assessment is needed before using the data for a given task to ensure that the data has an adequate quality level. Further, the results of the assessment can be used to assist the process of improving quality by cleaning and repairing deficiencies in the data. The objective of the work presented in this paper is to provide a data profiling service with fine-grained information that can be used as input for many quality assessment tasks related to both these views of data quality.

Detailed data analysis is one common preliminary task in quality assessment, and data profiling is one of the most widely-used techniques for such analysis [3]. Data profiling is defined as the process of examining data to collect statistics and provide relevant metadata about the data [4]. Even though data profiling is widely used in quality assessment in domains such as relational data, we see a lack of usage of data profiling in Linked Data.

In this paper, we describe a Linked Data profiling service, the Loupe API, which provides access to the Loupe tool via a RESTful interface. The Loupe API may be configured to specify the source data as well as the profiling activities it should perform. As a consequence it can be used for different purposes. In recent years, Loupe has been used to assess the quality of datasets in several projects such as DBpedia [5] and 3Cixty [6]. A RESTful interface facilitates the integration of the Loupe profiling services to other systems. The Loupe API has been integrated with one of our ongoing projects, MappingPedia[1], a collaborative environment for R2RML mappings, in order to gather statistics and do quality assessment since R2RML mappings are themselves RDF/Linked Data datasets.

2   Loupe API

The Loupe API[2] is a configurable Linked Data profiling service. The three main phases in Linked Data profiling are (1) specification of input, (2) execution of data profiling, and (3) representation of profiling results. Figure 1a shows an example input of a Loupe API profile request. Users can specify their requirements (i.e., which profiling tasks to execute) and other configuration details such as how to access the data source (and which data to profile), or whether to persist the profiling results in the Loupe public repository (i.e., they will be available via search). The profiling tasks are grouped into four categories:

- **summary** - provides generic statistics on an RDF data source related to its size and the type of content it has, for example, typed entity count or distinct IRI object count.
- **vocabUsage** - provides information on the implicit schema of the data by analyzing how vocabulary terms such as classes and properties are used, their domains and ranges, cardinalities, uniqueness, among others.

---

[1] http://demo.mappingpedia.linkeddata.es/.
[2] http://api.loupe.linkeddata.es/.

- **languagePartitions** - provides information on multilingual content by analyzing the frequency of each language in language tagged strings.
- **valueDistributions** - provides information on the value distribution of a given property.

The results of profiling are represented in RDF using the Loupe ontology[3]. The main elements of the profiling results are illustrated in Fig. 1b; the complete results in RDF are available[4]; we also provide a set of cURL examples[5] for invoking the service.

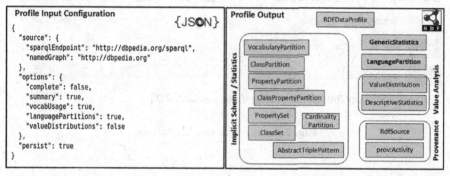

(a) Input Configuration   (b) Output Elements

Fig. 1. A summary of Loupe API input and output

These profiling results can be used for validating the quality of a dataset either by manual inspection or by specifying the validation rules in a language such as SHACL[6], ShEx[7], or SPIN[8]. Data profiling facilitates the manual inspection by providing a high-level summary so that an evaluator can adapt techniques such as exploratory testing [6] to identify strange occurrences in data.

Nevertheless, automatic validation is needed when a large amount of data is present and it is feasible in most situations. For example, data model constraints such as uniqueness of values, expected cardinalities, domains and ranges, inconsistent use of duplicate properties [5] can be easily validated by expressing those in a constraint language and automatically using profiling information.

Further, profiling results enable the analysis of a dataset over a period of time by periodically profiling data and performing the analysis on multiple profiling results. For instance, expected deletions of data or undesired changes can be detected by analysing the changes in the dataset profiles.

---

[3] http://ont-loupe.linkeddata.es/def/core#.
[4] https://git.io/vy1tO.
[5] https://github.com/nandana/loupe-api/wiki/examples.
[6] https://www.w3.org/TR/shacl/.
[7] https://shexspec.github.io/spec/.
[8] http://spinrdf.org/.

The Loupe API is implemented as a RESTful service and currently three operations are available as illustrated in Fig. 2.

Loupe Linked Data Profiler API

A REST API for profiling Linked Data with Loupe.

loupe-api : Profile RDF Data   Show/Hide   List Operations   Expand Operations

GET	/loupe/namedgraphs	Returns a list of namedgraphs found in a SPARQL endpoint
POST	/loupe/profile	Returns the profile information for a given RDF source.
POST	/loupe/search	Returns a list of dataset profile results based on the search criteria.

[BASE URL: http://api.loupe.linkeddata.es/ , API VERSION: 1.0.0]

Fig. 2. Loupe API Documentation

3   Related Work

Zaveri et al. [1] present a comprehensive review of data quality assessment techniques and tools in the literature, and propose a conceptual framework with quality metrics grouped in four dimensions: accessibility, intrinsic, contextual, and representational; in particular, it mentions the use of profiling by the Pro-LOD tool for Semantic Accuracy. The ProLOD tool [7] has a pre-processing clustering and labeling phase and a real-time profiling phase that gathers statistics on a specific cluster in order to detect misused properties and discordant values.

Tools that provide statistics on the Linked Open Data Cloud include Aether [8] that provides extended VOID statistical descriptions of RDF content and interlinking, and ExpLOD [9] and ABSTAT [10] that provide summaries of RDF usage and interlinking.

Differently from the other tools mentioned, the Loupe API is available as a RESTful web service where users can configure and generate Linked Data profiles in RDF using the Loupe ontology. Further, Loupe provides summarized information not only on explicit vocabulary, class and property usage as the other tools but it also facilitates the analysis of implicit data patterns by providing a finer grained set of metrics compared to existing tools, such as instance ratio (ratio of instances of a given class to all entities) and property cardinalities. Low granularity metrics and other capabilities of Loupe have been applied to the analysis of redundant information, consistency with respect to the axioms in the ontology, syntactic validity and detection of outliers.

4 Conclusion and Future Work

This paper presents the Loupe API, a configurable RESTful service for profiling Linked Data, where results can be used for quality assessment purposes. The paper illustrated its use, and motivated it with a discussion on how it can be integrated to the quality assessment process.

Nevertheless, there are several challenges in profiling large datasets using a service compared to a standalone tool. Thus, Loupe API is mostly suitable for profiling small datasets. Large datasets (e.g., DBPedia) could take a long time to profile and the requests might timeout. In the future, we plan to provide support for asynchronous executions for such cases.

Another challenge is to detect the capabilities and limitations of the SPARQL endpoint and to adapt to those capabilities. Loupe API uses SPARQL 1.1 features and some metrics are omitted if an endpoint only supports SPARQL 1.0.

In the future, we also plan to extend the profiling service to other Linked Data sources such as RDF dumps, SPARQL construct queries, and LDF endpoints. Further, we plan to allow users to specify their quality requirements in a declarative manner using formal languages such as SHACL, ShEX, SPIN or using an editor with common validation rules. This will allow the Loupe API to generate quality assessment reports based on those requirements.

References

1. Zaveri, A., Rula, A., Maurino, A., Pietrobon, R., Lehmann, J., Auer, S.: Quality assessment for linked data: a survey. Semant. Web 7(1), 63–93 (2016)
2. Defeo, J.A., Juran, J.M.: Juran's Quality Handbook: The Complete Guide to Performance Excellence, 6th edn. McGraw-Hill Education (2010)
3. Olson, J.E.: Data Quality: The Accuracy Dimension, 1st edn. Morgan Kaufmann, USA (2003)
4. Rahm, E., Do, H.H.: Data cleaning: problems and current approaches. IEEE Data Eng. Bull. 23(4), 3–13 (2000)
5. Mihindukulasooriya, N., Rico, M., García-Castro, R., Gómez-Pérez, A.: An analysis of the quality issues of the properties available in the Spanish DBpedia. In: Puerta, J.M., Gámez, J.A., Dorronsoro, B., Barrenechea, E., Troncoso, A., Baruque, B., Galar, M. (eds.) CAEPIA 2015. LNCS (LNAI), vol. 9422, pp. 198–209. Springer, Cham (2015). doi:10.1007/978-3-319-24598-0_18
6. Mihindukulasooriya, N., Rizzo, G., Troncy, R., Corcho, O., Garcıa-Castro, R.: A two-fold quality assurance approach for dynamic knowledge bases: the 3cixty use case. In: Proceedings of the 1st International Workshop on Completing and Debugging the Semantic Web, pp. 1–12 (2016)
7. Böhm, C., Naumann, F., Abedjan, Z., Fenz, D., Grütze, T., Hefenbrock, D., Pohl, M., Sonnabend, D.: Profiling linked open data with ProLOD. In: Haas, L. (ed.) Proceedings of the 2nd International Workshop on New Trends in Information Integration, pp. 175–178. IEEE (2010)
8. Mäkelä, E.: Aether – generating and viewing extended VoID statistical descriptions of RDF datasets. In: Presutti, V., Blomqvist, E., Troncy, R., Sack, H., Papadakis, I., Tordai, A. (eds.) ESWC 2014. LNCS, vol. 8798, pp. 429–433. Springer, Cham (2014). doi:10.1007/978-3-319-11955-7_61

9. Khatchadourian, S., Consens, M.P.: ExpLOD: summary-based exploration of inter-linking and RDF usage in the linked open data cloud. In: Aroyo, L., Antoniou, G., Hyvönen, E., Teije, A., Stuckenschmidt, H., Cabral, L., Tudorache, T. (eds.) ESWC 2010. LNCS, vol. 6089, pp. 272–287. Springer, Heidelberg (2010). doi:10. 1007/978-3-642-13489-0_19

10. Spahiu, B., Porrini, R., Palmonari, M., Rula, A., Maurino, A.: ABSTAT: ontology-driven linked data summaries with pattern minimalization. In: Sack, H., Rizzo, G., Steinmetz, N., Mladenić, D., Auer, S., Lange, C. (eds.) ESWC 2016. LNCS, vol. 9989, pp. 381–395. Springer, Cham (2016). doi:10.1007/978-3-319-47602-5_51

Workshop on Semantic Deep Learning (SemDeep)

Predicting Relations Between RDF Entities by Deep Neural Network

Tsuyoshi Murata[1]([✉]), Yohei Onuki[1], Shun Nukui[1], Seiya Inagi[2], Xule Qiu[2], Masao Watanabe[2], and Hiroshi Okamoto[2]

[1] Department of Computer Science, School of Computing, Tokyo Institute of Technology, W8-59 2-12-1 Ookayama, Meguro, Tokyo 152 -8552, Japan
`murata@c.titech.ac.jp`
[2] Research and Technology Group, Fuji Xerox Co., Ltd., 6-1 Minatomirai, Nishi-ku, Yokohama, Kanagawa 220-8668, Japan

Abstract. In the process of ontology construction, we often need to find relations between entities described by the Resource Description Framework (RDF). Predicting relations between RDF entities is important for developing large-scale ontologies. The goal of our research is to predict a relation (predicate) of two given entities (subject and object). TransE and TransR have been proposed as the methods for such a prediction. We propose a method for predicting a predicate from a subject and an object by using a Deep Neural Network (DNN), and developed RDFDNN. Experimental results showed that predictions by RDFDNN are more accurate than those by TransE and TransR.

1 Introduction

Ontology learning is one of the important topics for developing the Semantic Web. In general, there are many entity pairs where the relations between them are unknown [7,16]. If we can predict such relations accurately, we can augment a given ontology. Since many Semantic Web data (such as Google's Knowledge Graph) are already available, techniques for predicting relations between entities are important for developing large-scale ontologies.

The goal of our research is to predict relations between two given entities in Resource Description Framework (RDF) accurately. RDF is the framework for representing Web resources, and each triple in RDF is composed of three entities (subject, predicate, and object). Subject and object are entities, and predicate is the relation between the entities. Suppose (Tokyo, is-capital-of, Japan) is an example of such a triple. We would like to predict "is-capital-of" when "Tokyo" and "Japan" are given. For this purpose, we propose a method for predicting a predicate from a subject and an object by using a Deep Neural Network (DNN), and developed RDFDNN.

Freebase and Wordnet are used as the datasets of our experiments. The following experiments are performed: (1) comparison with previous methods

E. Blomqvist et al. (Eds.): ESWC 2017 Satellite Events, LNCS 10577, pp. 343–354, 2017.
https://doi.org/10.1007/978-3-319-70407-4_43

(Sect. 5), (2) failure analysis (Sect. 6), (3) embedding dimension and prediction accuracy (Sect. 7), and (4) embedding dimension and computational time (Sect. 8). As the results of our experiments, RDFDNN is more accurate than TransE [1] and TransR [10] for predicting a predicate from a given subject and object. We also propose a method for finding appropriate embedding dimensions in RDFDNN.

2   RDFDNN

RDFDNN predicts the relation between two entities represented as a RDF triple. When h and t of a RDF triple (h, l, t) are given as inputs, RDFDNN will output l.

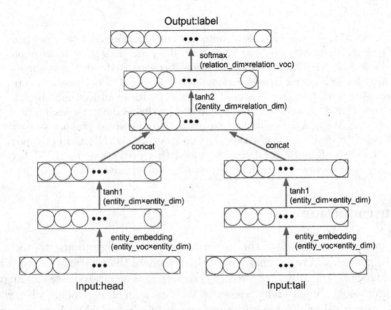

Fig. 1. The structure of RDFDNN

The structure of RDFDNN is shown in Fig. 1. Circles are nodes, rectangles are layers of DNN, and red arrows are the transformation of weight matrices. Its inputs are one-hot codes of h and t, and its output is the probability distribution of the one-hot codes of l. One-hot code is a sequence of bits for representing entities. For example, the following vector of length n (whose i-th bit is 1 and others are 0) is the representation of i-th entity among n entities.

$$(0\ 0\ \dots\ 0\ 1\ 0\ \dots\ 0) \tag{1}$$

entity_voc and *relation_voc* are the numbers of entities and relations, respectively. *entity_dim* and *relation_dim* are the dimensions of weight matrices.

Embedding is the transformation from RDF entities to their vector representations. The length of the transformed vector is called embedding dimension.

There are five weight matrices in RDFDNN: *entity_embedding*, *tanh*1, *concat*, *tanh*2, and *softmax*. *tanh*1 and *tanh*2 are the weight matrices for activation by tanh function, and *softmax* is the weight matrix for activation by softmax function. Concat is the composition of the embeddings of *h* and *t*. We employ simple concatenation of two embedding vectors for the concat. *entity_embedding* is the weight matrix for transforming an entity to its embedding. L2 regularization is used for the weight matrices of *entity_embedding*, *tanh*1, *tanh*2, and *softmax* in order to suppress overfitting.

Since the output of RDFDNN is the probability distribution of one-hot representation of relation *l*, the following cross entropy is used as the objective function for training RDFDNN:

$$E = - \sum_{(h,t,l) \in S} \sum_{k \in relation\_voc} l_k log P(h,t)_k, \tag{2}$$

where S is the set of triples in training data, $P(h,t)$ the output of RDFDNN when h and t are given as its inputs, k is the integer index that satisfies $0 \leq k < relation\_voc$. As the optimizer of the above objective function, Adam [8] is used.

3 Previous Methods for Predicting Relations

3.1 TransE

TransE [1] embeds both entities and relations in the same vector space. Based on vector operations of entities and relations, TransE predicts t from given h and l, and predicts l from h and t. It generates the vector space that satisfies the following equation:

$$d(h + l, t) = 0, \tag{3}$$

where d is the function of Euclidean distance between two given vectors.

TransE obtains a vector representation of entities and relations by minimizing the following objective function L by Gradient descent

$$L = \sum_{(h,l,t) \in S} \sum_{(h',l,t') \in S'} max(\gamma + d(h + l, t) - d(h' + l, t'), 0), \tag{4}$$

where γ is the margin for training, S is the set of triples in the dataset, S' is the set of wrong triples, E is the set of entities, and $S'_{(h,l,t)}$ is defined as follows:

$$S'_{(h,l,t)} = \{(h',l,t)|h' \in E\} \cap \{(h,l,t')|t' \in E\}. \tag{5}$$

3.2 TransR

TransR [10] is the extension of TransE, and it has the ability to learn 1-to-N relations, which is not possible for TransE. 1-to-N relation means that there are more than one ts for a given pair of h and l, such as (John, likes, pizza) and (John, likes, hamburger). In the case of TransE, learning 1-to-N relations is not possible because there is only one vector that satisfies $d(h + l, t) = 0$. In the above example, both pizza and hamburger are represented as the same vector, which is the problem of TransE.

In the case of TransR, h and t are mapped by means of the transformation matrix M_l which is unique to l and then vector operation is performed in order to avoid the above problem. TransR generates a vector space that satisfies the following equation:

$$d(hM_l + l, tM_l) = 0, \tag{6}$$

where M_l is the transformation matrix corresponding to relation l. TransR accepts vector representations of the entities obtained by TransE as its initial values, and it minimizes the following objective function L by Gradient descent in order to obtain vectors and matrices corresponding each relation:

$$L = \sum_{(h,l,t)\in S} \sum_{(h',l,t')\in S'} max(\gamma + d(h_l + l, t_l) - d(h'M_l + l, t'M_l), 0), \tag{7}$$

where $h_l = hM_l$ and $t_l = tM_l$.

4 Evaluation

4.1 Dataset

In our experiments, we have used the FB15k and WN18, which are the samples of the following two datasets. Details of FB15k and WN18 are shown in Table 1. The datasets are the same as the ones used in the experiments of previous research [1,10]. Original datasets of FB15k and WN18 are as follows:

Freebase [2]
   a large collaborative online knowledge base
Wordnet [11]
   a large lexical database of English

4.2 Criteria for Evaluation

We have implemented RDFDNN using keras and TensorFlow. Keras (https://keras.io) is a Python-based library executable on TensorFlow and Theano. Training of DNN by keras is done using CuDNN library on GPU. We use Python, keras and TensorFlow for the implementation. The CPU used in our experiments is Intel Xeon CPU E5-2609, and GPU is GeForce GTX 1080.

Table 1. Details of FB15k and WN18

	FB15k	WN18
Original data	Freebase	Wordnet
Number of entities (entity_voc)	14,951	40,943
Number of relations (relation_voc)	1,345	18
Number of triples for training	483,142	141,442
Number of triples for testing	59,071	5,000

We evaluated the results by *top-k accuracy*. After 10 times of training, h and t of a triple in the test data are given to RDFDNN as input, and its output l is evaluated by *top-k accuracy*, whose value is one if the correct answer is included in top-k plausible outputs, and is zero otherwise. This evaluation is done using all test data and results are averaged.

For the comparison of accuracy with previous methods, we set the parameters as $(entity\_dim, relation\_dim) = (30, 30)$ for FB15k and WN18. For failure analysis, we set the parameter as $(entity\_dim, relation\_dim) = (30, 30)$ for FB15k. For the experiments of embedding dimension and accuracy, parameters $entity\_dim$ and $relation\_dim$ are set as each of 2, 4, 6, 8, 10 for FB15k. For the experiments of relations between embedded dimension and computational time, $entity\_dim$ is set to 60, 120, 180, and 240, and $relation\_dim$ is set to 20, 40, 60, and 80 for FB15k.

4.3 Setting for Comparison

We have compared RDFDNN with TransE and TransR implemented by previous approach [10]. For TransE, the learning rate is set to 0.01, γ is set to 1, and embedding dimensions are set to 50 for FB15k, and 100 for WN18, respectively. For TransR, the learning rate is set to 0.001, γ is set to 1, and embedding dimensions are set to 50 for FB15k, and 100 for WN18, respectively.

When h and t are given, TransE computes $d(t - h, l)$ for all possible relations and selects the relation l of its minimum value as its prediction. This is because the vector space satisfying $d(t - h, l) = 0$ is generated in TransE, so the relation l that takes the minimum value of $d(t - h, l)$ for given h and t is expected to constitute a valid triple (h, l, t) rather than other relations.

When h and t are given, TransR computes $d(tM_l - hM_l, l)$ for all possible relations and select the relation l of its minimum value as its prediction. This is because the vector space satisfying $d(tM_l - hM_l, l) = 0$ is generated in TransR, so the relation l that takes the minimum value of $d(tM_l - hM_l, l)$ for given h and t is expected to constitute valid triple (h, l, t) rather than other relations.

5 Comparison with Previous Methods

For the dataset FB15k, we set parameters as $(entity\_dim, relation\_dim) = (30, 30)$ and compare the accuracy of RDFDNN with previous methods. For the dataset WN18, we set parameters as $(entity\_dim, relation\_dim) = (30, 30)$ and compare the accuracy of RDFDNN with previous methods.

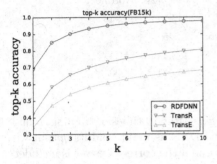

Fig. 2. Top-k accuracy (FB15k)   **Fig. 3.** Top-k accuracy (WN18)

Figures 2 and 3 are the results of comparison with the FB15k and WN18 datasets, respectively. The X-axis is k, and the Y-axis is *top-k accuracy*. For RDFDNN, we set parameters as $(entity\_dim, relation\_dim) = (30, 30)$ because its accuracy is the best when these values are used. As shown in both figures, RDFDNN is more accurate than TransE and TransR in both datasets. The results with FB15k dataset are a clear victory for RDFDNN. In the following discussion, we will discuss the results with FB15k data. The reason for the clear victory is that the number of relations in FB15k (1,345) is much higher than that in WN18 (18). Prediction of relations is harder when the number of relations is much higher.

6   Failure Analysis

Failure analysis is done in the experiments with FB15k when parameters are set as $(entity\_dim, relation\_dim) = (30, 30)$. RDFDNN's failed predictions can be classified to the following four categories:

- A: deceived by majority cases
- B: too abstract/too concrete
- C: structurally similar
- D: complete failure

For this failure analysis, parameters are set as $(entity\_dim, relation\_dim) = (30, 30)$ and 100 triples of RDFDNN failures are randomly sampled. Then the triples are manually evaluated and classified into the above four categories in order to obtain the results in Table 2.

As shown in Table 2, the most frequent failure is type A. As an example of type A, RDFDNN's prediction of relation between "Leslie Dilley" and "Raiders of the Lost Ark" is "performer", while its correct answer is "art director". This

Table 2. Types and the number of failed predictions

Type	Number of failures
A	<u>49</u>
B	14
C	5
D	32

is because the relation "performer" is the most frequent one for the relation between people and movies. The second most frequent failure is type D, complete failure. One of the examples is the prediction of the relation between "Iron Man" and "Stan Lee". The correct answer should be "creator", but the prediction by RDFDNN was "cause of death". The third most frequent failure is type B, too abstract or too concrete compared with correct answers. As an example of this type, RDFDNN predicts the relation between "Park Chu-yong" and "South Korea" as "citizenship", while its correct answer is "Olympic representative". The least frequent failure is type C, but this failure means that RDFDNN recognizes structural similarity between relations. As an example of this type, RDFDNN predicts the relation between "Washington Wizards" and "Michael Jordan" as "belonging states", while its correct answer is "team member".

7 Embedding Dimension and Prediction Accuracy

For the dataset FB15k, we set parameters *entity_dim* and *relation_dim* as each of 2, 4, 6, 8, 10, and observed the *top-k accuracy* of RDFDNN.

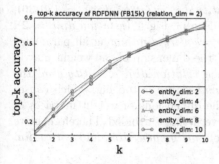

Fig. 4. top-k accuracy of RDFDNN (FB15k) (relation_dim = 2)

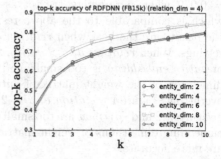

Fig. 5. top-k accuracy of RDFDNN (FB15k) (relation_dim = 4)

Figures 4, 5, 6, 7, and 8 are the results when *entity_dim* and *relation_dim* are set to each of 2, 4, 6, 8, 10, respectively. The X-axis is k, and the Y-axis is *top-k accuracy*. Results of the same *relation_dim* with five different

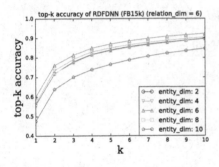

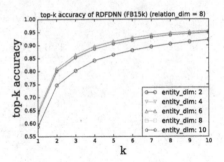

Fig. 6. top-k accuracy of RDFDNN (FB15k) (relation_dim = 6)

Fig. 7. top-k accuracy of RDFDNN (FB15k) (relation_dim = 8)

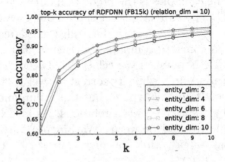

Fig. 8. top-k accuracy of RDFDNN (FB15k) (relation_dim = 10)

values of *entity_dim* are drawn in each figure. The best accuracy is obtained in Fig. 8 when parameters are set as $(entity\_dim, relation\_dim) = (10, 10)$, and its *top*-10 *accuracy* is 0.963. The best result in Sect. 5 is *top*-10 *accuracy* = 0.979 when parameters are set as $(entity\_dim, relation\_dim) = (30, 30)$, which is comparable to the above result. Except Fig. 4 (*relation_dim* = 2), the results are the best when *relation_dim* = *entity_dim* among all parameter settings. When *relation_dim* > *entity_dim*, the dimension of the weight matrix of *entity_embedding* is too small, and when *relation_dim* < *entity_dim*, the dimension of the weight matrix of *entity_embedding* is too big, which causes overfitting. Figure 4 (*relation_dim* = 2), the dimensions of weight matrices of *activation_2* and *softmax* are too small so overfitting is avoided. Therefore, more embedding dimensions of weight matrices of *entity_embedding* and *entity_dim* are more accurate.

Figure 9 aggregates all the results of Figs. 4, 5, 6, 7, and 8. The X-axis is k, and the Y-axis is *top-k accuracy*. Results with the same *relation_dim* are drawn with the same color, so five curves are drawn in each color. The difference of *top-k accuracy* with different *entity_dim* is 0.1 at most, which are quite small compared with the difference with different *relation_dim* values. In Fig. 9, curves of the same color (results with the same *relation_dim* value) are almost the same. *relation_dim* is more important for the accuracy of RDFDNN than *entity_dim*.

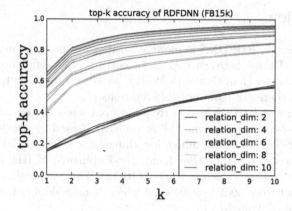

Fig. 9. top-k accuracy of RDFDNN (FB15k)

8 Embedding Dimension and Computational Time

For the dataset FB15k, we set *entity_dim* to 60, 120, 180, and 240, and *relation_dim* as 20, 40, 60, 80, and observed the computational time of RDFDNN.

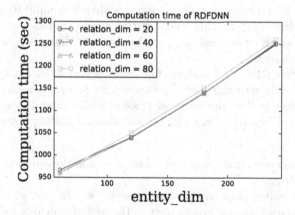

Fig. 10. Computational time of RDFDNN for different embedding dimensions

Figure 10 shows the computational times of RDFDNN for different embedding dimensions. The X-axis is *entity_dim*, and the Y-axis is the computational time (seconds). As shown in the figure, the value of *relation_dim* is not relevant to the computational time of RDFDNN. Only the value of *entity_dim* is relevant to the computational time. As shown in Table 1, *entity_voc* >> *relation_voc* is true in our experiments, which is the reason that *entity_dim* is relevant to the computational time of RDFDNN.

9   Discussion

As shown in Sect. 5, RDFDNN is more accurate than previous methods for the prediction of relations between two given entities. The difference of accuracy with FB15k is bigger than that with WN18, so we can conclude that prediction is harder when there are more possible relations.

The accuracy of RDFDNN is fairly good even when the embedding dimension is only one-fifth of the embedding dimension used in previous methods. In the case of TransR, the embedding dimension is set to 50 and its *top-k accuracy* is 0.808. On the other hand, *top-k accuracy* of RDFDNN is 0.963 even when $(entity\_dim, relation\_dim) = (10, 10)$. This means that the accuracy of RDFDNN is better than TransR even when its embedding dimension is only one-fifth of that of TransR.

As shown in Sect. 6, RDFDNN is more accurate when $relation\_dim$ is bigger, while the value of $entity\_dim$ is irrelevant to its accuracy. If $entity\_dim$ is bigger than $relation\_dim$, accuracy is not good because of overfitting. If $entity\_dim$ is smaller than $relation\_dim$, accuracy is not good because the dimension of the DNN weight matrix is not enough. Therefore, the values of $relation\_dim$ and $entity\_dim$ should be the same as initial setting.

As shown in Sect. 7, computational time of RDFDNN depends on $entity\_dim$, not $relation\_dim$, which is contrastive to the result in Sect. 6 that the accuracy depends on $relation\_dim$. Therefore, if we keep $entity\_dim$ small and make $relation\_dim$ bigger, better accuracy with less computational time will be achieved. However, in this case, $entity\_dim$ is smaller compared with $relation\_dim$, which causes less accuracy because the dimension of DNN weight matrix is not enough.

To summarize, RDFDNN achieves high accuracy with less embedding dimension with the following procedure. The reason for setting parameters as halves of previous values is that the range of possible embedding dimensions is fairly wide, so repeated bipartitioning will be desirable for finding better parameters with less trials.

1. Set the parameters $entity\_dim$ and $relation\_dim$ as those of previous methods as initial setting.
2. Set them as halves of previous values, keeping $entity\_dim = relation\_dim$.
3. Fix $relation\_dim$ and set $entity\_dim$ as the half of previous value.

10   Conclusion

In this paper, we propose RDFDNN for predicting relations of RDF from two given entities. RDFDNN is more accurate compared with previous methods (TransE and TransR). The following are the characteristics of RDFDNN.

– Bigger $relation\_dim$ for better accuracy
– Smaller $entity\_dim$ for less computational time

– Even when RDFDNN failed, more than half of its failed prediction are valid in some sense

In addition to TransE and TransR, there are some other related approaches [5,14,15]. The weaknesses of RDFDNN are as follows: (1) prediction of t from given h and l is not easy for RDFDNN, while it is possible for TransE and TransR. This is because RDFDNN cannot obtain embedded representation of relations, and (2) RDFDNN always predicts relations even when two given entities are completely irrelevant. These are left for our future work.

Acknowledgement. This work was supported by Tokyo Tech - Fuji Xerox Cooperative Research (Project Code KY260195), JSPS Grant-in-Aid for Scientific Research (B) (Grant Number 17H01785) and JST CREST (Grant Number JPMJCR1687).

References

1. Bordes, A., Usunier, N., Garcia-Duran, A., Weston, J., Yakhnenko, O.: Translating embeddings for modeling multi-relational data. Part Adv. Neural Inform. Process. Syst. **26**, 2787–2795 (2013)
2. Bollacker, K., Evans, C., Paritosh, P., Sturge, T., Taylor, J.: Freebase: a collaboratively created graph database for structuring human knowledge. In: Proceedings of the 2008 ACM SIGMOD International Conference on Management of Data (SIGMOD 2008), pp. 1247–1250 (2008)
3. Google, "Freebase Data Dumps". https://developers.google.com/freebase/data
4. Google, "Google Knowledge Graph Search API - Google Developers". https://developers.google.com/knowledge-graph/
5. Guo, S., Ding, B., Wang, Q., Wang, L., Wang, B.: Knowledge base completion via rule-enhanced relational learning. In: Chen, H., Ji, H., Sun, L., Wang, H., Qian, T., Ruan, T. (eds.) CCKS 2016. CCIS, vol. 650, pp. 219–227. Springer, Singapore (2016). https://doi.org/10.1007/978-981-10-3168-7_22
6. Hinton, G.E., Osindero, S., Teh, Y.-W.: A fast learning algorithm for deep belief nets. Neural Comput. **18**(7), 1527–1554 (2006)
7. Kavalec, M., Svatek, V.: A Study on automated relation labelling in ontology learning. In: Ontology Learning from Text: Methods, Evaluation and Applications. IOS Press, Amsterdam (2003)
8. Kingma, D., Ba, J.: Adam: a method for stochastic optimization. In: International Conference for Learning Representations, Published as a Conference Paper at the 3rd International Conference for Learning Representations, San Diego (2015)
9. Lassila, O., Swick, R.R.: Resource Description Framework (RDF) Model and Syntax Specification. https://www.w3.org/TR/1999/REC-rdf-syntax-19990222/
10. Lin, Y., Liu, Z., Sun, M., Liu, Y., Zhu, X.: Learning entity and relation embeddings for knowledge graph completion. In: Twenty-Ninth AAAI Conference on Artificial Intelligence, pp. 2181–2187 (2015)
11. Miller, G.A.: WordNet: a lexical database for English. Commun. ACM **38**(11), 39–41 (1995)
12. Nickel, M., Tresp, V., Kriegel, H.-P.: A Three-Way model for collective learning on Multi-Relational data. In: Proceedings of the 28th International Conference on Machine Learning, ICML 2011, Bellevue, WA, USA, pp. 809–816 (2011)

13. Russakovsky, O., Deng, J., Hao, S., Krause, J., Satheesh, S., Ma, S., Huang, Z., Karpathy, A., Khosla, A., Bernstein, M., Berg, A.C., Fei-Fei, L.: ImageNet large scale visual recognition challenge. Int. J. Comput. Vision **115**(3), 211–252 (2015)
14. Wang, Q., Wang, B., Guo, L.: Knowledge base completion using embeddings and rules. In: Proceedings of the 24th International Conference on Artificial Intelligence (IJCAI 2015), pp. 1859–1865 (2015)
15. Wang, Q., Liu, J., Luo, Y., Wang, B., Lin, C.-Y.: Knowledge base completion via coupled path ranking. In: Proceedings of the 54th Annual Meeting of the Association for Computational Linguistics (ACL), pp. 1308–1318 (2016)
16. Weichselbraun, A., Wohlgenannt, G., Scharl, A.: Refining non-taxonomic relation labels with external structured data to support ontology learning. Data Knowl. Eng. **69**(8), 763–778 (2010)

ELMDist: A Vector Space Model with Words and MusicBrainz Entities

Luis Espinosa-Anke[1]([⊠]), Sergio Oramas[2], Horacio Saggion[1], and Xavier Serra[2]

[1] TALN Natural Language Processing Group,
Universitat Pompeu Fabra, Barcelona, Spain
luis.espinosa83@gmail.com
[2] Music Technology Group, Universitat Pompeu Fabra, Barcelona, Spain

Abstract. Music consumption habits as well as the Music market have changed dramatically due to the increasing popularity of digital audio and streaming services. Today, users are closer than ever to a vast number of songs, albums, artists and bands. However, the challenge remains in how to make sense of all the data available in the Music domain, and how current state of the art in Natural Language Processing and semantic technologies can contribute in Music Information Retrieval areas such as music recommendation, artist similarity or automatic playlist generation. In this paper, we present and evaluate a distributional sense-based embeddings model in the music domain, which can be easily used for these tasks, as well as a device for improving artist or album clustering. The model is trained on a disambiguated corpus linked to the MusicBrainz musical Knowledge Base, and following current knowledge-based approaches to sense-level embeddings, entity-related vectors are provided *à la* WordNet, concatenating the id of the entity and its mention. The model is evaluated both intrinsically and extrinsically in a supervised entity typing task, and released for the use and scrutiny of the community.

1 Introduction

One of the earliest avenues for improvement identified in the otherwise powerful word embeddings [1,2] is that they tend to "conflate" (or agglutinate) in one vector the semantic representation of several meanings of a word or phrase [3]. In the last years, however, we have witnessed two parallel directions for alleviating this weakness. On one hand, what we could call *unsupervised approaches*, which usually cluster contexts in which a word appears and then obtain a representation of each cluster [4–6]. On the other hand, the so-called *knowledge-based approaches* exploit predefined semantic representations encoded in lexicons or Knowledge Bases (KBs) such as WordNet [7] or BabelNet [8]. Prominent examples include, *inter alia*, [9–13]. While these approaches have shown competitive results in some of the classic tasks in Natural Language Processing (NLP) like semantic similarity, whether these models would be truly helpful in restricted domains of knowledge remains an open question. In fact, they are inherently flawed by

© Springer International Publishing AG 2017
E. Blomqvist et al. (Eds.): ESWC 2017 Satellite Events, LNCS 10577, pp. 355–366, 2017.
https://doi.org/10.1007/978-3-319-70407-4_44

the natural incapability of current KBs and semantic lexicons to capture *all the knowledge existing out there*. While this is a problem theoretically addressed by the Open Information Extraction (OIE) paradigm [14–16], the truth is that current OIE systems are still too noisy and error-prone, and even approaches that have attempted to integrate them have had to deal with issues related with sparsity, redundancy and the lack of ontologization [17]. Another direction for improving *sense-level* vector representations in specific domains of knowledge is the construction and annotation of large domain corpora, and *transfer* the knowledge acquired from previously published (and highly successful) vector space modeling algorithms to a target domain. This is precisely the direction we adopt in this work.

In this paper, we present ELMDist[1] a *sense-level* embeddings model in the music domain, trained on a music-specific corpus of artist biographies, where musical entities have been automatically annotated with high precision against the musical KB MusicBrainz (MB) [18]. We evaluate this model in a twofold strategy. First, a qualitative evaluation of nearest neighbours to assess artist similarity. And second, a quantitative evaluation, in which we devise an *entity typing* strategy so that, for a given vector, we predict the probability of it being any of four of the most common entities in the music domain, namely `artist`, `album`, `song` and `record label`. Our results show a surprisingly good precision, especially considering the small size of the corpus, while coverage could be assumed to increase as additional corpora are incorporated to the model. We make available for the community a set of disambiguated pretrained vectors, as well as dumps of matrices trained to learn (`artist`, `album` and `record label`)-wise transformations.

2 Method

In this section, we first flesh out the different resources our approach consists of. First, we briefly summarize the approach followed to construct an automatic and fully disambiguated corpus in the music domain (Sect. 2.1). Second, we describe the linear transformation approach followed for assigning a music-specific type to any vector (Sect. 2.2). Finally, we provide evaluation results in Sect. 3.

2.1 Entity Linking in the Music Domain

While there is not a substantial work in applying current state of the art NLP systems in the music domain, this scenario seems to be gradually shifting, especially since exploitation of text mining techniques has proven to be useful for Music Information Retrieval (MIR) tasks such as artist similarity [19] or music recommendation [20,21]. One of the greatest challenges posed by the music domain for text understanding lies on the fact that musical entities show high variability, arguably higher than the regular entities with which evaluation is usually

---

[1] Available at https://bitbucket.org/luisespinosa/elmdist/.

concerned in Entity Recognition tasks, like Person, Location or Organization. Notable examples attempting Entity Linking (EL) (the task to assign to an entity mention its corresponding entry or uri in a predefined inventory) include the detection of music-related entities (e.g. songs or bands) on informal text [22] or applying Hidden Markov Models for discovering musical entities in Chinese corpora [23].

In this work, we use as training data an extended version of the ELMD corpus [24], which stems from the collection of biographies acquired from Last.fm[2]. The original ELMD corpus contains annotations mapped between inner last.fm links and their corresponding DBpedia URI thanks to the voting algorithm described in [24]. However, the whole motivation for this work is to model musical entities against a music-specific KB so that the coverage of entities is higher. Hence, we leverage ELMD2[3], an extension of the original annotated corpus, and take advantage of the fact that a large portion of last.fm annotations have a direct mapping to MB via its API. Furthermore, existing annotations in every document are propagated, assuming they appear in a one-sense-per-discourse fashion. For example, if the text span *The Beatles* is marked as an annotation in the first sentence of a document, and it appears again in the second sentence, but there is no annotation associated, an annotation is added. Finally, we look for mentions of the entity that constitutes the main theme of the biography, and annotate all its mentions within the biography, assuming unambiguity. The number of annotations and distinct entities are reported in Table 1. Note that MB has a coverage of 93.6% over all the annotations, and 91.1% over all distinct entities.

Table 1. Statistics of the ELMD2 corpus from which the ELMDist vector space model is derived. Annotations refers to all distinct mentions or apparitions of an entity of its corresponding type, whereas the Entities column refers to the number of distinct entities of each type.

	Annotations	Entities
All	144,593	63,902
Artist	112,524	39,131
Album	18,701	15,064
Song	9,203	7,832
Label	4,165	1,875

2.2   Training a Sense-Level Embeddings Model

Taking advantage of the mapping existing in ELMD between last.fm links and MB ids (mbids), we follow [25,26] and, for each entity mention in the ELMD corpus, we concatenate its mention with its corresponding mbid, so that this

---

[2] http://last.fm.
[3] Described in http://mtg.upf.edu/download/datasets/elmd.

"sense" (in an analogy with WordNet) is assigned one single vector. For instance, given the input sentence:

> *The Tools of the Trade* was never distributed outside the US, and yet again *Nocturnal Breed* would have to look for other business interests.

the resulting disambiguated concepts would result in (note that we also include the *type* of each entity)[4]

the_tools_of_the_trade_album_mbid:fb410e8f was never distributed outside the US, and yet again **nocturnal_breed_artist_mbid:f267a 071bb23** would have to look for other business interests.

We use the *gensim*[5] implementation of *word2vec* [27], and train a CBOW model of 300 dimensional vectors, filtering out tokens with a frequency less than 3, with a context window of 5 tokens, and hierarchical softmax (usually a better performing algorithm for infrequent words). Due to the nature of the corpus, we consider each disambiguated entity mention as a single token, and hence assign it a unique vector.

3   Model Evaluation

In this section, we provide the reader with the result of two experiments where we assess the fitness of the model, first, for artist similarity, and second, for named entity typing.

3.1   Entity Similarity

Artist similarity is an important task in MIR. Knowing, for instance, similar artists to the band ZZ Top (e.g. bands belonging to the jazz-rock genre), allows for a better music recommendation and playlist suggestion, and ultimately leads to a better user experience. While artist similarity has been approached looking at score, acoustic or even cultural features [28], text-based approaches have also played an important role in this task. For instance, by computing co-occurrences of artist names [29], leveraging search engines result counts [30] or introducing further linguistic analysis in the form of ngram, part of speech and TFIDF information [31].

---

[4] For readability purposes, we have shortened the mbid of the annotated entities.
[5] https://radimrehurek.com/gensim/models/word2vec.html.

Manual Evaluation. In the first experiment, we asked 2 human judges to assess whether, given an input artist, the disambiguated nearest neighbours in the vector space were *similar*[6]. We randomly sampled 10 instances of each type. Note that judging whether two songs are similar is much easier than judging whether two record labels are similar, and for the latter, we suggested that the judges looked at whether these record labels had a preference for a certain music genre, or if they were based (or originated) in the same geographical location. Then, for each test instance, we retrieved the top 3 entities returned by cosine distance. This results in 40 evaluation instances for each of the considered music types.

Results, shown in Table 2, show that the model clusters together not only vectors of the same type, but also sharing some kind of relationship, as assessed by the judges. Still, the outcome of this experiment is affected by subjectivity. For instance, given one of the randomly sampled instances for evaluation was the record label Universal Records, and evaluators were given as nearest neighbors other record labels which shared some features (e.g. also based in Paris or London), but which had little relationship from the musical standpoint. We show the behaviour of the model in Table 3, where the difference between the quality of *artist* and *record label* vectors can be clearly seen, as opposed to the quality of songs and albums. We plan to further investigate this notorious discrepancy.

Table 2. Average precision for the entity similarity task

artist	album	r.label
48%	20%	44%

We found surprisingly high results in the record label entity, despite the subjective nature of this classification, where almost half of the nearest neighbours were *similar* record labels to the input entity. However, we did encounter (also surprsingly) poor results in the song entity, where only 2 out of every 10 cases were deemed similar by the judges. There was an average observed agreement of 80% between both judges. Finally, in *all* cases the nearest neighbours to the validation album vectors we used were songs, and since we asked our judges to only consider similarity for entities of the same type (i.e., for albums, only albums), results for this entity type are not reported.

Automatic Evaluation. The literature in distributional semantics has in general explored whether *co-hyponymy*, the property of sharing the same hypernym, can be considered as a measure or indicator of similarity. Since the ELMDist vectors include type information, we conduct a similar experiment as the manual

---

[6] Since this judgement is, in the end, a subjective decision, we did not ask them to look at data such as listening habits.

Table 3. Examples of well known input entities for each type (in italics), showcasing the type of nearest neighbours that ELMDIST provides.

artist	album
Nirvana	*Heaven and Hell (Black Sabbath)*
Metallica	Shaman (Brazilian Progressive Rock Band)
Kinks	The Boys Next Door (Nick Cave Album)
Tiga	changing
NOFX	shortening
Megadeth	shortened
song	record label
Stand By Me (Ben E. King)	*London Records*
Gimme Little Sign (Brenton Wood)	Atlantic Records
doble	Epic Records
petite	Merge Records
zur	Elektra Records
rad	Universal Records

evaluation described in Sect. 3.1. In this case, for all vectors of any of the available types, we collect their five closest vectors by cosine score and assess their similarity. Without human intervention, we follow a coarse-grained classification in which we consider similar two vectors sharing the same type. We report two types of precision-wise evaluation: first, considering all neighbouring vectors as candidates (all vecs.), and second, considering only the disambiguated vectors (disambig.) as candidates (Table 4). In both cases, it is interesting to note the better performance of this approach for the artist and record label types. This is likely due to the fact that, in the former case, there are many more artist entities and therefore there is extensive corpus-based evidence in the form of word context to generate reliable representations. In the latter case, however, the better performance seems to be due to the less variability in how record labels are referred to in last.fm biographies, with less linguistic variability and therefore *better* vectors with substantially less data. Further discussion about the case of the record label type is provided in Sect. 3.2.

3.2 Named Entity Typing

Hypernymy is an important semantic relation that has to be accounted for in automatic text understanding. For instance, knowing that Tom Cruise is an actor can help a question answering system answer the question "which actors are involved in Scientology?" [32]. Similarly, in the music domain it is important to detect mentions of music entities such as bands or albums. This can be useful for automatically inserting new entries in existing KBs, or for improving any of the MIR tasks we have mentioned earlier.

Table 4. Automatic evaluation of the similarity experiment considering co-hyponymy as criterion.

	all vecs.	disambig.
artist	0.53	0.96
album	0.19	0.41
song	0.13	0.38
label	0.31	0.62

We thus proceed to evaluate our model in the task of automatic entity *typing* (restricting the number of available types to ARTIST, ALBUM, SONG and RECORD LABEL). The task consists in, given a *text-level* (non-disambiguated) input entity, predict its most likely musical type. To this end, we follow [33], who showed that semantically related pairs of linguistic items (x, y) could be modeled in terms of a linear transformation between them, having both items existing in two different analogous spaces. The original work by [33] used this intuition for modeling a transformation between English and Spanish (i.e., for word-level machine translation). This has been further explored for constructing semantic hierarchies in Chinese [34], Twitter language normalization [35], or for collocation discovery [36].

We follow this line of research, and construct an *entity matrix* $\mathbf{E} = [\boldsymbol{x}_1 \ldots \boldsymbol{x}_n]$ and a *music type matrix* $\mathbf{T} = [\boldsymbol{y}_1 \ldots \boldsymbol{y}_n]$, where $\mathbf{E}$ is our newly trained model, and $\mathbf{T}$ is the pretrained word2vec vectors on the Google News corpus[7]. These matrices are constructed as follows. We randomly sample musical entities from our musical model, and depending on their type (field *category* in the annotated corpus), we assign them a *set of prototypical words* for each type[8]. For instance, if we found the album *Nevermind* (by Nirvana), we would train with pairs such as $(Nevermind_e, album_t)$, $(Nevermind_e, release_t)$, or $(Nevermind_e, compact\_disc_t)$, where $e, t \in E, T$. As for the (exclusive) train-test split, we used at most 2k training pairs for each music type (although in the case of song these were 687 due to lack of enough song entities in the corpus), and evaluated on 500 entities, although again, the test size for the song type was smaller (229).

Then, under the intuition that there exists a linear function that *approaches* an unseen entity in our music model E to its most likely music type in the Google News corpus T, i.e., $\lambda(E) \approx T$, we train a linear regression model such that it minimizes

$$\min_{\lambda} \sum_{i=1}^{|E|} \|\lambda(e_i) - t_i\|^2 \qquad (1)$$

---

[7] https://code.google.com/archive/p/word2vec/.
[8] These were collected manually by inspecting nearest neighbours to the different types considered in the Google News model.

We train four regression models, one for each of the music types considered. Then, evaluation consists of, given an input entity's *text string*, applying each of the four models and assess which of them *approaches* the associated entity's type vector the closest, and then assessing correctness. Then, for each test sample, the result is the ranked position among four possible candidates in which the correct type was placed. For example, for the input string $s = $ 'let it be'[9] (type song), we rank the closest vectors in T of $\lambda(s)$ by cosine distance, and set the position of the correct type to 1. If in this specific case, the song function yields the *second* most similar vector to 'let it be', the result is $[0, 1, 0, 0]$.

We evaluate the result in terms of Mean Reciprocal Rank (see [37] for a description of this and other Information Retrieval metrics in a Natural Language Processing setting), a metric which takes into account the position of the first valid candidate in a ranked list of options. Formally,

$$ \text{MRR} = \frac{1}{|Q|} \sum_{i=1}^{|Q|} \frac{1}{rank_i} $$

where Q is a sample of experiment runs and $rank_i$ refers to the rank position of the *first* relevant outcome for the ith run.

Our results, provided in Table 5, computed over a sample of 100 entities per type, suggest that this is a promising approach, especially compared with approaches for similar tasks (hypernym discovery), which used much more training data coming from a wide range of resources such as Wikidata and the web [38]. Particularly encouraging are the results in the record labels entity type, although the fact that most record labels have words like 'label' or 'records' (e.g. *Epitaph Records*) most likely is being helpful to the model.

Table 5. Mean Reciprocal Rank for the entity typing task

artist	album	song	r.label
0.59	0.52	0.54	0.64

Visualizing *typed* vectors. The ELMDist embeddings are trained over a music-specific corpus, and clustered by type. While theoretically the type similarity should already provide some kind of semantic compactness or community to embeddings of the same type, this might not be necessarily true due to the different contexts in which each musical entity may occur. In a purely qualitative way we intend to explore whether the *typing function* described above affects equally all musical types. In the visualization provided in Fig. 1, we plot in red a sample of the original ELMDist vectors of the same type, and in green the same vectors (with labels for some of them for illustrative purposes) after combining them with the regression model. It can be clearly seen that artist and album

---

[9] For multiword entities, we average the corresponding vectors of each token.

vectors are scattered over the original space, which indicates that there is little corpus-based evidence for all artist names, for example, to be represented similarly. However, after training our typing function, artist names tend to cluster together, and while the semantics of these clusters remains to be explored in future work, it points towards an interesting "entity clustering" problem that can be approached similarly as in our proposed method. This phenomenon also applies to album names, although in this case there is clearly only one community. On the opposite side, songs and record labels seem to not benefit as much from the typing procedure, which may be due to the fact that their shared contexts are much more similar than in the other two entities. Another reason for the lackluster clustering in these two types is the much lower number of training pairs (due simply to ELMD2 having less entities of these types).

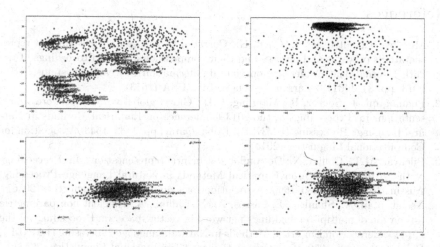

Fig. 1. Artist (top left), album (top right), song (bottom left) and record label (bottom right) embeddings before typing (red) and afterwards (green). (Color figure online)

4   Conclusion and Future Work

In this paper, we have described and evaluated a novel vector space model at the *sense* level in the music domain. It comes from running the word2vec algorithm over an automatically disambiguated collection of music texts collected from last.fm, where music entities are automatically annotated leveraging the degree of agreement between three well-known Entity Linking and Word Sense Disambiguation systems. The model is evaluated qualitatively, in terms of artist similarity, and quantitatively, in terms of its usefulness for musical entity typing.

We believe our results show a promising avenue of work, improving Music Information Retrieval with textual information. For future work, we would like to incorporate larger corpora, probably coming from heterogeneous resources, and exploit current neural architectures both for entity disambiguation and for typing. In addition, a mixed model that combines musical information (e.g. in the form of audio descriptors) as well as semantic information coming from text corpora, seems to be a promising and unexplored direction. Finally, it would be interesting to learn different embeddings for each musical entity type and evaluate these entity-specific models as compared with models containing all entities.

Acknowledgements. We would like to thank the anonymous reviewers for their very helpful comments and suggestions for improving the quality of the manuscript. We also acknowledge support from the Spanish Minmistry of Economy and Competitiveness under the Maria de Maeztu Units of Excellence Programme (MDM-2015-0502) and under the TUNER project (TIN2015-65308-C5-5-R, MINECO/FEDER, UE).

References

1. Mikolov, T., Sutskever, I., Chen, K., Corrado, G.S., Dean, J.: Distributed representations of words and phrases and their compositionality. In: Proceedings of the 26th International Conference on Neural Information Processing Systems, NIPS 2013, pp. 3111–3119. Curran Associates Inc., USA (2013)
2. Pennington, J., Socher, R., Manning, C.D.: Glove: global vectors for word representation. In: Proceedings of the 2014 Conference on Empirical Methods in Natural Language Processing (EMNLP), Doha, Qatar, pp. 1532–1543. Association for Computational Linguistics (2014)
3. Pilehvar, M.T., Collier, N.: De-conflated semantic representations. In: Proceedings of the 2016 Conference on Empirical Methods in Natural Language Processing, Austin, Texas, pp. 1680–1690. Association for Computational Linguistics (2016)
4. Neelakantan, A., Shankar, J., Passos, A., McCallum, A.: Efficient non-parametric estimation of multiple embeddings per word in vector space. In: Proceedings of the 2014 Conference on Empirical Methods in Natural Language Processing (EMNLP), Doha, Qatar, pp. 1059–1069. Association for Computational Linguistics (2014)
5. Tian, F., Dai, H., Bian, J., Gao, B., Zhang, R., Chen, E., Liu, T.-Y.: A probabilistic model for learning multi-prototype word embeddings. In: Proceedings of COLING 2014, the 25th International Conference on Computational Linguistics: Technical Papers, Dublin, Ireland, pp. 151–160. Dublin City University and Association for Computational Linguistics (2014)
6. Liu, Y., Liu, Z., Chua, T.-S., Sun, M.: Topical word embeddings. In: Proceedings of the Twenty-Ninth AAAI Conference on Artificial Intelligence, AAAI 2015, pp. 2418–2424. AAAI Press (2015)
7. Fellbaum, C.: WordNet, Wiley Online Library (1998)
8. Navigli, R., Ponzetto, S.P.: Babelnet: the automatic construction, evaluation and application of a wide-coverage multilingual semantic network. Artif. Intell. **193**, 217–250 (2012)
9. Jauhar, S.K., Dyer, C., Hovy, E.: Ontologically grounded multi-sense representation learning for semantic vector space models. In: Proceedings of the 2015 Conference of the North American Chapter of the Association for Computational Linguistics: Human Language Technologies, Denver, Colorado, pp. 683–693. Association for Computational Linguistics (2015)

10. Faruqui, M., Dodge, J., Jauhar, S.K., Dyer, C., Hovy, E., Smith, N.A.: Retro-fitting word vectors to semantic lexicons. In: Proceedings of the 2015 Conference of the North American Chapter of the Association for Computational Linguistics: Human Language Technologies, Denver, Colorado, pp. 1606–1615. Association for Computational Linguistics (2015)
11. Camacho-Collados, J., Pilehvar, M.T., Navigli, R.: NASARI: a novel approach to a semantically-aware representation of items. In: Proceedings of NAACL, pp. 567–577 (2015)
12. Bordes, A., Usunier, N., Garcia-Duran, A., Weston, J., Yakhnenko, O.: Translating embeddings for modeling multi-relational data. In: Burges, C.J.C., Bottou, L., Welling, M., Ghahramani, Z., Weinberger, K.Q. (eds.) Advances in Neural Information Processing Systems 26, pp. 2787–2795. Curran Associates Inc. (2013)
13. Pilehvar, M.T., Navigli, R.: From senses to texts: an all-in-one graph-based approach for measuring semantic similarity. Artif. Intell. **228**, 95–128 (2015)
14. Etzioni, O., Reiter, K., Soderland, S., Sammer, M., Turing Center: Lexical translation with application to image search on the web. Machine Translation Summit XI
15. Fader, A., Soderland, S., Etzioni, O.: Identifying relations for open information extraction. In: Proceedings of the Conference on Empirical Methods in Natural Language Processing, EMNLP 2011, Stroudsburg, PA, USA, pp. 1535–1545. Association for Computational Linguistics (2011)
16. Carlson, A., Betteridge, J., Kisiel, B., Settles, B., Hruschka Jr., E.R., Mitchell, T.M.: Toward an architecture for never-ending language learning. In: Proceedings of the Twenty-Fourth AAAI Conference on Artificial Intelligence, AAAI 2010, pp. 1306–1313. AAAI Press (2010)
17. Delli Bovi, C., Espinosa Anke, L., Navigli, R.: Knowledge base unification via sense embeddings and disambiguation. In: Proceedings of the 2015 Conference on Empirical Methods in Natural Language Processing, Lisbon, Portugal, pp. 726–736. Association for Computational Linguistics (2015)
18. Swartz, A.: Musicbrainz: a semantic web service. IEEE Intell. Syst. **17**(1), 76–77 (2002)
19. Oramas, S., Sordo, M., Espinosa-Anke, L., Serra, X.: A Semantic-based Approach for Artist Similarity. In: Proceedings of the International Society for Music Information Retrieval Conference, Málaga, Spain, pp. 100–106 (2015)
20. Sordo, M., Oramas, S., Espinosa-Anke, L.: Extracting relations from unstructured text sources for music recommendation. In: Biemann, C., Handschuh, S., Freitas, A., Meziane, F., Métais, E. (eds.) NLDB 2015. LNCS, vol. 9103, pp. 369–382. Springer, Cham (2015). doi:10.1007/978-3-319-19581-0_33
21. Oramas, S., Espinosa-Anke, L., Sordo, M., Saggion, H., Serra, X.: Information extraction for knowledge base construction in the music domain. Data Knowl. Eng. **106**, 70–83 (2016)
22. Gruhl, D., Nagarajan, M., Pieper, J., Robson, C., Sheth, A.: Context and domain knowledge enhanced entity spotting in informal text. In: Bernstein, A., Karger, D.R., Heath, T., Feigenbaum, L., Maynard, D., Motta, E., Thirunarayan, K. (eds.) ISWC 2009. LNCS, vol. 5823, pp. 260–276. Springer, Heidelberg (2009). doi:10.1007/978-3-642-04930-9_17
23. Zhang, X., Liu, Z., Qiu, H., Fu, Y.: A hybrid approach for chinese named entity recognition in music domain. In: 2009 Eighth IEEE International Conference on Dependable, Autonomic and Secure Computing, pp. 677–681 (2009)

24. Oramas, S., Espinosa-Anke, L., Sordo, M., Saggion, H., Serra, X.: ELMD: An automatically generated entity linking gold standard dataset in the music domain. In: Proceedings of the Tenth International Conference on Language Resources and Evaluation (LREC 2016) (2016)

25. Iacobacci, I., Pilehvar, M.T., Navigli, R.: Sensembed: learning sense embeddings for word and relational similarity. In: Proceedings of the 53rd Annual Meeting of the Association for Computational Linguistics and the 7th International Joint Conference on Natural Language Processing, vol. 1 Long Papers, Association for Computational Linguistics, Beijing, China, pp. 95–105 (2015)

26. Manicini, M., Camacho-Collados, J., Iacobacci, I., Navigli, R.: Embedding words and senses together via joint knowledge-enhanced training, arXiv prepring arXiv:1612.02703

27. Mikolov, T., Yih, W.-T., Zweig, G.: Linguistic regularities in continuous space word representations. In: HLT-NAACL 2013, pp. 746–751 (2013)

28. Ellis, D.P., Whitman, B., Berenzweig, A., Lawrence, S.: The quest for ground truth in musical artist similarity. In: ISMIR, Paris, France, pp. 170–177 (2002)

29. Cohen, W.W., Fan, W.: Web-collaborative filtering: recommending music by crawling the web. Comput. Netw. **33**(1), 685–698 (2000)

30. Schedl, M., Knees, P., Widmer, G.: A web-based approach to assessing artist similarity using co-occurrences. In: Proceedings of the Fourth International Workshop on Content-Based Multimedia Indexing (CBMI 2005) (2005)

31. Whitman, B., Lawrence, S.: Inferring descriptions and similarity for music from community metadata. In: ICMC 2002 (2002)

32. Shwartz, V., Goldberg, Y., Dagan, I.: Improving hypernymy detection with an integrated path-based and distributional method, pp. 2389–2398 (2016)

33. Mikolov, T., Le, Q.V., Sutskever, I.: Exploiting similarities among languages for machine translation, arXiv preprint arXiv:1309.4168

34. Fu, R., Guo, J., Qin, B., Che, W., Wang, H., Liu, T.: Learning semantic hierarchies via word embeddings. In: Proceedings of ACL, vol. 1, pp. 1199–1209. Association for Computational Linguistics (2014)

35. Tan, L., Zhang, H., Clarke, C., Smucker, M.: Lexical comparison between wikipedia and twitter corpora by using word embeddings. In: Proceedings of ACL (2), Beijing, China, pp. 657–661 (2015)

36. Rodrıguez-Fernández, S., Espinosa-Anke, L., Carlini, R., Wanner, L.: Semantics-driven recognition of collocations using word embeddings. In: Proceedings of the 54th Annual Meeting of the Association for Computational Linguistics (ACL): Short Papers, pp. 499–505 (2016)

37. Bian, J., Liu, Y., Agichtein, E., Zha, H.: Finding the right facts in the crowd: factoid question answering over social media. In: Proceedings of the 17th International Conference on World Wide Web, pp. 467–476. ACM (2008)

38. Espinosa Anke, L., Camacho-Collados, J., Delli Bovi, C., Saggion, H.: Supervised distributional hypernym discovery via domain adaptation. In: Proceedings of the 2016 Conference on Empirical Methods in Natural Language Processing, Austin, Texas, pp. 424–435. Association for Computational Linguistics (2016)

1st Workshop on Humanities in the SEmantic Web at ESWC 2016 (WHiSE 2016)

Linked Death—Representing, Publishing, and Using Second World War Death Records as Linked Open Data

Mikko Koho[✉], Eero Hyvönen, Erkki Heino, Jouni Tuominen,
Petri Leskinen, and Eetu Mäkelä

Semantic Computing Research Group (SeCo), Aalto University, Espoo, Finland
{mikko.koho,eero.hyvonen,erkki.heino,jouni.tuominen,petri.leskinen,
eetu.makela}@aalto.fi

Abstract. War history of the Second World War (WW2), humankind's largest disaster, is of great interest to both laymen and researchers. Most of us have ancestors and relatives who participated in the war, and in the worst case got killed. Researchers are eager to find out what actually happened then, and even more importantly why, so that future wars could perhaps be prevented. The darkest data of war history are casualty records—from such data we could perhaps learn most about the war. This paper presents a model and system for representing death records as linked data, so that (1) citizens could find out more easily what happened to their relatives during WW2 and (2) digital humanities (DH) researchers could (re)use the data easily for research.

1 Introduction

Lots of information about the WW2 is available on the web[1]. However, this information is typically meant for human consumption only. The underlying *data* is not available in machine-readable, i.e., "semantic" form for Digital Humanities research and use [3,5] and for end-user applications to utilize. By making war data more accessible our understanding of the reality of the war improves, which not only advances understanding of the past but also hopefully promotes peace in the future [6].

For the case of the First World War, the situation has started to change, with several projects publishing linked data on the web, such as Europeana Collections 1914–1918[2], 1914–1918 Online[3], WW1 Discovery[4], Out of the Trenches[5], CENDARI[6], Muninn[7], and WW1LOD [12]. A few works have used the linked

---

[1] http://ww2db.com, http://www.world-war-2.info, differentWikipedias, etc
[2] http://www.europeana-collections-1914-1918.eu
[3] http://www.1914-1918-online.net
[4] http://ww1.discovery.ac.uk
[5] http://www.canadiana.ca/en/pcdhn-lod/
[6] http://www.cendari.eu/research/first-world-war-studies/
[7] http://blog.muninn-project.org

© Springer International Publishing AG 2017
E. Blomqvist et al. (Eds.): ESWC 2017 Satellite Events, LNCS 10577, pp. 369–383, 2017.
https://doi.org/10.1007/978-3-319-70407-4_45

data approach to WW2 data as well, such as [1,2], the Open Memory Project[8], and WarSampo [6].

This paper discusses the publication and use of casualty (death) records as linked data, as one part of the larger WarSampo system. Here, a dataset of some 95,000 deaths in military action in the Finnish army is concerned. We first present the data, its modeling, the Linked Open Data (LOD) service, and interlinking the data with other WarSampo datasets. After this, two use case applications are presented: (1) analyzing the data for digital humanities research and (2) reassembling the biographical war history of individual soldiers and military units. The latter use case serves, e.g., laymen in trying to figure out what happened to their relatives in WW2. The WarSampo system[9] was published on Nov 27, 2015 and has had tens of thousands of end users indicating a large public interest in such applications.

2   Dataset, Data Model, and Data Service

Information about all known Finnish casualties of WW2 has been gathered in a relational database at the National Archives. This database contains 94,696 records of people that fought on the Finnish side, and died in 1939–1945 in the Winter War, the Continuation War, or in the Lapland War, or died of injuries obtained in those wars.

For use in the WarSampo project, the casualty database was first converted to CSV format, which was then converted to RDF format. Because the objective was to develop interactive applications directly on top of the large RDF dataset, it was important to keep the amount of RDF triples as low as possible without losing information and still linking the death records to ontological concepts. Thus, a simple data model was created for representing the data as linked data.

The data model is based on the CIDOC Conceptual Reference Model (CRM) vocabulary, which is designed for information exchange and integration of various cultural heritage information [4]. Each death record is represented as an instance of the Document class (crm:E31_Document) of CIDOC CRM.

A metadata schema was created that defines the properties used to describe each casualty with the information from the original database. The schema consists of OWL properties which have crm:E31_Document as the domain. A list of the properties and their rdfs:range constraints are shown in Table 1. The namespace prefixes used in this paper are:

: http://ldf.fi/schema/narc-menehtyneet1939-45/
crm: http://www.cidoc-crm.org/cidoc-crm/
skos: http://www.w3.org/2004/02/skos/core#
wat: http://ldf.fi/warsa/actors/actor_types/
wrank: http://ldf.fi/warsa/actors/ranks/

---

[8] http://www.bygle.net/wp-content/uploads/2015/04/Open-Memory-Project_3-1. pdf

[9] Including a semantic portal in use at http://sotasampo.fi and the underlying LOD SPARQL service at http://www.ldf.fi/dataset/warsa/

Table 1. Casualty metadata schema of all properties used for describing the death records.

Property description	Property name	Range
mother tongue	:aeidinkieli	:Aeidinkieli
occupation	:ammatti	xsd:string
principal abode	:asuinkunta	
first names	:etunimet	xsd:string
date of becoming wounded	:haavoittumisaika	xsd:date
municipality of becoming wounded	:haavoittumiskunta	
place of becoming wounded	:haavoittumispaikka	xsd:string
burial place	:hautapaikka	xsd:string
burial graveyard	:hautausmaa	:Hautausmaa
military unit	:joukko_osasto	xsd:string
military unit code	:joukko_osastokoodi	xsd:string
known military unit	:osasto	wat:MilitaryUnit
citizenship	:kansalaisuus	:Kansalaisuus
nationality at time of death	:kansallisuus	:Kansallisuus
date of becoming missing	:katoamisaika	xsd:date
municipality of becoming missing	:katoamiskunta	
place of becoming missing	:katoamispaikka	xsd:string
place of domicile	:kotikunta	
date of death	:kuolinaika	xsd:date
municipality of death	:kuolinkunta	
place of death	:kuolinpaikka	xsd:string
number of children	:lasten_lukumaeaerae	xsd:integer
perishing class	:menehtymisluokka	:Menehtymisluokka
marital status	:siviilisaeaety	:Siviilisaeaety
military rank	:sotilasarvo	wrank:Rank
last name	:sukunimi	xsd:string
gender	:sukupuoli	:Sukupuoli
municipality of birth	:synnyinkunta	
date of birth	:syntymaeaika	xsd:date
full name	skos:prefLabel	rdfs:Literal
WarSampo person instance	crm:P70_documents	crm:E21_Person

The default namespace corresponds to the casualty schema namespace. RDF Schema (RDFS), Web Ontology Language (OWL) and XML Schema namespaces are omitted.

In Table 1 there are a total of 31 properties that are used for describing the casualties. The properties are used only when there is a value for the property. Municipalities are currently linked to three distinct datasets, which is why their range is not defined. The place properties, which give a more specific place for the described events, are literals representing the place names of the original data. Original text representations of military units are also preserved and a new property :osasto is added for linking to WarSampo military units.

The Simple Knowledge Organization System (SKOS)[10] was used to define vocabularies to present the information found in the original database in RDF. The created SKOS vocabularies for describing the death records in the casualty dataset are listed in Table 2.

Table 2. SKOS vocabularies for describing the death records.

Vocabulary	Number of concepts
citizenships	10
genders	3
graveyards	802
marital statuses	5
mother tongues	11
municipalities	632
nationalities	11
perishing classes	7

A graveyard vocabulary was created to describe graveyards around Finland, and is also linked to ontologies of Finnish municipalities. These municipalities include current municipalities as well as historical municipalities, as some graveyards are located outside current Finnish borders, and often only the historical municipality of the graveyard is known.

The dataset is published on the Linked Data Finland (LDF) [8] platform, where it is openly available[11] for use via a SPARQL endpoint, with the Creative Commons Attribution 4.0 license[12]. The SPARQL endpoint[13] serves all WarSampo data, and has distinct graphs for each separate dataset and a default graph which contains all data. A Fuseki[14] SPARQL Server is used for storing and serving the linked data. The used URIs are dereferenceable and provide information about resources for both human and machine users.

---

[10] https://www.w3.org/2009/08/skos-reference/skos.html
[11] http://www.ldf.fi/dataset/narc-menehtyneet1939-45
[12] https://creativecommons.org/licenses/by/4.0/
[13] http://ldf.fi/warsa/sparql
[14] http://jena.apache.org/documentation/serving_data/

3   Interlinking with WarSampo Datasets

The RDF dataset has been enriched by linking it to other parts of WarSampo like military ranks, military units, information about people found in other sources, and municipalities of wartime Finland.

A figure displaying the external linking of the death records is shown in Fig. 1. Each casualty is linked to other related WarSampo datasets and to a common WarSampo military rank ontology. The annotated military rank represents the rank of a person at the time of death.

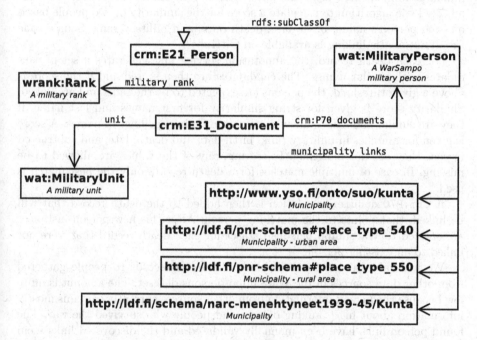

Fig. 1. External links from the death records, which are instances of crm:E31_Document. The properties are explained in Table 1. All WarSampo classes are aligned with the CIDOC CRM framework using rdfs:subClassOf relations.

Each death record is linked to a person instance (crm:E21_Person) of the WarSampo persons dataset via crm:P70_documents. So in our model, the death records are documents about the actual person. New information about people from other sources is not added directly to the casualty dataset, but to the WarSampo persons dataset, in order to maintain the integrity of the casualty dataset as a whole.

There are 3 municipality datasets, which include a dataset of contemporary Finnish municipalities, part of the Finnish Geographic Names Registry[15],

---

[15] http://www.ldf.fi/dataset/pnr

and two datasets that complement each other and consist of historical Finnish municipalities. These are the historical wartime municipalities registry [7] of WarSampo, and a municipality ontology based on the casualty dataset. The place properties are currently not linked to places available [7] in the Karelian map names in Finland and Russia, and the Finnish Geographic Names Registry. This is because finding the places to link automatically would result in a low precision due to the abundance of distinct places with identical names.

The death records are programmatically linked with people found in other WarSampo sources, which are gathered in the WarSampo persons dataset. The linking is implemented using the automatic annotation service ARPA [11], and a fuzzy logic algorithm to calculate a score for the similarity of two people based on each person's name, birth date, death date, and military rank. Source code for all automatic linking is available on GitHub[16].

For each death record, the annotation service first generates a set of candidates with similar names. The candidates are then scored and if the score is above a given threshold, the persons are expected to be the same and are linked. Similarity score is given for string similarity for first names and last name, if they are similar enough, to allow somewhat differing spellings of names. A score is given for matches in military rank, birth date and death date, and subtracted in case they are not matching. In scoring, any of the values are allowed to be missing. In case of multiple matches for a death record, only the best match is used.

A crm:P70_documents relation is then added to the death record that will be linked, that points to the matching person. After this new person instances are created to WarSampo persons dataset for each death record that were not linked to an existing person.

We were able to automatically link 118 death records to people gathered from other data sources in the WarSampo persons dataset. The amount is quite low because the person information from other sources currently contains mostly information about high ranking officers and people who survived the war. The found person links have been manually validated and the discovered links seem to be depicting the same people. Manual validation was also done to person pairs that were close to the score threshold but not linked, and these seem to either not depict the same persons or not have enough information to make an assumption either way. However, as the scoring is manually adjusted to work well for the current persons dataset, when new people from new sources are added to the persons dataset, the scoring may need readjusting.

Military units of casualties are also programmatically linked to military units described in the WarSampo army units dataset, which contains military unit information found in other sources. The linking is implemented using the ARPA service and is based on unit abbreviations found in the casualty dataset, which are matched against manually annotated unit abbreviations in the army units dataset. As the exact abbreviation formats vary somewhat in different sources, multiple different abbreviation formats are generated from the original

---

[16] https://github.com/SemanticComputing/Casualty-linking

one for use in the automatic linking. Some 66,700 death records were linked to WarSampo military units, so this accounts for 70% of all the casualties. Currently, military unit information in WarSampo is limited to units of the Winter War. Therefore not all casualties are linked to the military units of WarSampo.

Municipalities in the data are linked automatically based on the labels of the municipalities. As shown in Table 1, there are six properties that relate to municipalities for each death record. The automatic linking leads to 98% of all death records having at least one link to the known wartime municipalities, which is the primary municipality dataset of WarSampo.

4   Use Case 1: Studying Death Records

This use case studies how the data could be used for prosopographical digital humanities research. We present the casualties perspective of the WarSampo portal, which is a tool for interactively analyzing the data in order to find patterns in groups of individuals.

The dataset graph consists of almost 2.4 million RDF triples. Presenting the data in an online service for users to search and browse is not straightforward due to the large size of the dataset. Furthermore, there are lots of links to related data in other WarSampo datasets (people, places, military units, etc.).

Faceted search provides effective support for interactive information-seeking in information systems [13]. A faceted search application was developed for searching and browsing the dataset. The application[17] is part of the WarSampo portal, and provides the casualties perspective as one of the portal's different perspectives. Faceted search is based on displaying categories for each facet, from which the user can select one, which then narrow down the result set to include only the results that match the user selections.

Figure 2 shows a screenshot of the faceted search application in the casualties perspective. The data is laid out in a table-like view. Facets are presented on the left of the interface with string search support. The number of hits on each facet is calculated dynamically and shown to the user, and selections leading to an empty result set are hidden.

In Fig. 2, seven facets and the results are shown, where the user has selected "widow" in the marital status facet, focusing the search down to 278 killed widows that are presented in the table with links to further information.

The faceted search is used not only for searching but also as a flexible tool for researching the underlying data. In Fig. 2, the hit counts immediately show distributions of the killed widows along the facet categories. For example, the facet "Number of children" shows that one of the deceased had 10 children and most often (in 88 cases) widows had one child. If we next select the category "one child" on its facet, we can see that two of the deceased are women and 86 are men in the gender facet.

---

[17] http://www.sotasampo.fi/casualties/

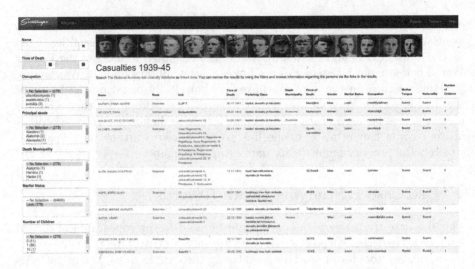

Fig. 2. The faceted search interface of death records with one selected facet. The left side contains the facets, displaying available categories and the amount of death records for each casualty. Death records matching the current facet selections are shown as a table.

The application is developed in JavaScript as a Rich Internet Application (RIA) on the client side, using the open SPARQL endpoint to fetch data according to user selections. The application is open source[18], and is based on our *SPARQL Faceter* tool [9], which is also open source[19]. When the user's selections of the facets change, an asynchronous SPARQL query is sent from the user's web browser to the SPARQL endpoint. The SPARQL endpoint returns results of the query to the user's browser, which does additional processing of the data before displaying the new results to the user. The system works well even with the large casualty dataset, because pagination is used to limit the amount of results that are queried and displayed at a time.

The faceted search application uses the AngularJS framework, and is based on two distinct components that together provide the needed functionalities: the main faceted search component, that handles the user interface, and a SPARQL service that maps results to JavaScript objects.

The application builds a single SPARQL query that retrieves the facet categories and the amount of results for each of them. Another query is built for the results display.

The shown facets are configured in the application and they directly use the properties of each death record instance. The categories shown in facets are values of properties of the death records, which may be resources selected from the corresponding ontologies, such as places, or plain literals.

---

[18] https://github.com/SemanticComputing/WarSampo-death-records
[19] https://github.com/SemanticComputing/angular-semantic-faceted-search

The interface contains 12 facets, of which nine are basic facets that display the values of a property as categories. In addition to the basic facets, there are three facets with different functionalities. The text search facet is used for finding people directly by name: the user just enters a person's name or a part of it into the search box. The date of death facet has a date range selector to filter the results. The military rank facet is a hierarchical facet, making use of the hierarchical nature of the military ranks. The used military rank ontology contains two hierarchies, one based on the actual rank, and one for grouping ranks to, e.g., generals, officers, and enlisted ranks. Of these, the rank group hierarchy is used in the facet. Selecting a category upper in the hierarchy also shows results for all the categories that are below it in the hierarchy. The hierarchy is flattened to show only two distinct levels. The level of the current selection, or initially the top level, is shown on an upper level and the values that are lower in the hierarchy are displayed on a lower level below the corresponding upper level categories.

Most of the facets are disabled by default, and the user has to click a plus sign on the facet to activate it. Activating facets makes the interface respond more slowly to user selections, as data for each activated facet has to be queried from the SPARQL endpoint based on user selections to show the facet categories. Normally when a user searches or browses the dataset, the facet categories and the results display are updated within a few seconds after the user has made a selection from one of the facets. With selections that have a large result set, and if additionally many facets are enabled, the user may have to wait more than ten seconds.

Another perspective of the WarSampo portal that makes use of the casualty data is the event perspective. The perspective displays wartime events on a timeline and map, as seen in Fig. 3. The casualty data is visualized by a heat map layer on the map, showing an overview of where casualties occurred during different time frames, and also which events happened nearby. The application also displays statistics regarding the casualties during the selected time frame: the total amount of casualties, and the amount per perishing class. People mentioned in the event descriptions are linked to the WarSampo persons dataset, and through this link to the casualties dataset for people that have died in the wars. The application provides hyperlinks to the linked entities shown in their corresponding perspectives. These other perspectives include applications for exploring places, photographs, military units, and magazine articles of the WarSampo system.

5   Use Case 2: Reassembling Soldier Biographies and Military Unit Histories

This use case studies how we can reassemble soldier biographies and military unit histories based on the information content available in the casualties dataset and linked information in other WarSampo datasets. This use case serves citizens and researchers who are interested in finding information about a person's involvement in the war.

Fig. 3. The WarSampo event perspective with casualties of an 8 day time period visualized as a heat map on top of Google Maps, and casualty statistics in the bottom right corner.

Linking the death records to information about the same people in other sources, events, military units, war diaries, photographs and wartime places provides new information about their activities, involvements in war events, whereabouts and movements during the war. By linking all these pieces of information together, we are able to construct partial biographies of individual soldiers, and the movements and actions of their military units. This allows an individual who is interested in investigating the biography of a relative who took part in the war to look at where the person probably fought, with whom, and when, and in what events his military unit participated. Also, the interlinked dataset, together with applications to effectively use it, provides digital humanities researchers with new perspectives to study the casualties, that would not be possible with a non-linked dataset.

Figure 4 shows a histogram of the amount of casualties per day of a single military unit, the Second Battalion of the 38th Infantry Regiment, and all of its subunits, which consist of 4 companies. The battalion existed during the Winter War, which was fought from 30 November 1939 to 13 March 1940. The time span in the figure covers the time from first casualty to the last, with the exception of one death that occurred much later in 1940, supposedly due to injuries obtained in the war.

Demonstrating the value of linking additional data to the death records, we have information of 19 events that are linked to the military unit and its subdivisions. They seem to explain quite well the casualties during the Winter War, as high peaks in casualties mostly occur when the unit is engaged in an assault. However, the second highest peak occurs during a long defensive battle just before the end of the Winter War.

Events of the whole 38th Infantry Regiment during the Winter War are quite well covered in WarSampo. The regiment's second battalion and its subdivisions are known to have participated in the following events:

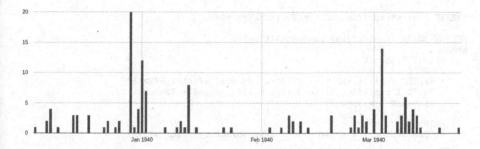

Fig. 4. A histogram visualization which shows casualties of the the Second Battalion of the 38th Infantry Regiment during the Winter War.

1. Defensive battle at Lavajärvi, 1939-12-06 – 1939-12-08
2. Battle at Lavajärvi, 1939-12-07 – 1939-12-08
3. Stalling battle at Lavajärvi-Lemetti, 1939-12-08 – 1939-12-10
4. Assault on Karjamökki, 1939-12-14 – 1939-12-14
5. Defense of Syskyjärvi sector, 1939-12-15 – 1939-12-28
6. Assault on Ruhtinaanmäki, 1939-12-29 – 1940-01-03
7. Assault on western Lemetti, 1940-01-06 – 1940-01-07
8. Assault battles at Repomäki, 1940-01-08 – 1940-01-12
9. Assault on Ruunaviita, 1940-01-13 – 1940-01-15
10. Battle at Koivuselkä, 1940-01-17 – 1940-02-06
11. Assault on Kehnovaara, 1940-01-18 – 1940-01-18
12. Assault on hill 63 and its defense, 1940-01-21 – 1940-01-24
13. Occupation of Pukitsanmäki and its defense, 1940-01-23 – 1940-01-26
14. Assault on Pujaski-Borisoff, 1940-01-25 – 1940-01-25
15. Destruction of Soviet elite ski unit at south of western Lemetti, 1940-02-06 – 1940-02-06
16. Capturing an encirclement northeast of Nietjärvi and destruction of a Soviet elite ski battalion, 1940-02-07 – 1940-02-09
17. Capturing 3 encirclements at Konnunkylä (Pujaski, Ahola and between railroad and road), 1940-02-18 – 1940-02-19
18. Capturing an encirclement south of point 26 (about 200 m east of Koivusilta), 1940-02-21 – 1940-02-21
19. Defensive battle south of Nietjärvi, 1940-02-24 – 1940-03-11

The histogram is created by reading data directly from the WarSampo SPARQL endpoint and visualizing it with YASGUI[20] online SPARQL tool. The SPARQL query for retrieving the casualties for this military unit and its subdivisions is the following:

```
PREFIX atypes: <http://ldf.fi/warsa/actors/actor_types/>
PREFIX crm: <http://www.cidoc-crm.org/cidoc-crm/>
PREFIX casualties: <http://ldf.fi/schema/narc-menehtyneet1939-45/>
```

---

[20] http://yasgui.org

```
PREFIX xsd: <http://www.w3.org/2001/XMLSchema#>

SELECT ?date (count(?cas) as ?casualties)
WHERE {
  { SELECT ?subunit
    WHERE {
      VALUES ?unit { <http://ldf.fi/warsa/actors/actor_972> } .
      ?unit (^crm:P144_joined_with/crm:P143_joined)+ ?subunit .
      ?subunit a atypes:MilitaryUnit .
    }
  } UNION {
    VALUES ?subunit { <http://ldf.fi/warsa/actors/actor_972> } .
  }
  ?cas casualties:osasto ?subunit .
  ?cas casualties:kuolinaika ?date .
  FILTER(?date < "1940-06-01"^^xsd:date)
} GROUP BY ?date ORDER BY ?date
```

All of the information about the Second Battalion of the 38th Infantry Regiment in WarSampo are available through the units perspective of WarSampo[21]. The units perspective visualizes the troop actions both on a map and a timeline, and shows the casualties of the unit as a heat map in the same fashion as in the event perspective. A screenshot of the perspective is shown in Fig. 5.

For even deeper understanding of the history, links to digitized images of the war diaries of the army units are provided, containing rich primary source descriptions of the events. By following the municipality links to the places perspective of WarSampo one can, e.g., study what kind of war events took place in the person's birth place, see photographs taken at specific locations the troops were located in, or read magazine articles depicting wartime events that took place in some specific place.

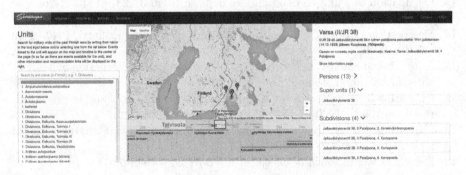

Fig. 5. WarSampo military units perspective displaying information about the Second Battalion of the 38th Infantry Regiment.

Figure 6 depicts an integrated view of information related to a casualty in the person perspective of the WarSampo portal. On the left side is a search interface for finding people by name, and on the right is information about the currently selected person. Basic information about a person (e.g., name, birth

---

[21] http://www.sotasampo.fi/en/units/?uri=http://ldf.fi/warsa/actors/actor_972

and death dates and places, occupation, marital status, military rank with promotion dates if available) is displayed on the top. After that, thumbnails of the linked photographs involving the person are shown. By clicking the thumbnails the user can explore the higher resolution versions of the photographs and their captions. Below the photographs are war time events of the person, his military units, military ranks, municipalities where he is known to have been and a link to a Wikipedia page about this person.

For some people, there is also a biography text from the National Biography of Finland shown on the page, and possibly further information like linked magazine articles.

In order to get further context for the person examined, the user can browse the army units the person belonged to during the war, and places related to his life events (e.g., birth and death municipalities on historical and contemporary maps). This way the user is able to track the person's participation in the war by investigating the movements of his army units and the durations of the battles the units fought.

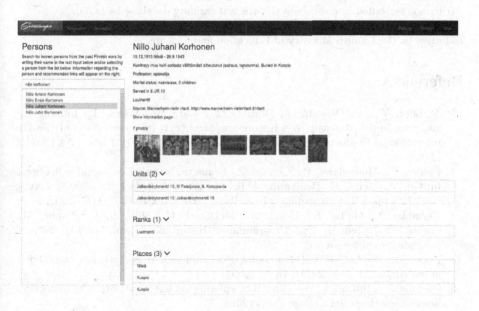

Fig. 6. A screenshot of the person perspective of the WarSampo portal depicting linked information related to a casualty.

6   Discussion

War history data is usually scattered in many isolated silos and may exist in totally different formats, e.g., books, paper archives, and databases. In this paper we have examined the benefits and challenges of linking casualty records of war to multiple related datasets, and publishing them as linked data for DH research and applications to use. Two use cases were studied related to supporting DH research and services for the public.

In the future, linking with other WarSampo data will be developed further as new datasets are added to the system. We plan to develop tools for statistical analysis of the data, and collaborate with humanities researchers in studying how linked data and our tooling can help to solve their research problems. A hierarchical occupation ontology is planned to be used and linked to the death records to provide insight into the social status of each casualty. Whether we could take advantage of existing occupation taxonomies, such as the Historical International Standard Classification of Occupations (HISCO) [10], will be explored.

It would be beneficial for research purposes to develop the casualties perspective to allow exporting the data based on facet selections, for use with other applications and visualization tools.

Acknowledgements. Tomi Ahoranta and Jérémie Dutruit from the National Archives contributed in publishing the original casualty database as LOD.

Our research is partially funded through the Finnish Open Science and Research Initiative by the Finnish Ministry of Education and Culture.

References

1. de Boer, V., van Doornik, J., Buitinck, L., Marx, M., Veken, T.: Linking the kingdom: enriched access to a historiographical text. In: Proceedings of the 7th International Conference on Knowledge Capture (KCAP 2013), pp. 17–24. ACM (2013)
2. Collins, T., Mulholland, P., Zdrahal, Z.: Semantic browsing of digital collections. In: Gil, Y., Motta, E., Benjamins, V.R., Musen, M.A. (eds.) ISWC 2005. LNCS, vol. 3729, pp. 127–141. Springer, Heidelberg (2005). doi:10.1007/11574620_12
3. Crymble, A., Gibbs, F., Hegel, A., McDaniel, C., Milligan, I., Posner, M., Turkel, W.J. (eds.): The Programming Historian. 2 edn. (2015). http://programminghistorian.org
4. Doerr, M.: The CIDOC CRM–an ontological approach to semantic interoperability of metadata. AI Mag. **24**(3), 75–92 (2003)
5. Graham, S., Milligan, I., Weingart, S.: Exploring big historical data. The historian's macroscope. Imperial College Press (2015)
6. Hyvönen, E., Heino, E., Leskinen, P., Ikkala, E., Koho, M., Tamper, M., Tuominen, J., Mäkelä, E.: WarSampo data service and semantic portal for publishing linked open data about the second world war history. In: Sack, H., Blomqvist, E., d'Aquin, M., Ghidini, C., Ponzetto, S.P., Lange, C. (eds.) ESWC 2016. LNCS, vol. 9678, pp. 758–773. Springer, Cham (2016). doi:10.1007/978-3-319-34129-3_46
7. Hyvönen, E., Ikkala, E., Tuominen, J.: Linked data brokering service for historical places and maps. In: Adamou, A., Daga, E., Isaksen, L. (eds.) Proceedings of the 1st Workshop on Humanities in the Semantic Web (WHiSe). CEUR Workshop Proceedings, No. 1608, Aachen, pp. 39–52 (2016). http://ceur-ws.org/Vol-1608/#paper-06

8. Hyvönen, E., Tuominen, J., Alonen, M., Mäkelä, E.: Linked data Finland: a 7-star model and platform for publishing and re-using linked datasets. In: Presutti, V., Blomqvist, E., Troncy, R., Sack, H., Papadakis, I., Tordai, A. (eds.) ESWC 2014. LNCS, vol. 8798, pp. 226–230. Springer, Cham (2014). doi:10.1007/978-3-319-11955-7_24

9. Koho, M., Heino, E., Hyvönen, E.: SPARQL faceter–client-side faceted search based on SPARQL. In: Troncy, R., Verborgh, R., Nixon, L., Kurz, T., Schlegel, K., Vander Sande, M. (eds.) Joint Proceedings of the 4th International Workshop on Linked Media and the 3rd Developers Hackshop, CEUR Workshop Proceedings. No. 1615 (2016). http://ceur-ws.org/Vol-1615/semdevPaper5.pdf

10. van Leeuwen, M.H.D., Maas, I., Miles, A.: HISCO: Historical International Standard Classification of Occupations. Leuven University Press, Cambridge (2002)

11. Mäkelä, E.: Combining a REST lexical analysis web service with SPARQL for mashup semantic annotation from text. In: Presutti, V., Blomqvist, E., Troncy, R., Sack, H., Papadakis, I., Tordai, A. (eds.) ESWC 2014. LNCS, vol. 8798, pp. 424–428. Springer, Cham (2014). doi:10.1007/978-3-319-11955-7_60

12. Mäkelä, E., Törnroos, J., Lindquist, T., Hyvönen, E.: World War I as Linked Open Data (2015), submitted for review. http://seco.cs.aalto.fi/publications/

13. Tunkelang, D.: Faceted search. Synthesis lectures on information concepts, retrieval, and services, Morgan & Claypool Publishers (2009)

Author Index

Printed in the United States
By Bookmasters